Public Policy and Regional Economic Development

Public Policy and Regional Economic Development

The Experience of Nine Western Countries

Niles M. Hansen, ed.

Ballinger Publishing Company • Cambridge, Mass.
A Subsidiary of J.B. Lippincott Company

The research for this book was prepared with the support of the Ford Foundation and the Centre for Environmental Studies, London.

International Standard Book Number: 0-88410-409-5

Library of Congress Catalog Card Number: 74-13819

Printed in the United States of America

Library of Congress Cataloging in Publication Data

Hansen, Niles M.
    Public policy and regional economic development.

    Bibliography: p.
    1. Regional planning—Europe—Case studies. 2. Regional planning—North America—Case studies. 3. Europe—Economic policy—Case studies. 4. North America—Economic policy—Case studies. I. Title.
HT395.E8H36   309.2'5'094   74-13819
ISBN 0-88410-409-5

Contents

List of Tables

List of Figures

List of Maps

Preface

Textbooks customarily introduce the discipline of economics as the analysis of What, How, and For Whom with respect to the allocation of scarce resources among competing uses. However, during the past decade pressing issues of population size and growth and of environmental quality have compelled economists and scholars in related fields to give increasing attention to the question of Where. At the same time, governments have shown an increasing tendency to attempt to alter the spatial allocation of resources in favor of patterns deemed more desirable than those which would result from market forces in the prevailing institutional setting. The general aim of this volume is to bring together within this context the theoretical and empirical contributions of economists and others engaged in related disciplines and the policy questions that confront public decision makers, to their mutual benefit.

This joint effort sought general conclusions and in some instances may have found them. However, it is evident that policy-related research and practice must be oriented toward the historical, social, and institutional perspectives of particular countries. The prospect that what we can learn from others may have to be modified for our own purposes—and vice-versa—may be disconcerting to those who desire immediate access to universal truths; but it is consistent with the less inflated notion that tolerance of diversity may in the long run be more consistent with the advance of knowledge, and perhaps wisdom.

The project was undertaken with the support of the Ford Foundation. It was carried out under the auspices of the Centre for Environmental Studies, London. I am grateful to the Centre's Director, David Donnison, for his generous cooperation. Christine Adnitt, Rowland Eustace, and John Kennedy, all of the Centre, also were most helpful. In addition I received valuable assistance from Rita Ellison, Pamela Pape, Carol Pfrommer, and Koren Sherrill, colleagues in the Center for Economic Development, The University of Texas. Finally, I am particularly indebted to William Pendleton of the Ford Foundation. This study is in many respects a result of his critical interest over a number of years in the issues raised here.

N.M.H.
Austin, Texas
September 1973

Public Policy and Regional
Economic Development

Chapter One

Preliminary Overview

INTRODUCTION

Since the Great Depression and the Second World War there has been a striking revolution in the degree of rational control that governments have exercised over aggregate economic variables. Despite the recent debates of both theoretical economists and political decision makers over issues surrounding the trade-offs between price stability and unemployment, essentially Keynesian policy measures have all but removed the old fear of recurrent and lengthy periods of high unemployment and generally depressed economic activity. In consequence, there has been a relative shift of interest in the industrial nations of the West toward issues involving the spatial distribution of economic activity, implying also a concern for population distribution. Thus, in one country after another regional policies have been adopted to aid economically lagging areas and, in some instances, to curb the growth of areas which are deemed to have become, or to be in danger of becoming, overconcentrated in terms of population and economic activity.

This book brings together critical examinations of these policies in Canada, Germany, France, Italy, The Netherlands, Spain, Sweden, the United Kingdom, and the United States. Mexico was not included with the other North American countries because of its essentially Latin American orientation. It was not feasible to include all of the smaller nations of Western Europe, even though several of those omitted have regional policies that would no doubt be of interest to many readers of this volume. The problem here is essentially one of scale; the regional problems of small countries and the policies which have been formulated to deal with them are more likely to be applicable to specific regions of larger countries than to larger countries as a whole. Nevertheless, Sweden and The Netherlands have been included to give an indication of the degree of sophistication that scholars and government officials in countries with relatively small populations have brought to bear on significant problems of spatial resource allocation. Eastern European countries were not included because of the numerous institutional differences between them and the countries studied here.

Unlike books which are collections of already published articles or of articles presented at conferences, the present volume was developed as a systematic cooperative effort of the authors. They were selected by the editor on the basis of their general scholarly contributions to the theoretical and empirical literature on spatial resource allocation and their intimate knowledge of regional issues and policies in their respective countries.

Before any of the articles were written, the authors met as a group to identify policy issues that were of significant interest in all or most of the countries represented. At this meeting it was decided that each chapter would consider the following topics: (1) general regional tendencies, (2) policy issues and goals, (3) regional development policies and tools for their implementation, (4) evaluation of policies, and (5) indications of likely future directions of regional policy. It also was decided to emphasize broadly regional considerations rather than specifically urban or rural problems and policies. The individual chapters are therefore not, strictly speaking, studies in either urban economics or rural development, though they do include these orientations in varying degree. Each author was, of course, free to exercise his personal perspective within the framework of the mutually approved broad constraints. First drafts for each of the chapters were submitted to other participants for criticism; the structure and content of these drafts were again critically discussed in a meeting of all the authors. Revisions based on these discussions were given final critical review by the editor and an anonymous reader.

GENERAL CHARACTERISTICS OF THE NATIONS STUDIES

The following section of this chapter presents detailed data directly relevant to regional problems and policies, as do the studies of the individual countries. However, to put these into their proper context it is also instructive to examine and compare briefly some of the countries' more general attributes. The data in Table 1-1 show that the countries range in geographic area from 37,000 square kilometers in The Netherlands to 9,976,000 square kilometers in Canada. France, with 549,000 square kilometers has the median area value. The figure for Canada is of course misleading because so much of its vast expanse is either unexploited or unexploitable. Thus, in terms of agricultural area and tillage the United States has a good deal more land than all of the other countries combined. The matter of differences in scale could mean that the experiences of smaller countries are more useful in relation to regions of bigger countries than to the latter as whole. (I am speaking here of regional issues, problems, and

Table 1-1.   Geographic and Demographic Characteristics, 1971

Country	Area (1,000 square kilometers)	Agricultural area (1,000 square kilometers)	Tillage (and temporary grassland) (1,000 square kilometers)	Population (thousands)	Population density (per square kilometer)
Canada	9,976	644	434	21,595	2
United States	9,363	4,356[1]	1,764[1]	207,049	22
Sweden	450	34	30	8,105	18
United Kingdom	244	191	72	55,668	228
France	549	330	190	51,250	93
West Germany	248	135	81	61,284	247
The Netherlands	37	22	9	13,194	360
Italy	301	192	142	53,899	179
Spain	505	364	206	34,003	67

Note: [1] Data for 1967
Source: OECD (1973), p. 20.

policies rather than of techniques of regional analysis, where generally high quality work often has been pioneered in the smaller countries.)

Although the United States has the largest population, its population density is relatively low, approximating that in Sweden. Four of the countries—France, Italy, the United Kingdom, and West Germany—have populations within the fifty-one million to sixty-two million range. The Netherlands has by far the highest population density, whereas that in France is quite low in comparison to other Common Market countries.

The data in Table 1-2 on per capita gross national product show considerable variation, ranging from $1,070 in Spain to $5,160 in the United States. In the perspective of the international monetary situation at this writing, the relative position of the United States is clearly overstated by these figures.

Table 1-2 also shows the broad relative structure of gross domestic product and employment for the relevant countries. The importance of agriculture and related activities remains particularly high in Spain and Italy. Although these activities make up 28.6 percent of Spanish employment, they account for only 13.5 percent of gross domestic product; in Italy the corresponding values are 19.5 percent and 11.5 percent. It is obvious that inevitable modernization in these countries will generate further larger transfers of workers from low-productivity agriculture to more productive sectors. The consequences of this phenomenon for regional policy are developed in particularly great detail in Vera Cao-Pinna's analysis of the problems of the Italian *Mezzogiorno*. It may also be noted that France still has 13.5 percent of its employed labor force in agriculture, although this accounts for only 6 percent of gross domestic product. On the other hand, in the United Kingdom 2.7 percent of total employment is in agriculture, which accounts for 2.9 percent of gross domestic product. Thus, as Gordon Cameron points out, regional problems in the United Kingdom are related to differences among industrialized areas rather than to the flight of redundant workers from agriculture, a process now virtually completed. The remaining countries represent intermediate situations but clearly are closer to the United Kingdom than to Spain or Italy.

In the past, regional economists and scholars in related disciplines often tended to associate the general economic progress of a nation with the degree to which the relative concentration of employment had progressed from the primary to the secondary sector, and from there to the tertiary sector. These three categories (which might also be termed, respectively, direct production from the earth, manufacturing activities that alter the form of the yield of the earth, and services in the broadest sense) correspond roughly to those listed in the last three columns of Table 1-2.

In the cases of Italy and Spain it is quite apparent that relatively low levels of per capita gross national product are associated with relatively high concentrations of employment in the primary sector and relatively low concentrations in the tertiary sector. Vera Cao-Pinna maintains that in the case of Italy

Table 1-2. Per Capita Gross National Product, Structure of Gross Domestic Product, and Employment Structure, 1971

Country	Per capita gross national product (at current prices and exchange rates, in U.S. $)	Structure of gross domestic product (percent) at factor cost			Total civilian employment (thousands)	of which		
		Agriculture	Mining, manufacturing, construction, and utilities	Other activities		Agriculture, forestry and fishing (percent)	Industry (percent)	Other (percent)
Canada	4,240	4.4	37.0	58.6	8,079	7.5	31.0	61.5
United States	5,160	2.9[a]	33.1[a]	63.9[a]	79,120	4.3	31.0	64.7
Sweden	4,400	4.4[a]	39.3[a]	56.2[a]	3,860	7.8	37.6	54.6
United Kingdom	2,460	2.9[b]	43.5[b]	53.6[b]	24,329	2.7	45.7	51.6
France	3,180	6.0[a]	48.4[a]	45.6[a]	20,518	13.4	38.6	48.0
West Germany	3,550	2.8[a]	53.5[a]	43.7[a]	26,673	8.4	50.1	41.5
The Netherlands	2,820	6.2	42.0	51.8	4,604	6.9	38.0	55.1
Italy	1,880	11.5	40.5	48.0	18,700	19.5	44.1	36.4
Spain	1,070	13.5	34.4	52.1	12,442	28.6	37.5	33.9

Source: OECD (1973), pp. 21-3.
Notes: [a] Gross Domestic Product at market prices.
[b] Includes stock appreciation.

high levels of agricultural employment in the *Mezzogiorno*, or South, are as much a result of regional problems, and the manner with which they have been dealt, as a cause of these problems. It also is true that the United States has the highest per capita gross national product, the highest proportion of the labor force in the tertiary sector and the next to lowest proportion in the primary sector. Canada also has a relatively high per capita gross national product, high tertiary employment, and low primary employment. On the other hand, per capita gross national product in the United Kingdom is below that of all the countries except Italy and Spain, although its proportion of employment accounted for by the primary sector is the lowest for any nation. However, relatively low prices make the purchasing power of a given dollar-equivalent income higher in the United Kingdom than in most other countries of Western Europe. The Netherlands, with a relatively high proportion of the labor force in the tertiary sector and the lowest European proportion in the primary sector except for the United Kingdom, also has a relatively low per capita gross national product. But here, too, lower prices make real purchasing power greater than it might seem. France, with the median per capita gross national product value, has a relatively high proportion of its labor force in primary activities but is close to the median with respect to secondary and tertiary activities.

Thus welfare, to the extent that it is a function of per capita gross national product, is related in a very loose manner to the primary-secondary-tertiary employment structure; but the relationship is by no means a necessary one with respect to each individual country. Nor does description of the employment structure reveal a great deal about the dynamic process of national or regional growth and development. Indeed, as Åke Andersson points out on the basis of Swedish data, questions of per capita income, employment structure, and accessibility to services are by no means independent of a community's place within a nation's communications network, broadly defined to include transportation, telecommunications, etc. Moreover, the notion that per capita gross national product reflects the overall quality of life—at least in nations whose people are far past the subsistence level—has been increasingly questioned. In many respects, the new concern for quality of life is related directly to the urbanization process and its consequences for the environment in which people live. What is at issue is not only urban congestion, but also the decline of economic opportunities and services in many rural areas. It is appropriate, therefore, to consider next data on urban growth and structure, and then some of the arguments which have influenced, and no doubt will continue to influence, the formulation and implementation of regional policies.

URBAN GROWTH AND STRUCTURE

Table 1-3 presents data on the rural-urban distribution of population in the countries discussed in this volume. (Although more recent data are available in some instances, the data shown in Tables 1-3 to 1-5 are utilized because of their standardization and comparability. A number of the contributors to this study expressed concern over the difficulty of making standardized comparisons of the sort discussed in this section. Davis, on whom I rely for the data, would probably be the first to agree. Despite the problems, I feel that these are the best estimates available, and refer the interested reader to Davis for specific criteria and definitions.) Urban class I refers to places defined as urban but having fewer than 100,000 inhabitants (these are referred to as towns in Table 1-4). Class II includes cities of 100,000 to 499,999 inhabitants; class III those of 500,000 to 999,999 inhabitants; and class IV those of 1,000,000 or more inhabitants. The term "rural" is a residual category comprising all of the nonurban population.

The highest proportions of rural population are found in Italy (48.5 percent) and Spain (41.2 percent). The lowest are in West Germany (17.8 percent) and the United Kingdom (20.9 percent). In the remaining countries the rural population represents between one-fourth and one-third of the total.

At the other end of the spectrum, the United Kingdom has 42.9 percent of its population in class IV cities. Over one-third of the population of the United States and West Germany lives in class IV cities. The corresponding proportion in Italy, Spain, Sweden, and The Netherlands ranges from 13.3 percent to 18.0 percent. The United Kingdom is the only country where over half of the population resides in class III and IV cities taken together, while in The Netherlands, France, and Sweden, class I and II cities together account for over 40 percent of the national population.

Table 1-3. Percent of Population in Rural Areas and in Four Urban Size Classes, 1970

			Urban Class		
Country	*Rural*	*I*	*II*	*III*	*IV*
Canada	25.3	25.4	14.5	12.0	22.8
United States	24.8	16.9	13.3	7.5	37.6
Sweden	33.9	33.4	8.0	8.0	16.7
United Kingdom	20.9	8.4	17.5	10.4	42.9
France	32.1	27.5	16.9	2.0	21.4
West Germany	17.8	28.2	9.2	9.3	35.6
The Netherlands	27.8	27.0	21.2	5.9	18.0
Italy	48.5	22.0	12.1	4.0	13.3
Spain	41.2	25.7	16.8	1.5	14.7

Source: Davis (1969), pp. 120, 132-3, 135.

Table 1-4 presents average annual population change in each country over the decades 1950-60 and 1960-70. The term "town" refers to an urban place with fewer than 100,000 inhabitants, while "city" refers to a place (or urbanized area) with that many people or more. These two categories combined constitute the "urban" population; the rural population is the total population minus the urban population.

With the exception of the total population growth rate in The Netherlands for the 1960-70 decade, it is striking that the growth rate in both North American countries was higher in each decade than was the rate of any of the European countries for either decade. However, the North American countries also were the only ones to register declines in the rate of growth between the decade of the 1950s and that of the 1960s. In other words, though Canada and the United States continue to grow at a faster rate than the European countries their rates of growth are rapidly falling toward European levels.

With the exception of a small increase in the United Kingdom and stability in Italy, the rural population of each country declined during the 1960s. The sharpest rates of decline were in West Germany, France, Sweden, and the United States.

The high urban growth rates of Canada and the United States slackened during the 1960s, whereas the corresponding values were fairly stable in the European countries. In The Netherlands, however, the annual urban growth rate jumped from 0.8 percent to 2.0 percent between the two decades, giving it the highest rate of any European country except France during the 1960s. In most cases the population in cities grew faster than that in towns during both decades. However, in the United Kingdom the growth rate of towns jumped from 0.2 percent to 2.9 percent while the city growth rate remained constant at 0.5 percent. The case of the United Kingdom in the 1960s is the only one where the city population growth rate was less than that of the nation's as a whole. In West Germany the growth rates of towns and cities are similar, though towns grew at a somewhat higher rate (1.8 percent) than cities during the 1960s.

Concern about urban problems and the growth of cities frequently is phrased in terms of the dominance of the principal city. The index values in Table 1-5 give an indication of first-city primacy. The values are simply the ratios of the population of the largest city to the combined populations of the next three largest cities. The principal city's share of the national population living in cities depends of course on the number of cities in a country as well as peculiarities of the country's urban hierarchy. The four-city index has the advantage of being independent of the total number of cities, while including enough cities to indicate the relative importance of the largest city. A larger number of cities could obviously be used, but Davis (1969) has found that the four-city index is highly correlated with a ten-city index as well as a two-city index.

Table 1-4. Annual Growth Rate of Population, 1950-1960 and 1960-1970 (Percent)

Country		Total	Rural	Urban	Town	City
Canada	1950-60	2.7	0.7	3.8	2.9	4.3
	1960-70	1.9	−0.3	2.8	1.9	3.3
United States	1950-60	1.8	−0.0	2.7	1.4	3.2
	1960-70	1.4	−0.6	2.1	−0.0	2.8
Sweden	1950-60	0.6	−0.7	1.6	1.1	2.3
	1960-70	0.8	−0.6	1.6	0.0	3.5
United Kingdom	1950-60	0.4	0.0	0.5	0.2	0.5
	1960-70	0.6	0.3	0.7	2.9	0.5
France	1950-60	0.9	−0.8	2.2	0.7	3.5
	1960-70	1.2	−0.7	2.2	1.2	3.0
West Germany	1950-60	0.9	−1.2	1.6	1.7	1.5
	1960-70	1.1	−1.2	1.7	1.8	1.6
The Netherlands	1950-60	1.3	2.2	0.8	−0.2	1.7
	1960-70	1.4	−0.2	2.0	0.4	3.1
Italy	1950-60	0.6	−0.1	1.4	0.5	2.4
	1960-70	0.8	0.0	1.5	0.1	2.8
Spain	1950-60	0.8	−0.2	1.9	1.4	2.3
	1960-70	0.8	−0.3	1.7	0.7	2.5

Source: Davis (1969), pp. 146, 155-58.

Table 1-5. Four-City Index of First-City Primacy, 1950, 1960, and 1970 (Percent)

Country	1950	1960	1970
Canada	0.69	0.68	0.63
United States	1.04	0.88	0.77
Sweden	n.a.	n.a.	1.14
United Kingdom	1.48	1.51	1.53
France	3.65	3.57	3.10
West Germany	0.85	0.96	1.03
The Netherlands	0.54	0.51	0.50
Italy	0.55	0.56	0.69
Spain	0.75	0.90	1.05

Note: n.a. = not available
Source: Davis (1969), pp. 244, 246.

The degree of primacy is particularly striking in the case of France. The dominance of the Paris region, though declining over time, has no counterpart among the other nations under discussion. In 1970, the four-city index for France was over twice that in the next closest country, the United Kingdom.

The annual percent growth rate of cities in the United Kingdom is remarkably stable. Each of the seventeen largest cities had the same rate of growth during the 1960s as during the 1950s, ranging from 0.1 percent in Manchester, Leeds-Bradford, and Sheffield to 1.5 percent in Coventry. The rate for London was 0.5 percent, the same as that for the entire city population (see Table 1-2).

The four-city index for The Netherlands is also stable over time, but at the lowest value of any of the nine countries. However, this gives a misleading picture of the actual situation. The four largest cities are located relatively close to one another and in many ways constitute an interrelated core within The Netherlands as a whole. The annual rate of growth of Amsterdam, the largest city, jumped from 0.2 percent during the 1950s to 2.3 percent during the 1960s. The corresponding rates for the next three largest cities were: Rotterdam, 0.6 percent and 4.0 percent; The Hague, 0.6 percent and 1.2 percent; and Utrecht, 2.5 percent and 1.4 percent. Thus, while the four-city index remained relatively constant and low, the degree of primacy of the "Rimcity Holland" complex actually increased substantially.

West Germany, Sweden, and Spain had similar four-city index values in 1970. As in the case of the United Kingdom, the growth rates of the largest German cities over time have been remarkably stable. Of the nineteen largest cities, all but one had the same annual rate of growth during the 1960s as during the previous decade, and the one changed by only one-tenth of one percentage point. The largest "city"—Essen-Dortmund-Duisberg—grew by 2.0 percent annually; West Berlin by 0.2 percent; Hamburg by 1.1 percent; and Stuttgart by 2.7 percent. Eight of the ten largest cities grew at faster rates during the 1960s than did the population of the nation as a whole, as did twelve of the largest fifteen. In Sweden, on the other hand, the annual rate of growth of Stockholm slowed from 2.2 percent to 1.6 percent, while the rates for Göteborg and Malmö increased respectively from 2.5 percent to 3.0 percent and from 2.3 percent to 5.2 percent. Each city grew considerably more rapidly than did the national population during the 1960s. Although the four-city index for Spain has been increasing over time, the growth of Madrid fell from an annual rate of 3.4 percent during the 1950s to 2.8 percent during the 1960s. The latter value was still higher than that in any of the other twelve largest cities, where, with the exception of Valencia, the growth rate also slackened between the two decades. Valencia experienced small population losses during both decades.

While the four-city index for Italy is relatively low, it is increasing over time. Rome's annual rate of growth increased from 2.3 percent during the

1950s to 3.8 percent during the 1960s. Meanwhile, the corresponding rates for the next three largest cities were falling: in Milan from 1.8 percent to 1.6 percent; in Naples from 1.6 percent to 1.1 percent; and in Turin from 3.4 percent to 2.0 percent. Nevertheless, in each case growth during the 1960s was considerably more rapid than that in Italy as a whole.

In the two North American countries, declining four-city index values were accompanied by slowing rates of growth of the largest cities. Montreal's annual growth rate fell from 4 percent during the 1950s to 2 percent during the 1960s, which was approximately the national rate of growth but well below the 3.3 percent Canadian city rate. Toronto's corresponding rates fell from 4.8 percent to 3.9 percent; Vancouver's from 3.5 percent to 2.6 percent; Winnipeg's from 3.0 percent to 1.6 percent; Ottawa's from 3.8 percent to 3.1 percent; and Hamilton's from 3.8 percent to 2.8 percent.

The five largest Standard Metropolitan Statistical Areas in the United States each had lower growth rates during the 1960s than the 1950s. New York's annual rate of increase fell from 1.4 percent to 1.3 percent, less than the national rate. The corresponding rates for Los Angeles were 4.9 percent and 3.9 percent; for Chicago, 1.9 percent and 1.6 percent; for Philadelphia 2.2 percent and 1.8 percent; and for Detroit, 2.9 percent and 2.3 percent.

Despite the variety of situations with respect to primacy and urban hierarchy structure and change, in most of the nations examined in subsequent chapters there has been a feeling that one or more of the largest metropolitan areas is, in some sense, too big. Usually the issue is put in terms of intrinsic problems of absolute size or density. But it may also be posed in terms of learning how to organize bigness, with the implication that the real problem is not so much one of size per se as of efficient planning and management.

Although there have been fugitive efforts to inhibit the growth of London, regional policy in the United Kingdom has been more concerned with working within the framework of a stable system of cities than with questions of bigness as such. The situation in West Germany is similar in this regard. Given the vastness of Canada, the fact that Toronto and Montreal have approximately 2.5 million inhabitants each does not appear to present cause for alarm, especially when their growth rates are declining. But in France, Italy, The Netherlands, Sweden, Spain, and the United States the assumptions that big cities are too big has had a significant impact on regional policies. It is therefore appropriate to consider this issue in some detail.

THE QUESTION OF CITY SIZE

The case for limiting the size of large cities is usually based on the notion that the marginal external economies of growth are outweighed by the concomitant diseconomies. External economies of agglomeration refer to cost reductions experienced by firms as a result of services or facilities which are available because economic activities outside the firms have already brought the services and facilities into being. External economies of agglomeration are thus external to the firm but internal to the city.

The problem arises because highly concentrated population and economic activity generate external diseconomies in the form of congestion; air, water, and noise pollution; social disorder; physical blight; high public investment requirements; inflation; and intense speculation. As Wilbur Thompson (1968) points out:

> The larger places have a clear and sizable advantage in such areas as cheaper and more flexible transportation and utility systems, better research and development facilities, a more skilled and varied labor supply, and better facilities for educating and retraining workers. Further, these economies of scale are captured by private business as lower private costs; at the same time private business is able to slough off on society various social costs that its presence imposes, such as its addition to traffic congestion and air pollution. If, then, the external diseconomies of business-created noise, dirt, congestion, and pollution are some increasing function of city size and/or density, factor market prices are biased in favor of large urban areas, and understate the true market costs of production in the metropolis. In the absence of sophisticated public policy and the even more sophisticated public management that would be needed to implement price reform, factor markets so biased promote urban growth and great size. (P. 60)

While some have argued that the growth of large cities should be checked when external diseconomies outweigh external economies, it might be preferable, even where the balance of external effects was positive, to encourage expansion in intermediate-size cities, particularly if, as many seem to believe likely, the net social product was potentially even greater there. This case rests fundamentally on the position that intermediate-size cities have most of the external economies of the largest cities, but they have not yet become generators of significant external diseconomies.

In support of the intermediate-size city, Neutze's (1967) analysis of Australian data indicates that most of the advantages of a city of 500,000 inhabitants probably also are found in a city of 200,000, but that if a city gets much beyond the 500,000 level external diseconomies are likely to begin to outweigh the concomitant economies. He suggests that many firms will maximize their profits in centers with populations between 200,000 and one million. Similarly, in an earlier study Clark (1945) examined structural differences in American, Canadian, and Australian cities of differing sizes and concluded that a city of about 200,000 provides nearly all of the important services and is nearly "full grown" with respect to manufacturing at 500,000.

Data with respect to the provision of public services indicate that both small towns and big cities fare worse than intermediate-size cities. For example, Hirsch (1968) estimates that the greatest economies of scale occur in the 50,000 to 100,000 population range, and cites a report of the Royal Commission on Local Government in Greater London which found the range to be from 100,000 to 250,000. Cameron (1970) finds a U-shaped infrastructure cost curve, with the minimum cost lying between somewhat less than 30,000 and somewhat more than 250,000. With respect to the findings of a research conference sponsored by the International Economic Association, E.A.G. Robinson (1969) reports that

> the general sense of our discussions was that the minimum size of growth points that experience had shown to be successful was nearer to a population of 100,000 than to one of 10,000 and that even 100,000 was more likely to be an underestimate than an overestimate. It must be large enough to provide efficiently the main services of education, medical facilities, banking, shopping facilities. . . . Above all, it must be large enough both to provide an efficient infrastructure of public utility services, and to permit the early and progressive growth of external economies for its local industries. (P. xvi)

In sum, while it is generally agreed that small towns rarely make efficient "growth centers," intermediate-size cities often have the necessary conditions. However, it would be a mistake to assume too readily that most big cities are too big. In the first place, as Alonso (1970) has persuasively argued, the minimizing of per capita public costs associated with urban size is a poor objective for public policy; rather, economic efficiency would be better served by maximizing the difference between income and costs. "We lack in this country [the United States] figures for the gross regional product of metropolitan areas, but German and Japanese figures show it rising more rapidly than public costs. In this country, using per capita income as an index, we find the same pattern: income rises sharply with urban size" (p. 2).

Alonso's more general argument can be summarized in terms of Figure 1-1, which shows a set of cost and product curves. The figure is analogous to the usual setting of costs and revenues for the firm except that the horizontal axis relates to population size rather than to quantity of output, and the returns to labor (total urban population) is the difference between the value of total output and total costs. The average cost curve (AC) rises after a certain population level; even though this may not always be the case, it tests more stringently Alonso's argument. The average product per capita curve (AP) rises monotonically, as suggested by empirical evidence.

Given this formulation, it is evident that the point of maximum local contribution to national income occurs at Pc, where marginal costs (MC) equal

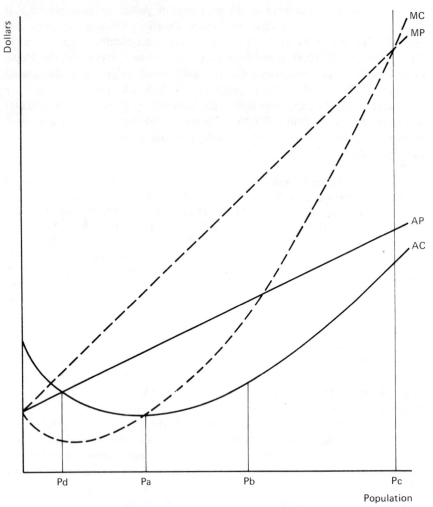

Figure 1-1. Urban Cost and Product Curves with City Size

marginal product (MP). The point of minimum per capita costs, Pa, is irrelevant from an efficiency viewpoint. A national government attempting to maximize total product would have Pc as its target, but with a limited supply of labor national product would be maximized at a smaller level, where the difference between MP and MC equals the opportunity cost similarly defined at alternative locations.

The inhabitants of the city would, however, have a different objective, namely, the maximization of per capita disposable income (i.e., the difference between AP and AC). This would occur where the rate of increase of AP and AC are the same. Because AP increases with population size, this point must lie at a point (Pb) above that where costs are at a minimum. Thus, the point of minimum costs does not coincide with the optimal population level from either a national or local viewpoint. The logic that would lead minimum cost theorists to tax new firms on the basis of the difference between MC and AC would lead just as well here to a justification for subsidies based on the positive externalities produced by the new firm. In general, any net tax or subsidy would be based on the difference between (MP-AP) and (MC-AC), which could be positive or negative.

Of course, no matter how fine the logic of these arguments, it is not possible at present to operationally quantify the key variables. And even if it were, on the basis of contemporary or historic data, for a given place, it should be recognized that the nature of the curves would change with different time horizon perspectives, which in turn would depend on the adaptability of the urban system. There also is a distributional problem. As Andersson points out in his paper, the marginal product benefits would tend to accrue to the owners of land and other fixed assets, whereas the marginal cost would tend to be borne by others, and particularly newcomers to the city.

Finally, the argument that income per capita rises with city size could be interpreted to mean not only that larger cities are more productive, but also that firms that benefit from external economies do so only because they bribe workers to leave smaller (and presumably more satisfying) places by paying higher wages. Wingo (1972) points out that if this is the case, it follows that (1) each worker relocates in keeping with his own trade-offs between money and psychic income, and (2) the extra wage required to compensate workers for living in big cities is included in the costs of production in big cities. When the goods and services produced in big cities are sold in the local market, the diseconomies are reflected in a higher cost of living. When they are exported, the purchasers bear the costs of these diseconomies, as they should. The market mechanism thus in part reflects the nonmarket costs and benefits of big city externalities; and to the extent that it does so it will promote upward pressure on big city wages or outmigration of workers who give relatively greater weight in their preference maps to the psychic income of smaller places.

Wingo also considers the impact of externalities on firms with differing factor cost structures, but like Alonso he concludes that there is no reason to believe that externalities necessarily result in cities of larger than optimal size as long as labor and capital are mobile. Moreover, from a national viewpoint the optimum size of a city can only be defined within the context of the total national settlement pattern, which rules out any conceptually optimal city size per se. This viewpoint appears to be gaining increasing acceptance in many national regional policies, but apparently not in policy approaches favored by the Common Market. More will be said in this regard in the final section of this chapter.

OTHER REGIONAL POLICY ISSUES

Of course, the efficiency of large cities is by no means the only or even the major concern of regional policy. Brown (1972) has argued that "regional economics starts from the existence of grievances that are identified with particular parts of the country, and from conflicts of economic interest between the predominant parts at least of different regional communities" (p. 1). Whether or not this is true of regional economics as an academic discipline, it is true of regional policy. Moreover, while the redress of regional grievances is often presented as being consistent with economic efficiency from a national viewpoint, the fundamental issue is more likely to be equity. Thus, in all of the countries considered regional policies have, in varying degree, been responses to demands from regions with relatively low per capita income and/or high unemployment that "something be done." These regions tend to fall into one of two categories. The first are rural areas characterized by relatively low-productivity agricultural employment, or by surplus labor that has been released from agriculture as a result of technological advance (mechanization, chemical fertilizers, etc.) but is unable to find local employment opportunities. The second are older industrial regions with an overdependence on declining sectors.

What Gordon Cameron (1970) states about the case of the United Kingdom would apply to most of the cases considered. "It would be naive and quite erroneous to detect a pursuit of national efficiency as the major justification for national measures to aid the peripheral regions." Cameron further points out that

> although political pressures give regional policy its main justification and its ever-changing vitality, *efficiency arguments* are never far beneath the surface. There are two possible meanings of efficiency in this context. The first is concerned with questions of how to devise regional policies which maximise the growth in real GNP, probably with a long-term perspective in mind. The second is concerned with using public resources and public policies in such a way that the goals of regional policy are achieved efficiently. This might imply a rule of minimum social costs for the achievement of a given "quantum" of regional goals.

In addition to the equity versus efficiency question, regional policies are complicated by a number of other factors. For example, sectoral policies that were not specifically designed as regional policies nevertheless may have important differential regional consequences. Agricultural policy in the United States has contributed heavily to a process whereby some forty million people have been transferred from rural farm areas to cities and suburbs during the past three decades. On the other hand, in countries such as France and West Germany direct and indirect agricultural subsidies have served to keep more people in rural farm areas than would have been the case if only market forces were operative. Similarly, subsidies to the shipbuilding sector in the United Kingdom have served to prop up employment in the industrial centers of western Scotland.

Yet another motive behind some regional policies is the desire to decentralize decision making with respect to regional and local problems and their solution. The nature and importance of this issue is very largely conditioned by the institutions and administrative structure of each nation. France, for example, has a highly centralized system of government, and most decisions that would have significant consequences for the respective regions are made wholly or in part in Paris. Despite a great deal of rhetoric surrounding the importance of the twenty-one planning regions into which the country has been divided, Rémy Prud'homme argues that there has in fact been no progress toward giving the regions the fiscal capacity to be more independent. Italy has recently made some progress in this respect, but it is too early to evaluate the consequences. On the other hand, regional planning is decentralized in West Germany because of the federal structure of its government. However, a federal structure does not necessarily guarantee decentralized decision-making authority. In the United States the national government has acquired increasing control and influence over regional matters, although the present administration is trying to reverse this process by substituting revenue sharing with state and local governments for categorical grant programs. It should also be noted that some regions with strongly held grievances about real or alleged neglect want funds from the central government but prefer to be their own masters in other respects, even at the cost of some degree of economic disadvantage. These regions often have large concentrations of national minority groups—e.g., the French in Canada, the Basques and Catalans in Spain, and the Indians in the United States. Finally, although the term "planning" is invoked again and again in discussions of regional policies, a word of caution is in order. The degree of formal planning with respect to regional problems varies considerably among the relevant countries, but in fact it is rather weak in most. Only The Netherlands and Sweden could be said to have strong de facto planning, perhaps because they are relatively small and homogeneous.

OUTMIGRATION FROM LAGGING REGIONS
AND PUBLIC POLICY

If regional policies have been primarily conceived and developed in response to allegedly undesirable disequilibria in spatial resource allocation patterns, it can safely be said that no issue is more representative of this concern than population migration from lagging areas to growing areas within countries (and, in the case of Italy, to other countries). With the possible exceptions of West Germany and Canada, the migration question is clearly a major focal point of regional policy formulation in the countries examined here.

After all of the many studies that have been made of the directions and magnitude of migration flows we still know remarkably little about whether and under what conditions migrants would have preferred to have stayed at home; the reasons for their choosing one destination over another; the means by which they adapt to new environments; their overall impact on their destinations; or the conditions under which they would return to their regions of origin.

While outmigration may well benefit the persons who are moving, the economic conditions of those who remain behind may either improve or worsen, depending on whether the local labor market adjusts to the new equilibrium or whether there is a cumulative downward disequilibrium. Outmigration from lagging areas can benefit the workers left behind by lessening the competition for jobs. Indeed, although migration is never forbidden, efforts which inhibit migration from areas with little economic opportunity can be a serious impediment to necessary adaptations. However, the selective nature of outmigration from lagging areas means that they lose their most vital people—the best workers, the young, the better educated. In addition to the initial reduction in employment (or, if the migrants were unemployed, the reduction in transfer payments of a welfare nature) there may well be adverse multiplier effects. If outmigration leads to absolute declines in population, the tax base will be decreased (to the extent that the region depends on revenues from within its boundaries, which of course varies among countries), leading in turn to higher average tax levels or to a deterioration in public services. If there are economies of scale in the provision of public services, a declining population would increase per capita public costs in any event, apart from the issue of a declining tax base. Some marginal firms may leave the region, creating further adverse multiplier effects. This situation may also be complicated by the business cycle, though the evidence is mixed.

Günter Krumme's review (Chapter 4) of the effects of business cycle fluctuations on industrial location in West Germany concludes that

> part of the industrialization of rural areas may not have been a structural "filtering" process where labor-intensive industries are filtered into low wage peripheries in order to survive, but merely temporary . . . and costly capacity expansions *at the margin* conditioned by urban labor shortages and the existence of pockets of underemployment in the rural periphery. In addition, firms affected by Germany's overemployment conditions have learned to cherish monopolistic flexibilities in isolated small community labor markets where, contrary to their situation in larger cities, they are better able to lay off workers temporarily without losing them permanently.

Although the opinion is occasionally expressed in Germany that purely production-oriented plants do not tend to leave during recessions, the best evidence supports a contrary view. On the other hand, in the context of cyclical downturns Gordon Cameron notes with respect to the United Kingdom that "a study of industry-specific closure rates in plants which migrated to the development areas suggested that these were not particularly high as compared to the closure rates at the national level."

If areas are experiencing population loss, the value of real estate may decline, causing banks and other financial institutions to be more strict in granting credit. In the final meeting of the contributors to this volume there was a general consensus that commercial banking systems have a strong tendency to transfer funds from lagging regions to support growth in other regions. To the extent that this is the case, problems of financing local development probably would be exacerbated. I (1971) have presented evidence elsewhere concerning this phenomenon in the United States. In addition, depopulation and declining purchasing power may cause some market-oriented producers to curtail production, resulting in still more unemployment.

The experience of the United States has indicated that when employment opportunities appear in a lagging or declining region there may be a return movement of workers who had once migrated from the region. Because these returnees are frequently more highly skilled than members of the local labor force, the hard core of the locally unemployed and underemployed labor force may not be helped. This remigration problem indicates that one of the major difficulties in lagging regions may be underinvestment in human resources in these regions rather than migration as such, which may be more a symptom than a cause of local distress. Of course, increased investments in human resources without a concomitant increase in local employment opportunities in lagging areas is likely to increase outmigration. This may explain the emphasis given by so many rural development advocates to highways, ports, industrial sites, and power facilities. Such investment in infrastructure, or social overhead capital (SOC) to use Hirschman's term, may also reflect other motives. Hirschman (1958) points out that there frequently is little possibility for evaluating objectively how much investment in SOC is really indicated in any given situation.

> The absence of ex ante criteria is compounded by the weakness of sanctions when mistakes have actually been made. Underutilized port installations, highways, and even power plants do not present nearly the same administrative and public relations problems as a factory that is idle or suffers losses because of insufficient demand.
> Perhaps it is this absence of criteria and of sanctions that has endeared SOC so much to the developers. Development planning is a risky business and there is naturally an attraction in undertaking ventures that cannot be proven wrong before they are started and that are unlikely ever to become obvious failures. (P. 85)

Investment in SOC may also appear to be safer than that in directly productive activities because it is diversified investment in general economic growth rather than in the growth of one specific activity. But as Hirschman notes:

> many SOC investments do not represent similarly diversified risks, and are rather narrowly tied to the anticipated rising fortunes of one city, one valley, or one traffic route; in such cases, it is questionable whether SOC investment is less risky than, for example, investment in an industry whose products might have a nationwide market. (P. 85)

There is yet another important reason why SOC may be overstressed in regional development programs. In countries such as those considered in this volume directly productive activities are largely in the hands of individuals or private firms. Development planners are principally concerned with allocating public investment funds among activities that are considered to be the responsibility of government agencies. Because economic planners spend most of their time on infrastructure projects in the narrow sense it is only natural that they should claim that these projects have primary importance. Alternative projects and programs which may be more desirable are simply not within their frame of reference.

In contrast, it has been claimed that regional economic planners will tend to stress investment in human resources. Newman (1972) writes that

> In the face of uncertainty, the surest investment is in human resources. No one can know now what the future economic activity or geography or aggregates of economic statistics for the region will look like. Uncertainty pervades the decision concerning which investments, of what scale, sequence and timing, will do most to develop the full potential of a selected area. The most that can be done is to operate on the best information currently available and to recognize that adjustments are most easily made through mobility of the population. Hence, the emphasis on preparation of the region's citizens to compete for opportunities "wherever they may choose to live." Uncertainty persists but is lessened when the decision is to enhance the inculcated qualities that individuals must possess if they are actually to have options in their decisions about their lives. If for no other reason, a regional development program will be drawn to investments in human resources. (P. 150)

In fact, a broad acquaintance with regional policies, including those discussed in this volume, would reveal that they do tend to stress investment in economic infrastructure rather than investment in human resources. Newman's case is based on the experience of the Appalachian Regional Commission, the most innovative of the regional development agencies that have functioned in the United States. But even the Appalachian program began with a heavy emphasis on economic infrastructure, principally highways. The reasons why the commission shifted its relative emphasis toward human resource development have never been fully developed, but one may be sure that those who have given the main political support to the program (i.e., the elected officials from the region) would not espouse a policy that implies substantial outmigration from the region.

Here we come to the heart of the problem of investment priorities in lagging regions, and especially in those that have never been developed industrially. Regional policies are invariably place-oriented rather than people-oriented; even where outmigration of people is considered to be a problem, it usually is assumed that economic opportunities are to be created for people *in* the regions in which they live. (As the next section of this chapter indicates, some migration may be tolerable, but in favor of regional centers rather than large, distant cities.) This position is stated with particular vigor in Vera Cao-Pinna's study of regional policy in Italy. She maintains that Italian regional policy should be considered a failure so long as massive outmigration from the South persists. Despite the liberal economist's faith in resource mobility as a major means for reducing regional economic disparities, it is difficult to deny that massive outmigration over many decades has left the South in a state of disequilibrium, and that it has had adverse social and institutional consequences. On the other hand, efforts to induce general economic development in the South have not yet been successful, and on the basis of the evidence in Cao-Pinna's study it would seem that many of the preconditions for economic development have been in doubtful status in the region. Nevertheless, she maintains that it is now possible for the South to attain a satisfactory equilibrium among population, employment, and gross product, and that even from a national viewpoint this should be the principal general objective of regional policy.

Italy has been singled out for attention because it most sharply represents the migration problem perceived within most of the countries studied here. To complicate matters, relocation assistance is, or recently has been, given to workers in The Netherlands, Sweden, Canada, the United Kingdom, and the United States. It is not altogether clear whether or to what extent aid is intended to promote labor mobility or merely to ease the difficulties involved in a more or less inevitable process. Whatever the ambiguities surrounding the migration issue it remains a mainstay behind most regional policies. Only in Sweden and The Netherlands has it been clarified to the point where net migration targets have been established by region.

THE ROLE OF GROWTH CENTERS

Growth center policies have been adopted in all of the countries studied, although the extent to which they have been influenced by growth center theory has varied considerably. Detailed consideration of the history, nature, and significance of growth center theory is beyond the scope of this chapter, but such studies are available elsewhere (Hansen, 1972; Kuklinski, 1972).

It should be emphasized at the outset that the growth centers which are the objects of public policy are not simply urban centers that already are growing rapidly—i.e., spontaneous growth centers. Indeed, one of the principal arguments for investments in induced growth centers is that population can thereby be diverted away from allegedly overcrowded metropolitan areas toward smaller cities. On the other hand, growth center theory quite explicitly recognizes the existence of economies of agglomeration. It maintains that the most efficient way to generate development in lagging regions is to concentrate projects in a relatively few places with genuine growth potential. Ideally, public investments in these places would initiate a kind of chain reaction of mutually induced public and private investments. (Some writers have made a distinction between growth poles, defined in terms of the expansion of interrelated economic sectors, and growth centers, defined in terms of geographic location. Because growth center policies rely on the concentration of sectoral activities within very specific geographic places, I use the terms "growth center" and "growth pole" interchangeably.) However, the benefits realized by a growth center approach are supposed to be regional in nature, and not just limited to the few select centers. In theory, economic expansion in the growth centers, or poles, is linked to similar expansion in their hinterlands by means of "spread effects," or "trickle down effects." A growth pole has been defined (Nichols, 1969) as "an urban centre of economic activity which can achieve self-sustaining growth to the point that growth is diffused outward into the pole region and eventually beyond into the less developed regions of the nation" (p. 193).

Most countries that have adopted growth center strategies have done so for the purpose of eventually generating economic expansion in lagging hinterland areas. With some exceptions in small countries, these strategies have not been successful, usually because they have suffered from a tendency toward proliferation of a large number of relatively small centers incapable of effectively performing the role attributed to them. This certainly has been the case in Canada (although many of the so-called "special areas" are not conceived as "growth centers") and the United States, where more than a few "growth centers" have actually been declining small towns. In West Germany growth centers are represented by over three hundred urban centers with an economic infrastructure emphasis and literally thousands of central places with a service function. The United Kingdom undertook some tentative experiments with growth centers but has now abandoned them. The Italian experience has been similar, even though some growth center approaches are still being carried out in the South. Italy's new "80 Project" calls for special projects in specific areas, including those that Cao-Pinna describes as "the most promising points of the South." In Spain the growth center notion inspired a series of policies designed first to develop regional capitals, then other provincial cities, and then growth axes in relatively poor areas. Spain now has a national spatial policy based on broad tiers in the urban hierarchy: metropolitan labor market areas, urban service centers, and finally local market towns. Growth center strategies related to various tiers of the urban hierarchy have been used in both The Netherlands and Sweden with some apparent success. In Sweden, as Åke Andersson's study reports, "A growth center strategy has been decided on and all municipalities have already been classified into four different groups of centers: metropolitan areas, primary centers, regional centers, and municipal centers. Projects connected with medium term regional economic policy will be concentrated in primary and regional centers. The problems of municipal centers in lagging areas will be dealt with in the framework of short term regional economic policy." In France, where a great deal of the growth center theory has been developed, the Fifth Plan (1966-70) gave considerable emphasis to eight *métropoles d'équilibre* that were to provide a counterweight to the Paris region and serve as growth centers for the provinces. Elaborate plans have been formulated for the *métropoles*, but their privileged status has been more one of principle than of implemented investment projects. In addition, the *métropoles* strategy has been somewhat confused, or at least diluted, by the demands of other centers for priority development. These include nine new towns (five in the Paris region and four elsewhere), the cities of the Paris Basin, and other cities scattered through the country. Some powerful voices also favor continuing support for the primacy of Paris in view of its European and world roles.

If one may generalize, there is increasing realization that viable growth center strategies demand greater selectivity in choice of centers and of activities. Despite some local successes it is still uncertain whether spread effects from induced growth centers can really raise income and employment opportunities in lagging or declining regions to levels comparable to those in more advanced regions. In some cases it is possible that the economic infrastructure bias that has accompanied growth center policies has done a disservice by shifting attention away from the critical health, education, and social problems that plague less developed regions. Preoccupation with spread effects also has hindered efforts to explore the role of induced growth centers as migration centers. In many of the countries considered here the fastest growing urban areas are neither the largest metropolitan areas nor the small towns and cities, but rather, intermediate-size cities. In the last, public funds could be integrated with existing or potential external economies to produce more rapid growth with a minimum of diseconomies of congestion. Although such places do not "need" growth center subsidies, it may be easier to accelerate their growth than it would be to accelerate growth in a lagging region. However, the accelerated growth of intermediate growth centers should be made conditional to the granting of newly created employment opportunities to a significant number of workers from lagging areas who could either commute or migrate. This approach would serve to keep workers from areas with poor growth prospects at least relatively close to their original homes. Moreover, if the government knows what places are going to grow it can provide public facilities in advance of demand. In other words, a growth center strategy can be integrated with rational physical planning to the greater benefit of both. It is evident that a successful growth center strategy would have to be based on careful analyses of data on employment growth prospects, commuting, migration, and the location preferences of people in the context of actual opportunities available in alternative locations. Even so, however, political realities may make it impossible to implement a development strategy based on only a relatively few urban centers.

Finally, it should be noted that the location of public services is often overshadowed by discussions of public investments. For example, Rémy Prud'homme finds that "there is, in France, a complete dichotomy between investment decisions and expenditures on the one hand, and operating decisions and expenditures on the other. The idea that there are relationships between the two types of expenditure, and that, in many cases, one may be substituted for the other has not yet gained much recognition in France." This neglect, which characterizes not only growth center discussions but also other regional development strategies, is of course by no means limited to France.

THE TOOLS OF REGIONAL POLICY

Regional policies usually assume that when undesirable disequilibria occur in spatial resource allocation patterns it is the task of policy to redress the situation by promoting the movement of economic opportunities to people. Despite some approaches that explicitly or implicitly emphasize the movement of workers to jobs—worker relocation assistance, some manpower and training programs, and the limited use of growth centers as migration centers—most of the tools of regional policy are used to subsidize capital expansion in areas where labor is relatively unemployed or working at relatively low wages. The objective is not only to encourage capital to move to target areas but also to induce local capital in these areas to be invested locally rather in more advanced regions where, under market conditions, rates of return are higher. The arguments for capital subsidies often are reminiscent of the "infant industry" arguments for national protectionist policies.

It is beyond our scope to review the various tools of regional policy in great detail. They tend to be complex and to vary over time. (The interested reader can obtain updated versions of specific regional legislation and decrees from the relevant agencies in the various countries or from international bodies such as the Commission of the European Communities in Brussels or the Organization for Economic Cooperation and Development in Paris.) However, the general nature of these measures in each country is discussed in the following chapters.

The mechanisms by which capital is subsidized vary considerably, but they usually involve a package of tax and credit advantages, direct grants, and technical assistance. In most cases areas eligible for aid are designated on the basis of one or more criteria, usually unemployment, low income, heavy outmigration, or lack of resources and infrastructure. The amount of subsidy available usually varies according to the zone where a project is located—i.e., the worse the conditions in an area, the greater the available subsidy. At times, (e.g., in the United States) this approach has been inconsistent with an ostensible growth center orientation. It has also, as in Italy, been compromised by the diversion of funds to less needy areas having influential political pressure groups.

Subsidies may also take indirect forms. For example, the government may use its influence over the location of infrastructure to create conditions favorable to the location of private investment, or it may deliberately decentralize some administrative activities. In cases where the government owns or partly owns firms engaged in directly productive activities, direct political pressures may be employed to locate plants in target areas. Institutional factors are of course critical here. Thus, the options available in a country such as Italy are greater than those in a relatively laissez faire country such as the United States. In addition to positive incentives to locate in target areas, there may also be negative restrictions on locating in some areas—for example Paris.

In view of the diverse nature of planning goals and economic systems, it is to be expected that policy tools which are effective in one country may not be in another; of course, this may also be true with regard to different regions within the same country. Within any given country, as Smith (1971) points out,

> it may seldom be possible to use an econometric model to test the efficiency of specific instruments prior to their application, but there are still rational ways of judging the merits of different measures in relation to a certain goal. For example, if the objective is to reduce unemployment it would seem reasonable to use a labor-cost subsidy to encourage the hiring of more workers or the location of new labor-intensive firms. . . . there is a certain irony in the use of capital investment inducements by so many governments as an instrument in depressed-region policy. They will tend to favor capital-intensive firms who may have few workers when the stated policy goal is the reduction of unemployment, and such inducements could in fact lead to some substitution of capital for labor. (Pp. 451-52)

Åke Andersson refers to a Norwegian econometric study indicating "that employment subsidies are three to fifteen times more efficient than capital subsidies as a means of regional policy, with the relative efficiency depending on the character of the production functions of the individual industries." Labor cost subsidies do seem in fact to be viewed with increasing interest in some countries, and in the United Kingdom they now are equivalent to the subsidies given to capital. There remains the problem of using labor subsidies in the most efficient manner. Subsidies based on average costs would be, in effect, similar to capital subsidies. What is needed is a relatively simple administrative device to allocate marginal labor subsidies so that only genuinely new employment is covered.

It may of course be questioned whether the goal of decreasing unemployment is the best objective for depressed regions in advanced countries. Policy instruments used toward this end may bring about short run improvements but not create the conditions necessary for self-sustained long run growth. Richardson (1969, p. 402) argues that relative growth in per capita output is a more rational objective, and that the relocation or expansion of firms should be evaluated in terms of future income growth and the creation of external economies rather than in terms of number of new jobs created and their cost. For example, even if few new jobs are created directly, the complete transfer of a plant and its workers would be justified if it leads to an inflow of other firms—e.g., suppliers to the original plant. The problem lies in the deficiencies of the analytic and predictive tools of regional economics and related disciplines. It is difficult enough to make accurate estimates of the new jobs attributable to regional policies with other things held equal and thus of the cost per job. But it is even more difficult to project future production structures and potential external economies and the degree to which and conditions under which they may be realized.

It must be admitted that there are major deficiencies in our ability to forecast with respect to variables of major importance to regional policy. Our methods too frequently are not well enough developed to pick up accurate signals of changing situations to which public policies should respond, given the objectives that have been specified. Moreover, when reasonably good methods are available there often are severe data limitations.

In many cases well-meaning hope has been more instrumental than critical analysis in the process of policy formulation; and while policies have had positive results there is general agreement that these results appear small in relation to policy objectives. Some would argue that success indicators have been too narrowly defined, in terms of employment, income, or net migration. But the wider criteria, including improvement of environmental quality, and greater regional and local self-determination, that are emerging in many countries are even more difficult to deal with from the standpoint of success indicators.

Some facets of regional science may appear to be preoccupied with endless refinements of professors' irrelevant games. Yet regional science has provided tools which in turn have proven valuable in the formulation and implementation of regional policies. The degree to which this is so has depended on particular national circumstances. In Sweden, relations between regional scientists and government decision makers have been relatively close, but in most other countries regional policies appear to have been more influenced by immediate political and administrative pressures than by objective research, even if the research has been extensive and well articulated. Because regional policies have broad social and political, as well as economic, implications it is not to be expected that they will take their primary orientation from economics and allied disciplines. Nevertheless, one may speculate that the next major advances in regional science will probably occur in response to real problems; the works in the history of economic thought that still interest us were, after all, addressed to immediate problems of political economy. I suggest that the clearest generalization that can be drawn from the diverse country studies is that what is needed most from the whole range of persons concerned with regional policies is not hasty selection of general "goals," but a better elucidation of what the problems really are.

A NOTE ON THE EUROPEAN COMMUNITY

Five of the countries considered in the following chapters—Italy, France, West Germany, The Netherlands, and the United Kingdom—account for by far the major part of the population and territory of the European Community, which also includes Denmark, Belgium, Luxembourg and Ireland. Because regional problems in Western Europe cannot be divorced from their international setting, and in view of postwar efforts to promote greater economic integration in the area, it is instructive to examine briefly regional policies in this context.

Map 1-1 indicates the degree of population concentration in the various regions of the community. It is immediately apparent that there is a zone of relatively high population density in roughly the central part. It includes the northernmost region of France, most of Belgium, The Netherlands (excluding four northern provinces and Zeeland in the south), the heavily industrialized regions of West Germany, and in England, the South East (London), West Midlands, East Midlands, North West, and Yorkshire-Humberside. The average density in this area is 452 persons per square kilometer. Its ninety million inhabitants account for thirty-five percent of the community's total population, though the area represents only 13 percent of the total. There are also several other areas with high population concentrations, the most important of which are the Paris region, Lombardy and Liguria in northern Italy, and an area surrounding Rome on the west coast of Italy.

There are three relatively large sparsely populated areas in the community. The largest cuts obliquely across France and consists of regions with a population density of about fifty. The others are Scotland and nearly all of Ireland.

In all other regions the density varies from 100 to 200, except on either side of the French sparsely settled area, where it remains below 100.

The Treaty of Rome, which created the European Community, stated that "reducing the differences existing between the various regions and the backwardness of the less favoured regions" would be one of the community's principal objectives. A report of the Commission of the European

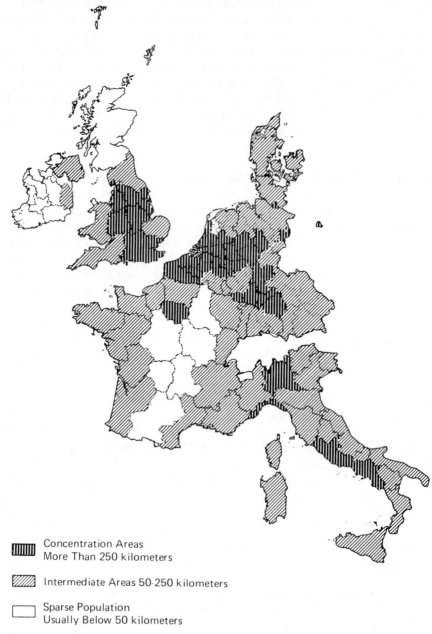

■■■■ Concentration Areas
More Than 250 kilometers

▨ Intermediate Areas 50-250 kilometers

☐ Sparse Population
Usually Below 50 kilometers

Source: Commission of the European Communities.

Map 1-1. Population Densities in Regions of the European Community

Communities (1973), referring to the period before the entrance of the United Kingdom, Ireland, and Denmark, states that:

> from 1960 to 1970 the gross national product of the Six increased in volume at a rate of 5.4% per year—and this was reflected in rising standards of living. It cannot be said, however, that economic activity throughout the Community has developed evenly, nor has expansion been geographically balanced. Indeed, despite positive interventionist policies by Member Governments, the gap with regard to comparative incomes between the regions has not shown any noticeable degree of change. The richest areas in the Community have an income per head about five times that of the poorest. (P. 2)

On the other hand, another study prepared by the commission (1971) reports that for the nineteen main regions in the Europe of the Six, the difference between the lowest-income (southern Italy) and the highest-income (Paris) regions declined between 1960 and 1969. The Paris region's per capita income index fell from 155.2 to 149.8 (community per capita income = 100), while that for southern Italy rose from 34.9 to 42.4. The coefficient of variation for all nineteen regions fell from .308 to .262. Using smaller regions, the highest index, that for Hamburg, remained virtually stable (209.7 in 1960 versus 209.6 in 1969). The lowest again were in southern Italy: 25.5 for Basilicata in 1960 and 33.2 for Calabria in 1969. The coefficient of variation declined from .323 to .284. In general, the modest reductions in the maximum differences between regions in the two cases was clearly due to index increases for southern Italy, but this region did not substantially improve its relative position within Italy. Thus, the increased values for southern Italy were primarily a consequence of the improved position of Italy vis-à-vis the other countries. Given this fact, as well as the somewhat uncertain nature of the data used in the foregoing analyses, it remains apparent that much remains to be done if regional per capita income disparities are to be reduced significantly.

The general concerns of the community with respect to regional policy are similar to those in most of the member countries. The Commission of the European Communities (1973), points out, for example, that "certain regions of the Community have always known structural underemployment and high levels of unemployment, and there has always been sizeable migration from some Community regions, in particular those at its periphery" (p. 3).

As Map 1-2 shows, there are six major areas of net outmigration. The most serious problem is in southern and south-central Italy (excepting Rome and Latium), where outmigration annually drains off an average of 260,000 persons. Of the forty-five provinces in the area, seventeen have an annual negative net outmigration rate in excess of fifteen percent. The other major areas are the north and northwest of the United Kingdom, particularly Scotland; eastern portions of West Germany; northwest France; and much of Denmark and

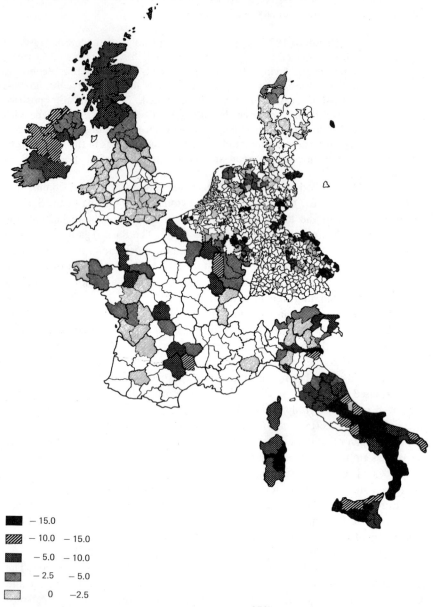

■	− 15.0	
▨	− 10.0	− 15.0
■	− 5.0	− 10.0
▦	− 2.5	− 5.0
▢	0	−2.5

Source: Commission of the European Communities (1973).

Map 1-2. Annual Migration Rates in the Regions of the European Community, 1973

Ireland. In addition, there are more modest population drains from the northeast of Italy to the Gulf of Genoa, and from the frontier zone of Belgium, France, and Germany.

Outmigration from peripheral areas tends to be associated with problems of traditional agriculture. In recent years these areas have experienced sharp rates of decline in the proportion of total employment accounted for by agriculture. They usually have high levels of structural underemployment and—in areas such as Ireland and the Italian South—there is also high, long term unemployment. While they have relatively low income per capita, they still have relatively high dependence on agriculture. The commission recognizes that "the need for this sector to modernize in order to integrate with an economy of high productivity and growth means that surplus manpower will be laid off and that there will be a continuous reduction in employment" (p. 131). Yet the commission fails to explore in any thorough manner the trade-offs between comprehensive worker relocation assistance and policies that would focus on development of the problem regions, including not only peripheral agricultural areas but also regions dependent on stagnant or declining industries. It obviously is the latter difficulty which is largely responsible for the fact that, according to commission (1973, p. 124) data, every region in the United Kingdom has a per capita income value below that of the community as a whole.

At this writing the commission has proposed that a Regional Development Fund be established before the end of 1973. The fund would be the principal vehicle for mobilizing community resources for regional development, apart of course from the programs already being carried out by the relevant governments. The fund would be entirely devoted to assistance for the long term development of the lesser developed and declining regions in the community, with the aim of inducing self-sustaining growth in these regions. Again in keeping with the intranational policies of many countries, the commission maintains that:

> Community regional policy is not only in the interests of those living in the areas of relative poverty, high unemployment, underemployment and mirgration. It is equally in the interests of those who live in the great conurbations with their increasing congestion. The physical poverty of the underprivileged regions is matched only by the mounting environmental poverty of the areas of concentration. The pressure on housing, the miseries of commuting on overloaded roads or overcrowded trains, the pollution of the air and the water—all these developments mean that the environmental case for closing the geographical gaps is as powerful a one for those who live in the so-called prosperous areas of the Community, as it is for those in the poorer regions. The Regional Development Fund, the machinery for coordination to be created and other Community instruments, which could be created, should therefore be seen not as a method by which the better-off regions are forced to subsidise

those less fortunate; they will in fact be contributing to a richer quality of life for themselves. Indeed, a Community regional strategy must ensure that efforts to attract new development in the problem regions are accompanied by "decongestion" arrangements which will make for the efficiency and coordination at a Community level of the present policies of Member States in order to discourage excessive industrial congestion in areas where this congestion can only lessen the quality of life, and encourage decentralisation of these industries and of other activities towards regions which need them. At the same time care must be taken lest the development of the poorest regions leads by ill-considered industrialisation to the destruction of their environment. These are the environmental considerations on which a Community regional policy should be based. (P. 5)

The commission believes that community regional policy should not be a substitute for the regional policies of the member countries, but should rather complement them. The community is reluctant to accept a common regional policy; rather, the issues raised and the approaches taken will simply mirror those now found in the respective member countries. Whether and to what extent this is wise may and indeed should be debated. Hopefully, this volume will contribute constructively to this debate.

Chapter Two

Regional Economic Policy in France, 1962-1972

INTRODUCTION

Regional economic policy in France (and elsewhere) is as old as economic policy. Transportation networks, for instance, have always been decided upon by some political authority; from Julius Caesar, who gave Gaul its first road system, to Baptiste Legrand, who designed the well-known Paris-centered plan for railways, France is a case in point. Yet, until the late forties, French policy makers practiced regional policy without, in fact, realizing it. To take only one example, the relocation or the creation in the west and the south of arms and ordnance factories (whose only client was the government) was systematically encouraged between 1935 and 1940; but this action, which happened to be largely successful, (over sixty factories and 15,000 jobs were concerned) was undertaken for purely strategic reasons. Regional economic policy was a means, and a by-product, not an end.

It was only after the war that regional policy became a policy as such. Two men played a decisive role in its early development. In 1947 a history and geography teacher, M. J.F. Gravier, published a book entitled *Paris et le Désert Français* (Paris and the French Desert). The thesis of the book was simple: the hypertrophy of Paris is a threat to the health of France. The development of this thesis, historical rather than economic in nature, was likely to be understood by the French elite. The title was a stroke of genius, like a great caricature. M. Gravier said what everyone thought, and said it well. He was to be listened to. He was, in particular, listened to by M. Claudius-Petit, then minister of reconstruction and urbanism. In 1950 Claudius-Petit published a short pamphlet entitled *Pour un Plan National d'Aménagement du Territoire* (For a National Plan of Regional Planning); he created, within his ministry, a division in charge of regional planning; and he had Parliament pass a bill creating a National Fund for Regional Planning (Fond National d'Aménagement du Territoire, or FNAT).

Many English-speaking observers hesitate over the expression *aménagement du territoire*, and often do not even translate it. The expression, which was coined by Claudius-Petit and has become widely used, is in French both vague and beautiful. It is made of two words. *Aménagement* means more than planning and designing; it evokes the idea of implementing a plan and hence the concept of policy. *Territoire* is not as abstract as "territory"; it can mean "land" (there is *terre*, or land, in *territoire*); it refers usually to the national space, but can also be used for smaller spatial units. *Aménagement du territoire* could then be translated by something halfway between "land policy" and "territorial policy." However, regional policy is probably as good a translation as anything else, and really captures much of the meaning of *aménagement du territoire.*

It can be said, then, that France has had a regional policy since 1950. Objectives have been specified and/or changed; tools have been diversified; institutions have been created; steps taken; and results obtained.

The first ten years were less interesting than the later period, though it is true that some of the major instruments of regional policy were created during this time. In 1954 and 1955 bills were passed that provided subsidies intended to induce manufacturing industries to move out of the Paris area and to locate in designated areas. A 1955 bill made special authorization necessary for a manufacturing firm to settle or to expand (over 500 square meters) in the Paris area. In 1956, "regions" were created. Since 1791, France had been divided into ninety "departments," which have been the basic administrative, and to some extent political, subdivisions of the country. It was felt that regional planning called for a smaller number of larger units, so the departments were then grouped together in order to form twenty-one regions which were supposed to have some sort of economic, geographic, or historic unity. It should be noted that the regions were by no means political units: nobody was elected at the regional level, and regions could not be considered as local governments. At this stage they were not even administrative units, since nobody was appointed at the regional level; rather they were mere planning units, which means that "development plans" for each region were to be drawn by the central government public administration. Such measures were not unimportant. But they were neither numerous, nor coordinated, nor successful.

In the early sixties, a number of steps were taken that gave regional policy in France a new start. The fourth national plan, covering the 1960-1965 period, was the first plan to explicitly tackle the regional aspects of economic development, to state aims, and to discuss means. In 1961, the twenty-one regions became administrative units; a regional prefect was appointed at the head of each region, with a certain degree of authority over the departmental prefects and hence over all the administrative agencies within the region. More important, a new institution that was to play a key role, DATAR (Délégation à l'Aménagement du Territoire et à l'Action Régionale, or Agency for Regional Planning and Action), was created in 1963. As Jérôme Monod (1971) puts it, this measure "marks an important stage, the move from mere intellectual speculations and specific measures to a coordinated action" (p. 37).

We shall therefore restrict our analysis of regional policy in France to what happened during the 1962-1972 period. We shall start with an overall picture of regional problems and trends at the beginning of the period, and then turn to the definition of regional economic policy in France and try to show who defined which goals. The fourth section is devoted to a critical analysis of the tools used, while the final section presents an evaluation of the policy actually followed.

REGIONAL PROBLEMS IN THE EARLY SIXTIES

The problems that regional policy has to solve stem, by definition, from the spatial distribution of men and activities. But these distributions, in turn, are nothing but spatial projections of the economy and the society as a whole. It is therefore necessary to start with a brief description of the changing patterns of the French economy. The three major features most pertinent for an under-standing of regional problems are (1) the demographic growth of the postwar period, (2) the decline of agriculture, and (3) the changing structure of manufac-turing activities.

Birth rates, which were about sixteen per thousand population during the prewar period—a level much lower than the levels found elsewhere—jumped to a high twenty-one in 1946 and remained at this level in the following years. The rate of natural increase, which was very low in the prewar period (and even negative between 1935 and 1944), climbed above seven per thousand. Such rates were and are to be found in many countries. What is noteworthy is that they were a new phenomenon in France. France had not experienced such a high rate of natural increase since the early nineteenth century. Consequently, whereas the population had stagnated between 1900 and 1945 at around forty million, it now started to increase. It reached forty-six million in 1961, and fifty million in 1968. In the twenty-five years that followed the end of the war, the French population increased twice as much as in the preceding century. This increase is in sharp contrast with the experience of most other developed countries, where regional problems appear in a context of slower, not faster, population growth.

The relative decline of agriculture is also a familiar story. It had of course commenced long ago in France, but, unlike what happened in most other developed countries, it accelerated during the postwar period. The share of value added contributed by agriculture to the total value added was cut down from a high of 15.3 percent in 1949 to a low of 8.7 percent in 1967. The number of farmers decreased greatly in relative and in absolute terms. The number of people who left farms for factories (or tertiary activities) increased from about 50,000 per year in the prewar period to more than 150,000 per year in the postwar period.

Productivity increases in agriculture (and the diminution in the agricultural labor force that came with it) were not enough for output per man in agriculture to equal output per man elsewhere. Agricultural incomes remained low, and farmers poor. Agricultural regions are low-income regions. Economic policy, then, had a threefold purpose: (1) to compensate for income differentials, (2) to promote productivity increases in agriculture, and (3) to promote the creation of jobs in the industrial and tertiary sectors for those people who had to leave agriculture.

Industrial employment did not increase very rapidly in postwar France, but industrial production and industrial productivity did. Over the 1949-1962 period, industrial production increased at a 5.5 percent yearly rate, and industrial productivity at a 5.1 percent yearly rate. A similar evolution could be—and actually was—projected for the following period. In the course of a few years, then, France was turned into a predominantly industrial country. In 1967 the share of industry in the GNP (47.3 percent) was higher in France than in all other countries (with the exception of Germany). But data for industry as a whole hide the most interesting part of the story. In some sectors, namely garments, textiles, leather, and mining, productivity increased faster than production, and employment declined, creating difficulties in the regions or areas where the share of such sectors was high. This growth has benefited some regions more than others; development has not been spatially "balanced." The major issues here are (1) interregional disparities and (2) centrifugal tendencies.

Data on income differentials in 1962 appear in Map 2-1. The striking features are (1) the considerable difference between income per household in the Paris region and income per household elsewhere; and (2) the low income of western regions relative to eastern regions. Such differences in income are easily accounted for by differences in sector-mix. High-income regions are regions with high productivity activities.

These century-old differences were not reduced in the 1954-1962 period. There is no reliable data available on the evolution of income differentials, but since low productivity sectors are also lagging or declining sectors, employment data gives an idea of the evolution. Total employment, which increased by one percent for France as a whole, increased by eleven percent for the Paris region and decreased by eleven percent for Limousin. In absolute terms, the number of jobs increased in the Paris region (+ 385,000), Provence-Côte d'Azur (+ 76,000), and Rhône-Alpes (+ 59,000), and decreased in Brittany (−81,000), Aquitaine (− 59,000), Pays de la Loire (− 46,000), Auvergne (− 45,000), Midi-Pyrénées (− 42,000), and Limousin (− 40,000). In the early sixties, then, western regions, which had the lowest income, were also losing jobs.

Income differentials are not the only measure of regional disparity. Other indicators (automobile ownership, infant death rates, etc.) tell very much the same story, though they do not give a complete picture of the difference that exists between Paris and the rest of France. Power—essentially political, but including economic, financial, cultural, and intellectual power—is heavily concentrated in Paris. Head offices of practically all major enterprises are concentrated there, and it has been estimated that in 1963 about thirty percent of salaried workers in manufacturing enterprises worked in "multiregional enterprises" with head offices located in Paris (Le Fillâtre, 1964; Anfré, 1969).

Such century-old disparities gave birth to (and were also caused by) important and continuous migrations, in which Paris played a key role,

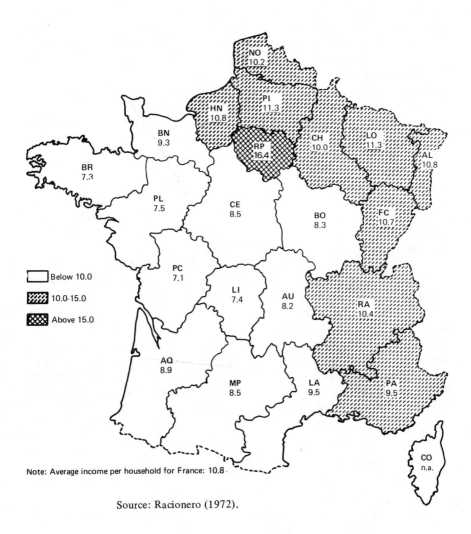

Note: Average income per household for France: 10.8

Source: Racionero (1972).

Map 2-1. Income per Household, by Region, 1962 (in 1,000 francs) francs)

absorbing all or most of the growth in the French population for a century (see Table 2-1). The growth of Paris cannot be explained by natural increase (birth rates were actually lower in Paris than in the rest of France) and is entirely accounted for by migration.

This secular pattern of migration continued after the war. Between 1954 and 1962, a time period for which there are matrixes of migratory flows available (INSEE, 1965, pp. 124-5), the Paris region was still the great beneficiary, but two other regions also exhibited important gains: Provence-Côte d'Azur and Rhône-Alpes. Losers were again the western regions: Brittany, Pays de la Loire, Basse-Normandie, etc., and also—this a new phenomenon—the north. It is also important to note that most of the important flows had Paris as origin or destination; this is additional evidence of the key role of Paris.

These flows group together people both in and out of the labor force; available data do not allow a detailed analysis of both groups of people. However, there are figures on total inmigrants and outmigrants for each region for labor force participants (INSEE, 1967, p. 223). The signs of net migratory flows are not changed but their magnitudes are. The net flow for Paris is relatively much more important; the net flow for Provence-Côte d'Azur is relatively less important (and less important than the one for Rhône-Alpes). This suggests that a good many people moving out of Paris are not members of the labor force, and, presumably, retired people. The "economic" attraction of Paris is therefore even greater than suggested by migration patterns.

Another major feature to be considered is urbanization. France was, until recently, rather a rural country. The ratio of urban to total population was below fifty percent until the thirties. Since total population was not growing, the rate of growth of urban population was fairly low. Between 1860 and 1960, urban population was multiplied by thirty in the United States, and only by three in France. However, after the war France dramatically entered the age of urbanization. The number of persons per year to be accommodated in cities jumped from about 200,000 before the war to over 500,000 in the 1950-1960 period. And it was easy to forecast that the movement would continue at about the same rate during the sixties and the seventies.

Table 2-1. Total Population, France and Paris Region, 1861-1962 (in millions)

	France	Paris region	Rest of France	Paris region France (percent)
1861	37.4	2.8	34.6	7.5
1901	40.7	4.7	36.0	11.6
1946	40.5	6.6	33.9	16.8
1962	46.2	8.4	37.8	18.2

Source: INSEE (1965), p. 59.

The process of change involved more than rural to urban migration. Data on migration among cities grouped by size-class shows that each category of cities had a net gain in its relations with all categories of smaller cities, and a net loss in its relation with all categories of larger cities (Schiray, 1970, p. 37). Backward migrations, when they existed, were in no case powerful enough to counterbalance migrations to larger cities.

DEFINITION OF REGIONAL ECONOMIC POLICIES

It is interesting to find out how the regional problems briefly described in the previous section have been assessed and dealt with. First, it is important to note that they have been recognized as problems. Regional planning as an economic policy concept did not lose momentum in the sixties. On the contrary, it grew in importance and gained an ever-increasing recognition in administrative and political circles. More and more references were made to *aménagement du territoire*, and decisions taken in the name of it.

It is all the more remarkable in view of the fact that, during this period, overall economic planning in France (again as a concept) was on the wane. The late fifties and the early sixties were the golden age of French planning; it attracted notice in the United States at about the time it started losing ground in France. Massé left in 1962, and no important figure was appointed to succeed him as head of the Planning Commission. Of course, the commission remained and kept producing plans, but in an atmosphere of disenchantment. If general planning was—and still is—out of fashion in France, regional planning was not. There has been a will, repeated again and again in official documents and speeches, to "solve regional problems," and to "take account of spatial dimensions of economic and social life." There has been a distinct refusal to let economic market forces shape the spatial distribution of activities and men. The rationale is that market forces result in (1) inequalities that could not be tolerated on an equity basis, and (2) externalities that should be corrected (or promoted) on an efficiency basis. The conclusion, and the dominant theme, is that public intervention in the spatial field—i.e., regional policy—is necessary, or to use a word from the title of a book by Labasse, geography should be "voluntary."

Everybody agreed then that "something had to be done." But what? How? For whom? And who should decide on these matters?

The latter question is essential. It soon became clear that regional policy could not be the responsibility of any one particular ministry. The regional dimension is to be found everywhere, in the policies of each ministry. Regional policy can hardly be thought of as a policy, but rather as a necessary component of other policies. The Planning Commission, which had always been directly under the prime minister, and whose task had been to coordinate and to orient the actions of all economic agents, was in a good position to take regional policy in its hands. It tried, and did not succeed.

A new organization, DATAR (Délégation à l'Aménagement du Territoire et à l'Action Régionale, or Agency for Regional Planning and Action), has managed to play the leading role. DATAR was created in 1963 and placed under the direct authority of the prime minister. As the founding decree puts it, DATAR was to be "an agency of coordination and impulsion" whose task was "to prepare and coordinate the information required for government decisions in regional planning and action, and to see that the various technical administrations would adjust their actions and use the means at their disposal in view of objectives beyond their respective responsibility—an interministerial task that requires the authority of the prime minister."

DATAR was—and still is—a small organization (approximately twenty to thirty professionals). It derived its influence and power from (1) the high quality of its staff, where some of the brightest young French civil servants could be found; (2) the money it could give (through FIAT—Fonds d'Intervention pour l'Aménagement du Territoire, or Regional Planning Fund); and (3) the political influence and importance of its leaders. The first director, Olivier Guichard, was a noted Gaullist politician who was later to occupy important cabinet positions. The second director, Jérôme Monod, has always been very close to Guichard, and is also a potential minister.

Officially, DATAR has no responsibility for setting goals. This is the task of the Planning Commission, which is supposed to integrate regional planning within the framework of overall planning. A special committee, CNAT (Commission Nationale de l'Aménagement du Territoire, or National Committee for Regional Planning), was set up to assist the Planning Commission in this task. The Planning Commission also developed within its structure an urban and regional division.

CNAT has not played a very important role, for two main reasons. First, it was concerned with long-term planning, and long-term planning strategies are rarely taken very seriously by policy makers. Second, CNAT was made up of seventy-seven members, from all regions and trades; such a "parliament" could hardly agree on clear-cut priorities and strategies, and the two CNAT reports (published respectively in 1964 and 1970) merely underline the necessity to do everything everywhere.

The Urban and Regional Division of the Planning Commission did not play an important role either. Its main responsibility was to "regionalize" the plan, i.e., to develop regional public investment plans for and by the different regions. But public investment planning was very firmly controlled by the various ministries, which were not willing to let the regions, let alone the Planning Commission, have their say. It was only at the time of the elaboration of the Sixth Plan, when regions were given more power, that the Urban and Regional Division of the Planning Commission could exercise a certain degree of influence. Moreover, the other divisions of the Planning Commission, and its leadership, were staffed with macroeconomists who were more interested in the sophisticated interplay of national aggregates than in regional problems.

In practice, then, regional policy was taken over by DATAR. The guidelines issued by CNAT for implementation by DATAR were vague enough to make it possible and even necessary for DATAR to develop its own objectives and its own actions. In addition there was a feedback mechanism, in that DATAR was influential at CNAT (the director of DATAR was vice-president of CNAT), and in a position to have its own views endorsed by CNAT and embodied in CNAT's plans. Moreover, there was nobody, except DATAR, empowered to say what was—or was not—regional policy. Lord Robbins once said that "economics is what economists do"; for very much the same reasons it can be said that regional policy was what DATAR did.

An important point to mention here is that regional policy was not inspired by a few broad objectives that could be easily stated, and compared with tools and results. DATAR undertook actions of all sorts (from initiating studies of the future of France, to providing incentives for the relocation of industries through the creation of national parks) that cannot be fitted easily into any coherent pattern. DATAR people themselves, however gifted, and despite many efforts, did not succeed in providing an overall framework that could serve as a blueprint for their actions; the abundant literature issued, or inspired, by DATAR is very disappointing in this respect. There is practically nothing on goals, and what little there is is usually vague, verbose, and even contradictory.

To quote Olivier Guichard (1965), DATAR's first director, who published a book on the subject, there were five objectives to regional planning:

> Public order objectives: disequilibria must not be aggravated dangerously; in some regions depopulation would be intolerable.
> Strategic objectives: we have already mentioned the removal of some defense industries.
> Social objectives: income disparities between regions must not be too great. This search for parity, more and more required by public opinion, has, however, some limits; it should not lead us to welfare policies or to noneconomic interventions that would freeze situations. . . . Constant restructuring, together with some geographic and social mobility, is indispensable.
> Cultural objectives: public authorities cannot neglect performing this mission, through, for instance, radio and TV regionalization; music and theatre decentralization; and the location of colleges and universities.
> Economic objectives: regional planning must promote better overall economic progress. (P. 25)

Other official documents are not much more explicit. The text of the Fourth Plan (1962-1965) states that "the goal [of regional policy] is not to guarantee every Frenchman a job wherever he happens to be born—this would create an unbearable rigidity for a growing economy—but is rather to limit migrations to a reasonable rate." The concept of a reasonable rate of migration as a policy objective is not particularly operational. But the vaguest definition is probably to be found in the first CNAT report: "Regional policy tends to improve the well-being of individuals by facilitating the choice of a place to work or to live, and by correcting geographic disparities that may result from growth."

To sum up, the two major goals ascribed to regional policy were (1) to maximize economic growth and (2) to minimize social costs. They were, however, conflicting goals. Migrations, for instance, involve considerable social costs (and in France are adversely felt by migrants) but are necessary for economic growth. Nor were they very useful for day to day decisions; the state of regional science is not very advanced, and no one can really predict whether GNP will benefit more from the location of a new automobile plant in Brittany than in the Paris region. Such goals were not specifically "regional goals"; they were also the goals of general economic policy. Regional policy, therefore, cannot really be defined in terms of broad goals. It is more easily defined in terms of sectors or of domains of intervention. In this regard, regional policy has been dealing with five major problems: (1) decentralization of industry and tertiary activities; (2) urban growth; (3) transportation; (4) rural activities; and (5) environmental protection. In each of these sectors, some goals can be identified more or less easily.

1. The first theme—decentralization of industries and tertiary activities—is probably the most important one. Regional policy in France started with this theme in the early fifties and it has never lost its importance—an indication that decentralization policies have not been very successful. Three major goals are explicitly stated: (a) to promote the creation of industrial employment in western, southwestern, and central France; (b) to facilitate the "reconversion" of the north and Lorraine, which are plagued with declining industries; and (c) to ease the difficulties of some particular cities located in the other regions. Decentralization implies a fourth goal: to restrict the growth of manufacturing industries in the Paris region.

2. The concern for urban growth did not lead to a very elaborate discussion of an optimal distribution of cities by size. Studies of the relative importance and role of French cities were undertaken in 1962 (Hautreux and Rochefort, 1963; Lajugie, 1968). Each city was graded according to thirteen criteria of importance or of influence; the nonweighted sum of grades defined the rank of the city in the hierarchy of French towns. This purely descriptive (and highly unsophisticated) classification was turned into a normative ranking. The eight first cities (excluding Paris)—namely, Lyon, Marseille, Lille, Bordeaux,

Toulouse, Nantes, Metz-Nancy, and Strasbourg—were taken as equilibrium metropolises. As such, it was said, they would benefit from special efforts and this was made a major commitment of the Fifth Plan. The rationale behind this goal was the idea—or the hope—that only large metropolises could counterbalance the influence and attraction of Paris. Similar studies were also undertaken at the regional level, and cities of various "levels" were identified. Such classifications were supposed to be instrumental in the allocation of public investment funds, but as a matter of fact, the goal of the equilibrium metropolises was difficult to maintain. In 1967 another conflicting goal appeared. It was decided that a special effort would be made for the medium-sized cities located within a radius of about 100-200 kilometers from Paris (like Rouen, Le Havre, Orléans, Tours, Amiens, Reims, Troyes), presumably on the basis that they could be a more effective deterrent to the growth of Paris. But even this was apparently not enough, and, in 1970, a new goal became fashionable: the promotion of medium-sized towns. Medium-sized towns in France are defined as cities with 50,000 to 200,000 inhabitants; they are said to be more "humane" than large metropolises, cheaper to develop, and growing more rapidly than other cities. Even the first major goal, restricting the growth of Paris, is now being questioned. As an official document puts it: "there are two ways of looking at the place of Paris in regional policy. Until recently, it was necessary to deal primarily with the disequilibrium between the Paris region and the rest of France.... But there is another aspect to the problem of Paris, namely, the role it can play in Europe and in the world," (DATAR, 1971, p. 24). As regards urban growth, France thus has three goals: (a) to promote Paris as an international center, (b) to promote the eight equilibrium metropolises, and (c) to promote medium-sized towns. A policy of promoting everyone is of course no policy at all.

But the above list of goals is incomplete. France has a fourth goal: to promote new towns. The idea of new towns emerged in 1964 in the context of a plan for the development of the Paris region. The main author of the plan, M. Delouvrier, then head of the Paris district, figured out that the population of Paris in 2000 could not realistically be expected to increase by less than five million, and suggested that a good share of this increase might be accommodated in seven "new towns" to be created about fifty kilometers outside Paris. The number of such new towns in the Paris area was later reduced to five: Cergy-Pontoise, Evry, Melun-Sénart, Saint-Quentin en Yvelines, and Marne la Vallée. In the meantime, plans were developed for new towns elsewhere in France: Villeneuve d'Asq, near Lille; Le Vaudreuil, near Rouen; L'Isle d'Abeau, near Lyon; and Fos, near Marseille. New towns are expected to reach about 300,000 to 500,000 inhabitants by the end of the century. These plans were accepted by the government, and are embodied in the Sixth Plan. They are, as a matter of fact, a major commitment of this plan, and their development is an active goal of regional policy.

3. Transportation has been a third concern of regional policy. No clear-cut objectives have been defined, but DATAR has been instrumental in coordinating, and, at times, in modifying the actions of such major investors as SNCF (the French railroads), the Ministry of Transportation and Equipment (responsible for highways, canals, and harbors), the Ministry of Telecommunications (responsible for telephone and telex networks), and chambers of commerce (responsible for airports). In particular, DATAR (a) promoted and assisted in the development of long term plans (completed by 1970) for highways and roads—very much in the spirit of the Interstate Highway System in the United States, for canals, for airports, and for telecommunications; (b) supported innovations by financing research and development, for new means of transportation such as aerotrain, naviplane, urba, continuous transportation, etc. (DATAR, 1969, pp. 67-69); and (c) altered the priorities of the ministries in favor of regions or cities where, from a regional policy point of view (and also, in some cases, a purely political point of view), action was badly needed.

4. The development of rural areas has also been explicitly a theme of regional policy. The rapid decrease of agricultural employment creates a number of problems in predominantly agricultural regions; these are exemplified and compounded by heavy outmigration. The promotion of industries in the western, southwestern and central areas of France is a partial answer.

It was felt, however, that this was not enough for some problem areas, and that a special program of "rural renewal," as it was called, was required (Rimareix, 1970). There are four such areas (which do not correspond to planning regions, but were specially designated in 1961 and 1962), as shown on Map 2-2: (a) Brittany and Manche; (b) Limousin-Lot; (c) Auvergne; and (d) "mountain areas" (Vosges, Jura, Alpes, Massif Central, Central Pyrénées, Eastern Pyrénées). These areas, covering about twenty-seven percent of the territory, are inhabited by about thirteen percent of the French population. Income levels are twenty-five percent to thirty percent below average French figures because the share of farmers in the labor force is much larger (thirty to forty percent versus sixteen percent for France as a whole), and because the average income of farmers is lower than the national average.

Four objectives have been agreed upon for these rural renewal areas: (a) to improve communications (roads, telephone, telex), which are usually particularly bad in these areas; (b) to invest in education and training; (c) to increase production and productivity in the agricultural sector; and (d) to develop industrial and tertiary (in particular tourism) activities.

Several other areas, although not particularly lagging, had specific problems that called for coordinated action. Special agencies were created to design and carry out integrated development plans. These areas (shown on Map 2-2) are:

a. The Rhône Valley: a special corporation, the Compagnie Nationale du Rhône (CNR), was created as early as 1921 to make as good use as possible of the Rhône river;

Map 2-2. Rural Areas and Special Development Areas

b. The Provence or Durance area: similarly, in 1957, another corporation, the Société du Canal de Provence, was created to develop the Durance basin, northeast of Marseille;

c. Bas-Rhône-Languedoc: the Compagnie Nationale du Bas-Rhône-Languedoc was created in 1955 to irrigate a very large area west of Marseille;

d. Gascogne: on a much smaller scale (and for much smaller areas), two agencies, the Compagnie d'Aménagement des Côteaux de Gascogne, and the Compagnie des Landes de Gascogne (later changed into Compagnie d'Aménagement Rural d'Aquitaine), are supposed to promote the agricultural development of the area;

e. Auvergne and Limousin: a special corporation, the Société de Mise en Valeur de l'Auvergne et du Limousin (SOMIVAL), was created in 1964 to develop these rural renewal areas;

f. Corsica: the Société de Mise en Valeur de la Corse (SOMIVAC), created in 1961, undertakes touristic as well as agricultural investments.

g. Languedoc-Roussillon coast and Aquitaine coast: in these two areas, ambitious touristic development programs (Languedoc-Roussillon has been called a planned French Florida) are being undertaken; they are sponsored by Missions Interministérielles (Interministerial Task Forces) which are more firmly controlled by DATAR than by development corporations.

5. A further domain taken up by DATAR and therefore considered regional policy, is environmental protection. Here again, no objectives have ever been defined, and what has been attempted is best described in terms of specific actions.

The two major points to be mentioned are (a) the creation of national and regional parks, and (b) the development of a water management policy. The latter is of special interest. For water management purposes France was divided into six "water basins," which correspond to the major water streams systems. In each basin, there is an agency that (a) undertakes studies of water quality, resources, and needs; (b) levies taxes on water consumption and pollution; (c) builds dams; and (d) helps finance antipollution equipment for local governments and industries.

IMPLEMENTATION OF REGIONAL ECONOMIC POLICIES

French regional economic policies have so far been described in terms of objectives. We must now see if, and how, these policies have been implemented. What tools have actually been used in order to achieve the goals stated in DATAR pronouncements and in the various plans? They appear to fall into three categories: (1) public investments, (2) economic incentives, and (3) direct controls.

1. Public investments are of course a major instrument of "voluntary geography." This is particularly true in a country like France, where the provision of many services, such as education, health, and, to a certain extent, culture, is considered a public responsibility. The location of public investments in a given area will improve the welfare of the people living in this area; it will also directly and indirectly influence the location of economic activities.

What really matters is the location of public services, not public investments. But there is, in France, a complete dichotomy between investment decisions and expenditures on the one hand, and operating decisions and expenditures on the other. The idea that there are relationships between the two types of expenditures, and that, in many cases, one may be substituted for the other, has not yet gained much recognition in France. The principal policy variable is therefore public investment, not the provision of public services.

Public investment decisions are largely made by the ministries in Paris. For those investments that are entirely paid for by the central government (about twenty-five percent of the total amount of public investments), the reason is obvious. It is also true, to a large extent, for the other seventy-five percent, which are investments undertaken by local governments and financed in part (twenty-five percent) by the local governments themselves, in part (twenty-five percent) by grants from the central government, and in part (for the remaining fifty percent) by borrowing. Grants and loans are negotiated piece-meal and there is a rule according to which a local government cannot, for a particular investment, get a loan unless it has received a grant; as a result of this rule the central government, or rather the ministries, can veto practically any project they do not like, and have rather firm control over most public investments.

Basically the real power resides in the ministries. The problem is that each ministry has its own rules and strategies concerning the allocation of public investments. These strategies may not coincide with regional policy strategies developed by DATAR, and they may not coincide with each other. DATAR will therefore try to influence investment decisions by ministries (and also by local governments) so that they will be coordinated and in accordance with regional planning goals set by DATAR.

This is not an easy task. Officially, the vehicles for such coordination are interministerial committees or task forces. The most important of these is the Regional Policy Interministerial Committee (Comité Interministériel pour l'Aménagement du Territoire, or CIAT); its membership includes all the principal ministers, with the prime minister (or his representative), as chairman. There are several other more specialized groups, such as the Interministerial Task Force for Water (Mission Interministérielle pour les Problèmes de L'Eau), the Committee for National Parks (Comité Interministériel des Parcs Nationaux), the Industrial Conversion Task Force (Groupe Central de Conversion Industrielle), the Interministerial Task Force for the Development of the Languedoc-Roussillon Coast (Mission Interministérielle pour l'Aménagement Touristique du Littoral Languedoc-Roussillon), etc.

In interacting with these interministerial committees DATAR has three primary means of influence. The first of these is power. DATAR is neither a particular ministry nor part of a particular ministry; it is directly under the authority of the prime minister, who, of course, has authority over all other ministries.

The second is information. DATAR has itself undertaken, or sponsored, a large number of studies, and has in particular launched long-range studies projecting France's future. The findings of these studies can provide useful arguments in interministerial discussions. DATAR has created, in each of the major urban areas, planning commissions (Organisations Régionales d'Etudes des Aires Métropolitaines, or OREAM) which have studied the problems of these areas rather extensively and have developed master plans that can also serve as vehicles for DATAR ideas. In addition, DATAR has helped nominate "commissioners" in the three rural renewal areas (Brittany, Limousin, and Auvergne) and in the three industrial conversion areas (the mining areas of North-Pas de Calais, Lorraine, and Saint-Etienne-Alès). The commissioners must find, suggest, and promote steps that could help their problem areas, and they must keep in constant touch with DATAR.

The third means of influence is money. DATAR controls a special fund for regional policy (Fonds d'Intervention pour l'Aménagement du Territoire, or FIAT). The sectoral breakdown of FIAT expenditures over the 1963-70 period (DATAR, 1972, p. 124) shows that transportation investments (roads, highways, canals, and harbors) accounted for forty-four percent of total expenditures, and received top priority. The regional breakdown (Ibid., p. 125) indicates that three regions, namely Midi-Pyrénées, Brittany, and North, were the major recipients of FIAT aid. It should be noted that the amounts of money involved are relatively small; for the Sixth Plan period (1966-1970), for instance, FIAT expenditures amounted only to 1.80 percent of central government expenditures for public investments, and 0.66 percent of public investment expenditures.

However, it is claimed that FIAT expenditures are "strategic." They are used to overcome bottlenecks, and for leverage in interministerial negotiations: "If you finance half of this budget, we shall finance the other half." Their importance may therefore be greater than the ratios would suggest.

Nevertheless, there are reasons to believe that, on the whole, the spatial distribution of public investments does not follow regional policy prescriptions (Prud'homme, 1972). For the Fifth Plan period (1966-1970), one obtains the regression

$$Dr = 2.355\,Pr + 21.515\,Gr - 6.777, \qquad R^2 = 0.974 \qquad (2.1)$$
$$\quad (0.0041) \quad\ \ (5.540)$$

where

      Dr = public equipment investments in region r;

      Pr = population of region r; and

      Gr = population increase in region r.

For a given region, the difference between $\hat{D}r$, the value calculated from Equation (2.1), and Dr, the actual value, tells us something of the impact of regional policy on public investments. When positive, it means that the region invested more than its share; when negative, it suggests that it invested less than its share. This difference can also be expressed in relative terms. Map 2-3 shows values for $Tr = (\hat{D}r - Dr) / Dr$, which can be taken as one measure of actual regional policy.

It is difficult—even impossible—to recognize a correspondence between the Tr values and the regional policy goals mentioned above. Western regions have not been systematically favored; three of them have a negative Tr. "Reconversion regions" have fared very badly; Lorraine, North, and Alsace each has a negative Tr, which is very large in the cases of North and Lorraine. These figures do not permit adequate evaluation of the equilibrium metropolises, but each of them (except Toulouse) is located in a region which has had less than its share of investments.

One could argue at this point that public investments are not entirely in the hands of the central government, and that therefore the Tr index is not a good measure of central government regional policy. Thus, another index was computed based on the regression

$$Cr = 1.139\,Pr + 1.855\,Gr - 0.037\,Ir - 430.5 \quad \text{where } R^2 = 0.980 \qquad (2.2)$$
$$(0.122) \quad (1.674) \qquad (0.378)$$

      Cr = central government expenditures for public investments in region r; and

      Ir = index of political influence of region r (relative number of representatives belonging to the political parties in office).

Equation (2.2) suggests that central government subsidies to a region *are* a function of the population of the region (which is obvious), but *not* of the increase in its population (which is surprising), or of its political influence. In other words, differences in per capita subsidies can be attributed to regional policy differences.

The index

$$T'r = \frac{Cr}{Pr} - \frac{\sum_r Cr}{\sum_r Pr} \qquad (2.3)$$

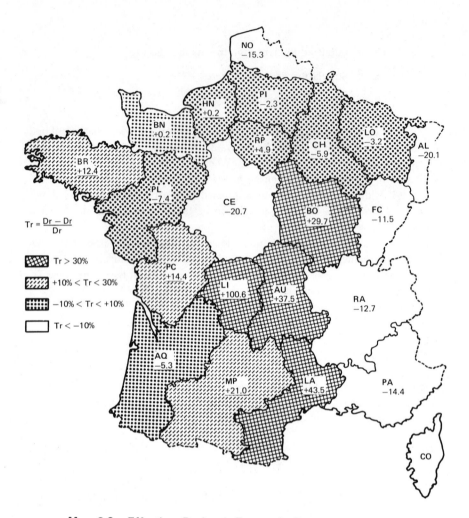

Map 2-3. Effective Regional Economic Policy During the Fifth Plan, 1966-1970

can be taken as a measure of effective central government regional policy. T'r values by region are shown on Map 2-4.

The picture that emerges from Map 2-4 is quite different from the one that emerged from Map 2-3, but it is equally alien to stated policy objectives. The goal of favoring the western regions has clearly not been implemented. The central government fared a little better with respect to the

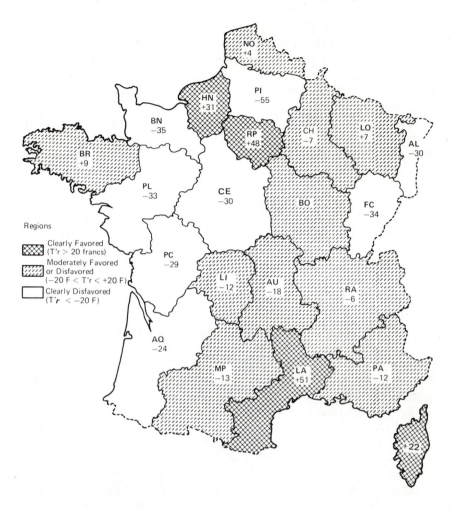

Map 2-4. Effective Central Government Regional Policy During the Fifth Plan, 1966-1970

objectives for North and Lorraine; both regions received, per head, more than the national average. But it is surprising to see that two of the most favored regions were the Paris region and Haute-Normandie, which, as the richest regions, are not supposed to receive special help.

2. Economic incentives are a second instrument of regional policy. As early as 1955 it was decided that investments in certain designated areas

would obtain (a) subsidies, (b) loans, and (c) tax reliefs (Durand, 1972, pp. 52-65; Lanversin, 1970, pp. 288-348).

The subsidy system has been simple in essence and complex in practice. France has been divided into several zones, which receive varying help from the central government. The system has been changed several times (in 1959, 1960, 1964, and again in 1972). The number and boundaries of the various zones have been modified, as have the types and the rates of the subsidies. The discretion of the relevant authority—the Ministry of Finance, advised by DATAR—has been modified, and distinctions have been introduced between investments creating new enterprises and investments extending old enterprises.

The 1972 system, which is simpler but not basically different from the previous ones, recognizes four zones (see Map 2-5). Zone I consists of several cities in western France (Cherbourg, Brest, Lorient, Nantes, Bordeaux, La Rochelle, Toulouse, Limoges, Bayonne, Brive, Castres, Mazamet); mining areas in northern and central France; and border areas in the northeast. Zone II consists of Brittany and Pyrénées-Atlantique (in the southwest of France). Zone III covers the rest of western France, and Zone IV the remainder of the country. The rates of the subsidy are as shown in Table 2-2.

In addition to this subsidy program, there has been a lending program that has never been quite so formal. FDES (Fonds de Développement Economique et Social), a budget-financed fund, has lent money at preferential rates for decentralization and reconversion investments. DATAR has also had a say in FDES decisions.

Lastly, tax benefits have been granted to newly created enterprises in aided areas. These enterprises can be exempted from the industrial property tax (*patente*) when both the local government and the central government agree to it. The same enterprises can also benefit from a lower rate of purchase tax (*droit de mutation*) on industrial buildings or equipment, and from a special depreciation allowance of twenty-five percent on industrial buildings.

The number and amounts of relevant subsidies and loans varied over time (Durand, 1972, pp. 68 and 74). Subsidies amounted to sixty to ninety

Table 2-2.   Rate of Investment Subsidies (Prime au Développement Régional), 1972 (in percent of total investments)

	Creations	Extensions
Zone I	25	20
Zone II	15	12
Zone III	12	12
Zone IV	0	0

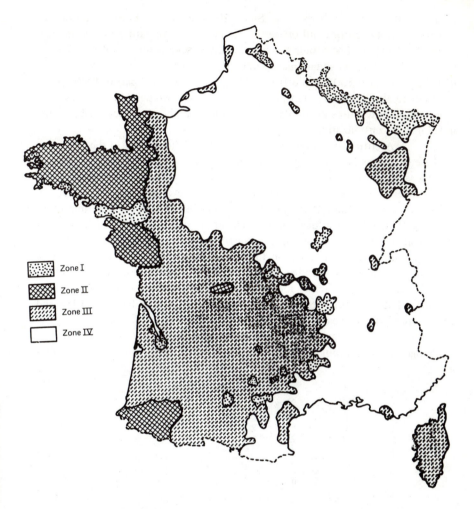

Map 2-5. Zones for Investment Subsidies, 1972

billion francs per year in the 1960-1967 period, and increased greatly after 1969, up to over 400 billion francs in 1970.

The regional distribution of subsidies has also undergone important changes. In the early sixties they primarily benefited western regions (Brittany, Aquitaine, Pays de la Loire). In more recent years the emphasis has shifted to "reconversion" areas in the North, Lorraine, and even the Rhône-Alpes regions.

In addition to the positive incentives just mentioned, there is a program of negative economic incentives, designed to discourage enterprises from investing in the Paris area. Since 1960 there has been a tax on the construction of factories and offices in the Paris area, or rather in certain areas of the Paris region. The system has been modified several times, but the rate was low (100 F or less per square meter) until 1971. It has been increased since, and in 1972 may reach 500 F (on office buildings in the western part of Paris). Since 1971, there also has been a transportation tax (about two percent of wages paid) levied on all enterprises in the Paris area, which should exert increased pressure in favor of decentralization.

A critical question that may be raised with respect to the efficiency of these programs is: have they influenced investors who have been in a position to choose a location? This question has in fact been asked of prospective and actual investors in several surveys. In some of these surveys (Strawczynoki, 1971; Falise and Lepas, 1970) investment subsidies appear to be an important factor in the choice of a location, second only to communications facilities and labor availability. But, according to others (Lamarre, 1972), such subsidies do not play a decisive role in locational decisions. Large firms are said to be more sensitive to investment subsidies than small firms. This contradicts the findings of a detailed study of actual location decisions in the electronics components industry. The fifty-three establishments that were created between 1954 and 1971 were distributed as shown in Table 2-3.

An important study by Aydalot and associates (1971) also throws some light on this problem. For each *département* he calculated a "mobility index":

$$S_i = \frac{\displaystyle\sum_j \left(x_{ij}^{t'} - \frac{\displaystyle\sum_i x_{ij}^{t'}}{\displaystyle\sum_i x_j^{t}} x_{ij}^{t} \right)}{\displaystyle\sum_j x_{ij}^{t'}} \underline{\quad} \tag{2.4}$$

where

x_{ij} = employment in sector j in *département* i,

t = 1962

t' = 1968,

and found that S_i was not significantly correlated with AI_i, an index of the level of subsidies in *département* i.

On the whole, the efficiency of the subsidy system on location decisions does not seem to be very great.

Table 2-3. Location of Electronics Passive Components
Establishments Created in France, 1954-1970, by Size of
Mother Enterprise and Type of Zone

Size of Mother Enterprise	High Level of subsidy	Type of Zone Medium Level of subsidy	Low Level of subsidy	No subsidy	Total
< 100	4	–	3	4	11
100-499	4	6	1	3	14
500-999	–	1	3	3	7
1000-4999	1	2	1	1	5
> 5000	3	–	3	10	16
Total	12	9	11	21	53

Source: D. Petitprez et D. Magdeleine, *Localisation de l'Industrie Electronique (branche des composants passifs)*, Mémoire de D.E.S. Université de Lille I, miméo, p. 32.

3. Direct controls are the third tool of regional policy in France.

As a general rule, it is necessary to secure an administrative authorization, known as a building permit, prior to the undertaking of any new construction. Regional policy makers were provided with this powerful tool by a 1961 law which specified that permits could and even should be denied to projects working "against regional policy." To make it sure (or surer) that regional policy objectives would be taken into consideration, at least in the case of large projects, it was decided in 1964 that DATAR approval would be necessary for industrial construction of more than 2,000 square meters.

A similar procedure has existed since 1955 for industrial construction in the Paris region. Building permits first have to be reviewed by a special Decentralization Committee (Comité de Décentralisation), controlled by DATAR. The law has been modified several times; for example, the minimum size for which review is necessary was changed from 500 square meters to 1000 square meters and then, in 1972, to 1500 square meters. The utilization of existing buildings has also come under the same rulings as the construction of new ones, and this special procedure was extended to the Lyon area from 1966 to 1970.

Foreign direct investments in France are subject to government approval. Until 1964 the criteria used were purely economic and financial; later DATAR insisted that regional policy be taken into consideration.

It is difficult to assess the efficiency of direct controls. Basically, they are tools that make it possible for DATAR to enter negotiations with large national or international enterprises: "We allow you to build another 2000 square meters in the Paris area provided you locate a new 2000-employee plant in La Rochelle. . . ." There are indications that this kind of bargaining has been important, and that the veto right on industrial development in the Paris area has been largely effective.

EVALUATION OF REGIONAL ECONOMIC POLICIES

It is not easy to evaluate a regional economic policy, especially when it comes to comparing what did happen with what might have happened if the policy had not been followed. The latter will of course always remain unknown and can only, at best, be conjectured. Even the former is not very well known in France, due to a lack of annual regional data. Evaluation can therefore only be tentative.

At first sight, regional economic policy seems quite successful. On several counts, the regional distribution of people and economic activities in the sixties was modified in the desired directions. This is particularly true of industrial employment, as shown in Table 2-4.

The change is dramatic in certain sectors, such as the automobile industry. The percentage of employment in the Paris area, which was about seventy percent in 1960, was reduced to fifty percent in 1970 and is expected to be below forty percent in 1975. Large new plants (over 1000 employees) were created in about twenty different cities, as shown on Map 2-6.

The patterns of migration have also been altered, as shown in Table 2-5. The change is particularly noteworthy for the Paris area; in the 1962-1968 period, it remained attractive, but not as attractive as before, and less attractive than several other regions, like Provence-Côte d'Azur, Rhône-Alpes, or Languedoc-Roussillon. There are indications that the change in attractiveness will continue and that, by 1972, the century-old flow of people from the provinces to Paris had been halted and possibly reversed (Bertrand, 1970).

Although several of the most important objectives of regional policy seem to have been reached, a closer look at the changes in the regional geography of France suggests a somewhat different appraisal. The patterns of growth in total employment were not really reversed. The regions that enjoyed the highest growth rates in the 1954-1962 period (g_1) are also the regions that

Table 2-4. Annual Growth in Industrial Employment, by Region, 1954-1962 and 1962-1968

	1954-1962		1962-1968	
	(1000)	*Percent of total growth*	*(1000)*	*Percent of total growth*
Paris	21	27.4	− 7	−13.5
East	40	51.6	32	60.4
West	16	21.0	28	53.1
Total	76	100.0	53	100.0

Source: Muel, Bolton, and Cazin, 1970, p. 42.

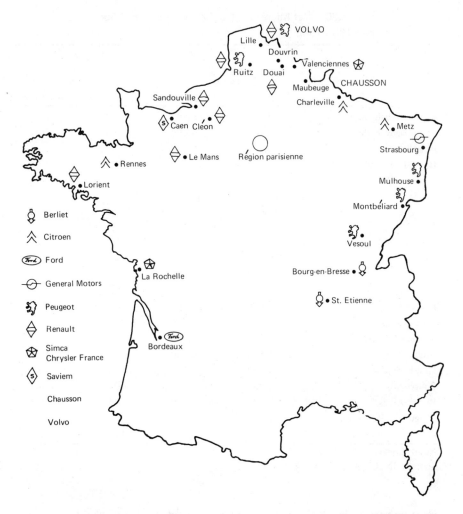

Map 2-6. Main Large New Plants in the Automobile Industry, 1960-1972

enjoyed the highest growth rates in the 1962-1968 period (g_2); the correlation between g_1 and g_2 is quite high:

$$g_2 = 0.627 g_1 + 0.790 \qquad R^2 = 0.785 \qquad (2.5)$$
$$(0.113) \qquad (0.079)$$

Although it is true that industrial employment increased more in the underdeveloped west than in the rest of France, it must be noted that it took

Table 2-5. Net Migratory Balance, by Regions, 1954-1962 and 1962-1968

	Migratory balance		Yearly net migratory balance (percent)	
	1954-1962	1962-1968	1954-1962	1962-1963
Région parisienne	+710,300	+365,400	+1.2	+0.7
Champagne-Ardenne	−9,400	+7.600	−0.1	+0.1
Picardie	−10,700	+18,600	−0.1	+0.2
Haute-Normandie	+9,500	+11,900	+0.1	+0.1
Centre	+20,400	+71,200	+0.1	+0.6
Nord	−20,100	−48,400	−0.1	−0.2
Lorraine	+50,600	−69,300	+0.3	−0.5
Alsace	+25,700	+36,700	+0.3	+0.5
Franche-Comte	+10,500	+14,400	+0.2	+0.3
Basse-Normandie	−55,500	−14,400	−0.6	−0.2
Pays de la Loire	−42,100	−10,600	−0.2	−0.1
Bretagne	−67,400	−12,500	−0.4	−0.1
Limousin	−6,700	+6,900	−0.1	+0.2
Auvergne	−1,500	+20,500	ϵ	+0.3
Poitou-Charentes	−26,900	−19,000	−0.2	−0.2
Aquitaine	+41,500	+96,800	+0.3	+0.7
Midi-Pyrénées	+34,400	+91,500	+0.2	+0.7
Bourgogne	+15,800	+28,900	+0.1	+0.3
Rhône-Alpes	+219,400	+224,500	+0.8	+0.9
Languedoc-Roussillon	+77,100	+122,900	+0.7	+1.3
Provence-Côte d'Azur (1)	+343,600	+390,200	+1.7	+2.2

Note: Corsica not included

Source: INSEE and DATAR, 1970, p. 60.

place primarily in those western regions closest to Paris, like Centre and Basse-Normandie, and also Brittany. Western regions far from Paris, like Midi-Pyrénées and Languedoc, did not enjoy high growth rates in industrial employment. Moreover, industrial employment actually decreased in North and Lorraine, an indication of the limited success of reconversion policy.

Data on increases in industrial wages by region during the 1962-1972 period (INSEE and DATAR, 1972, p. 252) do show that wages increased more slowly in the Paris region than in the other regions, thereby reducing the gap between Paris and the rest of France. But it does not follow that wages increased faster where they were lower; as a matter of fact there is no correlation between the wage level in 1962 and the overall wage increase during the 1962-1972 period. It cannot be said that wage differentials among regions—a major objective of regional planning—were reduced. In addition, such a correlation would only show a reduction in relative terms. In absolute terms it is likely that the gap between rich and poor regions widened over the period.

Data on incomes as a whole are not available for recent years and are at times contradictory. One source (Borel, 1969) concludes that differences in income by regions increased between 1962 and 1967; INSEE and other sources (DATAR, 1972, p. 42; Office Statistique des Communautés Européennes, 1972, pp. 34-37) claim that they decreased (for very much the same periods: 1962-1968 and 1960-1969). It seems fair to say that on balance the patterns of income disparities have not been changed dramatically.

One could conclude that the regional policy objectives concerning the spatial distribution of people and economic activities have only been partially met. But this does not tell much about the efficiency of the regional policy tools that have been used. One may well imagine that industrial growth would have spread out of Paris over the western parts of the country even if no regional policy had been carried out. The tendency of DATAR to establish a causal relationship between its action and actual developments is not well-founded.

On the other hand, several critiques can be formulated against the regional policy that has been followed. The first is purely theoretical and is not supported by any empirical study. The major tool used has been the incentive program. But it does not make economic sense to subsidize investment in order to create employment. Such programs lower the cost of capital relative to the cost of labor, and thereby tend to favor capital-intensive types of investment. In the aggregate, they should result in the creation of fewer—not more—jobs.

It is fair to mention a legal provision to deal with this problem; it is a ceiling imposed on the amount of money that can be given per job created. This ceiling was raised in 1972, and is now 15,000 francs in the case of a creation and 12,000 francs in the case of an extension. While this limits the negative effect of the investment incentive, it does not eliminate it. It may also be noted that this ceiling is quite high; in the case of a twelve percent subsidy, the investor will be encouraged to use a capital-intensive technology until his investment per job reaches 100,000 francs.

A second point to be made is that the policy followed was oriented primarily toward large corporations. According to the concept of regional development policy followed by DATAR, jobs are created by big national or international enterprises that create or decentralize large units. This is why DATAR created offices in the United States, Germany, Great Britain, and Japan to give prospective investors necessary information on investments in France. This approach may be consistent with export-base theory, but its accuracy may be doubted.

The mechanics of job creation are not very well known. However, some insights may be obtained by breaking down net growth in employment for a given period into several components. One such breakdown involves four categories: (1) growth in employment in establishments created during the period (creations); (2) growth in employment in establishments existing at the beginning of the period (extensions); (3) decrease in employment in establishments existing at the beginning of the period (reductions); and (4) decrease in employment by closing of establishments (closings). The relative importance of such flows appears in Table 2-6. It will be seen that employment resulting from the creation of enterprises is only a fraction of the net creation of employment.

Another breakdown involves net employment growth originating in small, medium, and large establishments. For France as a whole, over the 1962-1968 period, employment in large establishments (i.e. over 500 employees in 1962) increased by five percent; employment in medium-size establishments (50-500 employees in 1962) increased by twelve percent; and employment in small establishments (below fifty employees) decreased by ten percent.

An attempt was also made to break down net growth in employment in a given region into an "exogenous" component—i.e., growth originating in establishments financed and managed from outside the region—and an "endogenous" component—i.e., growth originating in establishments run from within the region. There are of course conceptual and statistical difficulties involved in deciding whether a given establishment is endogenous or exogenous. Data for the North region is given in Table 2-7.

The picture that emerges from these studies is quite different from that based on massive decentralizations by large firms. Rather, what accounts for the increase in industrial employment is typically a 100-employee firm that has gained another thirty employees.

One could argue that the figures given are misleading, and that growth in medium endogenous enterprises is only a consequence of growth in large exogenous establishments—an example of a multiplier effect. There are reasons to believe that this is not so. Large exogenous establishments located in a given region by large national or international firms are usually well-integrated into the other establishments of the firm, and keep subcontracting to a

Table 2-6. Growth of Industrial Employment, by Categories, 1962-1968 (Yearly growth rates in percentages)

	1962-1964	*1964-1966*	*1966-1968*
Creations	2.05	2.15	1.85
Extensions	7.30	6.00	5.25
Reductions	−4.20	−5.00	−5.50
Closings	−1.20	−1.45	−1.50
Total	+3.95	+1.70	+0.10

Source: Keller and Simula, 1971, p. 64.

Table 2-7. Endogenous and Exogenous Growth in Industrial
Employment in the North, 1962-1967 (in 1,000 jobs)

	Endogenous	*Exogenous*	*Total*
Employment, 1962	327	90	417
Creations, 1962-1967	+11	+3	+14
Extensions minus reductions, 1962-1967	+18	+7	+25
Closings, 1962-1967	−26	−2	−28
Net growth, 1962-1967	+ 3	+8	+11
Employment, 1967	330	98	428

Source: Centre d'Analyse du Développement, 1971, pp. 59-90.

minimum (the minimum required to absorb cyclical fluctuations). Their multiplier effect is probably smaller than the multiplier effect of smaller endogenous enterprises, as has already been suggested in the well-known paper by Chinitz (1961) on Pittsburgh and New York. In other words, locational decisions by big firms from outside a region or a city in need of employment opportunities may not be the strategic variable that it is commonly assumed to be; DATAR's big corporation policy may have been aiming at the wrong target.

A third point may also be raised. Industrial employment growth has usually been thought of in quantitative rather than qualitative terms, as if one job were always equal to one job. The picture given by figures on new jobs in the western regions must be qualified with some information on the types of jobs created. By and large these have been unskilled. A detailed study is available for Angers and Alençon, two cities in western France where several large new plants

were created in the early sixties (Bull and Thomson-Houston in Angers; Moulinex in Alençon); the breakdown of jobs by skill category in old establishments and in new establishments is shown in Table 2-8.

Table 2-8. Employment, by Skill Category and Type of
Establishment, Angers and Alençon, 1966

	White-collar	*Skilled*	*Unskilled*	*Total*
Angers:				
old enterprises	19.3	33.8	46.9	100.0
new enterprises	24.6	17.9	57.5	100.0
Alençon:				
old enterprises	14.1	37.2	48.7	100.0
new enterprises	14.3	14.2	71.5	100.0

Source: SODIC, 1967, p. V-14.

In both cases, the creation of new plants in glamorous sectors like electronics and light mechanical industry actually lowered the average level of skills. There is every reason to believe that these cases are by no means exceptional. The industrial development of the west is largely of a colonial nature. Large firms have exploited cheap sources of labor wherever they happened to be, but the main centers of power have not been decentralized and remain in Paris. This, by the way, tends to suggest that decentralization would have taken place in any event.

A fourth point to be made is that industrial rather than tertiary investment has been favored. This again may not have been the right target, even though it would have been suggested by economic base theory. In fact, for France as a whole the growth of employment comes primarily from the service sector.

This phenomenon received belated recognition. In 1967, the subsidy system was extended to include investments in the tertiary sector in nineteen cities (the equilibrium metropolises, plus Brest, Rennes, Dijon, Besançon, Poitiers, Clermont-Ferrand, Limoges, Montpellier, and Nice). However, this extension was not very successful; the number and amounts of subsidies for tertiary investments are ridiculously low. In 1972, the geographic areas for which investments in the tertiary sector are eligible for subsidy were extended to cover not only cities but the entire area in which industrial investments can be subsidized.

In the meantime, tertiary employment continued to concentrate in Paris. The balance of power was in no way altered. Although it is difficult to document, data on office buildings may be used as an indicator. Table 2-9 shows the relative importance of office space authorized for construction in the Paris region and in the rest of France. The share of office space authorized in the Paris region has increased in recent years; more than half of that now being constructed in France is located in Paris.

The restructuring of economic activities was only one objective of regional policy; to improve the quality of life was, as mentioned previously, another major objective. In the absence of pertinent indicators it is difficult to say whether this objective was met or not. It seems to have been largely met as far as water quality is concerned; the scheme that was introduced in 1964 works reasonably well and the trend toward deterioration has been halted.

But there is a widespread consensus that urbanization has escaped control. Local governments were not given the means necessary to implement a land use policy, and urban land prices have skyrocketed in sprawling cities. Public services of all sorts (schools, hospitals, etc.) have been lagging. Few parks have been created and the amount of park space per head has declined in many cities. Transportation policy relied heavily on the private automobile—in a country where many city centers date back to the Middle Ages—with the result that traffic congestion is the rule, and the length of work trips increased in most

Table 2-9. Office Floor Authorized, by Region, Selected
Years (in 1,000 square meters)

	Paris region	*Rest of France*	*France*
1965	556	650	1206
1968	564	864	1428
1971	1458	1236	2694

Source: Ministère de l'Equipement et du Logement, *Statistiques de la Construction*, various months.

cases. Lastly, spatial segregation by income, which was almost nonexistent in French cities (in the nineteenth century, there was a vertical segregation, with the rich in the first floors and the poor in the uppermost floors of the same houses—which is no segregation), has begun to appear.

CONCLUSIONS

Economic growth in France in the nineteenth and twentieth centuries has been accompanied by regional imbalance. After the war, policy measures were advocated to reduce or to limit imbalances which were felt (1) to be politically unbearable, and (2) to be a threat to economic growth itself. But it was only in the early sixties that a fairly efficient institution, DATAR, was created for the purpose of implementing policy, and that steps of some magnitude were actually taken.

Some positive results undoubtedly have been achieved. The industrial growth of the Paris region has been halted; outmigrations from the poorer regions have been reduced; income differentials have not increased and have probably decreased. The overall picture is therefore quite favorable.

However, limitations can be seen in three strategic choices that were made, which now appear to have been erroneous:

1. Efforts were focused on large firms, rather than on small or medium-sized enterprises, and there are reasons to believe that a large firm, merely by locating an additional factory in a given region, does not contribute very much to the region's development.
2. Efforts were centered on the number of jobs created, rather than on the type of jobs created, and as a result, many of the plants established in western France are merely producing units utilizing mostly unskilled and poorly paid labor.
3. Efforts were directed at industry, not at services, and at a time when the importance of the service sector is growing this could hardly—and did not—reduce the primacy of Paris.

The lessons to be learned from the French experience may relate more to such mistakes than to its achievements.

Chapter Three

Regional Economic Policy in the United Kingdom

INTRODUCTION

The history of regional policy in the United Kingdom is rather like that of a man with a grumbling appendix. Every now and again he feels acute pain and is forced to take a batch of medicines. Although his condition improves, he is never quite sure which of the medicines, singly or in combination with others, actually did the trick. However, at least he can forget about his discomfort and can turn his attention to other more pressing affairs. Then, sadly, his pain returns. This time he changes the dosage and hastily adds a few new medicines to his treatment. The new combination seems to work and once again he feels confident that the problem has been solved. Sadly, disillusionment is just around the corner.

Over the forty years during which British governments have sought to narrow interregional inequalities in employment opportunities, incomes, social service provision, and environmental quality, this ebb and flow of concern—the one bringing grateful detachment, the other political recriminations and frantic searches for new policies—is only too apparent to even the casual observer. However, despite these ebbs and flows, the long-run trend is unmistakable. Thus the three major political parties (the Conservatives, the Socialists and the Liberals) accept that the problems of restructuring the older industrial and largely peripheral northern areas—where the industrial revolution first bore fruit—have not been solved, and all are committed to powerful measures and large expenditures to improve their economic performance. In addition, all political parties, though with varying degrees of enthusiasm, accept the need to control the rate of development of the relatively prosperous core or central regions of the South and the West Midlands of England, with the overall objective of steering some new growth to the lagging peripheral areas. As a result of this continuous and continuing concern, the United Kingdom has developed a battery of inducements and controls which clearly have affected the spatial incidence of the demand for labor and, in consequence, the level of employment in, and the rate of outmigration from, these peripheral areas.

It would be naive and quite erroneous to detect a pursuit of national efficiency as the major justification for national measures to aid the peripheral regions. Whatever the form—the curbing of London's stranglehold over decision making, the pursuit of a "work to the workers" philosophy, or the blatant exercise of provincial bargaining power over the siting of public enterprise activities or central government facilities—equity arguments are constantly in evidence. On this level the regional problem consists of grievances, often ill-defined but acutely felt, which shower upon the heads of the government in the form of claims for the right to work, or the right to a secure future, or the right to a given standard of social service. Equally, the response to such claims is directly political and usually ad hoc.

It is not difficult to see why these grievances tend to meet a ready response among politicians of the Labour and Liberal Parties. McCallum (1973) has pointed out that in the 1970 general election Labour held 107 out of the 156 seats in the areas of greatest distress (the development areas) and no less than twenty-five out of the thirty-two seats in the areas which are showing symptoms of economic lag (the intermediate areas). Similarly, the Liberal Party, which won 6 seats, elected most of its members in development area constituencies.

The commitment by the Conservative Party to regional policy is slightly more difficult to explain. The results of the general election showed that the Conservative power base was overwhelmingly outside the lagging regions. Thus, they held almost two seats for every one held by Labour outside of development area and intermediate area constituencies (281 Conservative to 156 Labour seats). It is, however, a matter of fact that in the last phase of the Macmillan administration (1957-1964) a series of powerful regional measures were introduced after a period during the fifties of weak regional policy (McCrone, 1969). Similarly the Heath government (1970-1974), though originally professing a desire to disengage from activity which should more appropriately be left to private interests, and claiming that regional inducements should be tied more closely to performance, responded to high absolute levels of unemployment in the peripheral regions in 1971 by the introduction of a substantial package of regional inducements, many of which were not tied to performance. It also committed very large resources to propping up employment in sectors and companies which on strict market criteria should have been liquidated. Once again it seemed that no central government was prepared to countenance marked interregional variations in unemployment, nor, as we shall see, a policy of bringing workers to the work.

And yet, although political pressures give regional policy its main justification and its ever-changing vitality, efficiency arguments are never far beneath the surface. There are two possible meanings of efficiency in this context. The first is concerned with questions of how to devise regional policies which maximize the growth in real GNP, probably with a long-term perspective in mind. The second is concerned with using public resources and public policies in such a way that the goals of regional policy are achieved efficiently. This might imply a rule of minimum social costs for the achievement of a given "quantum" of regional goals. This chapter is primarily concerned with these two types of efficiency arguments.

THE CAUSES OF THE REGIONAL PROBLEM

Viewed from an economic point of view, the initial problem is a persistent tendency towards disequilibrium in the interregional labor market, with some regions operating at a level of unemployment significantly short of the full employment position despite continuous outflows of labor and other regions suffering persistent labor shortages despite continuous labor inmigration both from within the country and from overseas. The consensus is that the basic cause of this problem is found in interregional differences in the structure of industry and the differing increase in the demand for labor region by region, which is derived from this differential structure of activity. There is, however, a growing acceptance that, in particular regions, structure may not explain everything and that performance deficiencies in particular sectors may contribute to a low growth or even decline in jobs. Another accepted cause is the relatively high rate of natural increase in precisely the regions of job lag. The consequence of all of these factors is that employment declines and their inadequate replacement by growing sectors causes a slower growth in the demand for labor than in the supply of labor in these peripheral regions. Surpluses of labor grow and persist. By contrast, the central or core regions, which capture the bulk of the fast-growing manufacturing and service sectors, experience a growth in demand for labor which exceeds the available sources of local labor supply.

In these circumstances labor, and inactive population, tend to flow out of the peripheral regions and into the fast-growing regions. A reverse process, that of capital flowing to the regions of labor surplus and away from the regions of labor scarcity, is also set in motion. However, even in conditions of a high aggregate level of demand, these equilibrating mechanisms are never powerful enough to prevent persistent regional imbalance. This occurs largely because there are frictions which prevent adequate interregional flows of labor and of capital. With labor, the major constraint is the broad degree of regional uniformity in wages for given skills achieved by nationally organized trade unions. Thus, regardless of differences in productivity, cost of living, or demand

and supply conditions, wage rates within the lagging regions tend to follow the pattern set by bargains made in national negotiations or in the core regions. This effectively restrains the outflow of labor from the lagging regions and removes an obvious inducement which could attract large flows of capital to such regions. In terms of capital mobility, moreover, the possibilities of achieving an adequate rate of return within a lagging region may be clouded by personal prejudice or may appear insufficiently obvious when set against personal preferences for the known locale. In any event, capital may not flow into the problem regions on a scale sufficient to restore equilibrium. Thus, in the absence of any mechanism for adjusting regional factor prices, the structure of economic activity changes all too slowly and labor market disequilibrium persists. (McCrone, 1973)

In some circumstances, and apart from the social and political problems associated with marked disparities in employment conditions, this kind of interregional disequilibrium would not present a serious economic problem if

1. the absolute volume of unemployment and underemployment in the peripheral regions was small;
2. the natural growth in labor supply within the core regions was relatively large; and
3. there were large reservoirs of low-productivity agricultural labor which could be drawn into higher-productivity activities within the core regions.

None of these conditions apply to the United Kingdom. As we shall see, the peripheral regions contain large reservoirs of unemployed labor. According to a 1969 Department of Employment forecast, the growth in labor supply in the economy as a whole is expected to be only three percent between 1967 and 1981, whereas population is expected to grow by eight percent, and there are now no substantial reservoirs of agricultural labor available for transfer to urban-based activities. It follows that the reserves of labor which exist in the peripheral regions represent a valuable resource which, if drawn into employment, could make a substantial contribution to national employment and national output.

There are three alternative strategies by which this spare labor capacity could be absorbed into national production. The first is to permit unconstrained output expansion in the areas of labor shortage so that earnings for given skills are raised and migrants from the problem regions are sucked into these fast-growing regions. This movement could be stimulated by information, cash allowances, or other inducements to the migrants. A second alternative is to force activities to decentralize from major centers within the core regions either by physical controls of one kind or another or through a use of taxes, fees for development, and so on. The new location pattern may encourage short distance movements of labor from the surplus labor areas. The third alternative is to devise policies which directly raise the level of demand for the resources of the problem regions, at the source, so that unemployment is reduced, outmigration is curbed, and the structure of economic activity is adapted.

Although moving people to jobs is not a prominent feature of government policy there was a net movement from assisted to nonassisted areas of 6000 workers in 1972-1973, under the Department of Employment's transfer assisted scheme. (Expenditure Committee, Second Report, 1974, p. 39.) However, the preference of postwar governments for the second and third courses of action has been buttressed by a number of critical tenets of economic wisdom. The first argument concerns the generation of inflation. If the demand for labor within the core regions is expanded rapidly, it is assumed that migration from the labor surplus areas will not increase markedly in the short run. In conditions of a relatively inelastic supply curve of labor, large wage rate and earnings increases would be inevitable. These increases would then be spread quickly to all other regions of the country, including the labor surplus areas, by nationally organized trade unions. The obvious result would be that the marginal increment to national output could only be achieved with a very large marginal increase in labor costs. In contrast, a similar expansion of demand for labor in the surplus areas would not be inflationary, since there would be a far greater elasticity of labor supply at existing wage rates. This argument has frequently been used to justify control of industrial development in the inflation-generating regions.

A second set of arguments concerns the long-run effects of encouraging increased migration out of the labor surplus areas and into the core regions. While it is reasonable to expect that most migrants would be economically better off as a result of their move, their improvement in welfare would have to be set against losses incurred by others. For example, net outmigration would cause a reduction in expenditures for local goods and services (i.e., nonbasic production) and these negative multiplier effects could depress factor incomes and possibly employment levels. Moreover outmigration may result in an underutilization of social and economic overhead capital within the population-losing areas and a duplication of capital in the migrant-receiving areas. Over the longer run too, persistent net outmigration may be discriminant in that it creams off the most talented and vigorous sections of the labor force. Obviously, given the size (in millions, 1971 population figures) of the standard regions—Northern Ireland (1.53); Wales (2.73); Scotland (5.23); and in England: the Northern region (3.29); North West (6.73); Yorkshire and Humberside (4.79); East Midlands (3.29); West Midlands (5.10); South West (3.79); East Anglia (1.67); and South East (17.13)—the flows in and out are likely to be on a large scale. However, the assumption here is that the population-losing regions are liable to lose more from movement out than they might gain from movement in of the highly productive sectors of the labor force. If this is indeed the case, then the labor surplus areas are liable to have a diminished capacity for entrepreneurship and, *ceteris paribus*, a diminished appeal to mobile enterprises seeking reserves of proficient labor. Viewed from the fast-growing regions, on the other hand, any further inmigration is liable to increase the unwanted externalities of growth, such as traffic congestion, noise, air and water pollution, and possible environmental decay. More specifically, migration into London and Birmingham, which are assumed to have reached an excessive population size, could complicate the problems of dispersing population to planned overspill and new town settlements in the respective outer metropolitan areas.

The final and most critical assertion is that every major surplus region is urbanized, industrialized, and accessible to every region; has a labor force of broadly equal productivity (after training) for any given skill, and is open to the flow of general technological information and, more particularly, to knowledge on the 'best practice.' Accordingly, since the heart of the regional problem is how to adjust outdated industrial structures, each problem region possesses the necessary attributes to make this reconstruction possible and successful. This means that over the long run the bulk of British manufacturing capacity can operate just as profitably within the labor surplus regions as in the core regions. It follows that the use of government subsidies to encourage an inflow of capital to the problem regions need only cover the short run. Such subsidies are assumed to be needed partly to overcome ill-informed business prejudices or lack of information, partly to cover the real short-run costs of settling in, and partly to compensate for the short-run costs of an environment weak on specific or industry external economies. However, as these new industries expand and internal and external economies of scale are reaped, then continuing state support will become unnecessary. Of course, there is every reason to use subsidies to stimulate increments of expansion of the efficient firm once it is well established within the problem region. The objective here is simply to improve the rate of return from producing within the labor surplus areas relative to other unassisted areas, with the hope that this will result in a bigger share of expansion projects being undertaken in areas of labor surplus than would have occurred without the subsidies.

Therefore on all of these grounds—the more elastic supply of labor at existing wage rates, the relatively greater supplies of social and economic overhead capital, the possibilities of output expansion without unwanted externalities, and the underlying conditions for competitively efficient production—the assertion is that a given increment to national output can be achieved at a lower social cost by expanding the demand for labor within the labor surplus regions rather than within the core regions. Similarly over the long run such a policy can avoid the process of cumulative decline which is assumed to accompany persistent outmigration of the most talented.

In a later section we will attempt to evaluate the validity of these assertions but first we must provide some measures of the extent of the regional problem.

THE DIMENSIONS OF THE REGIONAL PROBLEM

Despite thirty years at, or close to, national full employment in which the annual unemployment rate has ranged from a low of 1.1 percent in 1955 to a high of 3.8 percent in 1972, certain of the peripheral regions (called officially development areas) have suffered persistently high unemployment, low female activity rates, relatively low per capita incomes, persistent net losses of population from outmigration, and severe environmental decay. All of Northern Ireland, and the bulk of the two other celtic regions, Scotland and Wales, together with parts of the north, northwest, and southwest regions of England tend to display all or many of these symptoms of economic distress. Taken together, these areas contain more than twenty percent of the United Kingdom's 55.5 million total population, a roughly equal proportion of its twenty-four million labor force, and forty percent of its land area.

Another type of problem area—often referred to as an intermediate area, since it is neither prosperous nor in deep economic distress—shows all the signs of incipient economic difficulties. Here, the symptoms are relatively low income growth, outmigration and environmental decay, and a general economic climate which does not seem conducive to new investment and a broadening of narrow economic structures. If these areas—which are largely concentrated in parts of Lancashire and the mining areas of South Yorkshire and North Derbyshire—are included in the problem category, then no less than forty-four percent of the United Kingdom's population is covered, according to mid-1971 population estimates (Parliamentary Question No. 2929, June 20, 1972).

In the development areas, unemployment rates typically run fifty percent to 100 percent above the national rate (Table 3-1). In contrast, the southeast has unemployment rates persistently and substantially below the national average. There is nothing ephemeral in this situation. Indeed, the persistency of the problem is shown by the fact that the regional rank order of unemployment rates has remained unaltered during the last fifty years (Brown, 1968).

The principal cause of this relatively high unemployment rate is not to be found in seasonal factors, labor market imperfections, or the incidence of unemployables. In large measure differences in unemployment levels, region by region, can be attributed to differences in the pressure of demand for labor and to a lesser extent to differences in natural increase which affect the supply of labor.* As a result, the growth in the employed labor force in the last fifty years

---

*Richard Crum has provided the author with estimates of the net increment to the labor force in Northern Ireland, Scotland, and England/Wales for 1970. These show that in Northern Ireland the labor force grew by 1.5 percent, in Scotland by 0.8 percent, and in England/Wales by 0.4 percent. His calculation process was (1) take all fifteen year olds and subtract all males aged sixty-five and females aged sixty; (2) express residual as a percentage of those aged fifteen to fifty-nine (females) and fifteen to sixty-four (males); and (3) the resulting percentage represents the approximate net increment to the labor force in 1970.

Table 3-1.   Unemployment Rates in the Regions, 1960-1972 (Percent Averages of Monthly Figures)

	1960	1961	1962	1963	1964	1965	1966	1967	1968	1969	1970	1971	1972
South East	1.0	1.0	1.3	1.6	1.0	0.9	1.0	1.7	1.6	1.6	1.7	2.0	2.2
East Anglia						1.3	1.4	2.1	2.0	1.9	2.2	3.1	2.9
South West	1.7	1.4	1.7	2.1	1.5	1.6	1.8	2.5	2.5	2.7	2.9	3.4	3.4
East Midlands						0.9	1.1	1.8	1.9	2.0	2.3	3.1	3.1
West Midlands	1.0	1.1	1.6	2.0	1.0	0.9	1.3	2.5	2.2	2.0	2.3	4.0	3.6
Yorkshire and Humberside						1.1	1.2	2.1	2.6	2.6	2.9	4.0	4.2
North West	1.9	1.6	2.5	3.1	2.1	1.6	1.5	2.5	2.5	2.5	2.8	4.1	4.9
North	2.9	2.5	3.7	5.0	3.3	2.6	2.6	4.0	4.7	4.8	4.8	5.9	6.4
Wales	2.7	2.6	3.1	3.6	2.6	2.6	2.9	4.1	4.0	4.1	4.0	4.7	4.9
Scotland	3.6	3.1	3.8	4.8	3.6	3.0	2.9	3.9	3.8	3.7	4.3	6.0	6.5
Northern Ireland	6.7	7.5	7.5	7.9	6.6	6.1	6.1	7.7	7.2	7.3	7.0	8.0	8.1
Total United Kingdom	1.7	1.6	2.1	2.6	1.7	1.5	1.6	2.5	2.5	2.5	2.7	3.7	3.9

Source: Department of Employment, *Gazette*, May, 1973.

has varied markedly region by region. For example, Table 3-2 shows the marked disparity between the growth performance of Northern Ireland, the northern group of regions, and Wales between 1921 and 1961 as contrasted to the southern and Midlands regions group. In Northern Ireland, Wales, Scotland, and the Northwest of England, there was either an absolute decline or a stationary condition, whereas all of the Midlands and southern group expanded their employed labor force markedly. Although these disparities in employment growth have been somewhat more muted in recent years, they still persist as Table 3-3 shows quite clearly.

Estimates of the number of unemployed workers actively seeking work who would be required to be employed before every region contained only unemployables or those affected by seasonal or frictional factors have varied enormously. However, a minimum of 100,000 jobs would have been required in the late 1960s to achieve this goal.

Accompanying high unemployment in many regions is a low regional activity rate, especially for females. With a national activity rate of just under forty percent in June 1968 for example, only thirty percent of the females aged fifteen and above were in the labor force in Wales, whereas no less than forty-three percent were economically active in London and the South East (Table 3-4). Given this degree of variation, one estimate has indicated that if every region had its age-specific activity rate raised to that of the highest attained anywhere within the nation then nearly 900,000 women would be added to the 8.8 million women in the twenty-three million labor force (Brown, 1972, p. 214).

Table 3-2. Percentage Increase in the Occupied Population at Work, 1921-1961*

Region	Percent Change
Northern Ireland	− 4.6**
Wales	+ 0.3
Scotland	+ 1.0
North West	+ 1.3
Yorkshire and Humberside	+ 7.9
North	+10.8
East Anglia	+20.4
East Midlands	+26.5
South West	+29.3
West Midlands	+39.9
South East	+41.3

Source: Lee, C.H., *Regional Economic Growth in the United Kingdom since the 1880's* (Maidenhead: McGraw Hill, 1971).

*As percentages of total employment in 1921.

**Period 1926-1961.

Table 3-3. Percentage Increase in Employees in Employment 1953-1966

Region	Percent Change
Scotland	+ 3.0
North West	+ 4.0
Wales	+ 6.6
North	+ 6.9
Yorkshire and Humberside	+ 9.1
East Midlands	+15.3
South East	+18.6
South West	+18.6
West Midlands	+18.9

Source: Brown, A.J. (1972), p. 30.

Table 3-4. Activity Rates, Standard Regions June 1968[a] (percent)

New Standard Regions	Male and female	Male	Female
South East	59.7	77.9	43.4
East Anglia	48.5	64.6	33.1
South West	47.0	63.5	32.2
West Midlands	60.2	78.4	42.6
East Midlands	56.3	74.1	39.3
Yorkshire and Humberside	56.1	74.7	38.8
North West	58.1	75.9	40.1
North	51.8	70.0	34.8
Wales	47.1	65.6	30.1
Scotland	56.4	74.5	40.4
Northern Ireland	48.9	64.0	35.2
Total United Kingdom	56.2	74.1	39.8

[a]Employees as a percentage of the home population aged fifteen years and over. See *Abstract of Regional Statistics*, No. 5, Her Majesty's Stationery Office, 1969.

Generally speaking the development areas not only suffer from a persistent underutilization of their human resources, they are also the poorest regions. Certainly, by comparison with many other advanced countries, the differences in real consumption per capita are not great and, if we exclude Northern Ireland, only range from a high of seven percent above the national norm in the South East to ten percent below the norm in the northern region (Table 3-5).

Table 3-5. Interregional Price Indices and Real Consumption, 1964

Price Indices (Great Britain = 100)	North	Yorkshire and Humberside	North West	East Midlands	West Midlands	South East	South West	Wales	Scotland
Food	99	101	98	100	102	99	99	104	105
Housing[a]	82	85	92	79	89	129	88	80	89
Fuel and light	95	96	98	93	96	109	112	102	101
Travel to work	80	89	96	90	92	119	78	104	89
All goods and services	96	97	99	97	98	106	97	98	99
Consumers' expenditure (United Kingdom = 100)	86	91	95	91	105	114	92	90	93
Consumers' expenditure valued at Great Britain prices	90	94	96	94	107	108	95	92	94
Consumers' expenditure plus beneficial current public expenditure[b]	90	94	97	94	105	107	95	94	95

Source: Brown, A.J. (1972). The figures are based on Central Statistical Office, *National Income and Expenditure 1964* (London: Her Majesty's Stationery Office, 1964); Ministry of Labour, *Family Expenditure Survey 1966* (London: Her Majesty's Stationery Office, 1967); Ministry of Agriculture, *Household Food Consumption and Expenditure 1964* (London: Her Majesty's Stationery Office, 1965); Ministry of Power, *Statistical Digest 1966* (London: Her Majesty's Stationery Office, 1967); Government Social Survey, *Labour Mobility in Great Britain 1953-63*.

[a]Including maintenance

[b]On goods and services

This narrow range is largely due to a high degree of uniformity in regional gross product per capita. Although this tends to have a wider range than that of real consumption, with a low in 1961 of eighty-five percent of the national figure in Wales and a high of 115 percent in the South East, this range is further narrowed by progressive taxation, central financing of the social services, and a relatively low cost of living in many of the development areas as compared to London.

Apart from the effects on the environment of dereliction and industrial obsolescence, of major concentrations of slum dwellings which once housed the artisans of the burgeoning Victorian cities, and of the limited range of services appropriate to relatively low incomes, the final indicator of development area malaise is found in the net migration trend. Three powerful processes are at work shaping the spatial distribution of British population. Of longest standing is the transfer of rural population to cities and small towns. This has occurred and continues to occur throughout every region but quantitatively it is largely a spent force. The United Kingdom now has one of the smallest agricultural and natural resource based populations in the world. For example, only 3.0 percent of the labor force is now classified as engaged in agriculture and forestry. The second major process is the dispersal of population out of the central cities of the major conurbations and into the outer conurbation areas. In part this reflects the scarcity of land within the central cities and the consequent spread of suburbs across central city boundaries; and in part the necessity for new and expanding population settlements to occur outside of the 'green belts,' many of which have been given statutory enforcement. However, in addition to these largely private movements, there are also large movements of population and of industry under planned overspill schemes, typically to 'close in' new towns and expanded towns, though sometimes, as in the case of London, to centers as much as 100 miles away from the origin of the migrants.

The final, and from our point of view, the most interesting process is the migration from the north to the south of the country. Between 1961 and 1966 over two million people moved across regional boundaries and changed residence. In terms of net flows, the figure was 200,000. Approximately half of these net flows consisted of gains made by the South West and East Anglian regions of England at the expense of the South East. In contrast, the South East gained almost 28,000 from Scotland. As Brown (1972) has noted:

> Scotland shows net emigration to every other British region, the North to every one except Scotland. There is a general tendency for each region to receive from those to the north of it and to give to the south as if they formed a cascade, until at the bottom, the South East's outflow surges into its westerly and northeasterly neighbours and even splashes into the East Midlands. (P. 80-81)

Taking internal and external migration together, the four regions north of the Trent—Yorkshire and Humberside; North West; Northern; and Scotland—tended to lose 50,000 people per annum over the period 1961-1966 whereas the rest of Britain was gaining over 75,000.

A number of points should be noted about this north to south migration pattern. It is clearly of long standing since it has occurred during periods of mass national unemployment as well as in the period of postwar full employment. Nevertheless, since the war no region has actually had a declining population. Apart from Scotland, where the net migration losses are very severe and almost equivalent to the natural increase, the internal growth in population in every other peripheral area has been approximately three times greater than the net migration loss (Table 3-6). Indeed, the actual gross movements of population across regional boundaries is, by the standards of most other countries, on a very limited scale with approximately 1.5 percent of the population crossing regional boundaries in any one year.

As a result of this relatively limited amount of interregional migration and the above average rates of natural increase in the two regions with the most serious losses of population from migration (Scotland and northern England) the actual share of each region in total national population has changed very little in the last fifty years. Recent official projections point to a continuation of this relatively slow process of regional population adjustment, for even the region with the most sizeable proportionate drop in population (Scotland) expects a population increase by 2001 of 750,000 inhabitants over the five million it had in 1951 (Table 3-7).

In sum, the differences in welfare across the British regions are small; rural depopulation has already occurred to a very great extent; the domination of the primate city has declined at least if measured in terms of population and despite interregional migration processes which constantly shape the balance of population in favor of the South East, the South West, East Anglia, and the West and East Midlands; and the overall regional changes in population distribution, both historically and forecast, are on a modest scale. However, a high level of unemployment in some regions, low activity rates, and generally appalling environmental conditions create a continuing need for active measures to improve regional economic performance and the regional physical environment.

NATIONAL GOALS FOR REGIONAL GROWTH

For reasons which are largely related to a desire to leave policy objectives as fluid as possible in the face of Britain's seemingly endless struggles with balance of payment deficits, rampant cost inflation, and puny private investment, both Labour and Conservative governments have resolutely shunned giving precise

Table 3-6. Change in Population, by Region, Mid-1961 to Mid-1971

Region	Mid-1971 estimated home population ('000)	Net migration ('000)	Average annual change mid-1961 to mid-1971		
			Natural change ('000)	Migration per 1000 population 1971	Migration as a percent of natural change
Scotland	5,217.4	−32.5	+34.3	−6.2	−95
North	3,293.5	−10.8	+17.4	−3.3	−62
North West	6,747.3	−11.4	+33.8	−1.7	−34
Yorkshire and Humberside	4,811.3	− 7.0	+26.5	−1.5	−26
Wales	2,723.6	− 0.4	+ 9.8	−0.1	−4
South East	17,288.7	− 3.7	+99.6	−0.2	−4
West Midlands	5,121.5	− 1.3	+39.8	−0.3	−3
East Midlands	3,390.2	+ 7.1	+22.2	+2.1	+32
East Anglia	1,686.0	+12.1	+ 8.4	+7.2	+144
South West	3,792.3	+22.4	+15.0	+5.9	+149
Northern Ireland	1,534.0	− 6.7	+17.3	−4.3	−39

Source: Abstract of Regional Statistics, No. 9, Her Majesty's Stationery Office, 1973.

Table 3-7. Projected Population Increase in the United Kingdom for 2001

Region	Population 1921 (thousands)	Percentage distribution					Population 1969 (thousands)	Projected home population 2001 (thousands)	Percentage distribution 2001
		1921	1931	1951	1961	1969			
England									
Northern	3,019	7.06	6.78	6.39	6.32	6.19	3,346	3,634	5.64
Yorkshire and Humberside	4,095	9.57	9.61	9.22	9.01	8.90	4,810	5,435	8.44
North West	6,022	14.09	13.83	13.12	12.73	12.53	6,770	7,431	12.31
East Midlands	2,337	5.46	5.61	5.92	6.05	6.20	3,349	4,472	6.94
West Midlands	3,504	8.19	8.36	9.05	9.27	9.52	5,145	6,235	9.68
East Anglia	1,211	2.83	2.75	2.84	2.90	3.07	1,657	2,261	3.51
South East	12,317	28.80	30.22	31.10	31.81	32.02	17,295	20,762	32.22
South West	2,725	6.37	6.24	6.64	6.69	6.91	3,730	4,714	7.32
Wales	2,656	6.21	5.79	5.29	5.13	5.04	2,724	3,096	4.80
Scotland	4,882	11.42	10.81	10.43	10.09	9.62	5,195	5,891	9.14
Total United Kingdom	42,769	100.00	100.00	100.00	100.00	100.00	54,022	64,431	100.00

Source: Department of the Environment (1971).

specification to the goals of regional policy and neither have shown any willingness to set quantified targets. Thus, vague terms such as the prevention of regional imbalance, the regeneration of the regions, and so on are in common parlance. Nonetheless, a careful reading of legislation, parliamentary debates, and government statements on regional development shows quite clearly that the implicit goals are a reduction in unemployment levels and an increase in activity rates of the peripheral regions. The slowing up of the drift of population out of the northern regions and into the southeast appears to be a complementary goal. Per capita income convergence is never specified as a goal, presumably because it is assumed that employment growth in the peripheral regions will occur in growing industries and that this by itself will mold the income-generating characteristics of these areas to correspond to those of the nation as a whole.

It is crucial to stress the totally unquantified nature of these goals. In forty years of regional policy, no central government has publicly announced targets for the number of jobs to be created in all the problem regions over a specified future period. Similarly although there are frequent regional population projections (made by the Registrar General and the Government Actuary; the latest projection is to 1991) which necessitate interdepartmental agreement on interregional migration assumptions and a never-ending stream of official plans for regions, subregions, and metropolitan areas, which include population assumptions, there are no regional population targets laid down by central government. This philosophy of nonquantified goals is best summed up by Anthony Crosland (1971), Secretary of State for Regional Planning in the 1964-1970 Labour Government. (Although Crosland seemed to argue at one point that the North West was overpopulated, he subsequently revised his argument.)

> I do not believe that . . . a case has been made out for precise regional population targets although all governments have formed the view that we want to stop the drift to the southeast. I believe we have not got the quantifiable factors which would lead us to set targets. We do not want to stop interregional migration. We live in a democratic society . . . where people are free to move from the places where they live . . . and there is no region which cannot cope with a very considerable increase in population. (P. 342)

Clearly this suggests that central governments tend to see no insoluble physical difficulties in accommodating the expected natural population increase of each and every region within regional boundaries. Moreover, although central governments have shown a preference for reducing the drift of the population from north to south, this is not seen as requiring precise migration and population targets for every region.

The desire of central governments to retain open-ended targets has been reinforced by the weakness of planning institutions at the regional level. In 1965 the newly elected Labour Government created a nationwide set of economic planning councils and economic planning boards within the eight planning regions of England, and within Scotland and Wales. The councils, which are not elected by the local population but appointed by central government, tend to be councils composed of private citizens, public officials, trade union representatives, and leaders of industry, all of whom are supposed to represent the key sectors of regional society. The boards, on the other hand, consist of senior government officials who direct a ministry's activities at the regional level.

When first established it was expected that these councils, with the assistance of the boards, would formulate long-term regional development strategies which could inform and help mold the medium- and long-term plans of the central government for each and every region. Over the longer run it was anticipated that these institutions would be the first building blocks in the creation of elected regional governments which would remove much of the planning and decision making from London. (Brown, Lord George, 1972)

The development of these institutions (which still exist) has been fitful. Their early strategies varied enormously in style, content, and sophistication and there is no unequivocal evidence that the central government took particular notice of their conclusions. Certainly, as their sophistication has grown, the councils have played a useful role in evaluating government proposals for given regions and the boards have provided a needed regional forum for the exchange of information across ministry frontiers. But these are minor achievements. The reality is that the Labour Government lost interest in the idea of powerful regional institutions. The last Conservative Government took a similar attitude. Thus, the councils remain purely advisory bodies, have limited financial resources, lack legitimacy in that their members are not elected, and have no rights to openly question central government decisions affecting a given region. (The chapter on the United Kingdom in J.L. Sundquist's forthcoming [Brookings] volume, provisionally titled *Population Distribution Policies in Western Europe*, provides a further study of these problems and limitations.) The result is that the real power over resource allocation, spatial planning, and inducements still rests at the center and especially in the Treasury, the Department of Trade and Industry, and the Department of the Environment.

THE NATURE OF GOVERNMENT MEASURES

Area Designation

Ever since the Town and Country Planning Act of 1947 successive central governments have used a 'carrot and stick' approach to encourage private enterprise to help solve the problems of the peripheral regions. The carrots consist of a whole range of incentives, backed up by a huge range of government actions, which seek to raise the level of investment and the demand for labor within the lagging regions. The sticks consist of controls over new industrial and office buildings in some of the full employment regions with the explicit objective of diverting some capital and enterprise to the problem regions.

Given this system of positive encouragements to growth and negative controls upon growth, the designation of areas as assisted or controlled is a crucial first step in a process which ultimately affects the spatial disposition of government resources; the spatial incidence of private investment; and the level of consumption, employment, and growth in the different regions.

The spatial building blocks are the ten economic planning regions—first designated in 1965—which are used as the basis for all regional administrative machinery, for regional economic planning, and for the subnational evaluation of government strategies which may affect the regions. Eight of these regions are in England, with Scotland and Wales making up the two other regions. Northern Ireland retains a large degree of planning and expenditure autonomy and is, to all intents and purposes, a separate entity (Map 3-1). Of these ten economic planning regions, only the South East of England and East Anglia do not have any areas in which some form of special government development assistance is available. In the remaining regions, part of the region, or in some instances the whole region, receives varying types and levels of assistance. Four different gradations of assisted area are currently used and these are listed in ascending order of available assistance and more generally of severity of economic distress (Map 3-2).

Derelict Land Clearance Areas: In areas where severe despoilation of the environment from mining or industrial work is currently creating difficulties in attracting and developing new sources of employment, the central government covers the bulk (seventy-five percent) of the costs incurred in approved clearance schemes. The northern parts of both the West and East Midlands are specifically covered by this designation.

Intermediate Areas: Large parts of the north of England show many signs of incipient economic distress. Typically, their economic structure is narrow, their physical environment is poor, income growth is lagging, and outmigration is a constant drain on population growth. The limited range of inducements and assistance presently on offer in these areas (which cover all of the North West, and Yorkshire and Humberside regions; parts of the South West, and the South East; and the northern coastal strip of Wales, and Edinburgh in Scotland) are designed to encourage new industrial building, retraining and training of labor, and derelict land clearance.

The Development Areas: Development areas (DAs), which represent the hard core of the regional problem, are primarily designated because of their level of unemployment. Here the full range of incentives and assistance are on offer. Currently, the whole of Scotland apart from Edinburgh, the whole of the Northern region of England, Merseyside, the bulk of Wales, and a large part of the South West region are development areas.

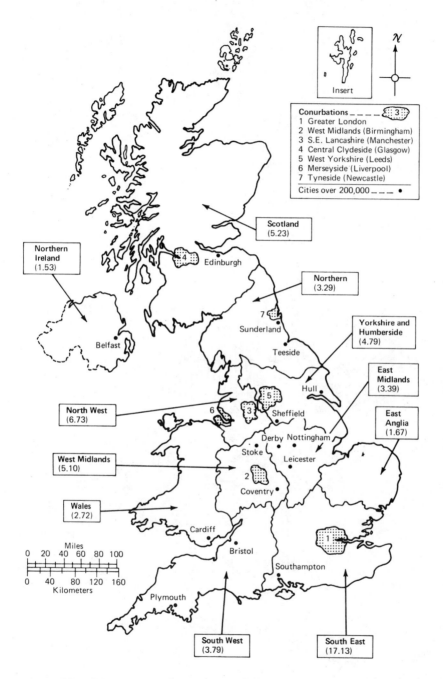

Map 3-1. Economic Planning Regions (1971 population, in millions)

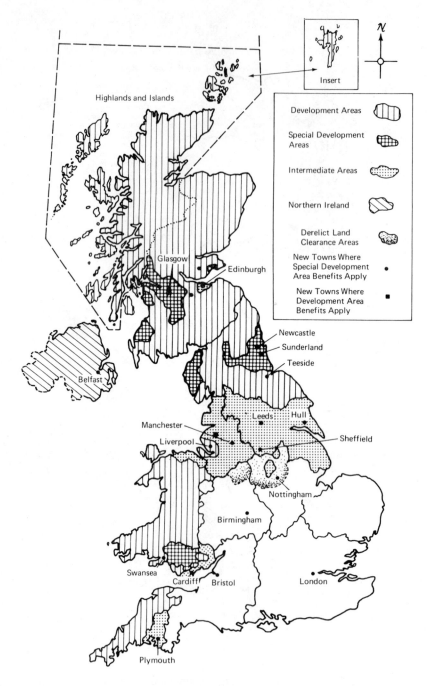

Map 3-2. Assisted Areas, 1972

The Special Development Areas: Within parts of the most northerly development areas (Northern England and Scotland) and in the valleys of Wales, the expectation is that severe unemployment will persist. In these special development areas, which originally embraced worked-out mining areas but now take in two major industrial areas in Scotland (Clydeside and Dundee) and in the northeast of England (around Newcastle and Sunderland), the highest rate of development grant is paid.

Taken together, these areas embrace almost half (48.2 percent) of the British population of over fifty-four million. Thus, in mid-1972, 4.0 percent of the population was in derelict land clearance areas, 21.7 percent in intermediate areas, 14.1 percent in development areas, and 8.4 percent in the special development areas.

Government Controls

Outside of development areas and special development areas, all new industrial building or extensions to existing industrial buildings of more than 10,000 square feet in the South East, and 15,000 square feet elsewhere, are subject to administrative scrutiny both by the Department of Trade and Industry and by the local planning authority. Before such developments are approved an industrial development certificate (IDC) is required and this can be refused if the production company "could reasonably be expected to set up in an assisted area . . . and, or . . . is likely to add appreciably to existing pressure on resources, principally on labour, in an area of labour shortage." (The best discussion of the use of IDC controls is in "The Intermediate Areas," Committee of Enquiry under the Chairmanship of Sir J. Hunt. Cmnd 3995, HMSO, 1969.)

In this system of controls the onus of proof rests upon the company (whether British-owned or foreign-owned) which must show that its long-run efficiency and/or its export competitiveness would suffer if it was diverted to a development or intermediate area. This proof must be based on calculations which include the benefits of government inducements associated with development in the assisted area.

Office developments in London are also subject to control through an office development permit system. Proposals to erect offices are scrutinized against the criteria of whether the development "would enhance London's prospects as an international financial and commercial centre."

Government Assistance

The central government seeks to favor the development of the assisted areas in four ways. The most obvious is the host of financial inducements aimed at encouraging private investment and an expansion of the demand for labor within these areas. A second method is through the disposition of spatially discriminant government expenditures on both capital and current account. The third and fourth methods use location of government offices and of the nationalized industries to favor the assisted areas.

Assistance to Private Enterprise: In the postwar period, the British method of encouraging private enterprises to help meet the government's objectives for the assisted areas has never included direct tax reliefs or tax holidays. Instead, varying combinations of subsidies for the use of new capital and of labor have operated. On capital investments, the initial allowance for depreciation purposes to be set against tax has also been used in a variety of ways. In addition, government grants to cover the costs of labor training or retraining are on offer and low interest loans may be obtained in special circumstances.

Three broad categories of assistance apply, the first being the assistance given to particular industrial sectors. For example, in circumstances where a key privately-owned industry within the development area has shown signs of imminent collapse, central government frequently has stepped in with either direct assistance for the industry as a whole or for particular companies. The classic case is the shipbuilding industry which has received substantial grants and reduced interest loans over a number of years.

The other principal method of encouraging private enterprise to aid in the achievement of the central government's regional goals is through a complex set of financial incentives. As we have already noted, postwar British governments have never used tax holidays, but employ instead a varying combination of financial incentives to encourage investment in fixed capital and in the employment of labor. Currently the key inducements consist of:

1. A regional development grant of twenty percent of the cost of new plant and machinery and of new industrial building with free depreciation on the plant and machinery, and an initial depreciation allowance of forty percent on buildings. This contrasts with a no grant situation in nondevelopment areas, but with free depreciation allowed on plant and machinery and a fifteen percent initial allowance on buildings. It is important to stress that the value of the grant can be offset against tax when depreciation is being calculated so that the real value of the grant for the company earning profits is approximately thirty percent. Secondly, grants are not conditional upon the creation of employment.

2. A regional employment premium (REP), an *ad hominem* subsidy, paid to manufacturing concerns which employ labor in the development areas. It was introduced in 1967 with an initial life of seven years and is due to be phased out after September 1974. When first introduced it represented a subsidy of approximately seven percent of the average earnings of male manual workers. Its current value (early 1974) is probably less than four percent.

3. Selective assistance, normally in the form of low interest loans but also by interest relief and removal grants, may also be paid to companies moving to a development area or already operating there. The criteria for allocation are

enormous, ranging from employment creation to employment stabilization. tion.

4. Training grants to offset the cost of training or retraining labor in the development areas can be paid in authorized schemes.

Taken together, the magnitude of these grants and loans is substantial. The official estimate is that, including REP, £410 million will be required in the financial year 1973-1974, although this largely depends upon the volume of new private investment. In fact, approximately £225 million will be available for development grants, £35 million for selective assistance, £96 million for REP, and a very small amount, £2-5 million, for training grants. The balance of £55 million is provided, under the local employment acts, for schemes which generate additional employment in areas of heavy and persistent unemployment. This type of assistance is due for phasing out almost entirely by 1975-1976. Measured in terms of total manufacturing costs Wilson (1973) has calculated that the development grant on its own will give development area producers a cost advantage of between 1 and 2.5 percent, or approximately 2.5 to 5 percent of net value added.

Government Expenditure: In very simple terms this can be broken down into expenditures on real assets such as our roads, advance factories, industrial estates, schools, ports; current expenditure from the government sector for specific goods and services; and equalization payments to supplement local authority resources. On the first two of these items regional criteria enter quite explicitly. For example, additional real expenditures for the development areas are typically allocated as a counter-cyclical device or, more normally, as an inducement to capital for population redistribution purposes or as a general method of improving the real standard of living. The government also favors the development areas through its own buying policy, giving special status to contractors in the DAs who are equally competitive with nondevelopment area bidders. There is little evidence on the effects of preference but two types of schemes are in operation:

1. In the general scheme, firms in development areas are given every opportunity to tender for public contracts from the government, public bodies, and nationalized industries. Where price, quality, delivery, and other considerations are equal, the DA firm is given preference.
2. In the special scheme, government purchasing departments review the initial competitive tenders and if at least twenty-five percent is not awarded to DA bidders then an offer is made to the first unsuccessful bidder in the DA, and, provided the overall cost of the project is not increased, an amount up to twenty-five percent of the overall purchase can be awarded to this bidder. If he refuses to accept the offer, the next lowest price tenderer is offered a contract and so on.

Once again the magnitude involved is very large. The government tends to spend more than £10 million each year on building factories which are let at noncompetitive rates and in its general spending on infrastructure clearly favors the DAs. For example, in 1968-1969 total public investment in new construction was £2,340 million, and if the DAs had received merely their per capita share, then £826 million would have come to them. In fact the figure invested was over £100 million more than this.

Government Offices: The government has dispersed its own offices in particular out of central London, and increasingly in answer to the claims of the DAs. Since the end of the war and up to October 1972, 48,000 government jobs were dispersed from London, roughly a third of them going to the assisted areas. In addition, almost 10,000 new jobs were created in these areas through deliberate decentralization policy. This policy is being continued and even strengthened. A further 16,000 jobs will be dispersed and created and it is likely that eighty percent will go to the assisted areas. Given that these areas have approximately one-fifth of United Kingdom employment, the degree of favorable treatment is large.

Nationalized Industries: It is extremely difficult to be categorical about the extent to which nationalized industries are used to achieve regional employment and development goals. Certainly, all nationalized sectors operate under profitability targets devised by central government. Accordingly, where specific loss-making activities are imposed upon an industry by the government, then it is the government which agrees to the nature of the service and assumes the subsequent losses. Apart from a few limited loss-making activities, such as the air and steamer links to the Scottish islands, there are very few explicit services which are exclusively or largely regional in their impact. However, the level of employment in the problem regions may enter into nationalized industry decisions in a way which is difficult to quantify but is none the less real. The most obvious example is the run down of employment in the coal industry during the 1960s. Both the relatively slow rate of run down and the personal subsidies which were used to induce early retirements, transfers to other coalfields, and retraining, together with the provision of advance factories and the highest level of development assistance within the areas of closure, largely reflected an awareness of the acute unemployment problems which the problem regions would face if the industry and the government had sought to achieve a fast run down.

Examples of where nationalized industries increase the growth of employment for explicitly regional reasons are harder to find, although the decision of the Conservative government (1970-1974) not to allow the British Steel Corporation (Maplin Sands) to consider a southeastern site for a new steel producing complex, and the company's subsequent choice of a development area site (Teeside), can be seen as an example of deliberate regional bias.

The Effects of Policy

It is obvious that the identification of the effects of policy is a particularly tricky exercise when policies have changed so frequently, companies may have made decisions favoring development in the assisted areas without receiving government aid, and the objectives of much government investment have been geared to long-run development goals.

Given these complexities we are fortunate in having two skillful and valuable exercises in measuring regional policy effects. A.J. Brown (1972), comparing the performance of the four major development areas—Scotland, Wales, and the North and North West England—over the years when policy was weak (1953-1959) and strong (1961-1966), concluded that *something* other than structure and changes in the characteristic performance of industries as such improved their relative performance by about 70,000 jobs per annum. This he ascribes to increases in mobile jobs (15,000 per annum), increases in new jobs associated with IDC approvals within the four regions (30,000 per annum), and multiplier effects in the service sectors (20,000 per annum). He concludes:

> It seems likely from our previous discussion that most of the change in patterns in moves and approvals was due to the strengthening of policy. If this is granted, it is very hard to suppose that the improvement in the relative performance of the assisted areas (after estimating structural factors) was not largely the result of strengthened policy also. (P. 318)

Brown has also concluded that if policy had not been strengthened, the GNP would have been reduced by the order of £150-£200 million per annum. This, of course, assumes that workers remain unemployed in the problem regions and do not migrate to the regions of labor shortage. However, the real economic question, as we have already pointed out, is how much GNP for a given social cost would be increased by raising the demand for labor in the problem regions as opposed to raising the demand in the labor shortage regions. No one, including Brown, has provided a definitive estimate of this kind.

The other careful estimate of regional policy effects has been made by Moore and Rhodes (1973). Using a modified shift-share technique, they concluded that over the years 1963-1970 employment in manufacturing within the DAs was twelve percent higher than it would have been if regional policies had been as passive as in the fifties and early sixties. In quantitative terms, and allowing for multiplier effects, they estimated that over 200,000 extra jobs were generated by the active regional policies in force over these years. As far as private manufacturing investment was concerned, the policy effect was an extra £90 million per annum or a thirty percent increase over the anticipated investment level.

Measured in more general terms, regional policy has contributed to an improvement in the regions' relative unemployment level, has underpinned a rate of per capita income growth which in most development areas has mirrored that of the nation, and has probably increased the flow into the DAs of talented personnel. The regions show different patterns of response to regional measures after 1963. For example, Scotland had a rate of unemployment roughly twice that of the nation between 1953 and 1966, but from 1967 onwards this relatively poor position improved. The same type of improvement occurred in Wales, but the North and North West showed no appreciable change, while Yorkshire and Humberside's position deteriorated sharply after 1965. Nonetheless, these measures can at least be regarded as a major holding operation pending the structural reform which is essential to the more rapid growth of the development areas. There are, however, more fundamental questions which must be asked of regional policy and these we discuss in the next section.

THE VALIDITY OF THE REGIONAL ARGUMENTS

In a country with as poor a postwar growth performance as that of the United Kingdom it is patently obvious that if policies which improve the economic performance of specified regions only do so by retarding the overall growth of GNP, then this should be clearly perceived and justified. We have already stressed that the economic case for raising the demand for labor in the high unemployment regions is that this is the most efficient method of raising both GNP and employment. The alternative method, it was argued, of allowing workers to migrate to the fast-growing regions could only generate additional economic costs, and therefore was less efficient. It is not difficult to develop an entirely different case which would substantiate Samuelson's (1969) verdict that regional aid typically results in a "sentimental distortion of the national production pattern." Here the real fear is that some quantum of new development is either being stifled altogether or forced to occur in locations which are not the best of the alternatives available. Both effects would reduce the rate of growth in the British GNP. In this section we try to reach some conclusion as to which of these views is more consistent with reality.

It is clear that some of the arguments which have been used against the movement of people from the problem regions have been rather poorly founded. The notion that outmigration results in severe negative multiplier effects in the population-losing regions has probably been overstressed. In terms of primary effects upon employment, A.J. Brown (1972) argued that in conditions of slack demand these effects will be minimal.

> Unemployed outgoers obviously do not ... [affect employment] while employed outgoers bequeath their jobs, in effect, to local unemployed. Incomers either stay unemployed or, more probably, get jobs that would otherwise have gone to local people. In these conditions the primary effect of migration is simply that the number of unemployed is reduced by the number of migrants in the region of origin, increased equally in that of destination. There are no primary effects on production in either region. (P. 275)

However, Brown concludes that there will be secondary effects as the spending power of the unemployed outmigrants (from unemployment benefits, supplementary benefits, and personal savings) is transferred to the region of destination. His calculation is based on the realistic assumptions that the average unemployed person spends between forty percent and sixty percent of the average employee in employment, and that forty percent of this expenditure goes into factor incomes within the region of the unemployed. Thus, for every unemployed outmigrant, eighteen to thirty percent of an average job might be lost. This means that for every 100 unemployed outmigrants, perhaps between eighteen and thirty jobs in the region of origin might be lost. This figure, of course, only relates to the short run. The migrants' spending power in the new region will be subject to normal leakages and this, in time, will have positive factor income and employment effects in the migrants' region of origin.

Therefore, although the loss of any jobs in labor surplus regions is unwelcome, the highly integrated nature of the British spatial economy, and the correspondingly large interregional leaks from any given regional expenditure, mean that reductions in employment following the migration of unemployed workers tend to be relatively limited.

A similar conclusion applies to the argument that outmigration results in the underutilization or even the redundancy of social capital in the migrant-losing area and its duplication in the migrant-receiving area. We know that the physical life of most forms of infrastructure, such as roads, schools, hospitals, libraries, and ports, is in excess of fifty years. Allowing for technological obsolescence and changing consumer preferences, perhaps an average of two percent social and economic overhead capital falls due for replacement each year. In broad terms this means that unless population as a whole is falling by more than two percent or, alternatively, unless there is a greater than two percent reduction in the numbers of specific age or social groups which use particular types of infrastructure, problems of redundancy and duplication do not apply. In fact, as we have already noted, no standard region has actually suffered a population decline in the last decade, and even in those subregions where population has declined, the percentage losses have typically been significantly less than two percent (Department of the Environment, 1971). We can therefore discount this argument as a major justification for preventing outmigration from the problem regions.

One other alleged cost of outmigration was that the migrants would crowd into congested centers and increase the unwanted externalities of noise, air, and water pollution; traffic congestion; and, perhaps, environmental overcrowding. There is simply no evidence on the magnitude of these effects, but two general points should be borne in mind. It is obvious that the migrants in leaving their home environment may, by this action, reduce the unwanted externalities there. Thus, before we could reach any definitive conclusion on the net costs of migrant moves (that is unwanted externalities created in the new location minus unwanted externalities diminished in the old location) we would require a substantial amount of information on the characteristics of both locations. A second point is equally obvious but has often been forgotten in British population analysis. The popular fallacy is that all migrants from the problem regions crowd into the most densely populated areas of the biggest cities of southern England. Inner Birmingham and inner London, on this reckoning, must be bristling with newly arrived Scotsmen, Tynesiders, and Merseysiders. The reality is more complex. If we take, as an example, the Census of Population figures on migration flows between England and Wales and Scotland over the years 1961-1966 we can readily dispose of the fallacy. During this period, Scotland lost 59,000 population from net migration flows. Over a third (thirty-five percent) of these net losses were to the Southeast region of England, while six other regions shared the bulk of the remaining net losses. The crucial point, however, is that in relation to the size of the population in the receiving areas, the biggest net loss went not to the South East but to the East Midlands, which picked up fifteen percent of the net losses although it had only seven percent of the population of England and Wales in 1966. The bulk of these net losses were concentrated in Corby New Town, where steel making has continuously attracted Scottish migrants ever since the 1930s. Even in the net losses to the South East, Greater London only picked up a thirteen percent share. The bulk of the net losses went to the fast-expanding outer metropolitan area and to the counties between London and Birmingham. A similar picture emerges in the West Midlands, with the conurbation only receiving 1.5 percent of the net losses, and with the remaining share, 9.5 percent, being concentrated in the outer conurbation area, especially around Coventry.

There is one further point to add. Even if peripheral region migrants crowd into the central parts of London or Birmingham, it does not follow that unwanted externalities will increase. London, in particular, has been losing population rapidly for several years as people move to suburban areas, new towns, and outer metropolitan areas. Thus, between 1961 and 1966 Greater London gained from inmigration, as a percentage of population, 4.1 percent but lost an equivalent of no less than 10.1 percent of its population from outmigration.

If none of these arguments carry weight, three other factors in favor of raising the level of demand for peripheral region labor have greater intrinsic merit. Although the evidence is by no means unequivocal, it does appear that wage inflation tends to be initiated in the South East and perhaps the West Midlands, and thereafter spreads to the other regions regardless of their factor market conditions. This has been corroborated in a general kind of way in a recent study which found that "unemployment dispersion [over the standard regions] exerted an upward pressure on aggregate rates of wage change of more than two percentage points in the post war period. . . ." (Thomas and Storey, 1971.)

If this finding is valid, then a reduction in the demand for factors in those fast-growing areas already at the margin of full capacity, and a transfer of that demand to the areas of labor surplus, would tend to slow the pace of wage inflation. The reasoning here is, first, that the bargains struck in the surplus areas would result in lower wage rates than would have occurred in the areas of labor shortage and, second, that the bargains struck in the shortage areas would ultimately reflect the relative diminution of the pressure of demand. To quote A.J. Brown (1972) once again, " . . . there seems to be a reasonable assumption that a more even spreading of the pressure of demand between regions would do something to reduce the speed of wage inflation, though it is difficult to quantify this effect" (p. 331).

Other crucial points relate to the nature and magnitude of migration flows. If outmigration from the problem regions is officially encouraged there is the real possibility that this process will cream off the most vigorous and talented members of the losing region. Once again the census figures for Scotland between 1961 and 1966 provide some justification for this argument. Scotland's net loss of people was largely made up of economically active persons (60.4 percent) who form only half of the overall population. Of these net losses, over sixty percent were in the socio-economic groups normally regarded as the most productive. These figures, of course, do not provide conclusive evidence that net outmigration has harmful long-run effects on Scotland's developmental capacity. At most, they indicate that there are some detectable differences in the socioeconomic characteristics of the outmigrants as compared to the inmigrants. Indeed, the whole subject of the effects of different degrees of outmigration on the economic structure and performance of losing regions requires much more thorough research.

A second more obvious possibility is that the scale of unemployment and even more especially of disguised unemployment as measured by low activity rates for females is such that only very large increases in outmigration would begin to bring the problem regions into demand/supply equilibrium. Thus, subsidized emigration is unlikely to solve either the immediate problem of surplus labor or the longer-term problem of how to recreate the economic base.

It is precisely at this point that the ground becomes particularly treacherous because what is at stake is whether (1) the cost in terms of growth foregone in controlling development in privately chosen locations is of a large magnitude; or (2) the real resource costs of manufacturing plants producing and distributing from lagging area locations are substantially different, over the long run, from the costs of producing and distributing in a preferred nonperipheral area locale. If the first type of cost is of a large magnitude then the GNP will be affected markedly. If the second type of situation applies, then central governments may be forced to provide long-run operating subsidies, simply to keep businesses competitive, rather than subsidies to cover short-run settling-in costs or subsidies to increase the share of national production occurring in the peripheral areas.

On the first question, the evidence is by no means clear-cut, but it does seem likely that the loss of growth caused by IDC controls is not large. Data from the controlling ministry, the Department of Trade and Industry

(DTI), show that in the two regions where controls have been most rigidly applied (the South East and West Midlands) an average of twenty to thirty percent of all employment associated with applications tends to be refused. Moreover the IDC system has been loosened considerably since 1971. In any event, the bulk of those refused projects go ahead in other parts of the nonassisted areas and only about five percent of all projects are abandoned or take place outside of the United Kingdom (Ibid., p. 304). However it is arguable that some projects are lost because manufacturers do not approach the DTI for permission to expand.

The Confederation of British Industry—the principal British employers' Association—looked into this point carefully. In reviewing their evidence, Brown came to the conclusion that this kind of potential loss of growth was of a very small magnitude indeed. Thus, we can probably discount the IDC control system as a major restraint on potential growth.

A verdict on the other possible undesirable effect—that of a misallocation of economic activity—cannot be given with such confidence. The critical question is whether the long-run costs of developing the new branch, new division, or transferred operation in an assisted area are higher than the costs associated with development in a nonassisted area which would almost certainly be more central to major centers of population and economic activity, and to international trade routes.

Some general points are worth bearing in mind. A proportion of mobile industry actually moves to the development areas to serve the local market there. Sometimes this is a general market coverage and sometimes it is production for a specific producer or producers within the development area. Evidence from a study by the author suggests that in the case of Scotland approximately ten percent of the moves arose from this kind of motive (Cameron and Clark, 1966). The second fact is that industries in which transport and communication costs form a relatively high proportion of total cost tend to avoid settling in the distant peripheral areas (Logan, 1972). To what extent this is because of the skillful administration of the IDC system or due to lack of growth in these industries so that new buildings are not required, the end result is that industries which might be particularly sensitive to distance from major markets and inputs tend not to settle in distant regions. A.J. Brown (1972), in a fascinating analysis, has also found no strong tendency for activities which are clustered together with others of the same industry to have significantly higher net output than activities which are not clustered. Indeed,

> an extra 10 per cent of a trade's national employment in a particular region seems to go with a raising of its net output per head in that region by about a seventh of one per cent. . . . [thus] so far as manufacturing industry is concerned . . . a move towards a new pattern of regional specialisation at all comparable to that of the nineteenth century is not visible. Dispersion and diversification rather are the rule. (P. 323-24)

It is also clear that mobile companies have shown a marked preference for the development areas which are most accessible to the core regions (Keeble, 1972) and from this one could conclude that what is happening is a natural extension of the boundaries of the core region.

Apart from these factors it does appear that the extra costs of operating a distant development area plant, as compared to an *in situ* extension or a more localized development, consist mainly of greater settling-in costs and perhaps some longer-run costs associated with duplication of staff and of buildings, extra transport and communication costs, and extra training costs. The most comprehensive evaluation of these extra costs has been made in a study by Luttrell (1962). Unfortunately, his study is now rather out of date since it dealt with moves in the immediate postwar period. Certainly Luttrell's findings were reassuring in that most mobile industries appeared able to operate, after the running-in stage, at a level of costs not markedly different from a potential location in a prosperous region and this "favorable" conclusion could be backed by a number of other more recent findings. There is no doubt that transport costs are falling in most industries as a proportion of net output (Logan, 1972). Moreover many British companies use average cost delivery charges so that the development area producers may not be at a disadvantage for inputs. Executive communication factors may present more serious problems, but once again these typically tend to represent a very small proportion of resource costs. Furthermore, if the development areas are marginal locations, then we could expect relatively high closure rates and a tendency to treat development area plants as the point of first redundancies during business downturns. This does not appear to be correct in terms of closures according to DTI data (Atkins, 1973). The DTI has also studied the decline in employment in branch plants within the DA's over a cyclical downturn and compared this to the decline at the headquarters plants of the parent companies located outside of DAs. This comparison showed that declines at the DA plants were considerably less than at headquarter plants. The evidence also suggests that there was no appreciable difference between the closure rates of DA branch plants and non-DA plants. Finally, studies by Hart and Macbean (1961) and by Mulvey (1974) suggest, for Scotland at least, that comparison of profitability with similar manufacturing sectors in England gave results which were not significantly different in the two countries.

In contrast to these studies, which all seem to point to the conclusion that the costs of developing in an assisted area are not significantly different from operating in a prosperous core region, there is a growing body of literature which claims that the United Kingdom cannot afford to have major companies suffer *any* degree of cost disadvantage (West, 1973). Memoranda to the Expenditure Committee of the House of Commons (1972-1973) from several leading manufacturers (particularly car assemblers) which had experience with operation in the development areas concluded that, even after allowing for government inducements, they had incurred sizeable cost disadvantages and these were normally caused by higher transport bills. When faced with these criticisms, the DTI could only stress that no company was forced to select a DA location, that there were a number of DAs which were highly accessible to the core regions, and that private manufacturers were not likely to pay attention to the inflationary effects on the labor market of expanding in the labor shortage regions.

Given this range of conflicting evidence, we must agree with Foster (1973) that regional policy cannot be securely based unless some of the crucial efficiency magnitudes are known. Thus, while the credit side of regional policy is fairly clear—unemployed and underemployed resources have been put to work, the pace of wage inflation probably has been reduced, and some of the undesirable economic effects of outmigration have been avoided—the debit side is not so clear-cut. Although the evidence suggests that the development control system has not caused a large volume of growth to be lost to the United Kingdom, it is not conclusive enough to permit any convincing statement on the degree of the private cost penalties suffered by companies which have been "invited" to develop in the problem areas. Indeed, until additional research has been undertaken, the economic justification for (or the case against) regional policy will remain tantalizingly in a state of "not proven."

THE FUTURE SCALE OF THE PROBLEM

Despite the obvious effects of powerful regional measures as indicated in the studies by Brown and by Moore and Rhodes, it is obvious that the regional problem has by no means been solved. The magnitude of the problem still seems enormous. One recent estimate has suggested that for the major problem regions—Scotland, Wales, northern Yorkshire and Humberside, and the North West—a job creation target of over one million may be required over the next ten years (Ridley, 1972). It is important to note how this target was derived. The first assumption was that the full employment rate for the nation is reached when unemployment falls to 1.5 percent. Assuming no regional policy, it was estimated that even if this rate was reached nationally these five regions would continue to have surplus labor. If the unemployment rates in these regions were to be equalized with the national rate, then 120,000 jobs would be required— e.g., approximately 60,000 jobs for those currently unemployed and a similar number to cover the reregistration of those currently unemployed but not officially registered as such. The second component of the target is made up of 250,000 extra jobs required to increase female activity rates. This in fact represents a halfway stage in a raising of regional activity rates to the highest level obtained anywhere. The third element comprised the expected growth in labor supply and the expected change in labor demand. Even if net migration continues at current rates (an average loss of 50,000 in the sixties) labor supply is expected to increase by 350,000 in the decade. In the absence of regional policy, the assumption was that aggregate demand of labor would be static but that 300,000 redundancies in the coal, steel, textiles, shipbuilding, and engineering industries would have to be filled to meet this static employment assumption.

It would be easy to quibble with some of these magnitudes. For example, the activity rate reduction could be regarded as an optional target. Clearly there is no compelling reason to assume that the same proportion of females in every region necessarily wish to be economically active. On the other side, a job reduction of only 300,000 over ten years may seem a ludicrously small estimate when seen against a reduction in the total number employed in these regions of 176,000 in the two years between 1969 and 1971. Thus, it seems reasonable to conclude that the overall magnitude of the problem has not been overstated, and a target of 100,000 jobs per annum seems a reasonable working assumption. To meet this target there are several obvious sources of employment growth:

1. Manufacturing activities moving from the nondevelopment areas of the United Kingdom;
2. International manufacturing companies being steered to the development areas;
3. Indigenous job creation from within the development areas themselves in the form of new manufacturing firms starting up as well as expansion of existing activities;
4. Public sector dispersion, particularly of central government office functions;
5. Private service sector dispersion; and
6. Indigenous growth in service employment.

Before we embark on a scrutiny of these possible sources of employment growth, one factor should be borne in mind. Like most other economically advanced nations, the balance of United Kingdom employment is constantly shifting towards the service sector. The last authoritative unofficial projection suggested that between 1968 and 1975 the number employed in services would rise by 900,000 but the number in goods-producing activities would fall by 300,000 (Cambridge University Department of Applied Economics, 1972).

Manufacturing Employment and Mobile Enterprise

With the economy expanding relatively rapidly, the development areas tend to pick up approximately 30,000 jobs per annum from mobile British enterprises—both transfer and branch type developments. Allowing for job multiplier effects within the receiving areas (a multiplier of between 1.15 and 1.20 is assumed) a total increase of approximately 35,000 jobs per annum might seem a reasonable expectation. This, of course, could be overly optimistic. We have already noted that IDCs are one of the influences in encouraging expanding companies to move to the development areas, but it should also be pointed out that the system has been considerably relaxed in recent years. Indeed in the last report on the United Kingdom economy the OECD (1972) warned of the weakening of regional policy if this course of action was pursued. Moreover, even when the system is applied, companies refused an IDC to expand in, say, the South East, may increasingly bluff the government into a favorable decision by threatening to open a plant on the Continent. It is also possible that the general rise in unemployment levels in the nonassisted areas, and the growing capital intensity of most manufacturing activities, may diminish businessmen's interest in the relatively more abundant supplies of labor in the development areas. Finally, the considerable improvement in communications brought about by the establishment of the main parts of the motorway network may mean that companies do not have the same incentive to establish branches in the development areas to service local customers. All of these factors would tend to reduce the magnitude of the mobile flow.

The other obvious source of mobile enterprise is from foreign companies setting up in the United Kingdom. British governments have been particularly successful in steering foreign companies to development areas, and of the regions, Scotland and Northern Ireland have gained most. Indeed, Scotland now has twenty percent of its manufacturing employment in United States-owned firms (Forsyth, 1972). Great faith is being pinned upon attracting European capital. It would, however, be overly optimistic to expect a large job flow from this source if the past few years are a valid guide. United States capital, some of it associated with North Sea oil and gas developments, and Japanese companies, seeking to offset their country's embarrassingly high balance of payment surpluses by establishing production bases within the EEC, could provide some new jobs, but even here the magnitudes will probably be small. Overall it seems unlikely that more than 3,000-5,000 jobs per annum will result from foreign investment, especially as DTI statistics show that only approximately 12,000 jobs were generated by overseas companies setting up plants in the DAs between 1965 and 1971. Obviously, we are still a long way short of the target.

Indigenous Growth in Manufacturing

This has two components—the creation and growth of new companies from within, and the diversification and development of existing companies. The evidence on the first is scanty and unsystematic, but work by John Firn, who is presently undertaking research into the formation of new companies in the Clydeside and West Midlands conurbations with a grant from the SSRC, on the Clydeside conurbation over the years 1958-1968 suggests that the flow of new enterprises has been minimal and that most of the new companies appear to be in local supply activities rather than basic activities (Table 3-8).

Table 3-8. Components of Employment Change in
Manufacturing Industry in the Central Clydeside
Conurbation, 1958-1968

	Scottish controlled plants	Externally controlled plants	All plants
Employment Growth			
a. .Overall	+32,192	+50,518	+ 82,710
b. In Existing Plants	+19,908	+29,350	+ 49,258
c. In New Plants	+12,284	+21,168	+ 33,452
Employment Decline			
d..Overall	−46,938	−57,842	−104,780
e. In Existing Plants	−18,900	−30,260	− 49,160
f. In Plant Closures	−28,038	−27,582	− 55,620
Net Employment Change			
g. Overall	−14,746	− 7,324	− 22,070
h. In Existing Plants	+ 1,008	− 910	+ 98
j. Stock Changes (ratio of c to f)	−15,754	− 6,414	− 22,168

Source: Firn (Forthcoming).

Data generated by the DTI also suggests that the assisted areas were particularly deficient in generating applications for IDC approval from the small firm sector. This, of course, embraces both new firms and expansion projects, but it does suggest that the small firm sector has tended to be weak in the development areas (Upson, 1974).

There are, of course, a great number of explanations of why this has occurred. The traditional answer is that the DAs simply do not generate sufficient new projects which could be profitable over the long run. Whether it arises from a diminution in the flow of entrepreneurial skill from persistent outmigration, a desire by individuals for security and the quiet life in regions prone to calamitous collapses of the leading industries, the difficulties of access to fast expanding markets elsewhere within the country, or the relative paucity of subcontracting opportunities, the real problem here appears to be how to create an atmosphere in which enterprise and risk-taking can flourish. The alternative explanation is that there are market imperfections, and perhaps policy barriers, which prevent the flow of new ideas from taking shape in the form of new companies and vigorous expansions. Not surprisingly, some critics have detected the root of the problem in the conservative local lending institutions which demand a higher rate of return from DA borrowers for a given degree of risk. Similarly some critics have seen the problem as the obvious outcome of excessive administrative concentration upon mobile capital, while neglecting locally initiated enterprise.

Whichever of these explanations is more accurate—and on balance it would appear that the first set of arguments "holds more water"—there is a real need for policy to take greater notice of the requirements of the new small firm sector within the DAs. Whether this will require a separate regional institutional framework is clearly a point yet to be decided, though the apparent success of a Northern Ireland agency specifically created for such a purpose perhaps indicates that the answer should be yes (Simpson, 1974).

When we come to the question of all other activity, apart from new mobile companies and newly created indigenous companies, we begin to enter a no man's land. Here the critical questions are how to encourage diversification, rationalization, greater competitiveness, and a host of other laudable objectives. Nonetheless, two general points are worthy of notice. First, it is a mistake to assume that all manufacturing enterprise in the development areas is collapsing dramatically. Apart from the half million jobs in over one thousand companies which have flowed to the development areas under postwar industrial mobility policy, many old established manufacturing sectors continue to thrive. The second point is that government aid in encouraging greater competitiveness and growth by indigenous (and other) activity must somehow avoid paying out subsidies for companies which would have taken such actions without this aid. Thus, the stress ought to be upon marginal cases wherever possible. This is of course easier said than done. The current approach, and indeed that favored by the last Labour Government, relies heavily upon standard grants for all investment-creating projects, regardless of employment created. REP is also a standard, "no strings attached" type of grant, since it is paid *ad hominem*. The advantages of this type of approach are obvious. The schemes are easily understood, and simple to administer, and the benefits to the recipients are fairly clear-cut. Moreover, such an approach is sophisticated enough to recognize that economic growth may come about without a growth in employment. It also avoids nasty equity questions since everyone is "equal before the law." However, this type of approach inevitably provides blanket benefits and favors those companies which may require no assistance. Standard grants may become an expensive system of overkill—and this may, in time, bring regional policy into disrepute.

Now it is true that under section 7 of the 1972 Industry Act loans and interest relief on especially favorable terms may be made available to companies expanding their employment. This certainly represents a type of discrimination but, although the government claims that 22,000 additional jobs will result from section 7 in the first year of the Industry Act (Guardian, June 28, 1973), it may not go far enough. This is not to argue the case for providing discriminatory assistance in growth centers. The structures of the lagging regions are so diversified, the trading interrelations between the regions so complex, and the spatial incidence of wanted externalities so changeable that no one could predict with any confidence where growth will be maximized, where the spread and backwash effects will be greatest, or where the creation of external economies will be largest (Cameron, 1969). Equally, there is no great interest in providing special subsidies for companies which are part of an integrated industrial complex. The administrative complexities alone seem to overwhelm any alleged advantages of faster regional growth for a given subsidy. However, Wilson (1973) has provided cogent arguments for a basic standard investment grant system topped up by regionally administered discretionary grants for those companies which increase employment markedly and for those which set up research and development divisions. The first kind of discretionary assistance might appropriately allow for direct and expected induced employment created by a given project. The latter is clearly aimed at stimulating the growth of those companies which provide opportunities for able people who might otherwise emigrate. In some regions where the problems of lag are particularly severe even discriminative subsidies may not get to the root of the problem. It could be that in regions like westcentral Scotland the decline in employment has been caused in part by the failure of major companies to exploit favorable market circumstances. If this is correct, the stress should be upon using government resources, probably through a semi-independent development corporation, to stimulate research, product innovation, industrial relations reform, better marketing, and so on. (West Central Scotland Plan.)

Services Growth

Here, the most obvious possibility is the dispersal of government offices, particularly of the standard decision-making type. Currently some 14,000 jobs are waiting to be dispersed or newly created in the development areas, and the Hardman Committee (1973), looking to the further dispersal of headquarters staff, has recommended that the DAs and intermediate areas receive a further 17,000 jobs. However, even if the government increases the latter figure it is unlikely that the problem areas will gain more than 3,000-4,000 jobs per annum, so this clearly cannot be a large contributor to regional equilibrium. This suggests that much greater effort should be given to encouraging private service activities to grow from within the DAs and to decentralize from the southeast of England, and especially from London. Certainly the success to date in achieving dispersal to the DAs has been minimal. This is regrettable since a major study by Rhodes and Kan has suggested that the subsidy cost of dispersing private sector office work could be much smaller than in the case of manufacturing. Until mid-1973 the Heath Government still appeared to think that services only supplied local needs, and it tended to argue that any aid, particularly to locally established services, would automatically result in local closures which would offset the benefits of the subsidy. Measures were belatedly introduced in June which could increase the flow of service activities out of the South East. These included rent rebates, transfer allowances for equipment and personnel, and offsets for relocation costs. However, until there is a far greater effort given to understanding how service industries operate and, in particular, which services are basic, as distinct from population-related activities, government promotional efforts are likely to remain puny and almost certainly inappropriate.

CONCLUSIONS

The new measures of March 1972, and the general support given to them by all major political parties, represent a consensus view that the regional problem has not been solved and must now be tackled with increased resources. Thus, while there is no doubt that policy did have substantial successes during the sixties, especially if measured in terms of extra employment created in the development areas, the task which still remains seems dauntingly large. Certainly the well-tried method of private industrial dispersal from the core regions will continue to provide a useful means of raising the demand for labor in the lagging regions, though the extent to which this affects private efficiency will have to be scrutinized much more closely. Moreover, government office dispersal will continue to provide some stable work. However, these components are clearly not sufficient, and the first is especially sensitive to success in maintaining a high rate of national growth and a system of industrial development controls. Considerable imagination will therefore be required if the base of the regional effort is to be successfully broadened. In particular, far greater effort will have to be given to encouraging that part of the private service sector which is not tied to local consumption requirements to locate or to expand in the development areas. There is also a clear need for greater discrimination in the use of financial subsidies if regional policy is not to fall into the evil company of other large programs which deliver the goods at a very high cost. Finally, the whole question of how to stimulate new growth from within the problem economies, and especially of how to encourage small new enterprises, should be given high priority.

ACKNOWLEDGEMENTS

The author is grateful to many people for reading and commenting upon an earlier draft of this study. Arthur Brown, Christopher Foster, Richard Crum, Kevin Allen, and Jim Sundquist all provided thoughtful and helpful criticism. The draft was also improved by an anonymous reader. Of course none of the above bear any responsibility for remaining errors of fact or judgment.

Chapter Four

Regional Policies in West Germany

INTRODUCTION

The origins of present-day regional and spatial planning in the Federal Republic of Germany can be traced to its constitution (the "Basic Law"), where it is explicitly stated that equality in living conditions has to be created and maintained in all parts of the country. The inability to define the meaning of equality in this context and to translate this mandate into a more operational framework which would be consistent with the prevailing antiplanning atmosphere of Erhard's "social market economy" long delayed any serious discussion about comprehensive spatial and regional planning schemes both in the scientific community and in the political arena. Whatever was done by the federal government in a regional context was either justified as an emergency measure or was politically motivated. Interventions in other spheres of the economy (sectoral tax preferences and agricultural market regulations, for example) tended to be more acceptable and less associated with planning, and justified as assisting in either (1) establishing, enforcing, and guaranteeing the rules of the market game; or (2) regulating the economic process to produce monetary and exchange rate stability, economic growth, and full employment. In general, any intervention tended to be individually aimed at specific, generally nonspatial or nonregional, targets, and any regional coordination between different government departments on the national level or between the federal and the state level tended to be frowned upon on ideological grounds. Comparing Germany with other European countries and the United States, Shonfield (1965) observed:

> Germany is seen to be better endowed . . . with the essential discriminatory equipment required for modern planning, especially planning of a long-term character. It seems unlikely that in the long run it will not be used. To adopt a principle of economic nonintervention by the state is at least intelligible; what does not make sense is to intervene constantly and yet not to plan. (P. 297)

In addition to ideological barriers of this kind, there was considerable uncertainty about the constitutional intent as to the extent to which the federal government should become active in a regional context. This uncertainty, although successively reduced by the Federal Spatial Planning Law of 1965 and by the actual operation of regional and spatial planning schemes, still presents a basis for occasional conflicts between the state and the federal level.

The Basic Law assigns to the federal level the right to establish a regulative framework for the sphere of spatial planning (*Raumordnung*). This right has been interpreted to mean the establishment of relatively broad but binding spatial planning guidelines. The federal government, apparently as a result of the activities of a number of states—particularly the passing of various state planning laws—was finally forced to take action which led to the passing of the *Raumordnungsgesetz* in 1965. This spatial planning law sets forth explicitly the planning responsibilities of the states in terms of establishing operational guidelines and regional plans. However, except for setting up various coordinating committees, it leaves the federal role comparatively ill-defined. In the field of regional economic policy, the federal government has accepted prime responsibility as part of its "structural policy."

Thus, in general, German regional and spatial planning and policy cannot be discussed without considering the roles of the states. Three relatively recent developments have further complicated a clear-cut division of national and state regional policy efforts: (1) under the leadership of the Federal Department for Economic Affairs, federal regional programs have expanded considerably during the past few years. These efforts are explicitly joint tasks with the states and require considerable coordination; (2) the Federal Spatial Planning Law, while spelling out responsibilities and guidelines for state spatial planning activities, nevertheless lacks specificity which in turn has led to considerable differences in interpretation and implementation by the states; (3) the states themselves, partly on their own initiative, and partly as a result of increasing federal interest in regional and spatial affairs, have accelerated their spatial and regional planning endeavors and complemented their traditional physical planning orientation by more functional social and economic planning approaches and concepts. In general, the states have taken this new orientation very seriously and have begun to develop and implement new planning concepts on their own.

GENERAL REGIONAL TENDENCIES

Three factors seem to be primarily responsible for the relatively favorable overall picture of regional development in Germany and the lack of really grave regional depressions (Commission, 1969, p. 88):

1. the relatively favorable pattern of distribution of towns and industrial centers;

2. the general climate of economic growth; and
3. the manpower shortage which has prevailed almost uninterruptedly since 1958.

In addition, overall (i.e., interstate) differences in productivity and income have—by and large—diminished over the past two decades. Predominantly rural, chronically lagging states such as Schleswig-Holstein and Niedersachsen (Lower Saxony) in the north, Bavaria in the south, and Rheinland-Pfalz in the west have reduced their per capita GRP (gross regional product) deviation from the federal average by between fifty and seventy-five percent (see Table 4-1), while the heavily industrialized Nordrhein-Westfalen has had to yield much of its lead.

And yet, in spite of the absence of large areas of economic depression there are significant pockets of low per capita income and structural decay and, in spite of the virtual absence of large-scale, long-term unemployment patterns, there are peripheral regions with remarkable seasonal unemployment. By its aggregate nature, state data do not reveal such peripheral regional problems. This is particularly true for the state of Bavaria, which encompasses the economic extremes for the whole of Germany—the wealthy, fast growing Munich region with its concentration of growth industries on the one hand; and on the other the low-income, economically highly sensitive region of eastern Bavaria, many parts of which have chronic seasonal unemployment and relatively high outmigration rates.

Table 4-1. Per Capita Gross Regional Product Deviation from Federal Average (in Percent)

	1950	*1960*	*1970*
Hamburg	+67.1	+48.4	+56.6
Hessen	−1.0	0	+8.1
Berlin	n.d	−3.3	+7.7
Nordrhein-Westfalen	+21.3	+6.7	+5.6
Bremen	+38.2	+15.1	+4.4
Baden Württemberg	0.2	+3.0	+0.7
Bayern (Bavaria)	−16.3	−11.3	−4.2
Rheinland-Pfalz	−15.0	−11.8	−6.4
Niedersachsen (Lower Saxony)	−18.5	−10.2	−8.6
Saar	n.d	−8.0	−12.5
Schleswig-Holstein	−28.6	−17.1	−14.0
Federal Republic, in DM	2386[1]	5958[2]	8530[2]

[1] 1954 prices

[2] 1962 prices

Source: Julitz (1972).

The 1966-1967 recession clearly demonstrated the severity of this continuing lag in development. Although the unemployment differences between the various regions had significantly declined before 1966-1967, the structural weakness only surfaced during this recession. The number of closures of plants has been relatively higher in these regions and the number of newly created jobs smaller. In addition, unskilled long-distance commuters whose employment in larger cities had contributed to the window dressing of the lagging regions' economic situation now returned to the local pool of the unemployed.

Selected Regional Development Patterns

The postwar partition of Germany into occupation zones and, subsequently, into two more or less sovereign states, had far-reaching consequences for regional development patterns in terms of population distribution, employment, and industrial production. The territory which is now the Federal Republic accounted for about sixty percent of the 1936 industrial production. Some industries (such as the iron, steel, and metal industries with seventy to seventy-seven percent) significantly exceeded this average, while others (such as the electrical equipment and clothing industries with thirty-eight to thirty-nine percent) were considerably below average. Such an unequal distribution resulted in very different starting positions among industries (as well as individual corporations), depending on whether they had lost more by losing a market (or production capacities) than they had gained by losing competitors in the eastern parts.

Subsequent structural changes were significantly influenced by refugee- and expellee-entrepreneurs. The British Overseas Economic Survey (1955) noted that a "remarkable number of these enterprises have succeeded in reestablishing themselves in Western Germany despite the immense difficulties which had to be overcome" (p. 77). However, the infant mortality (or re-establishment mortality) rate of these enterprises was remarkably high in rural areas along the periphery of the *Wirtschaftswunder* centers of reconstruction. Reporting on the Bavarian and Upper Palatine Forest Region, Böventer (1969a) points out that "many of these enterprises collapsed later because they turned out to be inefficient—the result of the isolated location of the region, its poor accessibility and its inadequate infrastructure" (p. 183). Indeed, in an ex post facto evaluation of this particular development phase, it is hard to escape the impression that here the federal government might have missed a rare and crucial long-run planning opportunity by not making better spatial use of the remarkable entrepreneurial potential in these rural areas.

Demographic and Employment Trends

The refugee problem was to a considerable extent also a regional one, since the overwhelming majority of refugees concentrated in the eastern portions of the British and American occupation zones—i.e., Schleswig-Holstein,

Lower Saxony, and Bavaria. Within these regions, refugees and expellees preferred the rural areas because of the more flexible food and housing conditions. This initial "misallocation" of millions of refugees was, no doubt, one of the reasons why, in the mid-fifties, the "population distribution in West Germany was still much more even than before the war" (Böventer, 1969b, p. 53). It presumably was also responsible in part for the subsequent development lags in many of the initially overpopulated regions. The refugee resettlement program of the early fifties, which was designed to lighten the burden of the rural eastern states, was not entirely successful; in fact, it has been called "a miserable failure" due to its overemphasis on spatially equal redistribution and its lack of consideration of regional growth potentials, resulting in subsequent secondary migration to the centers of economic growth (Gerfin, 1964, p. 572). Nevertheless, for the traditionally more industrialized states, and later for the country as a whole, the continuous stream of skilled workers represented only a temporary unemployment burden and soon turned into an important force for economic growth.

The inflow of Germans from East Germany was sharply reduced by the construction of the Berlin Wall in August 1961. The regional allocation, however, remained approximately the same, with Nordrhein-Westfalen, Bayern, Baden-Württemberg, and Niedersachsen leading the receiving states. Due to fairly high natural population increases (peaking in 1964) and rapidly expanding foreign inmigration, the sudden reduction of east-west migration was hidden in aggregate demographic data but, of course, it did leave its qualitative mark due to the high skill levels of the East German immigrants. The total number of births has been declining ever since 1964, reducing the surplus of births over deaths to 48,000 in 1971 and a surplus of deaths over births of 40,000 in 1972 (see Table 4-2). Regions with previously particularly high birth rates—Emsland, western Eifel, and parts of Baden-Württemberg—tended to have the largest decline in birth rates over the last few years. This regionally differentiated change in birth rates has been explained by economic factors, by regional lags in the reduction of family size, and by shifts in regional age structures resulting from internal and external migration.

Parallel to the reduction in births was the steady, only occasionally interrupted, increase in net foreign migration, which reached 574,000 or eighty-eight percent of the total German population increase in 1970. All states shared in this net foreign migration gain, although there was a marked preference among immigrants for the more industrialized states. While the state by state distribution of foreigners has since become slightly more even, the Nordrhein-Westfalen, Baden-Württemberg, Hessen, and Süd-Bayern labor districts, which each had a foreign employment rate 10.3 percent above the federal average in 1971, together still account for seventy-six percent of all foreign employment (see Table 4-3). On the level of the smaller labor office districts (*Arbeitsamtsbe-zirke*), the difference in distribution between the highest (Stuttgart, with 23.3

Table 4-2. Population Changes (FRG)

Total Population (FRG including West Berlin)

1950 (September 13)	50,184,700
1960 (monthly average)	55,433,000
1970 (May 26)	61,508,400

Year	Natural population change (Births–Deaths)	Total net external migration	Net migration gains From East Germany and former eastern territories	Foreign	Berlin (east and west)
1954	273,490*	221,130*	186,230**	−20,810	48,540
1956	271,200*	339,500*	260,200**	−5,950	77,710
1958	321,750*	328,960*	216,890**	50,560	61,260
1960	340,270*	364,030*	117,740**	176,850	70,610
1962	373,730	284,540*	16,420	238,210	27,620***
1964	421,310	276,490*	36,770	237,150	−22***
1966	364,020	131,620	36,380	93,560	—
1967	332,110	−176,920	27,060	−205,810	—
1968	235,780	278,140	23,500	253,210	—
1969	159,100	572,300	23,600	544,050	—
1970	76,080	574,050	23,580	547,090	—
1971	48,000				
1972	−40,000				

*Figures do not include West Berlin
**Figures do not include East Berlin
***From West Berlin only
Source: Statistisches Bundesant (1955-1972).

percent) and the lowest (Heide, in Schleswig-Holstein, with 1.7 percent) rates of foreign employment has increased (BAA, 1972, p. 16).

Spatial Patterns and Processes

An analysis of the spatial components of industrial patterns reveals certain trends in the sizes of new establishments and the sizes of cities and towns in which they located. These trends were strongly associated with changes in unemployment rates. Thus the period until 1959, the year when full employment had been attained in most regions, clearly was dominated by a process of agglomeration in and around established centers of industrial activities. The abundance of labor and the prevalence and importance of agglomeration advantages during this reconstruction period forced rural unemployed or underemployed workers to migrate to the cities or to commute over often

Table 4-3. Employment of Foreigners in Germany

State labor districts	1965* Share[1]	1965* Rate[2]	1967* Share[1]	1967* Rate[2]	1969* Share[1]	1969* Rate[2]	1971* Share[1]	1971* Rate[2]
Schleswig-Holstein (including Hamburg)	3.1	2.2	3.8	2.5	3.9	3.8	4.4	6.4
Niedersachsen (including Bremen)	6.8	3.0	5.9	2.3	6.1	3.6	6.9	5.9
Nordrhein-Westfalen	31.9	5.6	30.2	5.1	28.4	7.1	28.1	10.4
Hessen	11.1	7.0	11.8	6.0	11.7	8.9	11.9	13.2
Rheinland-Pfalz-Saar	5.1	3.9	4.9	3.3	4.3	4.3	4.5	6.6
Baden-Württemberg	26.4	10.0	26.8	8.5	27.4	12.5	24.6	16.0
Nord-Bayern	4.4	3.2	3.9	2.5	4.9	4.4	4.9	6.7
Süd-Bayern	10.2	6.5	11.0	5.7	10.7	8.1	11.3	12.3
Berlin	1.0	1.4	1.6	1.8	2.6	4.6	3.4	8.8
West Germany Total population (100.0%)			100.0% =991,255	4.7	100.0% =1,501,409	7.0	100.0% =2,240,793	10.3
1965	1,216,804	5.4						
1963	828,743	3.7						
1961	548,916	2.5						
1959	163,211	0.8						
1957	104,603	0.6						
1955	76,843	0.4						

*as of September 30 of each year

[1] Share: percent of total foreign employment in Germany

[2] Rate: foreign employment in percent of total employment

Sources: Bundesanstalt für Arbeit, *Ausländische Arbeitnehmer*, 1967, 1969, 1971.

substantial distances. The speedy restoration of prewar spatial and economic patterns was generally considered the most feasible path towards economic recovery and growth. Government interference in the form of investment subsidies and tax concessions generally discriminated in favor of what were believed to be key industries which tended to be fairly concentrated.

That such a policy might eventually lead to undesirable regional imbalances was recognized only after the agglomerative forces had already subsided considerably. Before 1957 there was hardly any movement of establishments from the agglomeration areas into rural areas. If such movement did take place, it was mainly because of the physical impossibility of expansion in the city. Only in a few relatively labor-intensive industries did the differential increase in the cost of labor result in first indications of a leveling off of the agglomerative tendencies. These were (1) industries having a relatively high proportion of jobs which were not very popular among the urban population, and which at the same time were not very well paid—for instance, textiles and leather, or (2) industries in which the raw material (and transport cost) orientation was relatively strong and already becoming dominant over agglomeration economies through small wage differentials—for instance, timber, furniture, and food, particularly fruit and vegetable processing (BAS, 1964).

Only after full employment was reached in the late 1950s did the dispersive tendencies become a significant force. The increasing labor shortage in the industrial centers led to highly competitive relocation games in many industries, with plants and "extended work benches" trying to locate ever closer to the source of long-distance rural-urban commuters, as well as to more peripheral areas where the agricultural labor force was underutilized or set free by mechanization. Between 1950 and 1970 the number of farms decreased by about a third from 1.94 million to 1.24 million. At the same time agriculture's share in the total gainfully employed labor force decreased from twenty-five percent in 1950 to 13.7 percent in 1960 and 8.8 percent in 1970. That the productivity problem in agriculture still exists is indicated by comparing the last figure with that sector's 3.1 percent share in 1970 GNP (BELF, 1971).

During the last few years of labor shortage before the 1966-67 recession, the size of communities selected for industrial plants had become remarkably small (see Table 4-4). In fact, forty-five percent of all new plants in 1964 and 1965 were opened in communities with populations of less than 3,000, with only eleven percent locating in cities above 50,000. However, it also was found that there was a general tendency for the smaller towns to be situated in the proximity of larger cities or at least within more densely populated areas. The Department of Labor speculated that these small localities participate directly in the locational advantages of neighboring cities but are able to offer more favorable and less expensive sites to new firms than the built-up cities (BAS, 1964, p. 13). Still, there were many small communities with less than 1,000 population in isolated locations, particularly Rheinland-Pfalz and Bavaria, which attracted industrial plants.

Table 4-4.   Relocated and Newly Established Plants and
Their Employment, by Type of Location

Community size class		Total		In agglomerated areas*		In rural areas	
		Number of plants	Average plant size	Number of plants	Average plant size	Number of plants	Average plant size
less than 1,000	a)	174	27.5	16	34.8	158	26.8
	b)	114	35.6	8	21.8	106	36.6
	c)	257	30.4	–	–	–	–
1,000-3,000	a)	379	40.6	70	40.7	309	40.6
	b)	244	39.7	52	55.4	192	35.4
	c)	502	39.1	–	–	–	–
3,000-5,000	a)	166	44.3	30	38.2	136	45.6
	b)	136	36.7	55	36.1	81	37.2
	c)	214	48.1	–	–	–	–
5,000-10,000	a)	238	55.7	56	64.3	182	53.1
	b)	165	44.5	60	41.7	105	46.0
	c)	256	50.2	–	–	–	–
10,000-20,000	a)	171	69.9	52	103.0	119	55.4
	b)	130	52.5	58	52.7	72	52.3
	c)	166	52.1	–	–	–	–
20,000-50,000	a)	172	66.9	90	73.0	82	60.1
	b)	88	89.4	51	99.5	37	75.5
	c)	119	65.6	–	–	–	–
50,000 and more	a)	250	103.9	240	112.8	10	34.5
	b)	160	65.9	156	66.2	4	52.0
	c)	186	62.4	–	–	–	–

[a]1968-1969
[b]1966-1967
[c]1964-1965 (further disaggregation was not available)
*Metropolitan Regions (*Stadtregionen*) using the delimitations of the Akademie für Raumforschung und Landesplanung (cf. *Stadtregionen in der Bundesrepublik Deutschland 1961*, Hannover: Jänecke, 1967).
Sources: BAS 1966; BAS 1968 and BAS 1971.

The most important reason for these location decisions was un-equivocally "availability of labor force" or, better, "unavailability of labor anywhere else." Relatively more branch plants were located in small communities (with less than 3,000 population), while newly founded and relocated firms were more frequently located in larger communities, particularly in the 3,000-10,000 size class (Jochimsen and Treuner, 1967, pp. 41ff.). It seems that the willingness of industries to shift into rural, village, and small town locations during this period of dramatic labor shortage significantly influenced subsequent small-center industrialization policies.

Not surprisingly, the attractiveness of rural areas and small communities for newly locating plants sharply declined during the 1966-1967 recession. The following two years (1968-1969) saw only a partial return to the old pattern. While industrialization in small communities did not regain prerecession levels, it more than doubled in larger cities (over 50,000) (see Table 4-4). This pattern was associated with a switch of the two principal reasons for site choice given by newly located plants ("available labor force" now being second and "physical expansion opportunities" first; see BAS, 1971, pp. 34f.) and was presumably also closely related to the increased inflow of foreign workers. The Federal Republic today is not any more agglomerated, in some respects, than in comparable prewar periods. Borries (1969, pp. 25ff.) identifies fifty urban agglomerations where 50.1 percent of the population lived in 1961 on thirteen percent of the total national area. The corresponding figures for 1939 and 1925 were 51.5 percent and 51.0 percent respectively. Other indices of dispersion or concentration applied on a county basis also indicate that postwar Germany did not reach the record highs of the late thirties, and that after the reconcentration of the 1950s a very weak equalization process can be detected in the spatial distribution of population. Not surprisingly, however, these index results hide two counteracting tendencies, namely, the continuing process of depopulation of already thinly populated isolated rural areas outside the agglomerations, and the process of deconcentration within agglomerated regions, with medium-size cities at the periphery growing and central cities declining.

Using the 1961 delineation of sixty-nine metropolitan regions for which the German Statistical Office is now supplying data, 54.1 percent (of a total of 60.65 million) of the resident population of the FRG are living in metropolitan regions (1961: 54.0 percent on the same area) which account for 17.4 percent of the total FRG territory (*Wirtschaft und Statistik*, 1972). The population increase in these regions since 1961 was 8.2 percent, only slightly higher than that in nonmetropolitan regions (7.7 percent). Not unexpectedly, the population in the core cities of the metropolitan area grew by only 1.2 percent (see Table 4-5), while the remaining *Umland* experienced a twenty-two percent increase. At the same time, population densities in metropolitan areas rose from 701 to 759 people per square kilometer (compared with an increase from 126 to 136 in nonmetropolitan areas).

Of the many other significant trends and developments which ought to be mentioned in this context one appears to be particularly important. It has been estimated that about twenty percent of all industrial investments in Germany are made by foreign-owned companies (*Wall Street Journal,* 1971). There are a variety of regional tendencies associated with the location of such firms, particularly with respect to newly founded ones: (1) American, French, and British firms tend to prefer locations in their former occupation zones, in

Table 4-5. Population Change in the Sixty-Nine Metropolitan Regions, 1961-1970

Metropolitan zone (1961 delimitations)	Residential population in '000s		Change in percent
	June 6, 1961	May 27, 1970	
Core cities	20,288.9	20,539.9	1.2
Additional core area	4,999.1	5,986.3	19.7
Total metropolitan core	25,288.1	26,526.2	4.9
Urbanized zone	3,545.3	4,541.4	28.1
Peripheral zone	1,505.9	1,749.9	16.2
Umland zones	5,051.2	6,291.3	24.6
Total	30,339.2	32,817.5	8.2

Source: *Wirtschaft und Statistik* 11 (1972): 628.

which these countries continue to maintain military bases; and (2) there has been a strong preference for the larger metropolitan cities with good communication and transport facilities (Frankfurt, Düsseldorf, Hamburg, and Munich) and a preference for cities where many other firms of the same nationality were already located (American firms in Frankfurt; Japanese firms in Düsseldorf; British firms in Hamburg; etc.). Production facilities, however, are increasingly decentralized, as with those of German firms. The oil refinery and chemical industries lead the list of industries; Nordrhein-Westfalen the list of states with newly established foreign production plants; and Switzerland, the United States, and the Scandinavian countries the list of countries of origin (BAS, 1971, p. 36).

GOAL FORMULATIONS FOR REGIONAL POLICIES

The mandate of the German Constitution calling for equal living conditions in all parts of the country was recast in only slightly more specific form in the 1965 Federal Spatial Planning Law where, in article 2, it is stipulated that:

> In regions in which the living conditions in their totality are significantly lagging behind the federal average, or in which such lags are to be anticipated, the general economic and social conditions as well as the cultural facilities shall be improved.

Since this proclamation, many of these rather vague criteria have been substantiated and guidelines developed for their implementation. Regional objectives have finally been accepted at the highest governmental levels as a high-priority policy field. In his "Policy Statement" at the beginning of the new legislative period (January 1973), Chancellor Brandt reiterated the constitutional mandate as well as his intent to continue the rapid expansion of regionally oriented policies.

It is our task to create and guarantee for all citizens in our federal state equal chances in life. To this end a concept for the regional development of the federal territory will be elaborated and federal measures better coordinated regionally. (Bulletin, 1973)

Regional policy in its broader meaning can—for the German scene—be roughly divided into three categories:

1. spatial planning policies in terms of government efforts designed to influence (quantitatively and qualitatively) the spatial structure of settlement patterns, population distributions, and systems of infrastructure facilities, generally referred to as *Raumordnungspolitik*: its major underlying objectives have been the improvement of living conditions in rural and depressed areas and the correction of socially unhealthy spatial settlement patterns, particularly in urban and industrial agglomerations;
2. regional economic policies principally in terms of fiscal measures aimed at industrialization processes in designated regions and centers: graduating from an emergency type of policy activity to a major position in federal economic policy after the emergence of bottlenecks in traditional growth regions, regional economic policy has been aimed at the mobilization of regional development potentials for national economic growth; and
3. other economic and social policy measures with varying regional or spatial significance, for example, sectoral subsidization and tax relief programs or transport investment policies.

Spatial Planning Goals

The concept of *Raumordnung* has the dual, interrelated meaning of "spatial organization" and "spatial orderliness" with an obvious difference in implicit goal orientation and an acceptance of a priori criterion of how spatial arrangements ought to look. The inherent terminological, conceptual, and ideological conflicts were not absent from the preparation and writing of the Federal Spatial Planning Law of 1965. The SARO Report submitted by a group of government-appointed experts in 1961 and generally considered the initial basis for the law reflects this division by identifying three meanings of the concept *Raumordnung*, namely, (1) spatial organization as an expression of factual aggregate spatial distributions; (2) spatial order, representing normative principles for a desired spatial pattern which corresponds to the economic, social, and cultural requirements of the population; and (3) spatial planning policy which reflects the task of the state to work toward reaching a more desirable spatial pattern.

Since this basic problem of definition was not solved before the formulation of the law, it is not surprising that the legislation was unable to provide workable planning concepts. A remarkably large number of fuzzy terms, without operational or even conceptual meaning, found their way into this law, leading to a scientifically awkward situation where vague formulations (such as "healthy living conditions," "convalescense of unbalanced structures," "spatial condensation," etc.) had to be justified and substantiated ex post facto; they not only had to be made operational, but often forced first into some theoretical jacket.

More recently, the need to implement such general concepts, and to reduce the range of different and uncoordinated interpretations by the states, has required the adoption of less pretentious and vague planning objectives. The simplicity, and simplistic implementation, of such "blanket" interpretations has, on the other hand, often created further disappointment: for example, the mandate of equalizing healthy living conditions in all parts of the country has been largely interpreted in terms of an equal distribution of social infrastructure facilities to be implemented through an hierarchical central place scheme.

The lack of operational planning objectives and guidelines has become particularly visible in the discussion about the desirability of further increases in the foreign labor force, which so far have occurred with very little government directive and few if any regional guidelines other than those suggested by the private sector. On the one hand, national economic projections are continuing to indicate labor deficits for the 1970s; on the other, there are indications that the emerging spatial pattern of foreign employment conflicts with spatial planning objectives. Generally, it seems that the relative ease of access to foreign workers by employers in urban areas has significantly slowed down the process of industrial decentralization and made it more difficult for planning agencies to influence this process qualitatively. In addition, the tendency of the foreign population to replace outmigrants from the central city and form national ghettos causes some concern. Chastising the unwillingness of the larger cities to use local taxes for appropriate social infrastructure facilities, the federal labor agency has repeatedly warned that further increases in foreign employment would likely lead to "misdevelopment" and social problems in urban areas. The agency suggests slowing down the rate of increase, and urges that a general decision be made on whether foreigners ought to continue to be considered "rotating guest workers" rather than citizens to be fully integrated socially (BAA, 1972, p. 16).

It seems that until very recently, the official German policy of encouraging and assisting foreign inmigration was almost an automatic response to economic demands. Government, employers, and German employees alike benefited from a continuing increase in the foreign labor force in that it (1) guaranteed the continued expansion of GNP; (2) contributed to anti-inflationary tendencies due to the high propensity for either saving or transferring earnings to families left behind; (3) permitted accelerated upward occupational mobility for German employees; (4) provided employment flexibility during recessions through hiring stops and attrition of foreign workers with relatively short-term contracts; and (5) helped to avoid extensive capital exports and establishment of branch plants abroad (which is opposed by the labor unions).

With the rapid increase of the absolute number of foreign workers in 1971-1972, and their increasing propensity to remain and be followed by their families, some of these advantages have diminished significantly while the burden upon local infrastructure facilities has increased dramatically and is now being "felt" by the population and government agencies.

Regional Economic Policy Goals

More limited in scope than the broad spatial planning goals, regional economic policy objectives are also more pragmatic and tangible since they are based on selected economic indicators such as gross domestic product (per county); unemployment and seasonal unemployment rates; percent of industrial labor force (*Industriebesatz*); and commuter and outmigration rates. However, there is as yet no specific legislation of these goals and the policy lacks precise formulation of overall objectives. However, the government does feel it has obligations in the field of regional policies (which, together with sectoral policies, comprise the *Strukturpolitik*) resulting from (1) the mandate of the German Constitution to guarantee equal living conditions; (2) the necessity to create an optimal economic structure in order to ensure that unused and underutilized factors of production are being mobilized for economic growth; (3) the task of facilitating adjustment processes which result from structural problems in already developed regions; and (4) the problems of Germany's division and the related separation of an integrated economic unit (economic assistance for Berlin and the *Zonenrandgebiet*).

These general objectives have led to specific regional policy measures. The authorizations for various assistance programs are based on certain principles which also have been accepted by the states. These principles emphasize (1) assistance for investments in promising, long-term growth industries; (2) assistance for the expansion of economic infrastructure facilities with the objective of improving the prerequisites for creating new industrial jobs; and (3) development of tourism in appropriate regions.

German regional policy started out as an area support scheme. Initially, only a few relatively small promotion centers were selected in addition to the promotion areas. Subsequently, there were indications of a "centralization upward" strategy in that area support slowly lost its significance (Krumme, 1972, pp. 228f.); at the same time the number of development centers mushroomed, their sizes became on the average larger, and certain hierarchical elements were introduced as larger and more strategic centers received additional aid.

However, in spite of its extended scope, this regional structural policy still exists at the periphery of economic policy in general. The so-called "magic polygon" of German economic policy goals is generally identified with full employment, price stability, a balance of external trade and payments, economic growth, and a socially just distribution of income and personal wealth.

Regional elements are introduced as constraints or regional subgoals, or as means to accomplish basically nonregional objectives. Regional economic policies are by and large interpreted as long-term structural policies and are as such associated with economic growth policies. Regionally significant conflicts have arisen, for example, when anticyclical fiscal measures (particularly budget cutbacks or temporary withholdings) were applied uniformly without regard to the significance of regional lags, different regional amplitudes, and the long-run damage of interruptions of particular projects; or when, as during the recession in 1966-1967, severe sectoral problems surfaced in larger industrial cities and agglomerations (Ruhr, Saar, Hamburg, and Kiel), forcing the government to support "orderly structural change" (and further agglomeration) in industrialized regions before the problem of lagging regions could be brought to a satisfactory solution.

A recent controversy has highlighted this conflict. In a confidential memo, the German Central Bank had recommended to the government a reduction of subsidies and tax concessions, including the regionally motivated investment grants; a reduction of the number of development centers; and, particularly, a reduction in regional funding during boom periods. One of the most critical responses to this memo, pointing out that there had been an earlier general agreement on the fact that regional development lags could be successfully attacked only during boom periods, came from the associations of cities and communities (*Welt*, 1973). On an earlier occasion, a German legislator had warned that "the regions with development lags have to pay the bill for the overheating of the agglomeration areas." He further pointed out that anticyclical policies could be regionalized by selective lifting of government spending cutbacks (FAZ, 1971). However, extensive but insufficiently known interdependencies and the fact that more than sixty percent of the federal territory belongs to federally supported regional programs would make such a differentiation possibly quite ineffective.

Sectoral Policy Goals

In Germany, as elsewhere, regional development problems are frequently closely tied to structural or locational problems of specific industries or sectors. Localized and resource-oriented activities supply specific examples. German agricultural policies of the postwar years were heavily influenced by a deeply ingrained conviction of the need for national self-sufficiency in food production. This inherent handicap was reinforced by the food shortages immediately following the end of the war and has been carefully cultivated and defended by conservative politicians and the farmers' associations ever since. Even leading agricultural economists (Weber and Meinhold, 1951) had pointed out that the

> continuing quantitative reduction of the rural population is a process which does not coincide with what ought to occur and which is one

of the gravest obstacles to a full development of the importance of agriculture [*landwirtschaftliche Bedeutungskraft*] . . . . agricultural policy must have as its goal the prevention of a reduction of personnel levels in agriculture which otherwise cannot fulfill its diverse tasks. (P. 101)

Although economists have probably not since espoused such a drastic case against structural change in the agricultural sector, and although German agricultural policies eventually supported structural adjustments, there has always tended to be a "policy lag" and a considerable lack of differentiation between the occupational and the spatial component of the *Landflucht* and the types and sizes of towns and cities which would be desirable or acceptable destinations for these rural refugees. Thus, it is not surprising that rural renewal has been strongly biased in favor of what is called "active" renewal. "Passive" renewal, the propagation of outmigration, had the stigma of a social uprooting contributing to the urban industrial proletariat. The possibility of maintaining a part-time farming structure by dispersing industries into rural areas—that is, industrialization without the loss of conservative rural voters—made structural adjustments acceptable to the Christian Democratic Government.

Such a retention policy was in direct conflict with the European Economic Commission's agricultural policy which, according to the Mansholt Plan, aims at a rigorous consolidation and rationalization of farms. The federal government now tolerates the part-time farming pattern existing in many parts of Germany, but appears to see it as a symptom of an unsatisfactory process of structural change, a temporary necessity for the support of insufficient incomes, and a potential source for the expansion of the "social fallow" and the erosion of the *Landschaft*. The comparatively conservative state of Bavaria has been most active in actually promoting the idea of part-time farming. In its 1970 Act for the Promotion of Bavarian Agriculture, two overriding goals of agricultural policy were specified: (1) to secure the position of agriculture through full- and part-time farms; and (2) to contribute to maintaining rural space as *Kulturland-schaft*. Further, the belief that an improvement of rural living conditions can be achieved by a combination of agricultural and nonagricultural employment was explicitly spelled out in the statement that everybody should have the "opportunity to retain his property and farm." The law also suggests that a basic network of full-time farms; basic agricultural and rural social infrastructure facilities; and cooperative arrangements for the use of agricultural machinery and marketing would have to be supported to achieve the act's two principal goals (Bayern, 1972, p. 119).

SPATIAL AND REGIONAL POLICIES

In many of the specific programs the federal government shares responsibility for policy formulation and execution with the states. While on the federal level these different policy categories have been separated with remarkable rigidity, and have only lately been integrated in the slowly emerging Federal Spatial Planning Program, the states have a longer history of integrated planning programs.

The 1965 Federal Spatial Planning Law indicated the necessity for consultation and coordination of spatial planning problems between the federal and state governments. In 1967 an administrative agreement between these two levels specified the details of this vertical and horizontal cooperation and also established the State and Federal Intergovernmental Cabinet Commission for Spatial Planning (MKRO), as well as several subcommittees. On the level of the federal government itself, coordination takes place within an Intracabinet Committee for Spatial Planning (IMARO). Regional economic policy projects, such as regional action programs which require federal assistance, are coordinated and approved by the Interdepartmental Committee for Regional Economic Policy (IMNOS) of the federal government.

Spatial Planning Policies

The Federal Spatial Planning Law identifies two regional categories (in addition to the eastern border zone) as its principal targets. In the first category are areas where the overall living conditions are significantly below the federal average, or where such a situation is to be anticipated. In order to reduce differentials in living conditions the states were asked to specify for their respective areas of jurisdiction central places within acceptable distances to all inhabitants, and to assist in the development of adequate infrastructure services for such central places. Subsequently, MKRO prescribed a four-level, hierarchical central place scheme and criteria for the selection of central places and their appropriate infrastructure facilities (Krumme, 1972). The second category includes areas in which the concentration of employment and residences has reached a level which could endanger healthy spatial living and working conditions as well as balanced economic and social structures. Additionally, there are regions where healthy living and working conditions already exist; these conditions have to be maintained and whenever possible, improved. In order to fulfill these stipulations, in 1968 MKRO identified twenty-four relatively compact *Verdichtungsräume* with 45.5 percent of the total population on 6.8 percent of the federal territory and an average population density of 1,555 per square kilometer (see Map 4-1).

Development and Agglomeration Axes: The central place and agglomeration policies are increasingly coordinated and integrated into a network system of axes linking major population concentrations, cities, and central places, and passing through, wherever possible, lower-order central places and development centers. Initially, the role of axes was restricted to a coordination and "bundling" of transport-related ribbons of infrastructure between major agglomerations. They now appear to assume a prime role in the general reorientation of settlement and industrial development policies from an indis-

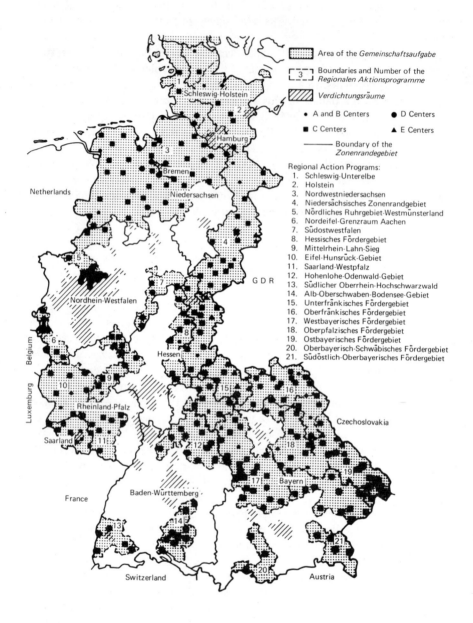

Area of the *Gemeinschaftsaufgabe*

Boundaries and Number of the *Regionalen Aktionsprogramme*

Verdichtungsräume

● A and B Centers ● D Centers

■ C Centers ▲ E Centers

Boundary of the *Zonenrandegebiet*

Regional Action Programs:
1. Schleswig-Unterelbe
2. Holstein
3. Nordwestniedersachsen
4. Niedersächsisches Zonenrandgebiet
5. Nördliches Ruhrgebiet-Westmünsterland
6. Nordeifel-Grenzraum Aachen
7. Südostwestfalen
8. Hessisches Fördergebiet
9. Mittelrhein-Lahn-Sieg
10. Eifel-Hunsrück-Gebiet
11. Saarland-Westpfalz
12. Hohenlohe-Odenwald-Gebiet
13. Südlicher Oberrhein-Hochschwarzwald
14. Alb-Oberschwaben-Bodensee-Gebiet
15. Unterfränkisches Fördergebiet
16. Oberfränkisches Fördergebiet
17. Westbayerisches Fördergebiet
18. Oberpfalzisches Fördergebiet
19. Ostbayerisches Fördergebiet
20. Oberbayerisch-Schwäbisches Fördergebiet
21. Südöstlich-Oberbayerisches Fördergebiet

Map 4-1. Action Program Regions and Development Centers as of January 1972

criminate area and small-center pattern to a decentralized system of increased population density.

Nevertheless, the concept still differs widely in content and terminology among those states which actually have referred to it in their development plans. These differences exist primarily in regard to (1) the mode of transport which dominated the determination of the axes; (2) the determination of different levels of axes; and (3) the objectives associated with these determinations. The federal government has only recently addressed itself to the notion of axes, but has not advanced much beyond a mere recognition of the states' initiative in this area. In a recent government brochure it was pointed out that the development of centers along axes radiating from agglomeration areas is preferable to a concentric expansion of these areas. The urgent need for federal coordination becomes apparent, for example, when one discovers that designated development axes abruptly end at state boundaries, as is the case between Rheinland-Pfalz and Baden-Württemberg. More generally, one receives the impression, supported by frequent references to cartographic presentation rather than to functional significance, that the prime role of the system of axes is to match the aesthetic elegance of the central place pattern in more densely populated nonrural areas.

Regional Economic Policy

In general, "regional economic policy is defined in a more restricted sense than in other countries" (OECD, 1970). It is considered to be only one of several methods available to correct interregional economic imbalances and should always be seen in conjunction with transport investment policies, housing policies, and, particularly, agricultural policies. In addition, authority for regional economic policy lies with the federal government as well as with the states, and it was only recently that the alleviation of regional problems was declared a *Gemeinschaftsaufgabe* (joint task) of state and federal governments. Some key regional policy programs of the federal government will now be discussed in some detail.

The Zonenrandgebiet: This is an approximately forty kilometer wide strip of land along the East German and Czechoslovakian borders and along the Baltic Sea in the north (with nineteen percent of the area and about twelve percent of the population of the FRG). The region has been supported since 1953 by measures such as freight subsidies, special depreciation allowances, and preferential treatment in the allocation of government contracts and infrastructure investments, all designed to reduce the economic impact of the political boundary and to maintain economic viability. The program has at times been attacked due to its highly political overtones and its lack of differentiation. In fact, the middle portion of the border strip has a comparatively central location within West Germany as a whole and Göttingen, Kassel, Wolfsburg, and Fulda are highly developed, relatively wealthy and industrialized cities. While, initially, additional funds were available through other regional programs only for the less developed parts of the *Zonenrandgebiet*, more recently the whole area has been included in various action regions, and all major towns and cities, including the ones mentioned above, are, as designated development centers, eligible for multiple support.

Federal Expansion Areas: The support of depressed areas began in 1951 as an emergency measure. The subsequent changes in terminology from "emergency areas" to "rehabilitation areas" to, in 1965, "expansion areas" reflect in part some of the changes in regional policy objectives during the 1950s and 1960s. The major features of this area support program were low interest loans or investment subsidies for the new establishment; conversion, rationalization, modernization, and expansion of production plants; and loans for tourist facilities. In three states, more than fifty percent of the total area qualified for this type of regional assistance program: Schleswig-Holstein (ninety percent), Niedersachsen (sixty-one percent), and Bavaria (fifty-one percent). With the change in emphasis from area to spatially more concentrated regional development assistance, this program slowly lost its significance and was merged into the regional action program after 1968.

Federal Expansion Centers: Deliberate spatial bundling of federal support in selected centers was first introduced in 1959 with the "development program for central places in rural, structurally weak areas." The number of these centers (their name was changed to "federal expansion places" in 1965) increased from an initial sixteen to eighty-one in 1970. Their size varied between 5,000 and 35,000, the larger ones being generally among the more recently selected. Their purpose was to complement the area support schemes and to initiate decentralized concentrations of nonagricultural job opportunities for rural areas with underemployment. Assistance was provided in the form of loans to newly locating firms and financial aid for developing industrial sites and infrastructure facilities. Initially, the size of subsidized industrial loans was dependent on the number of jobs created. After 1963, the amount of capital invested became the prime criterion. Most of the expansion centers were situated within the boundaries of the new "action program regions" and have since been incorporated into this program as "development centers."

Regional Action Programs: The regional action programs were initiated in 1968 after a new, Social Democratic secretary for economic affairs had taken office. It was part of a drive to intensify and coordinate regional and structural policies, particularly for lagging regions, and was basically an outgrowth of the rather unfavorable experience of the unexpectedly severe regional manifestations of the 1966-1967 nationwide economic recession. Initially, twelve regional action programs were accepted by IMNOS on the basis of development plans prepared by the states. By 1972, the then twenty-one action regions covered about sixty percent of the territory of the FRG with about thirty-two percent of the total population.

The main feature of this program is coordinated, regionalized, and spatially concentrated assistance to the former federal expansion areas. The focus for this concentration are industrial development centers (*gewerbliche Schwerpunkte*), 312 of which had been selected by 1972. In 1970 the average population of a development center and its commuting hinterland was 62,400 for the country as a whole. The Holstein action region in the north led with an average of 187,500 and Ostbayern (eastern Bavaria), where the individual minimum of 20,000 was often not fulfilled, was last with 29,400 (Albert, 1970, p. 249).

The regional action programs are jointly planned and financed by federal and state governments and projected for a period of five years. The vertical intergovernmental cooperation required a special prior constitutional amendment. In 1969, a new article was added to the Basic Law which reads in part: "The Federation contributes . . . to the fulfillment of the states' tasks, if these tasks are of overall significance and if the cooperation of the Federation is necessary for the improvement of living conditions." Subsequently, the specifics of cooperation have been codified by the Act for the Joint Task (*Gemeinschafts-aufgabe*) of Improvement of the Regional Economic Structure. This law, in turn, committed federal and state governments to come up with an overall regional policy plan which would set guidelines and allow for yearly revisions. The first version of this plan has been in force since January 1972.

The overriding objective of the "joint task" is the creation of new industrial jobs in development centers within designated action regions. Between 1972 and 1975, 464,000 new jobs are to be created and another 250,000 existing jobs "protected" (BfW, 1972, pp. 4-7). Before 1968, the yearly goal had been only 10,000 new jobs. With the introduction of the action programs the goal was doubled; however, even in the first year the government claimed that its financial support had in fact "created" 44,000. For the period 1969 to mid-1972, 363,000 new jobs were credited to government actions which supported a total of 12,700 private investment projects with a total volume of DM twenty-three billion. Thus, the rather ambitious goal of the first joint task plan (1972-1975) was based largely on this seemingly successful experience.

Among the government's arguments advocating its new joint federal-state regional assistance program were the advantages to be derived from improved clarity and coordination of the diverse regional support schemes, from their ex post facto evaluation, and from the expected stimulation of regional initiatives and competition among "action regions" fostered by the revolving nature of the five-year projections and planning allocations. On the other hand, strong criticism was voiced by the academic community which generally argued that the large size of the total area covered by the program (fifty-eight percent of the federal territory with about thirty-three percent of the population) and the large number (312) of often questionable development centers would dilute the total effect of the limited funds available; that the criteria for delimitation were too simplistic; and that the heterogenous nature of the different action programs would require rather vague supraregional guidelines and would not permit the desired intergovernmental coordination (see, for example, Jürgensen and Thormählen, 1972). Clearly, in view of the need for a policy of "fine tuning" rather than large-scale problem solving, the highly undifferentiated use of "jobs" as a policy objective was the single most disappointing aspect.

It is interesting to note that there are plans to check the success and reconfirm the status of development centers at regular intervals. More specifically, centers which after three years (with possible extension of another two years) have not reached their development objectives will lose their designation.

Federal funds for the regional programs (DM 266 million in 1972) are matched by the states and distributed to them on the basis of (rather controversial) quotas which are determined by the size of the population living in the designated regions. Only in the area along the Iron Curtain is the distribution of funds partially determined by the length of the boundary and coastline shared by the four relevant states.

Subsidies provided for industrial investments in development centers within the regions of the action programs consist of corporate income tax deductions, direct investment grants, and loans with favorable interest rates. The total value of this support cannot exceed a specific percentage (ten, fifteen, twenty, or twenty-five percent) of the actual investment outlays for any project. The percentage which applies to any specific center depends on whether or not the center is located within the Iron Curtain zone (where it is higher) and whether it is declared a higher-level center (see Map 4-1). Investment assistance is provided not only for establishing entirely new plants, but also to existing plants if they expand their employment by at least twenty percent. In addition, the joint task program includes the funding of local economic infrastructure projects (see Table 4-6).

Other Regional and Sectoral Programs: Among other federal regional policy measures, the regional programs of the Department of Agriculture deserve special mention. Here, the support of "naturally disadvantaged areas" is aimed primarily at the development of agricultural infrastructure such as drainage, flood, and tide control facilities. These measures had been codified in the early 1950s with regional development plans for four specific regions— namely, the *Küstenplan* (North Sea coastal areas); Programm Nord (northwest Schleswig-Holstein); Emslandprogramm, and Alpenplan (total investments through 1971: DM 3.9 billion; federal share: DM 1.9 billion).

The coal mining industry, heavily localized in the Ruhr and Saar districts, supplies a relevant example of a downward transitional industry in that it represents an old and established activity whose particular demand and

Table 4-6. Federal Support of Action Programs as Part
of the Joint Task Improvement of Regional Economic Structures

Allocation	1969-1972 (June)*	1972-1975 (projected)*
Private industry		
Total investment volume supported by tax deductions**	DM 22.9 billion	DM 11.8 billion
Additional regional subsidy grants***	DM 373 million	DM 718 million (fifty percent by states)
ERP-Marshall Plan funds (credit loans)****	DM 643 million	–
New jobs created or planned	363,433	464,300
Local economic infrastructure projects		
Total investment volume	DM 997.4 million	DM 2,245.2 million
Regional subsidy grants***	DM 320.8 million	DM 1,259.8 million (fifty percent by states)
ERP-Marshall Plan funds (credits)	DM 249.7 million	–

*The periods are overlapping for part of 1972.
**Such tax deductions (corporate income tax) are (on the average) subsidized by the federal government (forty-seven percent), the states (forty-seven percent), and local communities (six percent).
***Until 1972,*Regionales Förderungsprogramm*; thereafter, *Gemeinschaftsaufgabe*.
****Not separately listed after 1972.
Source: BfW (1972), pp. 4-7.

productivity combination "suggests as optimal a less intensive development than in the past." Instead of accelerating the reduction of old structures and improving the mobility of miners, the mining industry was for an extended period of time encouraged by the government to assume that federal assistance was a more or less permanent protection. During these years, capital and management proved to be considerably less mobile than labor which, at least during the years of full employment, has been easily re-employable. Finally, the government had to resort to financial incentives to close down most of the inefficient mines, a measure which, not surprisingly, did not eliminate the problem of surplus production (subsidies in 1968: DM 946 million; 1971: DM 339 million).

The shipbuilding industry is concentrated in a few cities along the northern coast in regions where other economic activities are suffering from peripheral location and sensitivity to fluctuating port functions. Shipbuilding itself is subject to significant employment fluctuations due to the nature of changes in shipbuilding technology, the investment characteristics of its output, strong international competition, and its dependence on political and financial support by the federal government. On the other hand, the industry is generally not affected by regional or even national business cycles. The recurring threat of massive layoffs of workers which could not be readily absorbed by other local firms, and the argument that all other countries subsidize their shipbuilding sector are skillfully used by the shipbuilding industry to obtain and maintain preferential tax treatment, investment subsidies, and low-cost loans from ERP funds (1970-1972: DM 173 million).

The federal government also supports, directly or indirectly, certain upward transitional industries with high capital needs or "overall significance for economic development" such as data processing, and the aerospace and atomic energy industries. Since these industries tend to be highly localized, generally in already congested, industrialized, structurally healthy urban areas (such as Munich and Stuttgart), such efforts have an inherent potential for policy conflicts. Finally, it has been estimated that the total yearly "spatially effective" federal expenditures amounted to about DM 20 billion in 1970.

EVALUATION OF PRESENT REGIONAL POLICY

Andrew Shonfield (1965) may have slightly exaggerated when he wrote about the German political scene:

> Subsidies, cheap loans provided by the state, and above all, discriminating tax allowances which support favored activities, are used with an abandon that could only be acceptable in a society where the average citizen expects the state to choose its favorites and to intervene on their behalf. . . . What emerges clearly from the comparison [with other countries] is the enormously greater German propensity to use public finance to discriminate in industry and trade. (P. 296)

However, the recent expansion of structural policies from primarily sectoral approaches to a proliferation of regional programs has underlined a basic concern, namely that of regional and fiscal policy efficiency. Growing as well as stagnating sectors are federally supported; about sixty percent of the federal territory and industrial activities in 312 development centers, and many additional state development centers and central places in rural areas, receive fiscal aid; and urban agglomerations are assisted in solving their structural and congestion problems. Thus, one is indeed inclined to wonder whether our theoretical insights about underlying regional economic and spatial processes, and our conceptual planning tools and implementing instruments, are well enough developed to justify the tangible and intangible, direct and indirect costs of these fiscal and redistributive mechanisms. A discussion of German interregional revenue sharing institutions might be in order, but it would explain only part of what appears on the surface to be a massive "cross hauling" of funds.

At the same time, far-reaching spatial settlement patterns are being designed on the basis of goals and assumptions which—in light of stagnating natural population levels—appear to be in conflict. Retaining the population in rural areas by means of central place schemes, while attempting to increase population densities along development axes in higher order central places and, at the same time, revitalize core areas of agglomerations, would require more people than will be available unless foreign inmigration continues at its present level. Increasingly, preferences for second residences in rural areas, extended weekend travel, and tourism will no doubt represent a solution to the problem of rural densities for some regions, but by their very nature, such preferences will also always discriminate between regions. Industrialization of rural areas has in the past had some statistical success but is impaired by cyclical instability. Cyclically stable rural industrialization seems to require larger industrial centers than are available or can realistically be projected in many parts of the lagging regions. The continuing economic expansion, with its accompanying over-employment tendencies, and the increasing centrality of the three major industrial agglomerations (Rhein-Ruhr; Rhein-Main; and Neckar) in a German and, more importantly, an expanding European setting, magnify the economic pressure for increasing employment and population densities in these areas via foreign inmigration. This no doubt will be a prime political problem in the very near future, and it will have to be resolved under conditions of rapidly increasing environmental constraints and public awareness.

Population Distribution Policies

It has become evident that the focal schemes of German regional and spatial policies, namely the central place and development center policies designed to bring about a socially desirable settlement pattern and an economically feasible pattern of moderately decentralized industrialization, are very much part of the modern welfare orientation of government policies in Western Europe. In Germany, the conservative interest in retaining the rural population has been replaced by the more social-oriented objectives of the Social Democratic government; the terms "maintaining," "securing," and "providing," which are so frequently used in the previously enacted spatial planning law have, however, only marginally different pragmatic meanings.

Thus, central places and development centers are supposed to be within normal commuting distances. Long-distance, long-period commuting patterns, as they are found in many of the lagging areas, have been considered signs of the strong desire of the rural population to maintain their rural residences. Migration has generally not been encouraged; in fact, one of the explicit objectives of the development center policy is the prevention of a "passive rehabilitation" (BfW, 1969, p. 21).

Within the framework of their central place policies, many states have assigned roles and sizes into which designated central places are supposed to grow. But in order to reach such planned sizes, which supposedly guarantee an efficient provision of social infrastructure facilities, inmigrants have to be attracted. Such an attraction process could either be based on the assumption that once the infrastructure is available migration will occur, or it could assume that migrants accept promises and are prepared to make the first move, thereby reducing the risk of overinvestment. Motivation research has been inconclusive as far as the effectiveness of infrastructure is concerned. Wieting and Hübschle (1968), in evaluating a survey of almost 5,000 representative migrants, attributed remarkably little significance to the available local infrastructure of communities as a migration motive. Instead, personal factors, and job opportunities or other professional reasons, as well as housing availability, each accounted for about a third of the primary migration factors. On the other hand, Zimmermann's (1972) research on mobility preferences identifies "residential satisfaction" as a prime factor; in turn, residential satisfaction correlated positively with locally available infrastructure facilities and negatively with infrastructure locally not available but highly regarded.

The differences could in part be explained by the different intent and focus of the studies. The first study was sponsored by the Department of the Interior, which is responsible for spatial planning and the federal coordination of the infrastructure-based central place program. Zimmermann's project was explicitly concerned with the basis for economic policy and led to a critique of the overemphasis on investment- and job-related regional measures and the lack of people-related, social infrastructure facilities. Interestingly, both studies agreed in their policy suggestions on the desirability and effectiveness of housing subsidies as a means to regulate migration streams and avoid misinvestments.

In spite of this inconclusiveness, German research results tend to verify that with increasing standards of living, professional status, and previous urban experience, proximity to an urban agglomeration becomes increasingly desirable for an individual and life in inaccessible villages and small towns less acceptable. More specifically, a recent study (Monheim, 1972) surveyed 1,070 entrepreneurs of small and medium-size firms (agencies and the like) from 244 different localities concerning their preferences for location of their residences and offices. Only nineteen percent of these entrepreneurs preferred nonmetropolitan areas (less than 500,000 population) for residential location (seventeen percent for location of firm, thirty-seven percent for retirement). Munich, Berlin, Hamburg, and Düsseldorf scored highest in entrepreneurial sympathies for all functions, while the Ruhr District, Frankfurt, and Cologne were rejected as undesirable residential locations although they did score as possible professional locations. The hypothesis that entrepreneurs and managers tend to impose their own metropolitan preferences on other groups of the population and thus contribute to urban agglomeration problems seems to be valid for Germany.

However, there is also some evidence for a not insignificant latent preference for large city proximity among the population in isolated, rural, low-income areas (see Table 4-7).

In this context, it has been suggested that better and more differentiated use be made of individuals' perceptions of and preferences for "proximity" to metropolitan areas. "Proximity" could possibly be "stretched" sufficiently to incorporate more distant areas and "ersatz centers" if such centers were to be appropriately tied to the metropolitan city (Zimmermann, 1972, pp. 395f.). This proposition is based on the frequently discussed phenomenon that small cities close to metropolitan centers are attracting more migrants and activities than their size class would suggest, mainly by participating in agglomeration economies without sharing many of the diseconomies and by providing intervening opportunities (Böventer, 1971). Only a few cities can realistically be expected to develop such "radiation potential" on a large scale, particularly Munich for eastern Bavaria, and Hamburg for Schleswig-Holstein and parts of Niedersachsen.

Table 4-7. Preferred Residential Location in Case of a Move (by Head of Household)

(Responses of residents and former residents of selected rural areas with below federal average economic indicators)

Preferred residential location	*Percent of those who have moved away (614 responses)*	*Percent of present residents (1614 responses)*
By distance to present residence		
Close proximity to present residence	25	20
In communities between 25 and 75 km.	9	9
More than 75 km.	6	5
Distance does not play role	56	51
Undetermined	4	14
By size of community		
Large cities	6	8
Peripheral communities close to large cities	30	21
Small and medium-size towns and cities with more than 10,000	33	28
Rural communities	14	11
Undetermined	17	32

Source: W. Stöckmann (1971), p. 65 and Appendix.

Regional Industrial Policies

Due to the economic and regional conditions in Germany, regional policy goals, as expressed abstractly by government officials and publications, call for more than merely alleviating unemployment or even increasing per capita incomes. The often expressed intent is to devise a set of regional policies and planning schemes that are differentiated but can be coordinated enough to be tuned to specific regional imbalances, without losing sight of overall goals and interregional effects. Policy intentions have thus increasingly shifted from attacking symptoms to correcting the structural origins of regional inequities— i.e., to guard against flaws in regional policies. Not surprisingly, however, more pragmatic identification of specific targets has proven to be rather conventional in terms of total numbers of jobs created, for example. No doubt, this lack of sophistication is due to the general uncertainty about the mechanism and effectiveness of various planning measures, particularly industrial subsidies which, in turn, readily lend themselves to criticism and controversy. A few of the most pertinent issues are related to (1) interindustry linkages; (2) the branch plant problem; and (3) the feasibility of investment subsidies.

Interindustry Linkages and Agglomeration Economies: Despite the sophistication of regional policy formulation on an abstract, general level, there has been almost no reference to industrial linkages and linkage effects à la Leontief and Rasmussen on the one hand, and Perroux on the other. In identifying the positive development factors of agglomeration areas, the spatial planning council merely stressed that the "sum of the infrastructure facilities and the large labor market in the development centers and along the agglomeration axes represent the most favorable conditions for an optimal combination of factors of production" (Beirat, 1972, p. 43). Provision of diversified job opportunities and efficient social and industrial infrastructure facilities requires specific sizes of development centers and specific degrees of population concentration. The general lack of evidence for linkage effects in industrialization may have been one reason for this neglect. In Germany, research of this kind was long hampered by the lack of general and regional interindustry data. The long delay in carrying out input-output research has been connected with the antiplanning attitudes of the former government, which considered such accounts as incompatible with the goals of a free market system (Krengel et al., 1968, p. 127).

It appears that planners and many scientists alike eagerly accepted relatively recent research findings which—at least on the surface—would seem to justify in retrospect the antilinkage bias in German spatial and regional policy discussions. Two studies deserve particular attention. Streit (1966) related input-output linkage intensity to the degree of spatial association of German industries and obtained generally rather low correlation coefficients. Although he identified a few partial industrial complexes dominated by the metal producing and processing industries, he nevertheless concluded that "in general, interindustry flows did not prove to be a central element in the statistical interpretation of the observed spatial distribution of industries in the FRG" (p. 56).

Brösse's (1971a) investigation was based on a questionnaire survey of firms in a variety of industrial branches (excluding the iron producing sector) in a selected number of chamber of commerce districts primarily in peripheral areas of the Ruhr agglomeration. Supply linkages were differentiated by raw materials, auxiliary materials, parts, and investment goods and spatially classified into (1) a thirty kilometer radius; (2) a 100 kilometer radius; (3) remainder of FRG; and (4) foreign (see Table 4-8). Brösse's conclusion is that "presently, and presumably also in the future, agglomeration economies resulting from spatial proximity between industrial suppliers and their customers have practically no relevance for their location selection. . . . an industrial policy which relies on such agglomeration economies of proximity is bound to fail" (Brösse, 1971b, p. 180).

These findings are in many ways questionable, and quite contradictory interpretations seem possible. In addition, specific limitations should be cited. Streit's results do not clarify the influence of historical inertia or that of other agglomerative factors such as the availability of a complementary labor pool. Brösse's research has been limited to specific types of ties, industries, and regions. One could also question the basis for defining proximate relationships in terms of a rather small thirty kilometer radius. Finally, it is by no means clear whether the relatively small number of proximate relationships found by Brösse (and others) may not deserve more than proportional weight due to their specific spatial sensitivity and their relative significance for the initial production and location decision.

Nevertheless, Brösse's findings have been readily picked up by planners and government officials. A high government official in the federal Department of Economic Affairs emphasized the scepticism with which regional policy makers view the notion of a "take off" based on agglomeration economies resulting from spatial proximity of industrial linkages. In reviewing Brösse's findings and claiming his department's development center policy a success, he concludes that "development centers develop special attractiveness for reasons not yet fully recognized. One of the reasons surely is the subsidy to the investor; another is the improvement of the industrial infrastructure" (Noé, 1971, p. 26f.).

If, in general, industries cannot be relied upon to attract additional industrial investments then the net benefits of public investment subsidies have to be generated more or less directly by the supported industry, and particularly by its own employment impact. The preference of German regional policy to support firms which do not depend on local linkages has been explicitly stated and is obviously related to the simultaneous preference for relatively small center sizes. That this bias will tend to favor large, multiplant corporations with well-established linkage systems has hardly been acknowledged in this context.

Table 4-8. Supply Linkages in Nordrhein-Westfalen*

Type of delivery	Number of surveyed plants receiving most of their deliveries from			
	Within 30 kilometer radius	*Within remaining 100 kilometer radius*	*Remainder of FRG*	*Abroad*
Raw materials	23	78	45	19
Auxiliary materials	52	39	20	–
Parts and components	21	45	50	7
Investment goods	7	21	80	5
Total	103	183	195	31

*Included were the chamber of commerce districts of Aachen, Arnsberg, Dortmund, Remscheid, Solingen, and Wuppertal
Source: Brösse (1971a), p. 26.

The Branch Plant Problem: To overcome the limitations of small center locations in lagging regions with relatively low population and market potentials, a relatively homogenous low-skill labor force, and a basic lack of external economies, newly induced firms are likely to be specialized in their local employment requirements. It will typically be the branch plant efficiently tied to a multiplant corporate system which is attracted to small and isolated development centers. This situation may have certain long-run development repercussions in addition to the short-term elimination of local under-employment.

Indeed, even in the highly industrialized state of Baden-Württemberg, considerable intraregional differences in wages and salaries have remained practically unchanged over the past fifteen years in spite of substantial statistical equalization of the rate of industrialization between different parts of the state. There were strong indications that the organizational structure of this industrialization process and the differentiated distribution of growth industries were largely responsible for sustained regional income disparities. A variety of German studies have suggested that there is a "spatial quality decay" (in relation to large urban centers) in the type of employee sought by industrial firms. The functional diversity of industrial establishments clearly diminishes with increasing distance from the core of the urban agglomeration. New firms tend to locate close to the core (or close to the owner's residence); relocating firms remain at the periphery of the agglomeration; and functionally balanced (i.e., occupationally diversified) branch plants stay within easy reach of the city. More isolated locations are sought mainly by the branch plants of larger corporations or by firms (of all sizes) of specific labor-intensive industries. While the former tend to depend on additionally available labor for expansion purposes, the latter tend to depend on low labor cost as a matter of survival. In a way, such industrialization successes in rural areas have been achieved by the often subsidized spread of relatively unfavorable organizational or industrial structures rather than by an improvement of local and regional location qualities.

Understandably, regional planning authorities have always been less than enthusiastic about such patterns of industrialization, although it has been realized that without more massive intervention this was the only possible outcome. The federal government has maintained that resettlement of plant establishments of "low-order production stages" during boom periods possibly reduces unemployment but tends to perpetuate the already existing "qualitative erosion" (BfW, 1969, p. 21).

The literature agrees in general with the government on this point in spite of the occasionally expressed opinion that purely production-oriented plants find a very appropriate location in rural areas and that branch plants do not tend to leave during recessions (Koch, 1968). Gerlach and Liepmann (1972) recently disproved this latter notion in a study of the business cycle behavior of the clothing and electronics industries in parts of eastern Bavaria, one of the most genuinely "lagging" regions highly sensitive to business cycle fluctuations. Employment time series revealed considerably wider fluctuations than for the remainder of Bavaria or the FRG both during boom periods and recessions. Focusing more specifically on the 1966-1967 recession, the authors traced most of the cyclical peculiarities in the region to the high proportion of branch plants (in these industries) with extraregional parent plants. While for the electronics industry the fluctuations were more pronounced for dependent branch plants at the high and low of the cycle, for the clothing industry only the downturn was significantly stronger for branch plants. These findings would suggest that, in the German case, part of the industrialization of rural areas may not have been a structural "filtering" process where labor-intensive industries are filtered into low wage peripheries in order to survive, but merely temporary (although in the German case rather extended) and costly capacity expansions *at the margin* conditioned by urban labor shortages and the existence of pockets of under-employment in the rural periphery. In addition, firms affected by Germany's overemployment conditions have learned to cherish monopolistic flexibilities in isolated small community labor markets where, contrary to their situation in larger cities, they are better able to lay off workers temporarily without losing them permanently.

Investment Subsidies: There has been little discussion of the effects of singling out one factor of production for preferential treatment (capital) with the expressed purpose of improving the general situation of another factor (labor). It seems plausible that the reduction in capital costs to the entrepreneur leads to (1) the selection of unduly capital-intensive investment goods for these areas, and (2) the selective location of those capital-intensive functions of large corporations which can operate independently of administrative and engineering personnel headquartered in the industrial agglomerations. The pull of unskilled labor and the difficulty of relocating salaried personnel would favor such a strategy. It has therefore been suggested that instead of investment subsidies the state should more directly support the creation of high paying jobs, for example by supporting the total paid-out wage volume (Kunz and Spöri, 1971). The empirical evidence for the effectiveness of any of these actual or suggested measures is sparse. The effectiveness of investment grants as a regional policy measure has been recently questioned by Blake (1972), admittedly on the basis of limited data collected in an environment where unemployment is more of a problem than in Germany. For the German scene, various studies have implied that the industrialization of rural areas does not automatically contribute to the regional equalization of income and prosperity due to the low skill and educational requirements for newly created jobs in branch plants of agglomeration-centered corporations, or in firms of stagnating industries which were forced out of the industrial districts. Stöckmann (1971), in his study of mobility in rural areas, maintains that too many marginal firms have made use of investment subsidies, leading to more than proportional closures of plants during recessions and structural crises. He claims that this pattern in turn leads to insecurity among the rural population, diminished job mobility, and a persistence of low productivity activities (p. 101). Unfortunately, no evidence exists that specific measures (such as wage subsidies) would cause expanding corporations (or their high wage and salary personnel) to relocate more balanced "bundles" of functions into rural areas. On the contrary, studies indicate the steadily increasing strength of preferences for large cities.

OUTLOOK

Among the pertinent policy developments currently underway is the redrawing of political boundaries for the consolidation of communities, counties, and states. This territorial reorganization has become necessary for reasons of administrative efficiency and interregional equity in the face of the progressing, relatively decentralized implementation of federal and state planning laws, guidelines, and joint tasks. Suggestions submitted by a "council of experts" early in 1973 for the consolidation of states into six or seven new units, and the attempt to reregionalize the Ruhr agglomeration, have received particular publicity and are, of course, highly controversial.

The publication of the long expected *Bundesraumordnungsprogramm* (Federal Spatial Planning Program), supposedly the guiding instrument for coordinating all federal government activities with spatial implications through 1985, is forthcoming and likely to supersede some of the criticisms expressed in this chapter. On the other hand, some basic dilemmas will continue to exist, such as the almost total reliance on planning and policy goals derived from vague and abstract constitutional mandates; the corresponding lack of public participation in goal formulations; the existence of basic, unresolved goal conflicts; the lack or inadequacy of scientifically established optimization principles; and certain constitutional limitations, particularly the restricted enforcing power of the federal government.

Otherwise, it is expected that the expanding federal role in environmental policies will lead to an increased integration of environmental and regional policies. In view of the present turbulence of the political and economic environment, this writer will refrain from any further predictions. Typically, regional problems and policies are again occupying the back seat as unemployment becomes a (admittedly small) national problem. Nevertheless, the new regional data will present some evidence of whether or not the policies of the last few years have indeed reduced the structural sensitivity in many of the problem areas.

Chapter Five

Regional Policy in Italy

THE ORIGIN OF ECONOMIC DUALISM AND
ITS EVOLUTION TO 1951

The problem of regional disequilibrium in Italy is very closely linked to the persistent dualism that has characterized the national economy. This introductory section attempts to explain—particularly to the new generation of economists—how this problem arose and why it has remained a critical issue.

It is now generally agreed that the lack of economic integration of the Italian South, or *Mezzogiorno* (an area that covers about two-fifths of the national territory), with the rest of the country arose from natural conditions inherent in the region, as well as its peripheral location. Indeed, long before the industrial "take off" of northern Italy the climatic, morphological, hydrological, and agronomic conditions prevalent in the Mediterranean "tail" played an important role in determining the region's economic inferiority in comparison with continental Italy (Fortunato, 1911; Luzzatto, 1962). When the seven Italian states (the largest of which was the old kingdom of the Two Sicilies, covering all the southern regions except Sardinia) were unified in 1861 agriculture was still the predominant activity throughout the country. However, the value of agricultural production (excluding forestry) per hectare was 75,000 lire (1961 prices) in Lombardy; 53,000 in Tuscany; and only 26,000 in Sicily and 7,000 in Sardinia (SVIMEZ, 1961). That the inherent disadvantages of the southern regions were aggravated by their peripheral location became evident when—during the last decade of the past century—the rapid industrialization of continental Europe began to spread to the neighboring Piedmont, Liguria, and Lombardy regions of Italy. Nevertheless, these factors were not exclusively responsible for the relative deterioration of economic conditions in the South following the creation of the new Italian state.

137

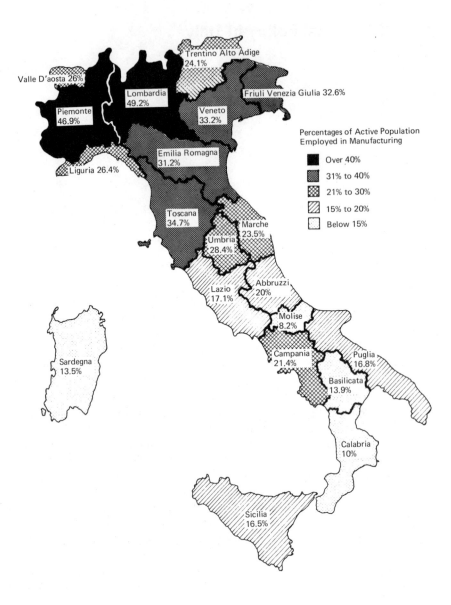

Map 5-1. Italy: Regional Intensity of Industrialisation in 1971

Most of the eminent southerners who first raised the "southern problem" maintained that the political unification implemented under the leadership of the Kingdom of Piedmont itself led to explosive "dualism" (Arfé, 1962). However, modern historians (Luzzatto, 1962) recognize that despite the elimination of interregional trade barriers, the leveling of taxation pressures, widespread social unrest, and severe repression, living conditions in the rural South really became unbearable only after 1887. At that time the moderate protectionism from which northern industry had benefited since 1878 was increased and extended to the agricultural sector in the form of a heavy duty on wheat imports. Disregard of the regional implications of those measures is now regarded as a major cause of the aggravation of economic disparities between the "two Italies" with all the tragic consequences for the people of the South, which became evident after the political unification. Dramatically increased outmigration from rural Italy—from the more slowly growing northern regions as well as from the South—occurred only after 1887, when the abrupt interruption of commercial relations with France, while favoring extensive wheat production, severely curtailed the export of specialized produce from small farms. The personal and social costs of outmigration were much greater for residents of the South. Redundant farm labor in other Italian regions was absorbed by the rapidly growing economies of continental Europe, but the massive exodus from the South found its main outlet overseas. From 1901 to 1913, when Italian outmigration was at its peak, over 3.4 million persons from the South (especially Sicily, Abruzzi, and Basilicata) streamed to the United States and other American countries; of the 4.4 million persons who left the rest of Italy (especially from the Venetian regions), seventy percent went to European countries (SVIMEZ, 1961).

The sacrifice borne by the South as a result of national fiscal and foreign trade policies was soon obvious. Loss of population was not accompanied by needed changes in the structure of agricultural output or in farming techniques, although there was some slight improvement in living standards and some reduction in unemployment in the largely abandoned villages. Meanwhile, the development of the railway system and continued protectionism further favored industrial concentration in the Turin-Milan-Genoa triangle. Thus, throughout the first decade of the century increasing differences between the social and economic conditions in the North and in the South became so apparent that the regional effects of protectionism became the major concern of the Italian Parliament and one of the main causes of its gradual disintegration.

This somewhat oversimplified sketch of the origins of Italian dualism might appear consistent with the conclusion that the first steps of national economic policy were perfectly in line with the fundamental principle that usually guides the growth of an open, dynamic economy—the strenuous defense of the so-called "national interest" over and above the local interests of regional components. However, the history of the political evolution of the Italian state (which for almost a century rejected all attempts to introduce a regional dimension into its highly centralized organization) reveals that the objectives underlying the apparently neutral central government's policies during the first five postunification decades were both more concrete and less "patriotic." In Italy, as in many developing countries, the "southern problem" has its own political background, one constantly dominated by the alliance between northern industrialists and southern landowners. In 1900 Salvemini noted that: "There is no warfare between North and South; there is warfare between the southern masses and the southern reactionaries and between the northern masses and the northern reactionaries. . . ." Moreover, these classes maintained their power intact under every regime. For example, it is perhaps ironic that the duty imposed in 1887 on imported wheat found its full application during the first experiments of a leftist government. The political and cultural dualism underlying that of an economic nature became especially clear during the first two decades of this century. Trade unionism started to take hold in the North, but its introduction was virtually irrelevant in the South due to widespread illiteracy, absentee ownership, and the general subjugation of the peasants.

The unfortunate situation in the South was not greatly changed after the First World War. Although fascism did somewhat control the insolence of Sicilian landowners, it wiped out residual leftism throughout Italy. Public works programs were extended to the South, but northern workers were the principal beneficiaries of the support given to heavy industry as a result of military adventures and Italy's participation in the Second World War. A foolish population growth policy, the world economic crisis of 1929-1934, and restrictions on internal migration gave the excess population of the South no other alternative than that offered by the temporary colonization of some African countries. The war also left northern industrial facilities virtually intact while ravaging the South, where the transportation and communication systems were so destroyed that the area was in effect isolated from the rest of the country for more than two years.

Unfortunately, available historical data are not sufficient to document fully the degree of dualism in the Italian economy through the Second World War. Nevertheless, to the extent that the changes in the distribution of active population, by economic sector, indicate the structural evolution of an economic system, the data in Table 5-1 illustrate the contrast between the regressive evolution of the southern economy and the dynamism of the growth pattern in the rest of the country throughout the first eighty-five years of Italy's history as a nation.

THE TENDENCY TOWARD INCREASING
REGIONAL DISEQUILIBRIUM

The Regional Components
of the Italian State

The emphasis throughout this section is on the persistent economic disparities among the four broad geographical areas into which the Italian territory is conventionally subdivided for purposes of macroeconomic analysis: the Northwest (covering the regions of Piedmont, Val d'Aosta, Liguria, and Lombardy); the Northeast (covering the regions of Veneto, Trentino-Alto Adige, Friuli-Venezia Giulia, and Emilia-Romagna); Central Italy (covering the regions of Marche, Tuscany, Umbria, and Lazio); and the South (covering the regions of Campania, Abruzzi, Molise, Puglia, Calabria, Basilicata, Sicily, and Sardinia). However, since more or less marked disequilibria are present even within these four areas, the analysis will be, as much as possible, developed also at the regional level.

Before bringing out the differences in the growth processes in the various regions, it should be made clear that the "regional" spaces considered here are *not* empirically determined subdivisions of the national territory,* but are rather the present geopolitical components of the Italian Republic, which, according to its constitution (1948), is subdivided into regions, provinces, and communes (article 114). It may also be noted that it took twenty-four years to implement fully the decentralization of public powers envisaged by the constitution (articles 115 to 133).

Before 1972, only five peripheral regions (Sicily, Sardinia, Val d'Aosta, Trentino-Alto Adige, and Friuli-Venezia Giulia) were constitutionally endowed with some more or less extended powers of self-government, delimited by respective "special" statutes. In 1972, the other fifteen regions were given functions previously exercised by the state and the other local administrations in the eighteen sectors that the constitution recognizes to be of "regional interest."

Each region includes several provinces, which in turn contain a large number of communes at varying distances from major urban centers ("provincial capital towns"). Thus, each Italian citizen belongs to the commune where he maintains his legal residence; to the province where this commune is located; and to the region that encompasses that province. There are now ninety-four provinces and 8,056 communes, of which 6,094 have fewer than 5,000 inhabitants and only six have more than 500,000 inhabitants. The local administrations exercise only those functions (mainly related to basic population needs) that are delegated to them by the central government or by the respective regional authorities.

Finally, it is necessary to point out that the autonomy of the three subnational government levels has in practice been severely limited. In particular, their capacity to raise revenues has been almost negligible, especially in the less developed regions. Central government funding of current expenditures has also been inadequate. Thus, the regions (and especially the southern ones) will continue to depend heavily on special allocations of national resources within the context of the goals of national economic plans.

---

*Among the many proposals formulated by geographers, demographers, and economists for restructuring the Italian economy on the basis of various "homogeneity" concepts, it is worth mentioning the one formulated (since 1961) by the European Community experts, in connection with a project aimed at harmonizing regional economic policies within the Common Market area. According to this proposal, the Italian economy could be subdivided in ten broad "programming regions."

Table 5-1. Distribution of Active Population, by Major Classes of Economic Activity, in Northern and Central Regions and in the South, for Census Years, 1871 to 1951

Northern and Central Italy

Years	Agriculture forestry and fishing	Industry	Trans- portation	Commerce	Other activities	Total	(Percent of total population)
\multicolumn{8}{c}{A) Thousand Units (of present population)}
1871	5,719	1,998	149	125	1,503	9,494	–
1881	5,482	2,441	170	190	1,470	9,753	–
1901	6,009	2,614	251	519	913	10,306	–
1911	5,578	3,136	332	606	939	10,591	–
1921	5,955	3,155	488	748	1,111	11,457	–
1931	4,898	3,780	483	905	1,303	11,369	–
1936	5,307	3,903	423	1,024	1,297	11,954	–
1951[a]	4,496	4,638	499	1,157	1,731	12,521	–
\multicolumn{8}{c}{B) Percentage Distributions}
1871	60.2	21.1	1.6	1.3	15.8	100	(57.9)
1881	56.2	25.0	1.8	1.9	15.1	100	(56.5)
1901	58.3	25.4	2.4	5.0	8.9	100	(52.2)
1911	52.7	29.6	3.1	5.7	8.9	100	(49.5)
1921	52.0	27.5	4.3	6.5	9.7	100	(49.9)
1931	43.1	33.2	4.2	8.0	11.5	100	(45.5)
1936	44.4	32.6	3.5	8.6	10.9	100	(46.4)
1951[a]	35.9	37.0	4.0	9.3	13.8	100	(43.7)

[a]Resident active population.

Source: Svimez (1962), pp. 50-51.

Population and Employment Shifts Among Regions

A variety of socioeconomic indicators can be used to represent, or explain, the many facets of regional disequilibrium. A useful starting point is to compare regional growth in population over a relatively long period of time. Between the last two census intervals (1951-1961 and 1961-1971) Italy's population grew by 6.6 million persons; this represented an increase of 13.6 percent—5.8 percent during the first decade and 7.8 percent during the second. Although all regions could not be expected to grow in population at the same rate, the magnitude of the differences is indicative of the importance of the factors causing disequilibrium. The data in the first three columns of Table 5-2 show that between 1951 and 1971 population grew rapidly in the two most

Agriculture forestry and fishing	Industry	Trans-portation	Commerce	Other activities	Total	(Percent of total population)
		Southern Italy				
2,981	1,327	122	75	1,029	5,534	–
3,117	1,956	143	90	1,056	6,362	–
3,657	1,376	173	255	506	5,967	–
3,508	1,268	212	313	478	5,779	–
3,886	1,246	267	300	494	6,193	–
2,970	1,245	267	343	549	5,374	–
3,197	1,257	239	401	513	5,607	–
3,627	1,493	254	433	756	6,563	–
53.9	24.0	2.2	1.3	18.6	100	(54.2)
49.0	30.8	2.2	1.4	16.6	100	(56.8)
61.3	23.0	2.9	4.3	8.5	100	(46.8)
60.7	21.9	3.7	5.4	8.3	100	(43.5)
62.8	20.1	4.3	4.8	8.0	100	(43.7)
55.2	23.2	5.0	6.4	10.2	100	(37.2)
57.0	22.4	4.3	7.1	9.2	100	(38.6)
55.3	22.7	3.9	6.6	11.5	100	(37.1)

highly industrialized regions, Lombardy (thirty percent) and Piedmont and Val d'Aosta (twenty-six percent), while the South as a whole grew by only five percent. The poorer southern regions—Abruzzi and Molise, Basilicata, and Calabria—experienced depopulation of ten percent.

The remaining columns of Table 5-2 present a more precise analysis of absolute and relative population shifts among sixteen regions (or groups of regions). The actual number of persons living in each region at the time of the 1961 and 1971 censuses is compared with the number which would have lived there if each region had grown at the national average rate of 0.6 percent annually during the 1950s and 0.8 percent annually during the 1960s. These calculations show that during both decades the greatest absolute and relative extra growth was experienced in the two most advanced regions of the industrial

Table 5-2.   Population Shifts Among Regions, 1951-1961 and
1961-1971 (000 Units)

	Present population at census dates[1]		
Areas and regions	November 4, 1951	October 15, 1961	October 24, 1971
	1	2	3
Area I (Northwest)	11,733	13,182	14,946
Piedmont and Val d'Aosta	3,641	4,052	4,573
Liguria	1,574	1,758	1,869
Lombardy	6,518	7,372	8,504
Area II (Northeast)	9,291	9,351	10,065
Venetian Regions	5,771	5,723	6,212
Emilia-Romagna	3,520	3,628	3,853
Area III (Central Italy)	8,702	9,386	10,387
Marche	1,349	1,313	1,351
Tuscany	3,185	3,293	3,502
Umbria	804	780	780
Lazio	3,364	4,000	4,754
(Rome)	(1,652)	(2,188)	(2,800)
Area IV (Southern Italy)	17,433	17,985	18,372
Campania	4,311	4,667	4,997
Abruzzi and Molise	1,620	1,460	1,432
Puglia	3,193	3,312	3,493
Basilicata	616	603	565
Calabria	1,983	1,937	1,887
Sicily	4,441	4,633	4,582
Sardinia	1,269	1,373	1,446
Italy	47,159	49,904	53,770

[1] At present boundaries

[2] Calculated on the basis of the increases that would have taken place if the population present in each region in 1951 and 1961 had grown at the national rates of 0.6 percent per year during the period 1951-1961 and of 0.8 percent during the period 1961-1971.

Source: Central Statistical Institute: Population Census of 1951 and 1961 and Preliminary results of 1971 Census.

triangle—Lombardy and Piedmont—and in Lazio, where the extra growth in the city of Rome amounted to 12.5 percent from 1951 to 1961 and 18.7 percent from 1961 to 1971. In the other three regions where there was a moderate upward shift during the 1950s—Liguria, Campania, and Sardinia—there was a downward shift in the following decade. The regions that experienced the most pronounced losses in relative or absolute terms, especially from 1961 to 1971,

Expected population²		Population shifts among regions		Relative gains (or losses)²		Percentage distributions of population shifts	
1961	*1971*	*1951-61*	*1961-71*	*1951-61*	*1961-71*	*1951-61*	*1961-71*
4	*5*	*6=2-4*	*7=3-5*	*8*	*9*	*10*	*11*
12,416	14,204	(+766)	(+742)	(+6.2)	(+5.2)	(+58.0)	(+60.1)
3,853	4,366	+199	+207	+5.2	+4.7	+15.1	+16.5
1,665	1,895	+93	−26	+5.5	−1.4	+7.0	−2.0
6,898	7,943	+474	+561	+6.9	+7.1	+35.9	+44.6
9,832	10,075	(−481)	(−10)	(−4.9)	(−0.1)	(−36.4)	(−0.8)
6,107	6,166	−384	+46	−8.3	+0.7	−29.1	+3.6
3,725	3,909	−97	−56	−2.6	−1.4	−7.3	−4.4
9,208	10,112	(+178)	(+275)	(+1.9)	(+2.7)	(+13.4)	(+21.6)
1,427	1,414	−114	−63	−8.0	−4.5	−8.7	−5.0
3,340	3,548	−56	−46	−1.7	−1.3	−4.3	−3.7
851	840	−71	−60	−8.3	−7.9	−5.4	−4.8
3,581	4,310	+419	+444	+11.7	+10.3	+31.8	+35.1
(1,747)	(2,358)	(+441)	(+442)	(+12.5)	(+18.7)	(+33.3)	(+35.1)
18,448	19,379	−463	(1,007)	(−2.0)	(−5.2)	(−35.1)	(−80.0)
4,562	5,029	+105	−32	+2.3	−0.6	+8.0	−2.5
1,715	1,573	−255	−141	−14.9	−9.0	−9.2	−11.2
3,379	3,569	−67	−76	−2.0	−2.1	−5.1	−6.0
650	650	−9	−85	−7.5	−13.1	−3.7	−6.7
2,098	2,087	−161	−230	−7.3	−11.0	−12.2	−18.3
4,699	4,992	−66	−410	−1.4	−8.2	−5.0	−32.6
1,343	1,479	+30	−33	+2.2	−2.2	+2.2	−2.7
49,904	53,770	±1,320	±1,258	0	0	±100	±100

were either the poorest southern regions—Abruzzi and Molise, Basilicata, and Calabria—or southern and central regions unable to offer new employment opportunities—Sicily, Marche, and Umbria.

Analysis of population shifts indicates that Rome has grown much more rapidly than the other provincial capital towns of the Lazio region. On the other hand, Milan, Genoa, Trieste, Venice, Florence, and Naples grew by less than their respective regional averages. The tendency for population to agglomerate in regional capital towns was especially marked in the South and in Umbria. In many regions important gains were recorded in provincial capital towns; this phenomenon was most evident in the South, since the redundant rural population finds its first, if often temporary, destination in such towns. Only in Lombardy and Liguria did the small communes gain more in population than the respective provincial capital towns; in almost all other northern regions this class of commune grew at much slower rates, and it showed heavy population losses in the South.

Analysis of regional growth in terms of employed labor force indicates that in Italy, as elsewhere, population movements are essentially explained by regional differences in job opportunities. The data presented in Table 5-3 show that total employment in Italy increased by 3.75 percent from 1951 to 1961, but declined by 5.1 percent from 1961 to 1971. Regional deviations from these national rates are quite similar to those relating to population change. Lombardy had the greatest expansion of total employment between 1951 and 1961 (fifteen percent), and even a small increase during the 1961-1971 period (+0.6 percent). Similarly, in these respective periods Piedmont and Val d'Aosta had an 8.5 percent increase and a 4.3 percent decline; and Lazio had an 11.5 percent increase and a 1.3 percent decline. Since 1951 the sharper total employment declines occurred in the poorer southern regions (Abruzzi and Molise; Basilicata; and Calabria) and in the less developed regions of central Italy (Marche and Umbria).

Increasing Differentials in Growth of Gross
Regional Product and Net Per Capita Income

Analysis of regional variations from the general growth pattern of the Italian economy is limited by the few crude statistical indicators available. A geographic breakdown of the Italian social accounts has been available since 1951, but unfortunately only at the level of the four large areas. The contribution of each region to national growth can only be analyzed on the basis of a series of unofficial estimates of net product, by province (Tagliacarne, 1972).

The data presented in Tables 5-4 and 5-5 indicate that between 1951 and 1961 the growth of both gross product at factor cost and net per capita income at market prices was considerably more rapid in the Northwest area than in the rest of the country, the respective annual rates being 6.2 percent and 5.6 percent as compared to the corresponding rates for the South of 4.8 percent and 4.1 percent. However, during the 1960s there was a tendency for area growth rates to converge toward the 4.8 percent annual rate of growth of gross national product, which left practically unchanged the contribution of each area to the growth in volume of the national economy.

The minor role played by the South in the growth of the national economy becomes even more evident when its share in total domestic product is compared with its shares of population and employment: between 1951 and 1971 the South's share of Italy's population fell from thirty-seven percent to thirty-four percent; its total employment share meanwhile dropped from thirty-three percent to thirty-one percent, and gross product at factor cost dropped from twenty-six percent to twenty-four percent. However, the most striking aspect of the data presented in Table 5-4 is less the leading role of the Northwest in the national growth process than the equilibrium maintained by the Northeast and Central areas between their almost identical shares of national population on the one hand, and their total employment and gross product figures on the other (all practically unchanged at the level of about twenty percent from 1951 to 1971).

The persisting relative economic inferiority of the South is also apparent from the data in Table 5-5 which show absolute and relative area differentials in net per capita income. While in the Northeast and Central areas this value has tended to bypass the national average, in the South it has remained well below this level in both absolute and relative terms.

Different Regional Growth Patterns

The agglomeration of manufacturing activities in a limited area of the national territory clearly lies behind differences in regional growth capacity. Despite government efforts, especially during the 1960s, to promote decentralization of manufacturing, fifty-two percent of the gross national product associated with this sector was still concentrated in the Northwest in 1971. A significant expansion of gross manufacturing product occurred only in the Northeast, where the national share rose from sixteen percent in 1951 to about twenty percent in 1971. In Central Italy it declined from sixteen percent to fifteen percent, while in the South it rose slightly from 12.4 percent to 13.2 percent.

Primary activities (agriculture, forestry, fishing) were uniquely important with respect to changes in the regional distribution of gross national product. The share of the Northwest declined from twenty-four percent in 1951 to eight percent in 1971, whereas in the South it increased from thirty-six percent to forty-four percent. In the other major areas it was almost unchanged.

The data in Table 5-6 show that agriculture remains the dominant activity in the South despite its sharp drop in share of gross product. In 1971 this sector accounted for eighteen percent of total southern gross product, compared to only eleven percent in the Northeast, seven percent in Central Italy, and five percent in the Northwest. While the relative importance of activities which primarily serve the local market has not changed much among regions, the government sector has grown rapidly in the central and southern regions; in

Table 5-3. Total Employment Shifts Among Regions, 1951-1961 and 1961-1971 (000 units)

Geographical areas and regions	Total employment (yearly averages)			Expected employment[1]		Employment shifts		Relative gains (+) or losses (−) %		Percentage distribution of gains or losses	
	1951	1961	1971	1961	1971	1951-61	1961-71	1951-61	1961-71	1951-61	1961-71
	1	2	3	4	5	6=2-4	7=3-5	8	9	10	11
Area I (Northwest)	5,343	5,998	5,868	5,543	5,693	+455	+175	+ 8.2	+ 3.1	+78.4	+46.5
Piedmont and Val d'Aosta	1,746	1,894	1,832	1,811	1,798	+ 83	+ 34	+ 4.6	+ 1.9	+14.3	+ 9.0
Liguria	706	781	692	732	741	+ 49	− 49	+ 6.7	− 8.6	+ 8.4	−13.0
Lombardy	2,891	3,323	3,344	3,000	3,154	+323	+190	+10.8	+ 6.0	+55.7	+50.5
Area II (Northeast)	4,048	4,078	3,873	4,200	3,872	−122	+ 1	− 2.9	+ 0	−21.1	+ 0.3
Venetian regions	2,390	2,392	2,266	2,480	2,271	− 88	− 5	− 3.6	−0.4	−15.2	− 1.3
Emilia-Romagna	1,658	1,686	1,607	1,720	1,601	− 34	+ 6	− 2.0	+0.4	− 5.9	+ 1.6
Area III (Central Italy)	3,811	3,986	3,696	3,954	3,783	+ 32	− 87	+ 0.8	− 2.3	+ 5.5	−23.2
Marche	683	660	547	708	626	− 48	− 79	− 6.9	−12.6	− 8.3	−21.0
Tuscany	1,351	1,402	1,307	1,402	1,331	0	− 24	0	− 1.8	0	− 6.4
Umbria	364	349	288	378	331	− 29	− 43	− 7.7	−13.0	− 5.0	−11.5
Lazio	1,413	1,575	1,554	1,466	1,495	+109	+ 59	+ 7.5	+ 3.9	+18.8	+15.7

Area IV (Southern Italy)	6,491	6,369	5,958	6,734	6,047	−365	− 89	− 5.4	− 1.5	−62.8	−23.6
Campania	1,598	1,674	1,602	1,658	1,589	+ 16	+ 13	+ 1.0	+ 0.8	+ 2.8	+ 3.5
Abruzzi and Molise	710	651	516	736	618	− 85	−102	−11.5	−16.5	−14.6	−27.1
Puglia	1,230	1,180	1,172	1,276	1,120	− 96	+ 52	− 7.5	+ 4.6	−16.5	+13.8
Basilicata	265	244	205	275	232	− 31	− 27	−11.3	−11.6	− 5.3	− 7.2
Calabria	771	675	595	800	641	−125	− 46	−15.6	− 7.2	−21.6	−12.2
Sicily	1,466	1,486	1,433	1,521	1,411	− 35	+ 22	− 2.3	+ 1.5	− 6.0	+ 5.9
Sardinia	451	459	435	468	436	− 9	− 1	− 2.0	− 0.2	− 1.6	− 0.3
Italy	19,693	20,431	19,395	20,431	19,395	+580 −580	+376 −376	0	0	±100	±100

[1] Calculated on the basis of the increases that would have taken place if total employment had increased, in each region, at the national average rates during the two periods.

Source: Central Statistical Institute: Proofs of "Occupati presenti in Italia, 1951-1971."

Table 5-4.   Percentage Distributions of Resident Population,
Total Employment, Gross Domestic Product, and Net Income, by
Major Geographical Area, 1951, 1961, 1971

| | | *1951* | | |
Areas	Present popula- tion[1]	Total employ- ment (yearly averages)	Gross product at factor cost	Net income at market prices
Area I (Northwest)	24.9	27.1	34.8	35.3
Area II (Northeast)	19.7	20.5	19.3	19.5
Area III (Central Italy)	18.4	19.4	20.1	19.9
Area IV (Southern Italy)	37.0	33.0	25.8	25.3
Italy	100	100	100	100
Idem, in absolute figures[2]	(47,159)	(19,693)	(14,460)	(14,501)

[1] At census dates: Nov. 4, 1951; Oct. 15, 1961; Oct. 24, 1971.
[2] Population and employment in thousand units; gross product and net income in billions of 1963 lire.
Source: Central Statistical Institute Yearbooks (1972).

1971 it accounted for sixteen percent of regional gross product in these areas, compared to eleven percent in the Northeast, and seven percent in the Northwest. In the area of its greatest concentration, the Northwest, the share of manufacturing in regional gross product dropped slightly from forty-three percent to forty percent between 1951 and 1971. The main beneficiary was the Northeast, where the corresponding share rose from twenty-three percent to twenty-seven percent. In Central Italy there was a decline from twenty-four percent to twenty-one percent; in the South it remained unchanged at the level of fifteen percent.

Changes in the composition of manufacturing gross product between 1951 and 1971 give some insight into the differing growth patterns of the four principal areas (see Table 5-7). Rapid manufacturing decentralization is taking place only in some traditional, relatively simple industries whose products have low demand elasticities in national and international markets. Examples are the textile and leather sectors. Decentralization is, instead, much slower in the most complex and advanced sectors—such as automobiles and other mechanical products—where expansion is largely dependent on exports to the rest of the world. Even though the South's moderate manufacturing growth was also essentially determined by the expansion of some advanced sectors (chemicals, petroleum refining, rubber, paper), the region's contribution to the national product in these sectors rose only from 7.5 percent in 1951 to 9.8 percent in 1971. It is particularly noteworthy that the sectors that registered significant

	1961				1971		
Present popula-tion[1]	*Total employ-ment (yearly averages)*	*Gross product at factor cost*	*Net income at market prices*	*Present popula-tion*[1]	*Total employ-ment (yearly averages)*	*Gross product at factor cost*	*Net income at market prices*
26.4	29.4	36.8	38.3	28.0	30.3	36.8	38.6
18.7	20.0	19.6	19.6	18.7	20.0	20.0	19.9
18.8	19.5	19.6	19.5	19.3	19.0	19.3	19.2
38.1	31.1	24.0	22.6	34.2	30.7	23.9	22.3
100	100	100	100	100	100	100	100
(49,904)	(20,430)	(24,843)	(25,626)	(53,770)	(19,395)	(39,878)	(41,204)

above average increases in the South—metallurgy and petrochemicals—are capital-intensive industries which generate little in the way of personal income and have limited linkages with other regional activities.

Although the sluggishness of structural transformations in the South remains the most visible problem of the Italian economy, the unsatisfactory growth pattern of the center should not be neglected. The center is, of course, heavily affected by the presence of Rome and the consequent "abnormal" expansion of service activities, which tends to keep the region's share of both traditional and advanced manufacturing activities at levels similar to those prevailing in the South.

The Social Consequences of Persisting Dualism

Because of the absence of reliable data by region on per capita personal income and its distribution by income bracket it is not possible to measure the critical interrelations between regional growth in gross product and population welfare. However, data on the average levels and consumption categories of total household consumption are available for the four major geographical areas. The data presented in Table 5-8 indicate that the only success so far achieved by regional policy has been to narrow the differences in household living standards between the northern and central areas, whereas (in spite of massive outmigration) the progress achieved in the South appears quite negligible, even from this point of view.

Area comparisons of deviations from average national per capita consumption levels show that the South is the only area where total outlays remains below (by about twenty-five percent) the corresponding national average. However, there are positive aspects to the South's evolving consumption pattern. There was a sharp decline in the percentages of expenditures on food and clothing (from fifty-two percent to forty-two percent, and from 12.6 percent to 9.8 percent, respectively, between 1951 and 1971), and a rapid increase in the share of total spending on less elementary needs (transportation and communications, health and personal care, household economy). Yet, in 1971 almost all these indicators of material advancement were below the levels attained in 1961 in the other areas, while infant mortality had attained the peak

Table 5-5. Growth of Gross Domestic Product and Net Per Capita Income in the Four Geographical Areas, 1951-1961, and 1971

Flows	Years	Area I (North-west)	Area II (North-east)	Area III (Central Italy)	Area IV (Southern Italy)	Italy
Gross domestic product, at factor cost						
	1951	5,029	2,797	2,905	3,729	14,460
billion lire, in 1963 prices	1961	9,136	4,873	4,870	5,964	24,843
	1971	14,666	7,958	7,716	9,538	39,878
Average growth rates, per year	1951-61	6.2	5.7	5.3	4.8	5.6
(percent)	1961-71	4.8	5.0	4.7	4.8	4.8
Net per capita income, at market prices						
	1951	436	302	334	208	306
000 lire, in 1963 prices	1961	749	530	532	312	507
	1971	1,072	820	772	488	765
Average growth rates, per year	1951-61	5.6	5.8	4.8	4.1	5.2
(percent)	1961-71	3.7	4.5	3.8	4.6	4.2
Absolute differentials, from national average (000 lire, in 1963 prices)	1951	+130	−4	+28	−98	0
	1961	+242	+23	+25	−195	0
	1971	+307	+55	+7	−277	0
Relative differentials, from national average (percent)	1951	1.42	0.98	1.09	0.68	1.0
	1961	1.48	1.04	1.05	0.62	1.0
	1971	1.40	1.07	1.01	0.64	1.0

Source: Central Statistical Institute: "Annuario di contabilità nazionale," vol. II, 1972.

of 3.3 per thousand of new born. Moreover, inadequacy of medical facilities is becoming more and more evident, especially in the largest southern cities.

On the other hand, the improvement of living conditions in depopulated regions is neither the only nor the most flattering indicator of social progress achieved as a result of a given regional development policy. From a social viewpoint, changes in the regional distribution of unemployment and net emigration are at least as important as changes in household consumption in measuring the success, or failure, of a national growth policy.

The unemployment data presented in Table 5-9 may appear in contrast to the reduction of total employment recorded during the past decade: between 1960 and 1970 there was an overall reduction of 221,000 registered job seekers who could not find employment and the unemployment rate fell from 4.1 percent to 3.1 percent. However, a word of caution is in order. The total labor force declined by 1.4 million persons as a result of net emigration of 1.1 million workers and of an increase in the rate of school attendance by juveniles. Unfortunately, no information exists on disguised unemployment, but there are sound reasons to believe that it has been increasing in all regions, including the most advanced ones. Labor demand is, in fact, concentrating on the more efficient and qualified workers, while it is increasingly difficult to find jobs for workers under twenty-five and over forty years of age. Examination of regional differences in unemployment rates reveals another negative aspect hidden by global figures.

The total share of unemployed job seekers accounted for by the South rose from thirty-nine percent in 1960 to forty-eight percent in 1970, and this despite a reduction of 700,000 in the area's labor force. Thus, while the rate of registered unemployment declined substantially in all other regions, it either increased or declined only marginally in the regions of the South. With the exception of Lazio, the unemployment rate for females declined in all northern and central regions; in the South it generally increased. The sharpest changes were recorded in Calabria (from 2.7 percent to 7.8 percent), Sicily (from 5.1 percent to 7.3 percent), and Sardinia (from 4.3 percent to 7.0 percent).

The deterioration of employment opportunities in the South is depicted somewhat more crudely in Table 5-10, which shows gross and net emigration flows, by region, from 1959 to 1969. It is particularly striking that eighty-one percent of the total net emigration from Italy was accounted for by departures from the South. The average annual net loss in population caused by net emigration from the South was 0.42 percent, whereas it was less than 0.10 percent in the rest of Italy. It is also significant that the most pronounced population losses due to net emigration in the South were not only in the most underdeveloped regions (Calabria and Basilicata), but also in Puglia and Campania, where government policy to promote a "take off" to autonomous development was focused.

Table 5-6.   Percentage Distributions of Gross Product, by Major
Classes of Economic Activity, in the Four Geographical Areas,
1951, 1961, 1971 (factor cost values at current prices)

Years	Agriculture, forestry, and fishing	Mining	Construc- tion	Electri- city, gas, and water	Commerce, eating and drinking places	Transport and communica- tions
Area I (Northwest)						
1951	14.4	0.8	3.6	2.3	12.6	5.9
1961	8.5	1.0	6.4	2.7	13.4	6.1
1971	4.8	0.6	6.6	2.4	14.7	6.2
Area II (Northeast)						
1951	28.7	0.5	5.8	2.2	12.4	6.9
1961	20.2	0.7	8.0	2.8	13.5	7.2
1971	11.4	0.5	10.1	2.2	14.1	6.7
Area III (Central Italy)						
1951	19.4	1.0	5.3	1.8	13.6	7.0
1961	12.4	1.1	7.5	2.2	14.4	8.5
1971	7.3	0.8	6.7	2.5	15.5	8.1
Area IV (Southern Italy)						
1951	33.9	1.6	5.9	1.5	11.0	6.2
1961	24.7	1.3	8.4	2.1	11.7	7.7
1971	17.9	1.0	8.8	2.4	12.5	7.1
Italy						
1951	22.9	1.0	4.9	2.0	12.4	6.4
1961	15.4	1.0	7.4	2.5	13.2	7.1
1971	9.8	0.7	7.9	2.4	14.2	6.9

Source: Central Statistical Institute: "Annuario di contabilità nazionale," vol. II, 1972.

GOALS AND INSTRUMENTS OF REGIONAL DEVELOPMENT POLICIES DURING THE FIFTIES AND SIXTIES

The 1947-1957 Period: Tentative Reorganization of the Agricultural Sector and Special Public Works in the Backward Regions

By the end of the Second World War, Italian policy makers were confronted with a critical choice between two alternative strategies for the recovery and development of the national economy. On the one hand was a desire to integrate the national economy into the international economic system

Credit and insurance	Rentals (actual and imputed)	Other market services	Government	Total	Manu- facturing	Percent	Total (billion lire)
3.1	2.9	6.0	5.3	56.9	43.1	100.0	(3,632)
4.2	5.4	5.4	5.4	58.5	41.5	100.0	(7,982)
6.0	4.8	6.7	7.0	59.8	40.2	100.0	(20,290)
2.7	2.8	5.7	8.9	76.6	23.4	100.0	(1,908)
3.8	4.9	5.2	9.4	75.7	24.3	100.0	(4,242)
5.2	4.3	7.1	11.1	72.7	27.3	100.0	(11,217)
3.5	3.9	7.1	13.4	76.0	24.0	100.0	(1,834)
4.3	6.5	7.1	15.4	79.4	20.6	100.0	(4,148)
6.4	6.7	8.7	16.3	79.0	21.0	100.0	(11,147)
2.3	4.1	5.9	12.8	85.2	14.8	100.0	(2,344)
3.3	6.6	6.4	14.6	86.8	13.2	100.0	(5,046)
4.8	6.1	7.8	16.5	84.9	15.1	100.0	(13,681)
2.9	3.4	6.0	9.3	71.2	28.8	100.0	(9,718)
3.9	5.8	6.0	10.3	72.6	27.4	100.0	(21,418)
5.6	5.4	7.5	12.0	72.4	27.6	100.0	(56,337)

as soon as possible via an immediate reactivation of the market mechanism and the liberalization of foreign trade. This approach relied essentially on the ability of individual entrepreneurs and on the expansion of demand for consumer goods. An alternative approach emphasized the seriousness of the internal problems posed by the historical dualism of the Italian economy, and the necessity and possibility of a profound reorganization of the agricultural sector and rapid industrialization of the backward areas. Of course, this strategy could only have been implemented within the general planning framework of either the public or private sectors (La Malfa, 1962).

The first of these alternatives was adopted not only with the full support of the entrepreneurial class and the great majority of Italian economists, but also with the approval of some of the most progressive political leaders, who

Table 5-7. Percentage Distributions, by Geographical Area, of the Gross Product of Traditional and Advanced Manufacturing, 1951, 1961, 1971

| | | | | | | *Traditional manufacturing* | | | |
Years	*Food and tobacco*	*Tex- tiles*	*Clothing and shoes*	*Leather*	*Lumber and furniture*	*Transforma- tion of non- metallic ores*	*Metal products*	*Other*	*Total*
Area I (Northwest)									
1951	30.3	70.0	35.8	63.6	34.9	34.7	66.5	56.9	48.6
1961	33.8	68.8	36.5	57.6	35.1	32.1	70.1	55.9	47.9
1971	33.2	59.3	32.9	41.7	32.4	26.9	60.3	57.1	42.2
Area II (Northeast)									
1951	23.2	15.1	18.3	6.1	22.4	22.9	10.5	11.9	17.8
1961	24.5	15.1	19.6	13.6	25.1	27.0	11.6	12.3	19.4
1971	26.6	18.6	22.5	23.6	29.4	30.5	12.7	14.1	22.5
Area III (Central Italy)									
1951	15.7	11.4	23.0	18.2	20.3	26.4	17.8	24.8	17.9
1961	13.9	12.6	22.8	20.3	19.8	23.4	12.0	25.5	17.7
1971	15.0	16.9	23.4	22.9	19.9	22.7	12.3	21.5	18.6
Area IV (Southern Italy)									
1951	30.8	3.5	22.9	12.1	22.4	16.0	5.2	6.4	15.7
1961	27.8	3.5	21.1	8.5	20.0	17.5	6.3	6.3	15.0
1971	25.2	5.2	21.2	11.8	18.3	19.9	14.7	7.3	16.7
Italy									
1951	100	100	100	100	100	100	100	100	100
1961	100	100	100	100	100	100	100	100	100
1971	100	100	100	100	100	100	100	100	100

Source: Central Statistical Institute: "Annuario di contabilità nazionale," vol. II, 1971.

felt that a disrupted economy, burdened with two million unemployed, galloping inflation, and a heavy balance of payments deficit, was too "immature" and unprepared for adventures into general planning formulation and implementation (Graziani, 1972).

The government decision not to interfere in the free choices of the most powerful social groups, and the fear of hindering the expansion of northern industries and their contribution to the readjustment of the balance of payments, heavily conditioned the first public policies with respect to sectoral and regional disequilibrium. The widespread conviction that the prospects for a rapid rehabilitation of the southern economy were slight, and that the excess population could not easily emigrate overseas, or even within Italy, induced the

| Mechanical products | Means of transpor- tation | Advanced manufacturing | | | | |
		Chemicals and petroleum products	Rubber	Paper	Total	Total
68.1	69.2	60.9	88.5	57.3	66.8	55.9
67.1	70.5	60.2	85.3	59.0	66.3	56.4
60.4	75.9	56.6	73.1	49.0	61.9	52.2
13.2	14.8	12.9	3.3	19.5	13.3	16.0
16.2	13.9	16.0	5.9	18.6	15.5	17.6
20.2	9.1	14.7	9.2	21.9	16.8	19.6
11.8	8.3	15.9	6.6	17.1	12.4	15.7
10.6	7.5	14.1	6.8	14.9	11.0	14.6
11.3	7.5	13.4	11.4	18.5	11.5	15.0
6.9	7.7	10.3	1.6	6.1	7.5	12.4
6.1	8.2	9.7	2.0	7.5	7.2	11.4
8.1	7.5	15.3	6.3	10.6	9.8	13.2
100	100	100	100	100	100	100
100	100	100	100	100	100	100
100	100	100	100	100	100	100

Italian authorities to adopt again for the South the type of relief policy experienced since national unification—i.e., a policy that simply offered to redundant rural populations the opportunity to be underemployed in primary activities and to urban populations more decorous living conditions (Graziani, 1968; see also Saraceno, 1961, for a review of the special policy measures implemented in the South by the new Italian state). The first acts issued in 1950 on behalf of the underdeveloped areas were in fact almost exclusively concerned with a more equitable distribution of agricultural revenues; a better exploitation of natural resources (land reclamation, aqueducts, river basins, irrigation, etc.); and increasing public overhead capital.

Various means were used to attain these objectives. Under the

Table 5-8.   Per Capita Private Consumption Levels and Structure
in the Four Geographical Areas, 1951, 1961, 1971

Areas needs	Years	Category needs — Food and beverages	Tobacco	Clothing and shoes	Household economy	Furniture and house equipment
Area I (Northwest)	1951	45.5	3.7	11.5	10.0	7.0
	1961	41.0	3.3	9.2	13.8	6.6
	1971	36.8	2.1	8.9	13.5	6.8
Area II (Northeast)	1951	45.6	4.2	14.7	9.7	5.8
	1961	43.7	3.8	10.4	11.7	5.5
	1971	37.9	2.8	9.4	12.0	6.2
Area III (Central Italy)	1951	42.8	4.4	14.2	10.4	6.5
	1961	40.7	3.9	9.5	13.5	6.0
	1971	37.3	3.1	8.7	13.4	5.5
Area IV (Southern Italy)	1951	52.3	4.0	12.6	9.1	5.1
	1961	46.8	3.8	9.6	12.5	5.4
	1971	41.1	3.2	9.8	12.5	5.4
Italy	1951	46.8	4.1	13.0	9.7	6.2
	1961	43.1	3.7	9.6	13.0	5.9
	1971	38.3	2.7	9.2	12.9	6.0

Source: Central Statistical Institute: "Annuario di contabilità nazionale," vol. II, 1972.

pressure of revolts in Puglia, Sicily, and Calabria, a land reform was implemented in 1950 over an area that, on the whole, represented about thirty percent of the total land in agriculture (acts of May 12, 1950, n. 230; Oct. 21, 1950, n. 841; and act of the regional government of Sicily, Dec. 27, 1950, n. 104). As a consequence of this reform, about 700 thousand hectares of poor land were expropriated and redistributed to peasants and farm laborers.

A special agency—the *Cassa*—was created in 1950 (act of August 10, 1950, n. 646) as an executive body under the control of a Committee of Ministers for the South, comprising the ministers of the treasury; agriculture and forestry; industry and commerce; public works; and labor and social security, which held parliamentary responsibility for the activities of the agency. Initially, the *Cassa* was only to execute a ten year program of extraordinary public works in the *Mezzogiorno* (an area covering all the southern regions, part of Lazio, and some peripheral territories of central Italy), in addition to those currently executed by central government departments. This special program received initially approximately $1.6 billion from various public resources and, partly, from IBRD loans.

Health and personal care	Transpor- tation and communication	Entertain- ment and leisure	Other goods and services	Total absolute values at current prices		Ratios Areas-Italy
				Percent	000 lire	
5.9	6.3	6.0	4.1	100	(209.2)	1.31
5.6	8.7	6.6	5.2	100	(390.4)	1.25
8.4	11.6	6.5	5.4	100	(904.7)	1.19
5.8	4.6	5.5	4.1	100	(161.5)	1.02
5.9	7.3	6.0	5.6	100	(325.9)	1.05
8.8	10.5	5.8	6.6	100	(809.2)	1.06
5.5	5.8	5.8	4.6	100	(174.4)	1.10
6.0	8.3	6.3	5.8	100	(349.1)	1.12
8.8	11.3	5.5	6.4	100	(852.3)	1.12
4.7	3.8	5.1	3.3	100	(117.1)	0.74
5.8	6.1	5.9	4.1	100	(228.4)	0.73
8.9	9.5	4.9	4.7	100	(569.4)	0.75
5.4	5.2	5.6	4.0	100	(159.1)	1.0
5.8	7.6	6.2	5.1	100	(311.1)	1.0
8.7	10.8	5.7	5.7	100	(760.0)	1.0

An additional program of public works was simultaneously insti-
tuted for the depressed zones of central and northern Italy; it represented
another $330 million burden on the national budget (act of August 10, 1950, n.
647).

Despite the *Cassa*'s public works program, the promotion of industrial activities was in fact very limited during this period (see DiNardi, 1960, on
the limited role and tasks originally assigned to the Cassa). The instruments used
for this purpose consisted of some tax benefits and a forty percent contribution
by the Cassa to the limited funds of the three financial institutions that were
enabled, as of 1953, to finance the investments of small and medium-size
industrial enterprises operating in the continental part of southern Italy and in
the two major islands (act of April 11, 1953, n. 298).

However, the need for assigning a less marginal role to industrial
activities in the South soon became clear. The positive effects of land reform
were felt almost exclusively in Central and Northeast Italy, where the first class
soils resulting from land reclamation could be more easily and evenly partitioned
among a relatively limited number of farm families. In the South, the necessarily
casual redistribution of uncultivated latifundia (representing about fifty percent

Table 5-9. Percentages of Registered Unemployed and Job Seekers, by Region, 1960, 1970

Regions	Men		Women		Total	
	1960	1970	1960	1970	1960	1970
Piedmont and Val d'Aosta	2.4	1.5	2.7	2.4	2.5	1.7
Liguria	3.1	2.6	5.1	3.6	3.6	2.8
Lombardy	2.3	1.5	2.9	2.3	2.5	1.7
Trentiño-Alto Adige	3.9	1.9	2.7	2.4	3.5	2.0
Veneto	4.5	1.0	3.2	3.0	4.2	2.1
Friuli-Venezia Giulia	7.3	2.8	6.9	3.8	7.2	2.0
Emilia-Romagna	4.5	1.9	4.3	2.8	4.4	2.5
Marche	3.1	2.3	2.1	3.3	2.7	2.7
Tuscany	4.1	2.0	2.7	3.7	3.7	2.5
Umbria	4.3	2.3	4.3	4.0	4.3	2.7
Lazio	4.8	3.4	4.7	5.5	4.8	3.9
Campania	6.0	5.7	4.9	5.3	5.7	5.6
Abruzzi and Molise	4.5	4.0	2.0	4.3	3.6	4.1
Puglia	4.3	4.5	4.7	4.8	4.4	4.6
Basilicata	6.8	7.4	7.2	6.3	7.0	7.1
Calabria	6.2	5.5	2.7	7.8	5.2	6.1
Sicily	3.7	3.0	5.1	7.3	3.9	3.7
Sardinia	5.5	4.6	4.3	7.0	5.1	5.1
Italy	4.1	2.3	3.7	3.9	4.0	3.1
Do, in 000 units	(604)	(407)	(232)	(208)	(836)	(615)
of which in the South (Percent)	(41.3)	(52.3)	(33.6)	(40.9)	(39.0)	(48.4)

Source: Central Statistical Institute: "Annuario di Statistiche del Lavoro," vol. XII, 1972.

of the total expropriated land) among a large number of peasants left the problem of rural unemployment virtually unsolved, especially in the internal areas (Rossi Doria, 1959).

A number of criticisms of the methods used to implement land reform in the South (Bandini, 1956; Valarché, 1956; and FAO, 1960) were very sound. These included the fact that political, rather than economic, criteria guided the redistribution of the expropriated land, leading to its excessive division into a great number of small and isolated plots (four to five hectares each on the average). Land also was redistributed before improving the crop yields, establishing the necessary physical infrastructures, or providing adequate technical training to the new land owners. Other points included the lack of an effective modification of labor contracts, and the high final cost of the reform (about $1.7 per hectare, as compared with the estimated cost of $0.7).

On the other hand, notwithstanding the concentration of the Cassa program in the agricultural sector (which indeed contributed to improving some basic infrastructure) and the important exodus of underemployed laborers, productivity levels remained very low, especially in the zones of extensive cereal cultivation. Moreover, the multiplier effect of extraordinary public expenditures was much lower than expected because of the increasing dependence of the South on the industrialized regions (Pilloton, 1960), thus justifying the impression that, after all, the South was continuing to "subsidize" the North through the exportation of labor surpluses and the importation of an increasing amount of consumer goods.

A nationwide debate concerning the evident deterioration of the southern economy and the additional measures needed to arrest it was instigated by the presentation to Parliament, in 1955, of the "Vanoni Plan." This document, which summarized the results of a research effort promoted by one of the most enlightened members of the government (Minister Vanoni) and carried out by the Association for the Industrial Development of Southern Italy (SVIMEZ, 1955), gave only an indication of a desirable pattern of growth of the national economy over a ten year period. However, it had the merit of introducing the spatial dimension into a quantitative analysis of potential development. Its principal purpose was to point out possible ways and means for solving the sectoral and regional disequilibria of the national economy. Despite a lack of solid data, it is worth noting the ambitious, if somewhat contradictory, goals of this attempt at a general plan for Italian development. Although these goals were at first pursued in principle only, they have represented concrete objectives in subsequent approaches to solving problems of a regional nature.

According to the Vanoni Plan the major aims of development policy were (1) attainment of full employment through the creation of four million new jobs, of which two million represented the elimination of unemployment; (2) restoration of equilibrium in the balance of payments; and (3) elimination of per capita income disparities between the North and the South.

The conditions that were judged necessary for the attainment of the last goal were a five percent annual growth rate of per capita income (eight percent in the South and four percent in the rest of the country), and the placing of forty percent of total industrial investment in the South. Unfortunately, the attempt to transform this scheme into a concrete plan of action failed, mainly because of the strong opposition of northern industrialists and the support that they found in the doctrine of neoclassical liberalism. It is, for instance, noteworthy that even some distinguished non-Italian economists (Lutz, 1962) supported the opinion that encouragement to labor mobility could be a more rewarding policy than that of subsidizing capital movements from the North to the South. However, it is equally relevant that other foreign economists

Table 5-10.   Emigration and Repatriation, by Region, 1959-1969 (000 units)

Regions	1959-1969			Yearly averages				Present population	
	Emigrations	Repatriations	Net emigration	Emigration	Repatriation	Net emigration (000)	Percent	Yearly average	Percent Net emigration
Area I (Northwest)	240.4	198.0	42.4	21.8	18.0	3.8	3.9	13,674	0.03
Piedmont and Val d'Aosta	49.6	41.8	7.8	4.5	3.8	0.7	0.7	4,149	0.02
Liguria	22.1	16.1	6.0	2.0	1.5	0.5	0.5	1,789	0.03
Lombardy	168.7	140.1	28.6	15.3	12.7	2.6	2.7	7,736	0.03
Area II (Northeast)	501.0	434.5	66.5	45.6	39.5	6.1	6.3	9,484	0.06
Trentino-Alto Adige	40.0	30.0	10.0	3.7	2.7	1.0	1.0	782	0.12
Veneto	260.0	232.6	27.4	23.6	21.2	2.4	2.5	3,850	0.66
Friuli-Venezia Giulia	127.7	110.3	17.4	11.6	10.0	1.6	1.7	1,161	0.15
Emilia-Romagna	73.3	61.6	11.7	6.7	5.6	1.1	1.1	3,691	0.03
Area III (Central Italy)	268.6	177.7	90.9	24.4	16.2	8.2	8.4	9,580	0.09
Marche	77.2	67.2	10.0	7.0	6.1	0.9	0.9	1,322	0.07
Tuscany	48.6	37.7	10.9	4.4	3.5	0.9	0.9	3,309	0.03
Umbria	25.7	22.3	3.4	2.3	2.0	0.3	0.3	773	0.04
Lazio	117.1	50.5	66.6	10.7	4.6	6.1	6.3	4,176	0.15

Area IV (Southern Italy)	2,137.5	1,264.2	873.3	194.3	114.9	79.4	81.4	18,921	0.42
Campania	483.8	314.7	169.1	44.0	28.6	15.4	15.9	1,992	0.77
Abruzzi and Molise	301.3	171.8	129.5	27.4	15.6	11.8	12.1	4,855	0.24
Puglia	514.2	355.2	159.0	46.7	32.3	14.4	14.8	3,427	0.42
Basilicata	134.3	90.2	44.1	12.2	8.2	4.0	4.0	618	0.65
Calabria	319.1	152.9	166.2	29.0	13.9	15.1	15.5	1,918	0.78
Sicily	327.9	145.9	182.0	29.8	13.3	16.5	16.9	4,700	0.35
Sardinia	56.9	33.5	23.4	5.2	3.0	2.2	2.2	1,411	0.16
Italy	3,147.5	2,074.4	1,073.1	286.1	188.6	97.5	100.0	51,220	0.19
of which toward:									
Common Market countries	(1,234.9)	(893.9)	(341.0)	(112.2)	(81.3)	(30.9)	(31.6)		
Other European countries	(1,271.1)	(1,002.9)	(268.2)	(115.5)	(91.2)	(24.3)	(25.0)		
U.S.A.	(177.6)	(10.3)	(167.3)	(16.1)	(0.9)	(15.2)	(15.6)		
Canada	(204.3)	(8.3)	(196.0)	(18.6)	(0.8)	(17.8)	(18.3)		
Latin America	(90.0)	(66.4)	(23.6)	(8.2)	(6.0)	(2.2)	(2.2)		
Australia and New Zealand	(147.0)	(13.6)	(133.4)	(13.4)	(1.2)	(12.2)	(12.5)		
African and other countries	(22.6)	(79.0)	(−56.4)	(2.1)	(7.2)	(−5.1)	(−5.2)		

Source: Central Statistical Institute: "Annuario di Statistiche del lavoro," vol. XII, 1972.

(Chenery, 1962), on the basis of more refined quantitative analysis of available information, arrived at the opposite conclusion. Of the three practical approaches to the solution of economic dualism—raising the productivity of agricultural activities, intensification of migration to the North, and accelerated industrialization—the third did not appear incompatible with the further progress of the Italian economy; and it was, in any case, an indispensable means for transforming the South into a vital area without forcing its people to leave their native places. The important point, however, is that the ideas contained in Vanoni's document contributed substantially to correcting the initial formulation of Italian regional development policy.

The 1957-1965 Period: Promotion of
Industrialization in the Backward Regions

The first attempt to promote the take off of the industrialization process in the South was made between 1957 and 1959. A series of acts (July 26, 1957, n. 634; July 18, 1959, n. 555; and July 24, 1959, n. 622) extended the activities of the Cassa to 1965, and increased its financial resources to about $3.5 billion. Among the most important new measures that appeared to be in line with the Vanoni Plan were:

1. an obligation that public and semipublic enterprises would locate at least sixty percent of their new investments in the Mezzogiorno;
2. inducements to local administrations and other public institutions of the southern regions to take the initiative in forming *Consorzi* for implementing (with the financial support of the Cassa) a program of public utility investments in those areas where industrial concentration appeared feasible;
3. the extension of Cassa programs to the construction and equipment of vocational schools and to public works necessary to develop tourism; and
4. grants to small and medium-size firms that would locate in communes with fewer than 75,000 inhabitants. These grants covered up to twenty percent of both relocation and equipment costs and were later extended to include communes with fewer than 200,000 inhabitants.

The objectives of this new policy were made more explicit by the interministerial committee in its instructions for the application of the law of 1957, especially with respect to the areas where industrialization efforts had to be concentrated. Initially, the criteria to be used for delimiting these areas were largely influenced by the new doctrine of "polarization," which proposed a model of regional economic structure based on a hierarchy of districts developing according to their capacity to attract new activities and thereby contribute to the transformation of whole regions.

In line with this approach, and an intensive research effort by SVIMEZ to identify potential growth poles in the South (Molinari and Turco,

1959), the interministerial committee decided to encourage the establishment of industrial development areas in only a few large and relatively homogeneous parts of the southern territory. However, by 1960 this policy of concentration was already diluted by local political considerations. Communes, or groups of communes, were authorized to constitute "industrialization nodes" in all southern areas where it appeared desirable to encourage the agglomeration of a few small firms willing to tap unused local resources or to supply the local market.

This ambitious program was destined to fail. The simultaneous encouragement of concentration and dispersion was contradictory from the start. Not only were there too many industrial areas and nodes without sufficient resources to execute the public utilities programs; there also was no coordination of direct and indirect public actions, which in turn resulted from the lack of a coherent plan for the development of the South. The kinds of private and public industrial activities located in the South—chiefly basic chemicals, metallurgy, and petroleum refining—did not have strong interindustry linkages with the various industrial nodes, and their capital-intensive nature did little to increase employment (Cacace, 1973). Even the distinction between industrial "areas" and "nodes" proved futile. The former experienced only a proliferation of small-scale and rather improvised efforts, whereas the latter benefited from the location of a few large firms, drawn principally to places with unexploited natural resources (Fiorelli and Novacco, 1963).

Moreover, the new provisions for the South were simultaneously extended to the depressed zones of northern and central Italy; central government subsidies were extended to 1965 and brought their total amount to $750 million for these zones (act of July 29, 1957, n. 635). In spite of the fact that these resources were too thinly spread over an excessively large number of zones (by the end of 1960, about seventy percent of the communes in central and northern Italy were recognized as depressed, and half of these were in the "industrial triangle") (Legitimo, 1960), these efforts were more successful than those in the South, because of the contiguity of communes receiving benefits with the most important industrial centers.

The 1965-1970 Period: Tentative Coordination of Projects and Actions within the Framework of National Economic Planning

The centenary celebrations of Italy's political unification gave the government an opportunity to emphasize the successes attained during the fifties in reaching the two major goals of national economic policy: a high rate of growth (about 6.5 percent per year) and a substantial reduction of registered unemployment, accompanied by price stability and the re-equilibration of the balance of payments. Satisfaction with these achievements (too early labeled the

"Italian miracle") was, however, tempered by the new problems posed by Italy's affiliation with the European Common Market, and used as justification for the delays in the adoption of a more effective regional development policy.

Despite the participation, since 1962, of the Socialists in a new governmental coalition, it took several years to reach a consensus on the need for implementing a planning strategy aimed at the elimination of regional disequilibrium (see Lombardini, 1967, and D'Antonio, 1967, for a review of the academic and political debates that accompanied the first, inconclusive, attempts at planning formulation prior to 1964). In fact, this goal was first formally set forth in the first national economic plan for the 1966-1970 period (Ministry of Budget and Economic Planning, 1965) and in legislation between 1965 and 1967 which provided for the coordination of public intervention in the South as a basic precondition for the plan's implementation.

The 1965 act and a subsequent series of legislative provisions concerning the Mezzogiorno (act of July 26, 1965, n. 717 and decree of the president of the Republic, June 30, 1967, n. 1523) established the institutional links between the national planning system and the various agencies responsible for the economic development of this area. A broader interministerial committee—including the ministers of the budget; state holdings; education; health; tourism; and transportation—for special intervention in the South, set up within the National Planning Committee (CIPE), was charged with the formulation of plurennial plans of action which were to be elaborated in cooperation with all the public administrations concerned and on the basis of proposals submitted by the regional authorities—i.e., by the local governments of the five autonomous regions, and by the presidents of the committees for economic planning that had been constituted in 1964, pending the institution of the regional administrations in all the other regions (decree of the minister of the budget, September 22, 1964). The chairman of the interministerial committee was charged with approving the annual programs of action of the Cassa and with the supervision and control of all its activities: the Cassa's activities were to extent to 1980, and it received an additional allotment of about $2.8 billion for the 1965-1970 period. The Cassa was charged with the execution of additional public works programs and the fulfillment of other new tasks, in conformity with the directions contained in the plurennial coordination plans formulated by the interministerial committee.

The major innovations introduced in the 1965-1967 legislation are worth mentioning. A broader role was assigned to special intervention in the agricultural sector, in addition to new actions to be undertaken by the Ministry of Agriculture for implementing the targets of the 1966-1970 national plan (act of October 27, 1966, n. 910). The new legislation for the South provided for the delimitation of "irrigation areas" and "zones for more intensive cultivation." The Cassa was authorized to form (mainly with public funds) a financial association for the promotion of cooperatives and associations of small and medium-size farms; to allocate grants and credit for the construction of food processing plants and for organizing the distribution of agricultural products; and to offer technical assistance to farmers. Certain reductions in transportation rates also were extended to agricultural products.

Meanwhile, promotion of industrial activities was intensified by a number of measures. All central government agencies were required to reserve a forty percent share of their public investments for the South, and thirty percent of their contracts for goods purchases were to go to the South. The Cassa was to aid regional financial companies for the promotion of industrial development, as well as to provide (within the limits established by the coordination plans) the funds necessary for equipping designated industrial areas and nodes. It also promoted the organization and operation of "consortiums"; financed a new institute for providing technical assistance services to industrial enterprises (IASM), and a center for training personnel for employment in industry and public administration; and provided for other educational and social services. Credit facilities and grants up to twenty percent of investment costs were extended to all new industrial plants and to the expanding ones, wherever located, provided that respective projects conformed to the criteria established by the coordination plans. The Cassa was also entitled to finance investments in tourist zones and, finally, the right to expropriate land and buildings was extended to 1980.

However, under pressure exercised by northern social and political forces, most of these measures (especially those concerning the financing of investments) were once more extended to the depressed zones of northern and central Italy (act of July 22, 1966, no. 614). Despite the moderate additional burden involved, this decision was and still is much criticized (Novacco, 1972). Actually, as was correctly pointed out by one of the major experts (Saraceno, 1968) engaged in the design of appropriate development policies for the South:

> industrial promotion is the modern substitute for the protectionism that many European countries implemented during the last half of the past century, to help the newborn industries to compete with those of the more developed countries. Thus, it is clear that this new form of protectionism cannot have the expected effects if it is accompanied by the extension of similar measures to other areas that are in a relatively better position than those of the regions to be developed.

On the other hand, the brave attempt at coordinating the actions of the southern area was destined to remain a political dream.

The evolution of Italy's economy between 1965 and 1970 demonstrated that the solemn enunciation of noble principles, the formulation of

national and regional plans*, and the enacting of legislation inspired by political
good will but not supported by adequate coercive powers are not sufficent even
to approach a satisfactory solution for the kinds of serious structural problems
that have confronted Italy for more than a century.

The comparison between the quantitative targets of the 1966-1970
national plan and the actual performance of the Italian economy during that
period offers a good example of the futility of planning exercises in mixed
economies when short term policies too often prevail over the goals of long-run
development strategies. The first set of data presented in Table 5-11 indicate the
situation which might have been attained through greater control of either the
market or the nonmarket forces of the national economic system. The second
set shows the actual results of a growth process that continued to be driven by
the rapid growth of a few leading industries on the one hand, and dampened on
the other by the inefficiency of marginal enterprises and the inertia of an archaic
bureaucratic apparatus that was not even prepared to utilize the resources
available for reaching the plan's worthy social goals.

NEW DIRECTIONS FOR THE PRESENT DECADE

A New Approach to National
Economic Planning

The new development strategy proposed for the seventies is outlined
in two official documents: the so-called "80 Project," and a "Preliminary Draft
of the Second National Plan for the Period 1971-1975" (Ministry of the Budget
and Economic Planning, 1969, 1971). These documents have not yet led to the
final formulation of a new economic plan, but it is worth sketching their
contents because most of their ideas and proposals were made part of a new Act
for the South, passed by Parliament in October 1971.

The first document begins with a tentative explanation of major
causes for the failure of the first national economic plan. They were identified as
a too lengthy process of legislation (the project approved by the Council of
Ministers in June 1965 was passed by the Parliament only in July 1967 [Act of
July 27, 1967, n. 685]), the critical situation during the 1963-1964 recession,
and the rigidities of an old administrative apparatus. The new planning concept
aimed at minimizing at least the last two types of shortcomings. A clear
distinction was introduced among the following three types of planning actions:
(1) those for attaining the targets for which the central planning system is
directly responsible (essentially in the area of social investment); (2) those
tending to influence and guide the behavior of the other autonomous decision

---

*For a review of the first Italian experiences in the formulation of regional
plans, see Indovina (1967, pp. 45-81) and Allione (1968, pp. 62-94); for the description of
the biregional model used to check the consistency of the first national plan, see Cao-Pinna
(1965).

centers by means of "negotiated planning"; and (3) those which should assure, through flexible use of the traditional policy instruments, coordination between the short-term behavior of the public and private decision centers and the long- and medium-term goals of planning policy.

The "80 Project" reiterated the three major goals of the first national plan and extended them to 1980. They were full employment, decentralization of productive activities, and higher quantitative and qualitative standards of social infrastructure. In addition, there were the conventional constraints imposed on all planning exercises—e.g., price stability and equilibrium of the balance of payments. However, the emphasis put on the long-term objective of eliminating regional imbalances (especially the disparity between the southern area and the rest of the country) was rather diluted in this document. On the other hand, having recognized the failure of an unplanned "polarization" process attenuated by the promotion of a spontaneous, casual proliferation of improvised initiatives all over the southern territory, it attempted to design a more comprehensive and rational space policy, along the lines indicated by a new approach to regional development. One of the most interesting sections of this document was, in fact, that dealing with environmental problems. A highly qualified team of urbanists, sociologists, and economists identified long-term solutions for the protection of the soil, the natural resources, and the artistic patrimony of the nation; the reorganization of the transportation and communication system; and a redistribution of the urban population among thirty interconnected urban systems, of which eleven new ones should be set up in the South (Centro di studi e piani economici, 1971).

Based essentially on the conceptual framework of the "80 Project," the preliminary draft for the Second Five Year Plan approached the development of the South as *a* (rather than *the*) problem of the national economy. The preliminary draft calls for the preparation and implementation of three types of concrete public programs. First are the "social projects." The targets, geographic distribution, timing, cost, responsibilities, and implementation procedures of public programs destined to satisfy collective needs are to be specified in quantitative terms. Second are the "promotion projects," which are to guide and coordinate the actions of the decision makers involved in the various industry sectors. Finally, there are the "special projects" of intervention in specific areas; those concerning the South were partially identified.

Without attempting to discuss the rationality of this pragmatic approach, one cannot help noting the contrast between the emphatic identification of the need to formulate a development strategy for the South, and the very cautious evaluation of the progress that could be achieved in the South up to 1975 and 1980. According to the most optimistic alternative assumed for GNP expansion (six percent per year), the share of the South was expected to increase from only twenty-four percent in 1970, to 24.4 percent in 1975, to 25.7 percent in 1980. (The region's population is expected to remain stable at thirty-five

Table 5-11. Quantitative Targets of the First National Economic Plan for the Period 1966-1970, Compared with Actual Performances

Targets (and restrictions)	Unit	Quantitative targets	Actual development
Full employment	000 units	+800	−172
to be achieved through growth rate of GNP	percent	5.0	6.0
to be achieved through growth rate of productivity	percent	4.2	6.2
Reduction of sectoral and regional disequilibrium			
Growth rate of national agricultural product	percent	2.85	2.15
Employment in Agriculture	000 units	−600	−1,273
of. which: In the South	000 units	−350	− 438
In the rest of the country	000 units	−250	− 835
Employment in other sectors	000 units	+1,400	+1,101
of. which: In the South	000 units	+ 590	+ 294
In the rest of the country	000 units	+ 810	+ 807
Ratios between			
Value added per worker employed in agriculture and in other sectors (in constant prices)	1	0.52	0.59
(in 1965)		(0.47)	(0.47)
Value added per worker employed in the South and in the rest of the country	1	0.85	0.16
(in 1965)		0.78	0.78

Increase of social capital

Gross investments	billions of 1963 lire	17,735	18,143
of which: Private housing construction (partly financed by the state)	billions of 1963 lire	9,125	12,315
Public investments		8,610	5,828
of which in: Education	billions of 1963 lire	(960)	(339)
Health	billions of 1963 lire	(360)	(125)
Transportation	billions of 1963 lire	(4,125)	(3,007)
Telecommunications	billions of 1963 lire	(715)	(927)
Public works	billions of 1963 lire	(2,270)	(1,312)
Other	billions of 1963 lire	(180)	(118)
Constraints:	billions of 1963 lire		
Increase of general price level	billions of 1963 lire	23	38
Balance of payments equilibrium (current transactions)	billions of 1963 lire	+0.5	+ 7.1
of which:			
goods	billions of 1963 lire	−2.7	+1.6
services	billions of 1963 lire	+2.3	+4.4
transfers	billions of 1963 lire	+0.9	+1.1

Source: Ministry of the Budget and Economic Planning (1971), Appendix II.

percent.) Moreover, despite the formal emphasis put on the need for accelerating the industrialization of the South, its contribution to the gross product of industrial activities (excluding construction) was expected to increase from 14.4 percent in 1970, to 16.4 percent in 1975, to nineteen percent in 1980. The outlook for the southern economy depicted by the most recent draft of the second national plan—which has been updated to cover the 1973-1977 period—is not much more optimistic.

1971 Law for the South

The reorganization of the national planning system and the administrative decentralization implemented in 1972 both accelerated the formulation and the approval of a new law for the South which has substantially changed the scope and the mechanism of public intervention in this area (act of October 6, 1971, n. 853). All of the Cassa's former responsibilities in the fields of agriculture and fishing, tourism, handicrafts, and vocational training have been transferred to the new southern regional administrations, as have the functions formerly exercised by the interministerial committee for the South and other ministries concerned with the industrial areas and nodes and the related physical planning activities.

To finance these operations, the southern regions have been allotted a sixty percent share of the national fund for financing regional economic plans, and the Cassa has been authorized to carry out their ordinary and special programs if requested to do so by the regional administrations. Another consequence of the partial transfer of powers to the regional administrations was the suppression of the interministerial committee for the South and its plurennial plans for the coordination of all the special projects in this area.

The role of all the southern regions (including the five self-governed by a special statute) in the decision-making process concerning their future development has been rather limited by the new law. The regional authorities are, in fact, entitled to meet periodically in a special committee, but only for the purpose of "formulating proposals and expressing opinions" on all the choices and proposals that the minister for special intervention in the South must submit to the National Planning Committee (CIPE). The continued centralization of ad hoc decisions on the future development of the South is indicated by the practically unlimited power of initiative given to this minister, especially for the selection and preparation of the multisectoral and/or multiregional "special projects" that the Cassa will have to implement in the southern regions.

For the time being, however, none of the twenty-one "special projects" approved by CIPE in 1972 can be classified as "strategic" for the future development of the regions concerned (see Table 5-12). Moreover, the validity of their design has not yet been tested on the basis of appropriate cost-benefit, or opportunity-cost, analysis (Leon, 1973), and the fear that their execution might be used for maneuvering electoral and political connections (Petriccione, 1972) is fully justified by past experiences.

Table 5-12. List of the First Special Projects to be Implemented in the Southern Regions

Number of projects	Scope of the projects	Regions concerned
7	Intensification of cattle breeding and meat production	Lazio, Abruzzi, Molise, Campania, Puglia, Basilicata, Calabria
1	Expansion, qualification, and higher competitiveness of citrus-fruit production	Sicily and Calabria
4	More extensive and multipurpose utilization of water resources	Molise, Basilicata, Puglia, Sardinia
2	Construction of landing places for tourist watercraft	Lazio, Calabria, Abruzzi, Puglia
2	Development of areas for tourism	Calabria, Lazio
1	Purification of the Naples harbor	Campania
2	Extension of interregional road transportation	Abruzzi, Marche, Campania
1	Construction of an industrial harbor	Sardinia
1	Construction of basic infrastructures for a new basic-chemicals concern	Sicily
21	Total	all the regions of the Mezzogiorno area

Source: Ministry of the Budget and Economic Planning, "Notiziario," no. 3 (1972).

On the other hand, the industrial localization policies adopted in line with the recommendations of the "80 Project" and the instruments envisaged to implement them appear to still be affected by the double ambition of achieving, simultaneously, the geographical concentration of the nationwide industrial concerns in the most promising points of the South and the maximum dispersion of industry, either along the eight predetermined geographical directions, or within the most internal depopulated zones of each region.

To achieve the first goal two important measures have been imposed, after a harsh political debate, by the new law. It is now obligatory for the first time for private corporations with assets over five billion lire (equivalent to about $8 million) and for public, or semipublic, enterprises to submit their investment programs to the minister of the budget and economic planning. This obligation also holds for any enterprise planning to create new industrial plants or to expand the pre-existing ones if the investment exceeds seven billion lire (equivalent to about $1.1 billion). The CIPE is entitled to express (within three months) a negative opinion if the projects increase congestion in certain areas or if new investments are not directed where there is an abundance of unemployed manpower. Firms which disregard the CIPE's negative opinion will be penalized by an amount corresponding to twenty-five percent of the total value of the programmed investment. Moreover, public administrations will not license, or authorize the implementation of, investment programs for which the CIPE has issued a negative opinion.

The share of the new investments of public and semipublic enterprises that must be reserved for the South has been raised (up to year 1980) from sixty percent to eighty percent, and the South's share of their respective total investments has been raised from forty percent to sixty percent. Moreover, every year these enterprises have to submit to the national planning authorities their five year programs of investments in the South, specifying value, locations, and employment targets, and plans for decentralizing their headquarters and sales departments. Finally, to promote industrial decentralization to and within the South, the CIPE is authorized to establish a special credit company for the South to help small and medium-size enterprises in particular to meet their current financial needs.

The other instruments to be used for inducing industrial expansion are largely traditional. They include the extension up to 1980 of the provisions assuring the South a forty percent share of the investments programmed by public administrations and thirty percent of the value of each contract concerning current purchases of industrial goods. Similar stipulations are made with respect to national funds for restructuring industrial and commercial enterprises and for the expansion of research activities.

An indication of the type of industrial pattern to be promoted in the South during the seventies can be derived from the new system of incentives established by the law of 1971 (see Table 5-13). The graduation of the shares of investments which will be financed according to their conformity with the sectoral and location priorities identified by the CIPE represents an important innovation compared with the indiscriminate use that has been made of this approach in the past (Ilses, 1965; and Graziani et al., 1973).

Finally, it is worth noting that in 1971 it was recognized that more incentives were needed to induce more labor-intensive industries to locate in the South. Toward this end, temporary exemptions from the payment of social security contributions were extended to 1980, and were raised to thirty percent (act of August 4, 1971, n. 589). The major problems in this inducement effort are the impressive amount of resources that will be required for the infrastructure in the areas where the new industries are to be located, and the heavy responsibilities that the Cassa will have to assume during the seventies. Although no longer responsible for the projects now under the authority of the regional administrations, the Cassa still has to (1) complete the many thousand programs begun before the new law was passed and, eventually, to execute new public utilities programs at the request of the regional administrations; (2) carry out the construction of the important basic infrastructures required for implementing the multiregional and/or multisectoral special projects; and (3) promote the diffusion of the industrialization process through construction of infrastructures, training of skilled personnel, marketing assistance to entrepreneurs, etc.

To perform these tasks, the Cassa will have about $13 billion for the 1971-1975 period, or much more than the total funds it had spent during the past twenty years. But it seems that half of this amount will be absorbed by the twenty-one special projects already approved up to the end of 1972; and that only the other half will be available for the promotion of industrial activities. Thus, a more accurate financial plan will have to be formulated if the Cassa is to fulfill all the major tasks that have been assigned to it by the new legislation (Vicinelli, 1972). There is, however, a widespread conviction in Italy that the major problem which might continue to delay the development of the southern area is *not* a financial one.

TOWARD REDRESSING PAST ERRORS

The political instability which has accompanied the economic crises Italy has experienced for the past three years adds further uncertainty to the outlook for the solution of its critical regional problem. Among the facts that might justify cautious optimism is official recognition of the shortcomings that have led to the failure of the first planning experiences, especially with regard to the goal of narrowing the disparities between the Two Italies (Ruffolo, 1973). It is now generally admitted that the specific factors responsible for the slow progress so far achieved in the South were:

1. the lack of a development strategy at both the national and the regional level, and government reluctance to control the growth of the North;

Table 5-13. Summary of the Incentives Established by the 1971 Act for the South[1] (in percentages of the fixed investment costs)

Classes and types of initiatives	*Credit facilities Favorable loans[2]*				*Grants[6]*	
	New Plants[3]		*Expansions and renewals[4]*	*Reactivation conversion or transformation[4]*	*New plants, expansions, and renewals*	*Reactivation, conversion, or transformation*
	in locations deserving priority[5]	*in other locations*				
Industrial Activities						
I. *Small initiatives* (up to about 2.5 million lire of fixed investments)	35	35	35	35	35	35
do, if localized in the territories experiencing progressive depopulation					45[7]	45[7]
II. *Medium-size initiatives* (from about 2.5 to 8 million lire of fixed investments):						
Mining or manufacturing activities deserving priority	50	45	50	50	20	20
Mining or manufacturing activities operating at high capital intensity	35	35	45	50	15	20
Mining, or manufacturing activities in sectors needing restructuring	35	35	35	35	15	15
All other industrial activities	45	40	45	50	20	20
III. *Large scale initiatives* (over 8 million lire of fixed investments)	30 to 50 (of total investments, including inventories)	30 to 50	30 to 50	30 to 50	7 to 12	7 to 12

IV. *Dessalination of sea water sent to the small islands*	35	35	35	50	50	50
Commercial Activities						
Cooperatives and small and medium-size shops	50	50	50	—	—	—

[1] The two types of facilities are allowed to single industrial units classified in categories I and II, after examination of their conformity with the CIPE directives; the contributions are allocated (on the basis of the works in progress) to firms possessing at least thirty percent of the programmed fixed investment. The additional financing of inventories varies from thirty to fifty percent of their values.

[2] Four percent for industrial initiatives classified in categories I and II; eight percent for the other industrial initiatives; three percent for commercial activities.

[3] Maximum period admitted: Fifteen years.

[4] Maximum period admitted: Ten years.

[5] Clusters (agglomerati) within the "industrial development areas" and the "industrial nodes" and territories situated along the eight axes established by CIPE.

[6] For the share of investments represented by purchases of machinery and equipment fabricated in the South and of antipollution equipment, the grant is raised by ten percent.

[7] Plus an additional five percent to be allocated for the cost of small specific infrastructures and training of manpower.

Source: Synthesis of the provisions issued for implementing the Act of October 8, 1971, no. 853 (see IASN: "Direttive e norme di applicazione della legge 853 per il Mezzogiorno," nov. 1972).

2. the excess confidence placed in the results obtainable in the South through the unplanned spending of a relatively limited amount of national resources (about $20 billion, representing less than one percent of the national income produced during the past twenty years);
3. the lack of coordination of the special programs in the South with the ordinary activities of central government administrations operating throughout the nation;
4. the discontinuity and incompleteness of approaches to the restructuring of southern agriculture;
5. the inefficacy of industrial incentives, which have been limited to the financing of equipment costs and the provision of similar facilities to enterprises located in the more advanced regions;
6. the kind of capital-intensive and nonpropulsive investments carried out by public enterprises in a few places in the South;
7. the role played by the commercial banking system in pumping savings from the South to support growth in the northern regions;
8. the sluggish pressure exercised by the trade unions to obtain a more equitable distribution of employment among the various regions; and
9. the extreme politicization of local authorities, which favored the misuse of significant amounts of resources.

Despite these deficiencies, demands for a more effective approach to the development of the South remained unheeded until August 1973, when the new (center-left) political coalition that again took responsibility for governing the country recognized the necessity for more energetic action in the South.

A first step in this direction was the preparation and approval, by the Council of Ministers, of a new law authorizing the government to coordinate, update, and integrate all the legislation promulgated after 1967 on behalf of the southern regions; and to revise again the system of incentives of the 1971 law, to adapt it to the fundamental objective of raising employment levels in southern industries. Among the expected modifications, the most significant is the reduction of the contributions for financing new capital formation, to be compensated by credit and fiscal means (primarily exemptions of substantial shares of social security contributions). This will primarily benefit small and medium-sized firms.

Another government initiative, evidently stimulated by the controversial evaluations of the role played by public enterprises in the process of industrialization of the South, is represented by the new directives issued by the minister for public enterprises. While recognizing the full operational autonomy of these enterprises, the minister has affirmed his right to exercise, in cooperation with the regional administrations and trade unions, political control of their investment programs, and has induced them to interpret the concept of "efficiency" in a less self-interested manner than that which guides the choices and actions of private firms.

From these signs of the government's resolution to remedy past approaches to the development of the South it might be inferred that Italian regional policy is finally headed in the right direction. Unfortunately, however, the political situation at this writing is not reassuring. It is difficult to predict how many political crises are to come, or if present and future Italian governments will be more successful than preceding ones in facing the problem of regional disequilibrium.

Equally uncertain is the success of the efforts that the European Community is making to establish effective cooperation among the nine member countries to accelerate the development, or the recovery, of backward regions. The decision to establish an ad hoc Regional Development Fund offers a gleam of hope. However, the magnitude of this fund and its division among the net contributing and the net benefiting countries are still the subject of hot disputes. On the other hand, it can hardly be expected that the provision of these additional resources will substantially contribute to solving European regional problems so long as the countries concerned hesitate to harmonize their economic and monetary policies.

In the present circumstances, it seems realistic to conclude by dampening any expectation for a rapid strengthening of Italy's regional policy, or for a rapid recovery of the time and opportunities that have been lost during the past twenty-five years.

ACKNOWLEDGEMENTS

My greatest debt is to Niles Hansen who exercised great editorial care in shaping and reducing the earlier drafts of my contribution and in clarifying the many stylistic imperfections and obscurities inherent in the use of a foreign language.

I am also deeply indebted to all my colleagues whose enlightened comments and suggestions were of great help in revising the manuscript for publication. My gratitude goes especially to G. Ammassari, F. Fiorelli, A. Graziani, A. Marzotto, N. Novacco, G. Podbielski, and G. Schachter.

However, I remain fully responsible for the opinions expressed in the text and for the inexactitudes that it may contain.

Chapter Six

Regional Policy in the Netherlands

HISTORICAL BACKGROUND

The approach to regional problems in a country shows the characteristics of its socioeconomic system and administrative framework. In the case of the Netherlands we are confronted with a relatively small but very densely populated country. Although distances are small and the national economy is in the same stage of development as that of other Western European countries, during the past decades continuous and growing attention has been paid to regional planning.

The interest in regional planning dates back to the years after the Second World War. While the country as a whole was enjoying a period of almost full employment, some areas in the north and south were suffering from lack of employment; these were the same regions that had shown the highest unemployment during the first part of the thirties (Table 6-1).

Research done by the Ministry of Economic Affairs on the region with the highest unemployment, southeast Drenthe, led to the conclusion that the basic problem in that region was the decline in the demand for labor in some traditional activities (agriculture, peat cutting), combined with rapid natural increase in population. On the basis of this a development plan for southeast Drenthe was formulated and approved by Parliament on July 13, 1951. This was, in fact, the beginning of regional policy in the Netherlands.

A second step was taken rather soon afterward. A number of criteria were formulated to decide whether or not an area should be given special assistance. These criteria were that

1. the problem of structural employment should be acute;
2. migration would not be a reasonable solution;

**Table 6-1.   Unemployment of Males as a Percentage of Male
Occupational Population in Some Regions**

Area	1950	1951
Southeast Drenthe	15.5	13.8
East Groningen	6.6	8.0
East Friesland	3.9	5.2
Southeast Noordbrabant	8.3	8.4
Northeast Noordbrabant	4.5	4.4
Netherlands	2.5	2.9

Source: Ministry of Labor.

3. industrialization might be expected to provide a solution; and
4. the costs of carrying out the development plan could be kept within reasonable and acceptable limits.

On the basis of these criteria the government designated, besides southeast Drenthe, eight other development areas (see Map 6-1). The law on regional development plans was passed by Parliament on June 23, 1952.

Thus, Netherlands regional policy started out as a campaign to combat structural regional unemployment. The special assistance given to development areas to make them attractive for industries consisted of:

1. construction of industrial sites;
2. improvement of transport infrastructure;
3. improvement of public utilities;
4. construction of industrial buildings;
5. training and retraining of workers; and
6. construction of houses for employees of new industries in development areas.

Furthermore, the government intended to grant an allowance to unemployed laborers who migrated out of areas with structural unemployment to other parts of the country. This measure, which was intended to stimulate the mobility of labor, was not very successful: from 1952 to 1958 only 3,466 persons made use of it, and in 1959 the whole scheme was dropped.

As we have seen, the concept of Netherlands regional policy was a simple one to begin with. Being confronted with areas suffering from lack of employment, the government tried to influence the mobility of capital in favor of these areas on the one hand, and the mobility of labor out of them on the other. Unemployed labor being in most cases not very mobile, the latter measure was not much of a success.

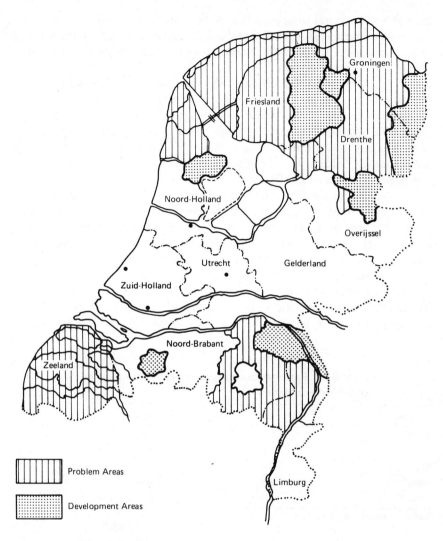

Map 6-1. Development Areas and Problem Areas

Before going on to discuss the subsequent stages in the evolution of Netherlands regional policy, let us first provide some factual information.

FACTUAL INFORMATION

If we divide the Netherlands into four different parts—i.e., North (the provinces Groningen, Friesland, and Drenthe); East (Overijssel and Gelderland); West (Utrecht, North Holland, South Holland, and Zeeland); and South (North

Brabant and Limburg)—it appears that in the North, regional unemployment has been high over quite a long period (Table 6-2). The income data (Table 6-3) lead to an analogous conclusion. The North proves to be the region with the lowest average income per taxpayer.

A more detailed review of the structure in the various parts of the Netherlands is given in Table 6-4, which consists of a number of key data concerning the year 1968. About half the population lives in the West on twenty-five percent of the country's area, where secondary and tertiary employment is highly concentrated. In fact, this concentration is limited to what is called Rimcity Holland—i.e., the quadrangle formed by the cities of Amsterdam, The Hague, Rotterdam, and Utrecht.

During the fifties, employment showed a tendency to decentralization from the West to other parts of the country. In analyzing the nature of decentralization from the West it is important to consider three types of industrial sectors: (1) growth sectors whose employment growth exceeds the total industrial average; (2) sectors of average growth; and (3) stagnating sectors.

Among the growth sectors, chemicals, paper, printing, and leather and rubber have shown only a slight tendency to decentralize. Most of these sectors are bound to specific areas: the chemical and paper sectors are located near deep water; the printing industry near its market; and the leather and

Table 6-2.   Regional Unemployment as a Percentage of the Employed Population

Area	1950	1960	1970
North	3.7	3.6	2.3
East	1.6	1.0	1.3
West	2.0	0.9	0.7
South	2.2	1.0	1.6
Netherlands	2.2	1.2	1.2

Source: Central Planning Bureau.

Table 6-3.   Index of Average Income (Netherlands = 100)

Area	1950	1955	1960	1963
North	96.5	88.8	90.1	90.9
East	92.2	90.8	91.2	93.2
West	105.6	107.1	107.4	106.2
South	92.9	93.7	92.8	94.8

Source: Central Planning Bureau.
Note: No more recent data available.

Table 6-4.   Indices of Key Regional Data for 1968
(Netherlands = 100)

	North	East	West	South	*Netherlands* Relative	*Netherlands* Absolute
Area (excluding water)	25	29	25	21	100	338 x 10⁴ hectares
Population	11	19	49	21	100	1266 x 10⁴ million
Population density	44	64	193	102	100	375 per square kilometer
Occupational labor	10	18	51	21	100	447 x 10⁴ million
Total employment	10	18	52	20	100	439 x 10⁴ manyears
in agriculture	18	27	35	20	100	
in industry	10	20	45	25	100	
in services	9	15	60	16	100	
in government	11	16	54	19	100	

Source: Central Planning Bureau

rubber sector near sources of cheap labor. In contrast, the metal industry has experienced substantial decentralization from the West. The South in particular has gained in employment due to the expansion of the metal industry there.

On the whole the industries from the average group have shown a slight tendency to decentralize, due, in general, to the increase in population agglomerations outside the West, which in turn has attracted some service sectors. The decentralization of stagnating industries, mainly the textile sector, from the West can also be considered slight. Since the share of this industry in the West was very small, its gradual contraction there did not have any significant impact on the general decentralization process.

One of the measures used in determining the degree of concentration of certain industries is the coefficient of location. This coefficient is a measure of regional concentration based on the regional distribution of an industrial activity compared to some total national quantity such as population, land area, etc. Vanhove (1962) calculated this coefficient for thirty-five sectors for the years 1953 and 1960, in order to determine more explicitly the tendency of some sectors to concentrate in certain areas. He found that twenty-eight out of thirty-five sectors had lower coefficients of location in 1960 than in 1953. Since larger coefficients mean high concentrations, this indicates that the tendency to concentrate decreased during that period. The main sectors showing the largest decreases were the mechanical and electrotechnical, clothing, and timber sectors.

Thus it can be concluded that the process of decentralization was not necessarily propelled by weak industries; indeed, one of the most important growth industries, the metal industry, had a major role in this process.

Among the factors which determine industrial location and influence decentralization are the following:

1. The costs of land and construction. These can be influenced by the availability and suitability of certain sites for an industrial estate.
2. The transport cost. The role of this factor in location theory is well-known from the pioneering work of Alfred Weber (1909).
3. The labor cost. This is also one of the general factors which Weber found to be important in connection with the location of industry. In this context the availability of labor with different skills plays an important role too.
4. Other costs of production. These include the costs of raw material, water, energy, etc.
5. Factors on the demand side. These have to do with the market for the goods produced by the industry.
6. Agglomeration factors. These include the presence of supplying firms, service and auxiliary functions, social and cultural amenities, etc.
7. Institutional factors. These concern the special treatment given to the areas in terms of premiums, subsidies, etc., and the location of governmental activities.

Since we are trying to find an explanation for the general process of decentralization from the West only the factors that affect industry in general—rather than a specific sector—are relevant. The following equation is used to explain the relative decentralization from the West:

$$D = f(A, T, S, G) \qquad (6.1)$$

D is the decentralization index per industry, defined as the ratio between, on the one hand, the difference in the shares of the West in the employment in a given industry in, respectively, 1953 and 1960, and on the other hand, the share of the West in this industry in 1953. Thus,

$$D = \frac{\dfrac{E_i^W (53)}{E_i^N (53)} - \dfrac{E_i^W (60)}{E_i^N (60)}}{\dfrac{E_i^W (53)}{E_i^N (53)}},$$

where E_i^W and E_i^N respectively denote employment in industry i in the West and in the whole of the Netherlands.

A is the share of wages in the gross value added. This variable reflects both the quantity of labor and the wage level.

T is the weight of material used per worker. It is the most representative measure of the difference between a light and a heavy industry. This variable contains the elements of transport costs, since a major part of the materials comes through the ports of the West. It is used as a substitute for the true transport cost factor because the shares of transport costs of raw materials and products cannot easily be isolated from the prices of products.

S represents the share of skilled workers in the total labor force employed. This factor has a qualitative element and is supposed to inhibit the decentralization process, since the market for skilled labor is concentrated in the West. While variable A will influence D positively, S will influence D negatively.

G is the percentage increase of employment in a given industry between the years 1950 and 1960. This is included in the regression equation because, as shown in the foregoing section, growth sectors tend to have wider choice than others in locating their factories.

The result of the estimation is:

$$D = 0.556\,A - 0.327\,T - 0.211\,S + 0.118\,G - 20.63 \qquad (6.2)$$
$$\quad (0.238) \qquad (0.149) \qquad (0.105) \qquad (0.062)$$

$$(R = 0.782)$$

It is clear that the labor intensity factor (A) and the growth factor (G) stimulate decentralization, while the transport cost factor (T) and the skill factor (S) inhibit this process. The negative sign of the constant term points to the fact that there are still other factors which can influence the choice of location, in this case a concentration in the West, to which all separate industries used in the regression react in a more or less uniform manner.

From this analysis we may conclude that the typical Weberian location factors of labor costs and transport costs are important factors in the explanation of the industrial decentralization process.

The provinces which benefited particularly from the decentralization out of the West were North Brabant and Gelderland, each of which experienced rapid increase in population. Both are situated not too far from the economic gravity point in the West.

REGIONAL POLICY ISSUES

National and Regional Economic Policy Goals

The goals of national economic policy can be specified as follows:

1. full employment;
2. stability of prices;
3. equity of the balance of payments;
4. economic growth; and
5. acceptable distribution of income.

As we have seen a few sections back, Netherlands regional policy is typically an employment policy. It is regional structural unemployment that provides the argument for government action. Stagnating regional economic growth and relatively declining income per capita are no reasons for special measures unless they go hand in hand with acute and structural unemployment. This makes Netherlands regional policy in fact a social rather than an economic policy, for it is intended to help those who are most backward, irrespective of their growth potential.

It would, however, be going too far to state that Netherlands regional policy is completely void of economic aspects. They are, in fact, represented in the form of attention paid to the growth pole concept. The basic idea behind growth pole theory is that growth is practically never widely dispersed but takes place in nuclei, in which each additional activity tends to improve conditions for further growth.

When a new activity is started in a given region, this has the effect of creating value added which, as far as it is spent locally, will give rise to new impulses. This income increase means an increase in the size of the local market and that makes the area more attractive for the location of new activities.

The problem remains, however, that this growth process does not take place to the same extent in all the regions of the country. The geographical situation, and autonomous trends in existing branches of activities (agriculture, for instance), as well as the infrastructural system, the location of government, etc., will all affect the extent of regional growth. In a diversified region where goods and services needed are produced locally, a larger proportion of the growth impulses will remain in the region itself than will be the case in a one-sided economy where the effects will leak out to other regions.

A second effect has to be mentioned. Increases in income and employment in a region will influence the demand for amenities such as education, medical care, housing, etc. Expansion of the available amenities will again increase the attractiveness of the area concerned for the location of new activities.

These two effects call for a regional development policy directed toward nuclei, and it is this nuclei policy that has played and still plays an important role in Netherlands regional economic policy. In 1953 there was added to the existing instruments that of granting direct financial support to companies locating in certain designated nuclei in development regions. This premium amounted to twenty-five percent of the construction costs of new industrial buildings up to a certain maximum, which was raised periodically. Thus the concept of regional dispersion by concentration entered Netherlands regional planning as a strategy. The government introduced this concept on the considerations that (1) centralization of amenities makes for sizable economies of scale; and (2) the effectiveness of the support given to development regions might be improved by this new strategy.

The Effectiveness of Dutch Regional
Policy in the First Period

Has regional policy as described so far been successful? Vanhove (1962) attempted to measure the effects of this policy by means of an equation explaining the percentage growth of industrial employment in seventy-eight economic-geographic areas in the period 1950-1960. He began by using four explanatory variables:

U   = average unemployment between the years 1950-1960

S   = average share of employment in the chemical and metal
       sectors in total employment

I   = degree of industrialization in 1950

L   = average income per taxpayer in industry in 1955

However, he arrived at the following equation, with two highly significant explanatory variables:

$$Y = 7.613\,U - 10.178\,L + 43.80 \qquad\qquad (6.3)$$
$$\quad (1.300) \qquad (3.857) \qquad\qquad\qquad (R = 0.815)$$

where Y is the percentage growth of industrial employment in the period 1950-1960.

The significant role of the rate of unemployment variable (U) points to the fact that the situation in the regional labor markets in the Netherlands between 1950-1960 varied widely. Generally, these markets were rather tight and the limit of full employment (three percent unemployment) was overstepped only once, in 1952. This created considerable tension in the labor market and suggests the important role of U in explaining the growth of employment. The significant role of the variable L testifies to the fact that industries are still attracted by markets with cheaper labor.

Although the above equation generally provides sufficient explanation for Y in the sample of seventy-eight areas, it is interesting to find out how far it can explain Y in development areas. This is of some importance in connection with regional policy regarding these areas. According to Vanhove, the efficiency of the policy can be read off from the residuals—i.e., the difference between the observed and the estimated values of Y. Table 6-5 contains these figures for the nine main development areas.

These results show that on the whole the estimated equation does not adequately explain Y in the development areas. Vanhove cautiously concludes that east Friesland, northeast Overijssel, the northeastern part of North-Brabant, and north Limburg would not have attained the actual growth of employment without the measures of regional economic policy. This conclusion is based on the large and positive residuals seen in these areas. For the southwestern part of North Brabant a similar conclusion applies, when the area is redefined to comprise only the true development region in the area.

For southeast Drenthe, regional policy can also be considered effective if we allow for the fact that unemployment in Drenthe—and to a lesser extent in a few other northern areas—has a character somewhat different from that in most other areas. In Drenthe and other northern areas most of the unemployed are aged workers who had always been employed in traditional activities that are now disappearing; moreover, it is difficult to retrain them for other jobs. Their presence, represented by variable U in Equation (6.3), does not stimulate the expansion of industrial employment to the extent suggested by the

Table 6-5.   Observed and Estimated Growth of Industrial Employment in the Development Areas, 1950-1960

Development area	Observed Y percent	Estimated Y percent	Residual
Southwest Groningen	11.2	17.0	− 5.8
East Groningen	20.5	36.0	−15.5
East Friesland	63.1	42.6	+20.5
Southeast Drenthe	64.8	64.0	+ 0.8
Northeast Overijssel	51.2	37.1	+14.1
Eastern part of West Friesland	7.9	13.2	− 5.3
Southwestern part of North Brabant	28.8	20.0	+ 8.8
Northeastern part of North Brabant	86.4	23.5	+62.9
North Limburg	77.8	20.3	+57.5

equation. In spite of a large negative residual for east Groningen, Vanhove suggests that there, too, regional policy has been effective, the lagging "observed employment growth" being due to factors similar to those in the case of Drenthe.

Although these conclusions sound quite credible, the way they have been reached calls for some reservations. Vanhove, realizing this, twice warns the reader with the term "cautious" in connection with his judgment. For one thing, the economic-geographic division of areas can sometimes lead to inconsistencies. We have seen this in the case of the southwestern part of North Brabant, which is composed partly of development areas and partly of normal areas. Moreover, the relevant labor market of a given area may be wider than the economic-geographic area to which it belongs. This is particularly true when the pace of development is rapid. In addition, there might easily be some other significant explanatory variables besides the two used in Equation (6.3). The pattern of residuals could change if such variables were included. We have seen in the foregoing section that many factors can be influential in the determination of industrial location. It is possible that these influences are caught up in the residuals of the equation, which uses only the labor market factors.

Population Distribution

After the Second World War, the Rhine became even more important as a link between the world's most intensively sailed sea—the North Sea—and the continent of Europe. Amsterdam and Rotterdam in particular have developed their seaport functions, while the third main center, The Hague, has flourished on the strength of its administrative and diplomatic functions. Within the urban environment of these cities many other activities also have sprung up. Because of the enormous concentration of economic activities and population within the Amsterdam-The Hague-Rotterdam-Utrecht area, it has come to be known as Rimcity Holland—the economic gravity center of the Netherlands.

One of the problems in the Rimcity is that urban radiation increasingly affects its inner belt, which rightly is called the Green Heart of Holland, an area which is considered essential to the whole region from the point of view of living environment. Another problem is that the regional cities are becoming less and less attractive as residential areas. Among the reasons for this phenomenon are smaller families, increasing demand for separate homes for independent individuals, and demand for more space per household member. Also, housing conditions in the existing centers are considered insufficient; growing economic activities (offices, shops) in the inner cities and heavy traffic flows require so much space that there is a severe shortage of space for residential purposes.

In 1956 two governmental institutions, the Central Planning Agency and the National Spatial Planning Agency, jointly published a booklet entitled "The West and the Rest of the Netherlands." This first report on national spatial planning argues the urgency of a government policy that would promote a better distribution of economic activities and of population over the country. Since that time the Netherlands government has taken a more active approach to spatial planning. A Spatial Planning Act was passed in 1962, and in 1966 a program of positive policy was formulated in the Second Memorandum on Spatial Planning, in which the government defined the purpose of spatial planning to be "promotion of the best spatial structure to serve the development of the people's welfare."

The goals to be achieved were:

1. prevention of the strong outmigration of population threatening to drain the economic and social life of peripheral areas;
2. prevention of excessive income differences among regions; and
3. prevention of excessive congestion in concentrated areas.

The only quantitative criterion concerned population distribution. Table 6-6 shows the aims of population dispersal policy. In the North, population was to increase from 1.3 million in 1965 to 3 million by 2000, meaning that the population share of this part of the country would increase from 10.7 percent of the national population in 1965 to 15.4 percent by 2000.

The instruments for achieving these goals are virtually the same as those used for government action to combat regional structural unemployment—i.e., they emphasize housing, investment promotion, and transport facilities. We may, in fact, conclude that one policy (stimulating capital mobility) has evolved to deal with a combination of two problems (structural unemployment in certain areas, and the need to prevent further congestion of population in the Rimcity). Mobility of labor is encouraged only inside "development" or "problem" areas, and then only with respect to movement to development nuclei and mobility from declining occupations to those with a more promising future (with the aid of retraining assistance).

The Administrative Framework

The administrative organization in the Netherlands is centralized to a relatively high degree. Between the central government and the over 800 municipalities there is an intermediary level, represented by the provincial

Table 6-6. Population Distribution in the Netherlands, 1965 and 2000

Regions	Actual 1965		Desired 2000	
	in millions	in percent	in millions	in percent
North	1.30	10.7	3.00	15.4
Rest	10.80	89.3	16.50	84.6
Netherlands	12.10	100.0	19.50	100.0

authorities. Because taxes are nearly all collected centrally, local and provincial governments have only limited financial resources of their own, which makes them highly dependent on allocations of centrally administered funds. Nevertheless, there are opportunities for local initiative, which finds expression in the form of recommendations to the national government; on the other hand, the latter frequently employs lower authorities to implement its policies.

To understand how the system works in the field of regional planning, one should call to mind the two main lines of regional planning followed in the Netherlands: regional industrialization policy and spatial planning.

The regional industrialization policy leans heavily on the Ministry of Economic Affairs. It is the minister of economic affairs who, albeit after consulting the provincial authorities, decides upon the designation of development or problem areas and development nuclei. Only against this background can one understand that the first designation of development nuclei comprised forty-two towns, later to be reduced to twelve by writing off the less successful ones.

While the allocation of migration allowances is a task of the Ministry of Labor, the spatial planning system comes under the control of the Ministry of Housing and Spatial Planning. Under the Social Housing Act the latter ministry is authorized to assign extra housing quotas to development nuclei in order to support the migration of industries. Moreover, this ministry formulates the objectives to be achieved through nationwide redistribution of population. The Ministries of Agriculture, Social Affairs, Labor, and Economic Affairs together have formed an interministerial committee with a view to coordinating regional policies. The Ministry of Agriculture is involved in this committee on the strength of its reallotment program; the Ministry of Social Affairs has additional funds available for stimulating social amenities in development nuclei.

The Spatial Planning Act of 1962 authorizes local and provincial governments to prepare and decide on plans for the spatial organization of their own area or parts of it. In every province, the Ministry of Housing and Spatial Planning has its inspectors to make sure that such plans are in line with the objectives of the national government.

The Second Phase of Regional Economic Policy

In 1959 the government declared that henceforth regional policy was to aim not only at combating regional structural unemployment, but also at the dispersion of industry and economic activities. At the same time a much larger portion of the peripheral areas was designated for special assistance. Next to areas with structural unemployment, areas showing population losses were to be considered as problem areas. Maintaining the principle of freedom of location for companies, the government continued to use the instruments of direct (premiums) and indirect (improvement of infrastructure) subsidies. The subsidy for construction costs, available to industries locating on a designated municipal estate, was complemented by a fifty percent reduction in the price of land. Both new companies and existing firms extending their establishments were subsidized. Migration allowances became available to unemployed laborers migrating inside problem areas to development nuclei as well as to employed laborers migrating with their companies from the West to a development nucleus in a problem area.

The policy based on development nuclei underwent yet another change when the minister of economic affairs stated in the Sixth Memorandum on Industrialization "that only a limited number of development nuclei are to be designated and that only such towns must be designated as offer the best chances to attract employment for the occupational population of the area concerned." The minister made a distinction between primary and secondary nuclei, considering as primary nuclei those towns which had already shown important industrial development in the past and where, according to the authorities, conditions justified the expectation of a reasonably successful policy. Assistance to secondary nuclei was gradually brought to a conclusion by diminishing the stimulating efforts, but final termination of support to these centers was postponed until 1972 because the recession of the years 1967 and 1968 caused a rise in unemployment precisely in some areas around such secondary nuclei.

The Third Phase of Regional Policy

A third phase in Dutch regional policy began in 1969. Contrary to the expectations awakened by certain publications about problems faced in the congested areas in the West, the minister of economic affairs, in his memorandum on regional policy for the years 1969-1972 issued at the end of 1968, said that the structural unemployment prevailing in certain areas must remain the government's primary concern. In view of the high unemployment figures of the preceding years this statement is understandable, but it is possible that the financial support given was confined too strictly to industrial companies that created new employment opportunities. In periods of economic boom the West is confronted by tight labor markets, and it is at such times that western companies are apt to delegate work to contractors in more peripheral areas where labor is more plentiful, or to locate affiliated companies in development areas. Labor-intensive industries are particularly interested in such opportunities. When, however, a subsequent recession brings a decline in contract work or causes labor-intensive affiliates to close down, then the consequences for the supported region tend to be all the worse. Such phenomena are not unknown in the peripheral areas of the western economic gravity centers.

Another unfavorable development is the continuous migration of higher skilled people to the West. The education system is the same all over the country, but labor-intensive companies searching for locations in development areas mostly create a demand for lower skilled personnel. This explains why demand for labor and migration of unemployed labor can go hand in hand.

The point is that government regional policy has been directed only slightly towards investments in depth, so that very few companies with technologically complicated production processes have been induced to locate in supported areas. Recognizing these weaknesses, the government stated in a Memorandum on the North of the Country (1972) that "attention should be drawn to the location of industries with very capital-intensive production processes. The primary goal of such attention is not the creation of new jobs, but first and foremost the creation of opportunities for other activities which may stimulate each other." To realize this intention, the existing policy instruments were extended by a so-called investment premium scheme. Thanks to this scheme it is now possible to get a subsidy not only on construction and land costs but also on the price paid for machines and industrial equipment. The premium amounts to twenty-five percent of the total investment costs up to a maximum of Dfl. 3 million. The scheme applies to service industries, too.

For the sake of completeness it has to be remarked that in a number of cases companies may obtain a state guarantee on loans and credits and that the state is permitted to participate in companies as a temporary shareholder. Apart from this, opportunities have been created for an interest subsidy of up to three percent.

Although some spatial differentiation has been introduced into regional planning (for instance the distinction between primary and secondary nuclei), regional differentiation has been, in fact, lacking. The successive premium schemes were highly objective: every location or extension that met the conditions formulated had to be subsidized, whether or not its location in a certain region was appropriate. No attention had been given to the special needs and problems of each development area individually. We will see that recent trends in regional planning do take this point into account.

Recent Trends in Regional Planning

Regional planning in the Netherlands became a topic for discussion in Parliament at the end of 1973 when the government introduced a bill and presented two memoranda on the subject. The bill aimed at limiting by a selective procedure the investments in congested areas, more precisely in the Rimcity, so as to decrease the disadvantages bound up with continuous concentration of people and activities in those areas. The law, since passed by Parliament, contains a system of licenses required for every investment which involves more than a certain minimum amount of money. Whether such a license can be granted is to be judged on the basis of what the investment implies for the concentration of activities and population, for the economic structure of the area, and for its labor market. In the meantime, the investment's implications for the spatial structure of the Rimcity will be evaluated, in order to prevent the green heart of the Rimcity from falling a victim to further urban sprawl.

In one of its memoranda, the government draws attention to the special problems of the region around the city of The Hague, where a population growth up to one million inhabitants was expected in a region which can accommodate no more than 650,000. The government intends to intervene by checking private investments (with the help of the above-mentioned law) and dispersing governmental institutions to more peripheral parts of the country, in particular to the North and to south Limburg.

The second memorandum concerns the North; in it the government designated this region as a problem area and also as an area to which people and economic activities from the Rimcity should be directed. At least one urban agglomeration in the North is supposed to grow to such an extent that it can serve as a countermagnet to the Rimcity. The city of Groningen has been selected to fulfill this function, and, toward this end a special regional development program has been announced.

CONCLUSION

The general direction of Dutch regional planning can be sketched as follows. It began as a program to combat structural unemployment in a number of lagging regions. Regional industrialization policies proved more successful than migration policies, so more and more attention was given to the task of bringing jobs to the people rather than bringing people to jobs. Toward the middle of the sixties, the disadvantages of the heavy concentration of people and economic activities in the Rimcity became apparent, and the allowances which had been paid to those migrating to the West from backward regions were restricted. Meanwhile, subsidies on land and investment costs were added to the instruments of regional industrialization policy, which until then had consisted of subsidies on construction costs. The growth pole concept was introduced to make regional policies more effective. Owing to political pressure from lower governmental levels, too many growth poles (or development nuclei) were at first selected; to remedy this, a distinction between primary and secondary development nuclei was subsequently introduced. At the same time, the definition of "supported areas" was extended to include not only regions with structural unemployment (development regions) but also regions with loss of population; now, the expression "problem areas" has become the vogue. All these measures and developments must be seen against the background of the congestion problems in the West.

Recently, it became clear that more and more attention must be given to the problems of the Rimcity. Instruments to brake investments in the Rimcity were introduced, as well as a policy of dispersion of governmental institutions. An attempt has been made to solve the problems of both the Rimcity and the North by designating Groningen as the potential countermagnet to the attraction of the Rimcity. This adds a new dimension to regional planning in Holland: regions are no longer perceived as separate entities but as parts of a system of regions.

The announcement of a special development program for the North also means that the principle of nondiscriminating policy instruments has been abandoned in favor of growing attention to each region's specific characteristics and its potential within the national framework. This evolution may be expected to continue in the near future, with respect both to problem areas and to the Rimcity and its central cities. Urban renovation and attempts to channel the outflow of population and economic activities towards a limited number of subcenters (the policy of clustered deconcentration) in order to save the remaining green areas from further urbanization are driving in the same direction. A third Memorandum on Spatial Planning is in preparation and will present a new set of instruments to achieve these goals.

Chapter Seven

Regional Economic Policy: Problems, Analysis, and Political Experiments in Sweden

REGIONAL CONCENTRATION AND INSTITUTIONAL CHARACTERISTICS

Sweden is a long, narrow country and is sparsely populated. The country is divided into twenty-four administrative counties with significantly different population densities. Even the most densely populated county—Stockholm— has, however, a lower density of population than the average for the whole of Great Britain. The differences between counties are illustrated in Figure 7-1.

In 1870, when the process of industrialization started in Sweden, the population distribution was rather different. The most remarkable difference was the relative size of Stockholm county. At that time only approximately seven percent of the total population in Sweden was living in that area. In 1972 the Stockholm share of a much larger national population had increased to approximately eighteen percent.

The general urbanization did not create any serious political problem until the beginning of the 1960s, when the northern counties faced accelerated outmigration. This development is illustrated in Figure 7-2.

Interregional policy is implemented at several different levels, but has generally a very short history. A few institutional facts will illustrate some notable differences between Sweden's and other countries' interregional policy programs.

In Sweden comparatively large powers have been given to local governments at the county and subcounty levels. The two local government bodies (counties and municipalities) together levy a local income tax of approximately twenty-three percent of total household income, which gives them a relatively large share in total government spending. This is the main reason why subsidies to local governments in the poor parts of the country were among the first means used to further regional equality.

The Proportional Area of the Counties   The Proportional Population of the Counties

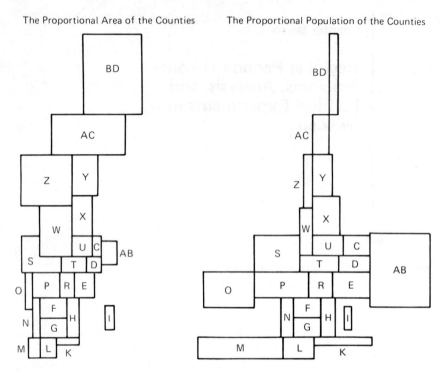

The letters stand for the individual counties, which are referred to throughout this chapter in this way or by their names, as follows:

AB	Stockholm	K	Blekinge	T	Örebro
C	Uppsala	L	Kristianstad	U	Västmanland
D	Södermanland	M	Malmöhus	W	Kopparberg
E	Östergötland	N	Halland	X	Gävleborg
F	Jönköping	O	Göteborg and Bohus	Y	Västernorrland
G	Kronoberg	P	Älvsborg	Z	Jämtland
H	Kalmar	R	Skaraborg	AC	Västerbotten
I	Gotland	S	Värmland	BD	Norrbotten

Figure 7-1. Two Pictures of Sweden

      Although Sweden in all fundamental respects must be regarded as a capitalistic country, there are some government-controlled investments which in most other capitalistic countries are freely planned within the private sector. Construction, and especially housing investment, is firmly controlled by the central government through the Housing Board and the Labor Market Board, with local offices reporting on local employment and investment demand and supply capacities all over the country. Rent control—hidden or overt—in connection with quantitative construction control, and the presence of eco-

Percentage of Population   Counties = National Zone

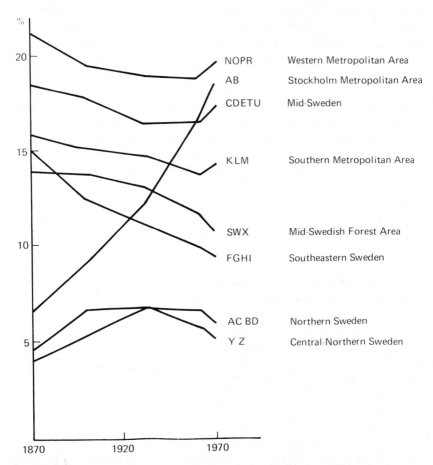

NOPR	Western Metropolitan Area
AB	Stockholm Metropolitan Area
CDETU	Mid-Sweden
KLM	Southern Metropolitan Area
SWX	Mid-Swedish Forest Area
FGHI	Southeastern Sweden
AC BD	Northern Sweden
YZ	Central-Northern Sweden

Figure 7-2. Breakdown of the Population by National Zones in the Period 1870-1970

nomically strong local governments, has made it possible to plan local infrastructure investment together with housing investment in close alignment with relocation of industry and population. This system has in some instances and in some regions meant a balanced expansion of private and public capital. In other regions, and especially in those with a very rapid expansion of industry and population, severe imbalances in local housing markets have developed.

It should also be noted that professional economists and politicians participate more closely in the development of economic policy in Sweden than they do in most other western countries. This is a tradition inherited from the 1930s and the Stockholm School of Economics, with Bertil Ohlin, Gunnar Myrdal, Erik Lindahl, and Erik Lundberg as some of its leading exponents. These economists actively participated in the formation of modern stabilization policy during the 1930s and introduced a principle of government economic research reports as the conventional background to all new economic policy acts. A large number of economics dissertations have been published as government research reports in the SOU series (*Statens Offentliga Utredningar*). Regional economic policy is no exception to this rule. Since the start of the modern location policy, in 1965, practically all research workers in regional science have worked (some only briefly, others over long periods) for the Ministry of Labor and Housing, which is the ministry responsible for regional policy.

The active participation of research workers in policy formation implies that most of the means discussed in this paper can be—and have been—derived from some of the rather formal analyses performed by scholars directly or indirectly employed by the Ministry of Labor and Housing.

PROBLEMS OF ACHIEVING REGIONAL EQUALITY IN INCOME AND EMPLOYMENT

Urbanization and the Development of Regional Inequality in Sweden

At the beginning of the twentieth century half of Sweden's population was engaged in agriculture and forestry. About a third of its working population was employed in manufacturing and construction. The primary communications system was already almost fully developed and all parts of the country were connected by a railway network.

From 1920 to 1970 agriculture and forestry declined from approximately forty percent to eight percent of the working population and in the same time services expanded from approximately thirty percent to more than sixty percent of the working population. Under these circumstances a natural hypothesis would be that the contraction of the relative importance of land-oriented sectors and the corresponding expansion of labor- and capital-oriented sectors would have resulted in a regional concentration of production. Such an hypothesis is however not correct. The relative importance of the different geographical areas remained practically constant during the whole period 1920-1970, as is seen in the data in Table 7-1.

The table shows that the initially dislocated areas in the southeast and the far north have expanded their shares in total income, but the main impression is a very strong tendency to stability in the regional pattern of production. There seem to be strong forces working for stability in the regional allocation of production and capital, although there have been large economic, social, and political changes in the country as a whole.

Table 7-1. Regional Shares in Production Measured as Percent of Total Assessed Income for Sweden in the Period 1920-1970

	Groups of counties	1920	1930	1940	1950	1960	1970
(AB)	Stockholm metropolitan area	26.1	28.7	25.9	23.8	23.4	24.4
(CDETU)	Mid-Sweden	15.1	13.9	15.8	15.8	15.9	16.0
(FGHIR)	Southeast	8.3	8.8	9.6	10.7	10.6	10.8
(KLM)	Southern metropolitan area	14.2	13.6	13.6	13.5	13.2	13.7
(NOP)	Western metropolitan area	17.2	15.7	16.3	15.9	15.4	15.9
(SWX)	Mid-Swedish forest area	10.5	9.8	9.6	10.2	10.3	9.3
(YZ)	Central Northern.	4.7	4.8	4.1	4.7	4.9	4.3
(AC, BD)	Northern	3.6	4.6	5.1	5.3	6.1	5.5

Source: SOS Skattetaxeringarna 1920-1970

It would nevertheless be wrong to conclude that Sweden has been a country without problems of urbanization. There has been a balanced structure of development between the different parts of the country with respect to production and investment but not with respect to the regional allocation of the population. Stockholm had a share in the national production of about twenty-five percent in 1920 but a share in the population at the same time of no more than eleven percent. This is, of course, a measure of great economic inequality. The normal reaction to this inequality would be either a decline in the share of production through outmigration of capital from the Stockholm metropolitan area or inmigration of labor to the same area (or both). Table 7-2 shows that the adaption has been almost totally in the form of migration of labor to the Stockholm area, mainly from the southeast and the Mid-Swedish and Central Northern areas.

Table 7-2. Regional Shares in National Population in the Period 1920-1970 (percent)

	Region	1920	1930	1940	1950	1960	1970
(AB)	Stockholm metropolitan area	11.2	12.2	13.7	15.5	16.8	18.2
(CDETU)	Mid-Sweden	17.3	16.7	16.3	16.5	16.6	17.0
(FGHIR)	Southeast	15.5	15.0	14.4	13.9	13.2	12.8
(KLM)	Southern metropolitan area	14.8	14.7	14.5	14.1	13.7	14.0
(NOP)	Western metropolitan area	14.8	15.0	15.2	15.3	15.6	16.1
(SWX)	Mid-Swedish forest area	13.4	13.1	12.5	11.8	11.7	10.7
(YZ)	Central Northern.	6.7	6.7	6.5	6.1	5.7	5.0
(AC, BD)	Northern	6.2	6.5	6.8	6.7	6.7	6.1

Table 7-3.   Share of Income in Relation to Share of Population
1920-1970

Region		1920	1960	1970
(AB)	Stockholm metropolitan area	2.330	1.393	1.341
(CDETU)	Mid-Sweden	0.884	0.958	0.941
(FGHIR)	Southeast	0.535	0.803	0.844
(KLM)	Southern metropolitan area	0.959	0.963	0.978
(NOP)	Western metropolitan area.	1.162	0.987	0.987
(SWX)	Mid-Swedish forest area	0.783	0.880	0.869
(YZ)	Central Northern.	0.701	0.860	0.860
(AC, BD)	Northern	0.581	0.910	0.902

The two tables of the development of regional allocation of income and population can be combined into a table showing the share of income in relation to the share in population in the same period. Table 7-3 gives an indication of the long-term development of the regional income distribution in the country and shows that there was a spontaneous decline in regional income inequality from 1920 to 1960. The table also shows that there has been a stagnation in the process of equalization in the 1960s, which is the period of *explicit* regional policy.

It is my opinion that failure to achieve income equalization during the first period of regional economic policy in Sweden has been mainly a consequence of the failure to cope with short-run regional unemployment problems and to coordinate long-run communication and location policies.

The following sections of this chapter will deal successively with short-term, medium-term, and long-term regional economic policy from this background.

Modern Labor Market Policy as a
Means to Achieve Equality of
Wages and Employment

Already in the 1930s Swedish politicians adopted the Keynesian means to reduce unemployment on a national level. Their policies were concentrated on expansion of government expenditure without any corresponding increase in the rate of taxation. The expansion of government demand was consciously used to stimulate general demand through the working of the multiplier. In this way firms could be induced to reengage the unemployed.

At the end of the 1940s unemployment had been reduced to a comparatively low level, with corresponding general inflation and increasing problems in the balance of payments. The problem which is often illustrated in the Phillips curve was thus a political issue in Sweden at the end of the 1940s. A group of economists—mainly Bent Hansen, Erik Lundberg, and Gösta Rehn—

became engaged in the discussion of the conflict between stable prices and unemployment. It was realized that a low level of registered unemployment at the national level coupled with an implied high rate of inflation was normally accompanied by extensive unemployment in certain industrial sectors, occupations, and regions. This regional and sectoral unemployment problem seems to have been comparatively pronounced in countries like Sweden, which has a long, narrow geographical form and a history of development from a technologically backward and very dispersed agrarian and forestry economy to a modern postindustrial state within eight decades.

As early as 1950 two economists working within the Swedish association of labor unions—Gösta Rehn and Rudolf Meidner—developed the theory of Modern Labor Market Policy (MLMP). MLMP had the following theoretical foundation: Suppose that there is a centralized wage policy working for an equalization of wages in the whole economy (called "the solidarity principle") subject to constraints imposed by the development of prices, and influencing the terms of trade with other countries and the desired rate of growth of the national product. The negotiated general increase in wages would be rather large, implying a sharply declining demand for labor in certain regions and sectors facing low productivity, and low income elasticity of demand in the product market. The government could then act in two ways: it could either subsidize the firms in order to prevent shut downs or it could increase the sectoral and regional mobility of the people in danger of becoming unemployed. Actual policies in the period 1955-1965 show that mobility measures were favored politically, which means that the Meidner-Rehn model was never followed completely.

The increased mobility of labor would be the means to:

1. avoid unemployment in the stagnant sectors and regions;
2. avoid excess demand for labor in the advancing sectors and regions, thus checking inflation; and
3. increase the rate of reallocation of labor, thus increasing the rate of economic growth in the economy as a whole.

Swedish politicians demonstrated their willingness to experiment on the basis of a theoretical model when, in 1955, the AMS (Labor Market Board) gained the financial ability to launch a system of subsidies to increase the geographical, occupational, and sectoral mobility of labor.

The budget of the AMS increased from 0.8 percent of the federal budget in 1955 to five percent in 1965, the year of reorientation of Swedish regional policy. After ten years of increasing subsidies for the mobility of labor there were still large discrepancies between different parts of the country. These differences in conditions of the local labor markets are illustrated in Table 7-4.

Table 7-4. Situation in Different Local Labor Markets, 1965

Agglomeration group	Number of regions in agglomeration group	Situation in labor market
Number of persons living within a radius of approximately twenty miles around the central place		Number of registered unemployed as a percentage of the number of vacant jobs
1,340,000 or more	1	15
197,000-646,000	3	22
133,000-184,000	8	52
96,000-132,000	11	49
60,000-92,000	17	87
29,800-59,000	30	96
The country as a whole	70	53

Source: AMS: Meddelanden från utredningsbyrån, 1966.

Statistics of this kind indicated that mobility measures would not be sufficient to reduce regional disparities in potential employment. In 1965 the political catch phrase in regional policy was changed from "men to jobs" to "jobs to men." The main means for obtaining this new end was a capital subsidy scheme which, during its first period of use, had the structure shown in Table 7-5, where only the means of location policy and not the means of MLMP are shown.

After seven years, the use of these mainly capital-subsidizing means in regional policy has been highly disappointing. The regional variation in employment, which was reduced during the period 1950-1965, increased in the period 1965-1970. The still severe regional unemployment problem is illustrated by the data in Table 7-6.

The development of the regional problem in Sweden during the 1950s and 1960s shows that a regional policy concentrating on subsidies to labor mobility in the expanding regions and subsidies to capital formation in the lagging regions is insufficient as a means of reaching the most vital of regional policy goals—the goal of full employment in all regions.

MLMP, Unemployment, and Wages:
An Econometric Study

Although a number of measures aimed at increasing the mobility of labor were introduced between 1955 and 1965, the effect on regional income and employment equality was disappointing. MLMP was built on a theoretical foundation that was partly neoclassical; firms were assumed to have downward sloping demand curves with respect to real wages, and labor was assumed to have

Table 7-5. The Structure of Regional Subsidies, 1965-1971

Type of subsidy	Proportion in total federal regional policy budget (percent)
Subsidies to local government expenditure	58
Subsidies to investment in private firms	36
Subsidies to education within private firms	5
Subsidies to local employment	1

Source: DS: Ministry of Labor and Housing.

Table 7-6. Unemployment as a Percentage of Total Labor Force in Different Regions, 1971

H1 Stockholm metropolitan area	2.7
H2 Göteborg and Malmö metropolitan areas	3.2
H3 Municipalities with populations of more than 90,000 within a distance of twenty miles	4.0
H4 Municipalities with populations of 27,000 to 90,000 within a distance of twenty miles and with more than 300,000 within sixty miles distance	3.9
H5 Municipalities with less than 300,000 within sixty miles distance (northern coastal regions)	9.4
H6 Less densely populated areas (northern inland regions)	11.2

Source: AMS: Meddelande från utredningsbyrån, (1972), p. 34.

a positively sloping supply curve. The wage negotiations according to the solidarity principle would then have a strong tendency to cause unemployment in stagnant sectors and regions. The main remedy was subsidies to labor mobility.

It is of considerable interest to test the assumed covariations in an econometric interregional labor market model in which I have used data for the Swedish counties in 1970. In this linear model, supply in a given region is assumed to be determined positively by the level of wages and negatively by the level of unemployment. Demand is determined negatively by wages and positively by the relative communication advantages for the region. Total employment in a region is assumed to be determined by the level of demand at a given level of wages and a given level of communication advantages. The difference between supply and demand is the level of unemployment.

A linear estimation of the supply and demand relations (performed in reduced forms) gives the expected results. The supply relation has the following structure:

$$S_i = 0.01 \ w_i - 10 \ U_i + k \qquad (7.1)$$

where
S_i = supply of labor in region i (normalized with respect to differences in population)

w_i = level of wages in region i

U_i = level of unemployment in region i (normalized)

k = a constant

The demand relation has the following structure:

$$D_i = -0.01 \ w_i + 1.15 \ T_i + h \qquad (7.2)$$

where
D_i = demand in region i (normalized)

T_i = accessibility in region i, as measured by air distance

k = a constant

A similar model with other accessibility arguments gives a better fit in the wage-determination equation and as good a fit in the employment equation. Two measures of accessibilities are considered in this context:

P_1 = accessibility to population within approximately twenty miles radius of the regional center

P_2 = accessibility to population within approximately sixty miles radius of the regional center

The reduced forms give the following estimates:

$$\bar{w}_{it} = 485 \ U_{it} + 7 \ P_{1 \cdot it} + 2 \ P_{2 \cdot it} + k_1; \qquad R^2 = 0.74$$
$$\quad\quad (4.5) \quad\quad (5.4) \quad\quad (3.4)$$

$$L_{it} = 6 \ U_{it} \qquad\qquad + 0.03 \ P_{2 \cdot it} + k_2; \quad R^2 = 0.79$$
$$\quad (4) \qquad\qquad\qquad (3.4)$$

$$(7.3)$$

The t-values are given below each parameter. It is not possible to identify the original supply and demand equations, but the coefficients on the unemployment variables are sufficiently close to estimates of the former equations to allow a partial identification of the wage elasticities of supply and demand.

An inclusion of regional differences in the stocks of capital and in the structure of industry should further increase the capacity to explain the regional differences in employment (see pp. 218-220).

Elasticity of labor supply with respect to wages: +0.25 to +0.38
Elasticity of labor supply with respect to unemployment: −0.6 to −0.8
Elasticity of labor demand with respect to wages: −0.36 to −0.42
Elasticity of labor demand with respect to first model
  accessibility: +0.1 to +0.2

The estimated functions show that there is a clear conflict between the three goals of full employment in all regions, equality in wages among regions, and stable population in all regions.

The period between 1955 and 1970 witnessed an ever-increasing emphasis on the "solidarity principle" in regional wage determination. The Swedish association of labor unions (LO) has thus in its centralized negotiations increasingly demanded wage increases in inverse relation to the wage rate in the previous negotiation period.

According to the estimated functions this has increased unemployment and consequently outmigration from areas with a low accessibility index (which in the long run also further decreases the accessibility index). The MLMP with its subsidies to interregional migrants could thus be looked upon as a collective means for those employed after equalization of wages to compensate the unemployed through the wage equalization policy.

According to the estimates the spontaneous migration in the case of "full" employment in all regions and correspondingly larger income differences should be greater than under the present system of equalized income and large differences in unemployment.

It is also obvious that migration selectivity would, given the present ystem, help to reduce welfare. High levels of local unemployment hit mainly the oldest employees. Private benefits minus costs of migration for these employees are often exceedingly small or even negative, which means that they tend to prefer to remain unemployed until they get their retirement pensions. Firms, on the other hand, prefer the potential outmigrants below thirty-five years of age. Thus, there seems to be a marked intergenerational distribution problem associated with the system of wage negotiations according to the solidarity principle when applied to the adversely located region. Both the estimations show that the short-run regional economic policy has to work with means to reduce wages as costs to firms, and that regional development in the long run can be influenced through communications policies.

EVALUATION OF SHORT-TERM REGIONAL
POLICY IN SWEDEN, 1950-1970

No real regional policies were used in the period 1950-1955 to reduce the large discrepancies among regions in standard of living as reflected in income per capita and employment opportunities. At the theoretical level these problems were, however, intensely discussed, and the introduction of modern labor market policy in 1955 provided for both industrial and regional policies. This set of instruments was mainly designed to increase the mobility of labor in order to avoid sectoral and regional unemployment as a consequence of solidarity-based wage negotiations.

This system was crucially dependent on the assumption that all categories of labor could be induced to migrate between low-productivity and high-productivity regions in response to unemployment differences and reasonable subsidies to migration. The actual development of unemployment differentials among regions and the econometric study presented in this paper indicate that MLMP has been insufficient as a means to achieve regional equality in income and employment opportunities, although it rests on a theoretically and empirically sound basis. Those groups of the labor force that live in a locally stabilized family environment live mainly in the less productive regions, and they seem to be hurt by MLMP, especially when a majority of young and unmarried members of the labor force have outmigrated. Under these conditions the solidarity-based wage increases create increased unemployment, and the subsidies through MLMP are too small to motivate individuals to migrate to other regions with high productivity. In these regions MLMP should have complementary policies designed to create local jobs. Such an approach was designed in 1963-1964 and implemented in 1965, not only because of the partial failures of MLMP but also because of accelerated outmigration from the northern counties.

The complementary means were mainly designed to stimulate investment in manufacturing industries in the lagging regions. Approximately six percent of total manufacturing investment in the country as a whole has received investment subsidies, and the total expansion of employment in the firms receiving subsidies has been 12,800 jobs, according to official estimates. The total sum of location loans and grants has amounted to approximately 1,900 million Swedish kroner; their success has been only moderate in view of the needed increase of 170,000 jobs estimated by the Ministry of Labor and Housing.

The development of general indices of interregional inequality in income and employment does not indicate that these capital-oriented subsidies have contributed significantly to the achievement of equal opportunities of income and employment in all regions. Modern labor market policy—introduced in 1955—and location policy—introduced in 1965—must be complemented by still other means if the equalization goals of Swedish regional policy are to be fulfilled with reasonable social and economic efficiency.

Transfers from the central government to local governments in the poor areas have contributed much to the equality of public consumption, but large discrepancies still remain. The policy of increased subsidization of local government consumption seems efficient because it goes directly to the areas in need, and because it contributes to a balanced expansion of private and public consumption. Marginal subsidies to industrial employment have been used to a very limited extent, though there are strong reasons to believe that a partial switch from capital to employment subsidies would be desirable for short-term regional policy.

The main goal of Swedish regional policy in the short run is the equality of wages and employment in different regions. The different regions have, however, unequal accessibility and unequal stocks of capital. This means that regions with a high level of accessibility and large stocks of capital will have high marginal productivity of labor and a better capacity to pay wages at all levels of employment than the more remote regions which lack capital. The conflict between goals for a disadvantaged region can be illustrated in Figure 7-3.

It is obvious that a marginal employment subsidy to the firms working in the disadvantaged region could provide simultaneous fulfillment of the two goals. The total sum of marginal employment subsidies should equal the shaded area in the figure. The main advantage of a scheme of employment subsidies is the quick effect of such an instrument in comparison with subsidies to capital which have to work through a necessarily slow investment process, and which also tend to have a very limited effect on employment because of the lowered price of capital, which induces firms to overmechanize. The Swedish forest industries are a prime example of subsidization which has led to excessive mechanization and severe unemployment of old workers specialized in the old techniques.

A Norwegian econometric study of the relative advantages of employment and capital subsidies also indicated that capital subsidies have a large relative disadvantage in short- and medium-term regional equalization policies. The study was based on a productivity analysis of manufacturing industries and it used an assumption of embodied technological growth. It indicated that employment subsidies are three to fifteen times more efficient than capital subsidies as a means of regional policy, with the relative efficiency depending upon the character of the production functions of the individual industries.

MEDIUM-TERM REGIONAL POLICY

Planning and Regional Hierarchies

In most countries population distribution of commuting regions follows the Pareto or rank-size rule. Sweden is no exception. The population distribution of the seventy commuting regions in 1965 could be described by the following formula:

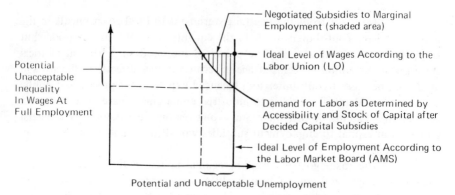

Figure 7-3. Conflicting Goals in Disadvantaged Regions

$$B \quad = \frac{900\ 565}{r^{0.72}} \ ; \text{coefficient of correlation: } -0.98 \text{ (log), where}$$

B = population, and r = rank.

In the 1965-1970 discussions of regional economic problems the commuting regions were divided into six groups according to the population of the region.

A grouping of the regions according to their population size indicated that many regional economic problems are closely correlated with each other and with the degree of agglomeration. Table 7-7 gives a statistical picture of these differences when the commuting regions are grouped without consideration of differences in accessibility in the national communication system.

Since 1970 this division of regions according to degree of agglomeration has been further refined to partly include accessibility. This statistical principle was used in Table 7-8. The new grouping of data according to agglomeration and partial accessibility of the different regions further emphasized the structural character of the regional policy problem and the need to formulate a regional economic policy in close coordination with the general medium-term economic programs of the country.

The kind of statistics used in SOU 1971:16 (from the Ministry of Labor and Housing) to demonstrate these structural regional problems are illustrated in Tables 7-8 and 7-9.

The broad spectrum of economic problems in each of the size classes caused the government, in 1972, to classify each center of the country within one of the following four functional categories:

Metropolitan areas   (3)

Primary centers   (23)

Table 7-7.   Labor Market Conditions and Migration Flows in Size Groups of Swedish Commuting Regions

Size group	Participation in labor force (percent)	Average domestic yearly migration 1961-1965 (per thousand population)	Nominal taxed income per capita (index)
29,000-59,000 inhabitants	41.4	−7.0	100
60,000-92,000 inhabitants	41.4	−4.0	101
96,000-132,000 inhabitants	42.6	−1.4	105
133,000-184,000 inhabitants	43.8	+0.4	111
Two second-largest metropolitan areas	45.9	+6.8	134
Stockholm metropolitan area	47.6	+6.9	158

Source: AMS: Statistical Reports, 1966-1968.

Table 7-8.   Population Change in Groups of Regions in Sweden, 1960-1970 (1960=100)

	1960	1965	1970
H1 Stockholm metropolitan area	100	109	116
H2 Göteborg and Malmö metropolitan areas	100	109	117
H3 Municipalities with populations of more than 90,000 within a distance of twenty miles	100	107	111
H4 Municipalities with populations of 27,000 to 90,000 within a distance of twenty miles and with more than 300,000 within sixty miles distance	100	99	101
H5 Municipalities with less than 300,000 within sixty miles distance (northern coastal regions)	100	97	99
H6 Less densely populated areas (northern inland regions)			

Source: SOU 1971:16.

    Regional centers   (76)
    Municipal centers   (114)

In short, the medium-term regional problem was defined as the problem of its main center. Regional economic policy should, according to Prop 1972:111, gradually be developed to meet the need for structural redevelopment of the main center of each region.

Table 7-9.   Change in and Level of Structural Variables in
Swedish Regions

Region	Domestic net migration, 1967-1969 (per 1,000 inhabitants)	Net immigration, 1967-1969 (per 1,000 inhabitants)
H1 Stockholm metropolitan area	+ 5.95	+3.17
H2 Göteborg and Malmö metropolitan areas	+ 6.44	+3.77
H3 Municipalities with populations of more than 90,000 within a distance of twenty miles	+ 1.77	+3.26
H4 Municipalities with populations of 27,000 to 90,000 within a distance of twenty miles and with more than 300,000 within sixty miles distance	− 3.98	+2.64
H5 Municipalities with less than 300,000 within sixty miles distance (northern coastal regions)	− 3.04	+0.88
H6 Less densely populated areas (northern inland regions)	−19.93	+1.28

Source: SOU 1971:16

The problem of the metropolitan areas was considered to be excessively rapid expansion, leading to congestion, air pollution, noise, and other environmental problems. A too rapid decline of manufacturing was also considered to create problems for the older age groups in the labor market. On the whole, though, the labor market situation was considered to be close to the ideal. Political means should be used to curb the growth of these areas.

The "primary centers" were considered to have most of the advantages of the metropolitan areas except for a wide range of choices in the labor market. In order to develop these centers, and consequently their regions, economic activities should be so located as to increase the demand for skilled labor and to increase the possibilities for female participation in the labor market. The relocation of central government activities was directed to these centers as a first step in this direction. The primary centers and their surrounding regions were to be the main receivers of the migrants who would otherwise go to the metropolitan areas.

It was also decided that the central administrative units of a manufacturing industry could receive location aid if they decided to move to the primary centers.

Employment participation (percent)	Employment in agriculture 1965 (percent)	Relative share of administrative employment in total manufacturing employment (percent)	Index of municipal expenditure per capita, 1969	Index of income per capita, 1967
48	1.5	38	202	163
47	4.3	29	200	141
44	10.5	25	120	122
45	16.1	23	104	111
42	15.7	21	128	115
37	28.1	18	100	100

"Regional centers" were defined as commuting centers providing public and private services for a number of municipalities. Although such regional services are usually well developed, and although these centers perform these functions with sufficient efficiency, their potential as focal points of their labor markets is often insufficiently developed. It is to be expected that these centers—especially the regional centers in the north—will receive most of the future location aid to investment.

"Municipal centers" are lowest in the hierarchy. Most of them are located in the vicinity of regional primary centers and do not play any significant role in the labor market of their respective regions. These centers will not be of any interest for regional policy at the national level. Some of the municipal centers in the forest areas (mainly in the north of Sweden) are, however, the only centers of any kind in the entire region. Regions of this type are rapidly declining in population and suffer from severe unemployment, low income, and other structural problems. The government has decided to use a variety of instruments with immediate effect in these cases, but with very moderate expectations of success concerning the general goals of regional policy. Very recently these regions were given the right to use employment subsidies for manufacturing as direct location subsidies to local service facilities. A major part of the subsidies to local government is also directed to these regions. However, most of them seem to be regarded as "lost" by the central authorities, and their medium- and long-term problems are mainly handled with short-term means to alleviate the most pressing problems of the labor market.

The government has also declared that regional policy should not aim at long-term solutions for the problems in the metropolitan areas or in the areas with administrative centers of the highest order. A recent official publication on regional policy even concluded: "The intention is to concentrate a major part of the public investments and, to a large extent, the measures for location aid in the places that have been designated primary centers and regional centers."

The Regional Distribution of Public Services in Medium-term Regional Planning and Policy Making

In the formulation of medium-term regional policies the central government has put great emphasis on the regional allocation of private investments. One should, however, not get the impression that this is the major area of medium-term regional policy. The public sector of the Swedish economy has a larger share in the national product than in any other market economy. Indivisibilities in the public sector create a major problem in government policy both with respect to allocative efficiency and equality in the spatial distribution of services. The central government uses heavy subsidies to local governments in order to reduce the distributional consequences of a small local income tax base and indivisibility of public equipment. General subsidies to local government do in fact amount to larger sums than the total location subsidies going to the private sector.

In nonspatial economic theory there has been a rather common belief that public sector products are automatically distributed rather evenly among households. This belief turns out to be wrong as soon as space is explicitly considered. One of the main reasons for public provision of services is indivisibility of equipment, which reduces or even prevents private supply. The consequent decline in the long-run marginal cost of production and the low pricing policy gives transaction costs—and thus location policy—a central role in the distribution of these services. Table 7-10 gives an indication of regional inequality in spatial distribution of government services.

There are two kinds of distributional problems connected with the allocation of government supply points in space. The first is the distribution of government services among groups of the population in different locations; and the second is the influence on the level and distribution of land rents associated with differences in government supply capacity between different areas. The use of transaction costs as a major means to restrict the demand and use of government services necessarily implies a complete price discrimination system. A person living very near to a supply point will have a lower price per unit of the service than a person living a long distance from the supply point. A reallocation in space will thus always lead to a change in the cost of government services to consumers and a corresponding change in the use of services. If the consumer of the service in question faces an increased distance and has a high (absolute) elasticity with respect to transaction cost, his service use will go down while the amount of money and time used for private consumption will increase. If the demand is completely inelastic (as for instance in primary education) his level of services will remain on the same level, but the money and time left for private consumption will decrease. This means that discrimination will always be a factor for those who live farther away from the government supply points, unless there is a compensatory increase in other consumption.

In the vicinity of a city it is always possible to get compensation in the form of a lower price on land, and such a compensation can also be observed in land price statistics. However, in most countries the price of land very near to the urban concentration points will drop to the agricultural price, while it will be equal in the rest of the countryside irrespective of the distances to government supply points. A number of studies have shown that there is no compensation in higher private consumption, but rather that the converse is the rule. The correspondence between private consumption inequality and public consumption is indicated in Table 7-11, which shows the changes in regional inequalities in Sweden over a period of forty-five years.

There seems to be a fundamental inequality among the regions both in the provision of government services and in the distribution of private purchasing power. These differences cannot disappear through migration within a reasonable time period, although a reduction has been observed. The variation in municipal expenditure per capita, for instance, decreased from 0.5 to 0.2 between 1930 and 1970, but is still considered to be a severe problem for distribution policy.

Investments in the communication system in order to increase the service areas is one way to reduce these inequalities. The TV system is an example of a communication reform giving a spatially more equalized service.

Table 7-11 shows that there has been a decrease in regional inequality in the public sector between 1920 and 1965. It also shows that large inequalities remain despite ever-increasing subsidies from the central government to local governments.

These figures also indicate that the interregional inequalities tend to be more persistent in the government service indicators studied than in private purchasing power as indicated by income variation. A consequence for planning and policy should be that the public expenditures have to be properly included in the methods and models used as tools of decision making in medium-term planning.

Table 7-10.   Relative Supply of Service Units per 100,000 Inhabitants Within 30 Kilometer Radius in the Sparsely Populated Areas in 1970 (percentages of the supply in the Stockholm metropolitan area)

	Dentists	*Doctors*	*Clinics*	*Libraries*	*Technical colleges*
The sparsely populated areas in the north	19	11	35	66	0

Source: Appendix to the Swedish long-term program for economic growth. SOU 1971:16.

Table 7-11.   Interregional Coefficients of Variation in Selected Per Capita Variables

	Municipal consumption	*Number of doctors*	*Number of hospital beds*	*Number of college students*	*Income*
1920	0.5	0.69	0.99	0.98	0.44
1965	0.2	0.62	0.55	0.27	0.19

Sources: L. Jörberg, "Svensk ekonomi under 100 år," *Svensk Ekonomi*, ed. B. Södersten (Stockholm, 1970), and SOS, Kommunernas finanser.

Regional Differences in Productivity in Manufacturing Industry as a Constraint on Regional Policy

The empirical analysis in the first part of this chapter showed that there are substantial differences in income per capita among different regions. These income differences can to a considerable extent be explained by differences in accessibility and in the level of local unemployment. A large part of the recorded differences in income cannot, however, be explained by these factors. The most densely populated area, Stockholm county is the most remarkable case. Its income per capita according to the identifiable regression equations is twenty percent below the actual value. This is a finding in close accordance with other estimates. Normally productivity indices show a marked jump at a population figure well above 500,000 inhabitants within the commuting region. A recent study in regional productivity in Swedish manufacturing industry (which is leaving the metropolitan areas) confirmed this finding. The study was performed according to the following hypotheses:

1. Educational, managerial, and material capital is mobile among regions according to marginal profitability.
2. Pure labor is fully employed in each region at the residual wage rate.
3. Product prices are equal among regions.

Hypothesis 2 gives a particular bias to the estimates because it amounts to a complete neglect of the potential wage decreases if unemployment is reduced.

Firms were assumed to have the following production function:

$$q_i = A_i \ k_i^\alpha \ S_i^\beta \tag{7.4}$$

where q = value added per employee

k = capital in use per employee

S = size of the firm in number of employees

Wages were determined by the following relation:

$$w_i = \overline{p}q_i - \overline{r}k_i \tag{7.5}$$

where w = wage rate for unskilled labor

$\overline{p}$ = predetermined level of prices

$\overline{r}$ = predetermined level of rate of interest

The ratio (A_i/A_j) is a measure of regional productivity differences and can be approximated by the wage rate ratio raised to an exponent which is equal to the labor elasticity of production.

The result of the estimates was that differences in capital intensity and size of production units could explain two-thirds of the total regional productivity differences. The rest was attributable to regional factors. Thirteen percent higher regional productivity was recorded for Stockholm county than for the sparsely populated regions. This difference is practically unaffected by disaggregation into subsectors of manufacturing. It is obviously not sufficiently large to make these sectors compete for space and labor with other sectors in the metropolitan regions, which are growing at the expense of manufacturing industry.

Measurements of this kind give no real explanations of the regional differences in income and productivity, a problem already encountered. Differential accessibility provides a good partial explanation. Another explanation lies directly in the size of the commuting region itself. The consumer in the densely populated region lives a more collective life than the consumer in a sparsely populated region. Collectivity in consumption means nothing else than a higher level of capacity exploitation. Collectivity in consumption through the use of services instead of household private ownership means, accordingly, a total saving of capital resources, giving a higher standard of living, *ceteris paribus*. The same phenomenon of collectivity in use of indivisible resources also holds true for the firms producing in the metropolitan regions. Instead of holding their own mostly idle capacity in educational or material capital, firms take advantage of resource sharing through a large market for producer services. The differences in this respect are hard to demonstrate empirically, but the occupational register for the Stockholm metropolitan telephone area records more than ten times as many service sectors as an ordinary medium-sized region.

Medium-term Regional Allocation Policy
Coordinated with Medium-term
Industrial Policy at the National Level

Since 1967, all the county administrations have been engaged in a medium-term planning procedure. Its main focus is on population change in the next ten-year period. The population planning levels decided on at the county level are afterwards revised at the central government level to attain consistency with the forecasts of national population and employment growth, and in the light of the regional policy instruments that can be used in the planning period. One should expect the corrections needed at the national level to be large, but this has not been the case in the work on plans in 1970-1972. This is illustrated in Table 7-12.

Industrial policy is formulated in the Ministry of Finance every five years in a program giving the projected development of the different industrial sectors without any explicit consideration of the regional consequences of the industrial development. The constraints on labor supply given by the county plans and the industrial program are not sufficient to determine the development of individual sectors within individual counties. A program of optimal, or at least consistent, sectoral development in the different planning regions is needed. This need for a consistent analysis of sectoral and regional development was formulated by the minister of labor and housing in his proposition to the Parliament in 1972.

> As I have mentioned earlier economic policy has a great influence on regional policy. There is thus a natural connection between the long-term economic judgment contained in the long-term economic programs and the planning within the framework of regional policy. A model of planning that simultaneously considers the judgments in the long-term economic programs and in regional development planning would be very hard to manage. Furthermore, the data needed for such integrated planning is lacking. On the other hand, time schedules for both planning activities should be coordinated in order to facilitate consistency in testing and reasonably frequent exchange of information.... I would in this connection like to mention the research projects within ERU that aim at a demonstration of the methods that should be used for a unification of the results of the long-term economic programming and regional development planning.

Table 7-12. Population Goals for 1980 in the Planning of Swedish
Counties (thousand inhabitants)

County	Countyplan (1970)	Minister's proposition (1972)
Stockholm	1,727	1,600-1675
Uppland	256	225-235
Södermanland	279	250-260
Östergötland	440	390-410
Jönköping	333	305-320
Kronoberg	186	170-180
Kalmar	256	245-255
Gotland	56	52-55
Blekinge	168	155-165
Kristianstad	279	265-275
Malmöhus	850	760-790
Halland	229	210-220
Göteborg	811	760-790
Älvsborg	440	410-430
Skaraborg	276	260-270
Värmland	292	280-290
Örebro	300	280-290
Västmanland	301	270-280
Gävleborg	314	290-300
Kopparberg	286	270-280
Jämtland	144	125-135
Västernorrland	281	260-270
Västerbotten	250	230-240
Norrbotten	259	250-260

ERU—the group of experts on regional problems in the Ministry of
Labor and Housing—has administered a large research project intended to
develop models for medium-term regional planning, and to coordinate planning
in the counties with the projections done at the national level for the
development of sectors. These models have mostly been formulated according to
the theory of programming, with an explicit goal function that is to be
optimized subject to constraints. The counties make their own preliminary plans
for the growth of total labor force and income per capita, while the Ministry of
Finance makes a medium-term projection for the development of the different
sectors. The consequences for some national welfare indicator are then tested in
an optimization procedure under the constraints given by the counties and the
Ministry of Finance. The interrelations are illustrated in Figure 7-4.

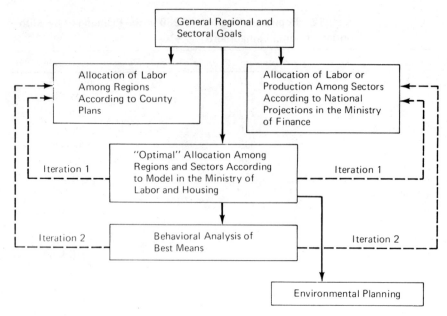

Figure 7-4. Interrelation Between National and County Labor Allocations

All the models have the following general structure:

Goal: Maximize a national goal function depending on the allocation to individual sectors in individual regions.

Constraints: The allocation of individual sectors to individual regions should be in accordance with employment goals given by the county plans and the production goals given by the national economic program under the technical conditions given by the statistically predetermined production functions.

The goal functions have been proxies for national product or total consumption at the national level. Linear and nonlinear optimizing models of this kind are now being implemented by ERU within the Ministry of Labor.

The Problem of Land Rents and its Connection with Medium-term Communication and Location Policy

It has been shown that the differences in accessibility to persons and to capital lead to site rents, in the form of differences in wages due to immobility of labor. There is always a problem of distribution of site rents, even in the case of full labor mobility. Any increase in accessibility in a region would be reflected in the rising price of land use in that region. If there is a distinct group of people owning land, as in Sweden, this group would get a large share of the profits resulting from the changed accessibility.

In Sweden this problem has mainly been discussed from the distributional point of view, as "the problem of rising prices of land." Rising prices of land should, of course, be no problem, if the distributional consequences could be avoided. Maximal increases in the value of land could instead be regarded as a goal in communication and capital location policy. The distributional problem in rising values of land points to a fundamental conflict between a system of socially planned communication and infrastructure investments and privately owned or controlled use of land. This conflict is illustrated in Figure 7-5.

The figure illustrates the fact that socially planned investments in infrastructure capital and communications links lead to income to the land owners, who never take any active part in the investment decisions. In a country with a rapidly growing share of public investment in total capital formation this could create a considerable distributional problem. Acquisition of land does in these cases become a very profitable financial investment as compared to investment in buildings and machines. In order to avoid the distribution problem caused by increasing values of land, the local governments in expanding regions have bought land, but this has not solved the problem. Because the municipalities have to pay full market value, all known investments will already, at the time of acquisition, have influenced the price of land.

Even in those cases where the government has used its superior knowledge of the development of accessibility, the distributional problem has often remained afterwards. The level of municipal yearly charges has usually been determined according to some bookkeeping rule of thumb, without consideration of the actual development of accessibility.

Because of the distribution argument and for reasons of efficiency of allocation there is a need to rearrange the original system into a taxation system such as that shown in Figure 7-6.

The figure illustrates a system of taxation of land according to its realized accessibility. In such a system there would not be any gain from speculation in land, because any realized investment increasing pure accessibility or the part played by accessibility in economic potential would automatically be reflected in increased taxes on land. There would also be considerably increased efficiency in the planning of locational patterns and communication systems, since the quality of planning would be reflected in the level of income from the site rent taxation system.

A tax system of this kind has a general advantage in its effects on allocation in the private sector. No negative reallocation in order to evade the tax is possible. All that firms can do is to get rid of land that cannot be used profitably and to get the highest possible productivity out of sites in use.

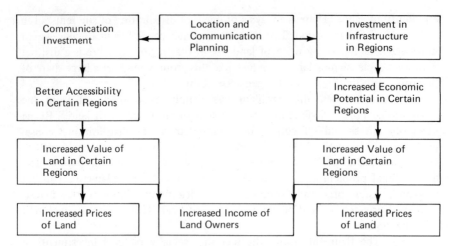

Figure 7-5. Factors Contributing to Increased Values and Uneven Distribution of Land

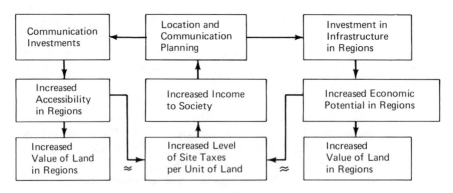

Figure 7-6. Proposed Reformed System of Real Estate Taxes

Conclusions on Medium-term Regional Economic Planning in Sweden

The main part of regional economic planning is now performed by the Ministry of Labor in cooperation with the county administrations and the municipalities. This regional planning system concentrates on actions within a medium-term time perspective of five to ten years. It provides the guidelines both for government actions to redistribute public services spatially and for the allocation of location grants to the private sector. In these respects regional economic planning runs into considerable problems of consistency with *national* medium-term economic planning. Extensive work on models for consistent planning at the regional and national-sectoral levels has been done within the relevant ministries, but these models have not yet been used in connection with the preparation of the medium-term economic program for the country.

A growth center strategy has been decided on and all municipalities have already been classified into four different groups of centers: metropolitan areas, primary centers, regional centers, and municipal centers. Projects connected with medium- term regional economic policy will be concentrated in primary and regional centers. The problems of municipal centers in lagging areas will be dealt with in the framework of short-term regional economic policy.

Measurements of productivity have shown that there are sizable economies of agglomeration in the Swedish economy. Agglomeration economies in conjunction with accessibility differentials create significant problems of land and other site rents. These problems have been discussed extensively at the political level but as yet there has been no taxation reform. Such a reform would be distributionally and allocationally efficient and would provide a reasonable financial base for medium term regional economic policy.

LONG-TERM REGIONAL POLICY BASED ON ECONOMIC GOALS

Present Long-term Location and Communication Policy in Sweden

Up to this point it has been pointed out that the regional inequality problem, both in real income and in employment opportunities, is to a large extent a consequence of regional differences in accessibility. A country like Sweden has naturally, as a consequence of its long, narrow geographical structure, a relatively strong tendency to regional inequality. A rectangular area with the Swedish relations between the sides means that the corner points have more than fifty percent longer distances to other points than if the same land area had been square. One should, accordingly, expect Swedish communication policy to be integrated or even unified with location policy and with MLMP. This, however, is not the case. Planning of investments in the communication system is performed in the Ministry of Communications without any explicit consideration of the consequences for the general economic development of regions. The communications planners normally plan their investments according to a procedure described in a simplified manner in Figure 7-7.

Long-term locational planning, as performed in the Ministry of Labor and Housing, is normally built on a reversed chain. In order to analyze the optimal pattern of location, the communication system is assumed to be given according to long-term plans. Figure 7-8 illustrates the different steps of locational planning.

The planning techniques described in Figures 7-7 and 7-8 often run into inconsistencies, which becomes obvious if simplified versions of the two figures are connected to each other, as in Figure 7-9.

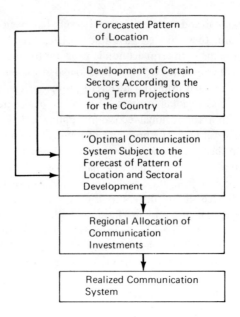

Figure 7-7. Communications System Planning

The firm basis of planning in one ministry turns out to be the result of planning in the other ministry. There is no guarantee that such a system of one-way information in a planning system leads to an optimal or at least consistent chain of plans in the long run, especially not if the different objects are as interrelated causally as in the case of communications and location patterns.

The current system of consultations between the ministries has not been sufficient to secure integrated planning. Long-term planning of locations and communications needs to be unified within the same ministry, but there is no sign of such a reorganization.

In the development of models for integrated planning within the Ministry of Labor and Housing some significant steps have, however, been taken in the direction of a framework for coordinated communication and location planning. A research project conducted by Professors Törnqvist and Hägerstrand has provided a considerable amount of empirical knowledge about the Swedish communication system. This kind of knowledge is a necessary condition for meaningful development of planning models.

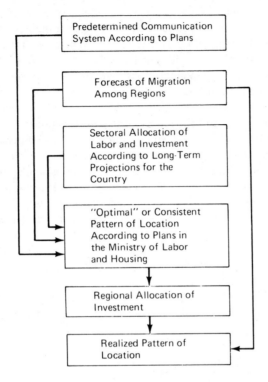

Figure 7-8. Locational Planning

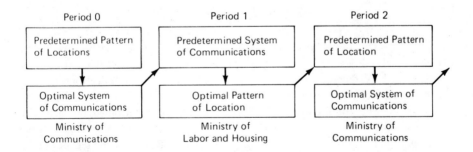

Figure 7-9. Relationship and Inconsistencies Between Communications and Locational Planning

One of the models for coordinated planning of communications and location is based on the same formulation of the goal function proposed by Beckmann and Koopmans in 1957. This type of model makes it possible to see the optimal development of the locational pattern under different investment and pricing strategies in the communications system. However, the model does not allow for an endogenous analysis of the growth effects resulting from different communication strategies. This latter problem is being studied in another research project within the same ministry by the author of this chapter. The study is based on the general equilibrium framework proposed by von Neumann. The main assumption is that sustained long-term economic growth must be proportional and must maintain constant relations among the different sectors and regions of the economy. The economy is divided into a number of sectors and regions. These sectors and regions are interrelated with each other by an input-output and a capital-output matrix with representative elements a_{ij}^{rs} and b_{ij}^{rs} respectively.

Some of these elements are predetermined as the consumption and labor input-output coefficients, which are determined in special regional studies and are supposed to be independent of the structure of the communications system. Most of them are, however, dependent on the structure of the communications system, because the coefficients are determined by the following formula:

$$a_{ij}^{rs} = \frac{\overline{a}_{ij}}{(d^{rq})^{\alpha_i} \ \Sigma \, (d^{rq})^{-\alpha_i} \ (\frac{x_i^r}{x_i})} \tag{7.6}$$

where

$$\overline{a}_{ij} = \text{the national input-output coefficient}$$
$$d^{rq} = \text{the distance between the two regions } r \text{ and } q$$
$$-\alpha_i = \text{the elasticity of distance for sector } i$$

This procedure is also used for the capital-output coefficients, which means that every interregional input-output and capital-output coefficient is determined by technical factors, the structure of the communications system, and the elasticity of transport with respect to relative communication distances.

The total growth of the system is thus determined by technical factors and the characteristics of the communications system. A communication reform could thus be traced all the way to its consequences for the balanced rate of growth and the relative shares in production, employment, and population of different regions and sectors.

This model has been implemented recently for the Swedish economy with a disaggregation of the country into eight groups of counties and thirty-two sectors, including the household sector as an endogenous variable. The balanced structure of production in regions and sectors for the beginning of the 1970s has been forecasted on the basis of statistics from the second half of the 1960s, and the results have been encouraging. Table 7-13 shows the distribution of assessed income among the different counties according to official statistics and the share in value-added predicted by the model.

This model predicts a regional hierarchical distribution of product in accordance with the differences in accessibility in the transportation system and the general elasticity of contacts with respect to distance. The model gives a very reasonable explanation of the stability of the regional distribution of production recorded in Table 7-1. The spatial distribution of production and income should be stable as long as the transportation network is stable. The stability in the interregional distribution of income is, according to the model, a consequence of the fact that the transportation network had its main structure determined at the beginning of the century and has not been significantly changed since.

The model also emphasizes the fundamental role of a coordination of transportation and location planning in long-run regional economic policy. The regional pattern of production could be significantly changed only by a major change in the transportation network.

Environmental and Cultural Problems
in Long-term Regional Policy

Most discussions in this paper are reflections of the predominant emphasis on economic variables in the formulation of Swedish regional policy. Political discussions have often tended to move in rather different directions. Differences in way of life and in cultural attitudes and the dynamic consequences of one or the other kind of regional population and production distribution among the regions have from time to time dominated the discussion—at least outside Parliament and the ministries. It must be admitted that Sweden has a long way to go to achieve a consistent long-term regional policy with an equal emphasis on economic, cultural, and environmental factors.

The differences in cultural habits among various parts of the country with different densities of population cannot be given an analytically satisfying description on the basis of statistical material discussed within the ministries and other government bodies formulating Swedish regional policy. Some steps are, however, being taken by the ERU research group to provide a better understanding of the more qualitative and environmental aspects of regional welfare.

The marked regional differences in income per capita have their counterpart in differences in private consumption per household. A recent study of consumption patterns at different levels of agglomeration showed that the one-third of the population living in the most densely populated parts of the country—the metropolitan areas—had a consumption per member of household which exceeded the consumption per member of household of the one-third of the population living in the sparsely populated areas—the forest areas—by approximately forty-five percent.

Table 7-13. The Regional Distribution of Production Predicted by the Regional Growth Model and the Recorded Distribution of Assessed Income According to the Taxation Statistics for the Same Year

Groups of counties	Share in assessed income (percent)	Predicted share (percent)
Stockholm (AB)	24	24
Mid-Sweden (CDETU)	16	14
Southeast (FGHIR)	11	10
Southern metro-politan area (KLM)	14	14
Western metro-politan area (NOP)	16	15
Mid-Swedish forest area (SWX)	9	10
Central Northern (YZ)	4	7
Northern (AC,BD)	6	6

The differences in consumption standards are, however, not only a quantitative but also a structural problem. The structure of consumption in metropolitan areas, compared to other areas, is illustrated by the data in Table 7-14.

The consumption of semicollective goods (or services) is concentrated in the densely populated areas, while the consumption of private goods (or goods which are mainly consumable within the home) are relatively more in demand in the sparsely populated areas. This bias towards collective consumption in the metropolitan areas in contrast to the family-oriented pattern of life in the sparsely populated areas can further be illustrated by material from the "low income group investigation."

The data in Tables 7-15 and 7-16 also illustrate the collective pattern of consumption in the densely populated areas, with its greater possibilities for commuting and cost-sharing between households, in contrast to the family-oriented pattern of consumption in the sparsely populated areas, with its use of privately owned equipment within each individual household.

These differences are explainable in the short run even with an assumption that utility functions are identical and that variations in demand are only consequences of interregional variations in income and prices. The income effect seems to be negligible because almost all the differences remain at all levels of income. The optimal quantity consumed by a household of a good is determined by the equalization of the marginal rate of substitution between the goods and the relation of prices at the preferred location of consumption, including all costs of transportation. The use of semicollective and collective

Table 7-14. Indices of Consumption per Member of Household in Regions at Different Levels of Agglomeration

	Metropolitan areas	Other city regions	Sparsely populated areas
Individual goods			
Food	116	102	100
Clothing	131	129	100
Household inventories	125	133	100
Liquor and tobacco	190	134	100
Housing	168	148	100
Total individual	137	123	100
Transportation	127	113	100
Semicollective goods			
Private health and beauty services	208	122	100
Amusements	163	144	100
Restaurants and processed food	223	161	100
Trips to other countries	377	227	100
Total semicollective	199	151	100

Source: Meuller-Johnsson, "Interaktioner mellan konsumtion och storstadstillväxt," (Göteborgs universitet, September 1972). Mimeographed.

Table 7-15. Dominant Activities in Sparsely Populated Areas

	Northern forest areas (percent of population)	Stockholm metropolitan area (percent of population)
Own daily paper	88	76
Own radio	94	82
Own TV	84	78
Own telephone	85	81
Own weekly journal	77	68
Receive relatives in own home	90	84
Receive friends in own home	96	92
Work in garden	50	40
Hunting	17	3
Fishing	50	36

Source: Urbaniseringsprocessen: 50. Bearbetningar av levnadsnivåundersökningen, mimeographed, (Stockholm 1972).

Note: All statistical figures describe behavior.

Table 7-16. Dominant Activities in Densely Populated Areas

	Northern forest areas (percent of population)	Stockholm metropolitan area (percent of population)
Owns a small library	49	77
Have made trips to		
Central Europe	1	10
Eastern Europe	0	2
Southern Europe	2	12
Nordic countries	50	60
Other countries.	1	2
Visits theatre, museums, etc.	19	61
Visits cinema	27	55
Visits public dancing or restaurants	59	74
Participates in musical activities	12	19
sports	20	30
evening studies	17	22
hobbies	52	59

Source: Urbaniseringsprocessen: 50. Bearbetningar av levnadsnivåundersökningen, mimeo-graphed, (Stockholm 1972).

Note: All statistical figures describe behavior.

goods always implies personal transportation to the supply points, which is much more expensive in sparsely populated areas than in the densely populated regions. This means that the cif-prices of collective and semicollective goods in relation to the cif-prices of private goods fall with increased density of population, implying increases in the share of collective consumption.

If there is any learning by doing in consumption there will also be a cumulative effect on the utility function leading to a reinforced regional discrepancy in ways of life. The problem of differences in consumption is therefore not only a distributional problem, but also a problem of the development of the cultural values of society. As a response to these aspects of regional development there has been growing opposition—mainly formulated by social anthropologists—against the purely quantitative formulation of the redistributional goals of Swedish regional policy. It is obvious from Tables 7-14, 7-15, and 7-16 that there could be connections between the regional pattern of population dispersion and the structure of behavior, and possibly also cultural attitudes. The formulation of such anthropological and cultural policy goals consistent with a more general political ideology is, however, an unsolved problem.

Conclusions on Long-term Regional Policy in Sweden

The structure, capacity, and user rules of the communications system are the main factors determining the pattern of location and regional development. Changes in the structure of the communications system can, however, only be made through investment in other large and indivisible projects. This implies that communications investments must be planned as an integrated part of long-term regional policy.

This kind of long-term integrated communications and location planning has not been implemented in Sweden. Formal analytical techniques for integrated communication and location planning based on the theories of location and economic growth are at the moment being developed by the research groups in the Ministry of Labor and Housing. The main reason to suspect a long period of introduction of such an integrated planning system is thus not of an analytical nature, but seems to depend on organizational causes. Communications investments in roads, telecommunications, etc. are planned in the Ministry of Communications, which has no responsibility for regional policy goals, while the location of industries is planned within the Ministry of Labor and Housing. A reasonable organizational reform to achieve a coordinated long-term development of the communications system and the pattern of location according to regional policy goals might be to create a new ministry with responsibility to plan and implement both regional and communications policy.

The development of a long-term regional policy must consider variables that are of a more qualitative nature than those which are normally treated within regional economic theory. Some examples of regional differences in cultural and environmental variables have been given. The statistics indicate a larger share of collective consumption in the metropolitan areas but also a significantly larger consumption of alcohol per capita. These two phenomena are explained not only by higher per capita income but also by the more dense location of the service supply points. The larger share of collective consumption in the metropolitan areas implies that people congregate much more in large anonymous groups with higher risks of interpersonal conflicts. This is to some extent indicated by the higher rates of known criminality in the metropolitan areas. The differences among regions in the values of all the welfare indicators beside the purely economic ones suggest the need for a more general environmental and cultural approach to regional planning and policy. Some have suggested that such a generalized approach to regional planning would be most efficiently executed by a "softer" approach, without any explicit use of abstract models. This is not my opinion.

A wider cultural and environmental approach to regional planning demands a relevant and broader—but still theoretical—framework, one that is capable of simultaneously dealing with cultural and environmental variables as well as the economic variables which are now the focus of regional policy.

Chapter Eight

Spain's Regional Growth

INTRODUCTION

The present study attempts to do several things, and is, perhaps, a somewhat ambitious undertaking. It aims first at presenting briefly and explaining succinctly the long-run historical evolution of Spain's regional growth; and second, it aims at describing and evaluating pre- and post-Civil War regional development policies, specially the latter, against the backdrop of previous long-run evolution.

In doing so, it is not possible to avoid the inevitable conclusion that the centuries-long evolutionary development pattern of Spain's regions has been affected primarily by long-run historical national policies, whose permanence goes a long way towards explaining the inertia of its regional structure. It is also safe to conclude that the effectiveness of modern regional policies has been heavily dependent on the manner in which the long-run historical national policies are presently defined in terms of national development policies.

Within this framework, formal regional development policies have played only a small part in shaping the regions' development. However, I give them as much space as seems necessary in order to explain the interaction between formal regional policy and the actual regional effects of the national development policies, and thus to pinpoint the regional variables most significant in formal regional policy. This, as I think the Spanish case proves, depends basically on the level of development achieved by a particular country and on the national development strategy being pursued.

The specific conclusions which I derive from the text are logically to be drawn after the whole argument has been presented. However, it seems pertinent to point out here that every type of country can learn from the description of Spain's long-run experience with regional growth. In fact, the Spanish data illustrates well the notion that regional patterns can be dramatically changed, both for better or for worse—but over a long period; hardly in the short terms of most present planning horizons.

Spain's modern regional growth experience does not offer many lessons to developed countries. The reasons for this are that the nation's problems and the manner in which they have been perceived by both policy makers and the public alike bear little resemblance to the regional problems, the available means for solving these problems, and the goals of the developed world. I am going to deal with this point at some length since it permits the reader to understand the Spanish people's present assessment of their country's development and the ways in which this self-assessment has affected regional development lately.

Although Spain will soon join the advanced countries, its economic progress has been the product of the sixties; as a consequence, its still lagging and underdeveloped infrastructure creates problems different in kind and magnitude from those of the affluent world (with the possible exceptions of Italy and Japan). Additionally, its even more underdeveloped cultural super-structure results in a public evaluation of its regional problems at variance on many points with that prevailing in the earlier developed countries.

Some data will illustrate the point being made. Official (Spanish government income data at current exchange rates) per capita GNP in 1973 will be around $2,000; the "real" figure (correcting for income undervaluation and for price differences) will be around $2,400. At the forecasted rates (and since the beginning of the sixties all official forecasts have been lower than the realized figures) it will attain a level larger than Ireland's in 1975 and larger than the United Kingdom's and probably Italy's in 1980 (Alcaide, 1973).

Though this growth pattern seems reasonable to most foreign observers of the Spanish economy, from recent *Le Monde* editorials to Herman Kahn, including the international financial community, it is not afforded much credence inside Spain (the latest work of Tamames [1973] is one of the few exceptions). The heart of the matter is that until 1972 the official income per capita figure was at least thirty percent below the real level, and this discrepancy went unchallenged in spite of the glaring differences between Spanish consumption levels and those of countries within the same income bracket.

Alcaide's above-mentioned estimates are in effect the result of a polemic on the subject, initiated by an indirect estimate of Spanish income and carried out with the Beckerman-UNRISD technique by my associates in EVP (1971) which I reported in *Informaciones* (1972). This, and the coincident industrial income estimates of the IBRD Industrial Mission (1972), resulted in a petition by several international agencies to the Spanish Statistical Office to revise its income figures upwards.

The emotional reason behind the disbelief concerning the country's actual and potential growth (which, in the view of many foreign observers and myself, will be the third ranking western European economy—after Germany and France—in the early eighties) is not hard to understand. According to Clark

(1957), Spanish income per capita in the thirties was larger than the Italian; one would therefore think that once the retarding factors—especially the political isolation—were removed, Spain would again reach the Italian level. However, the poor results of the forties and fifties did not permit Spain to reach the highest prewar income level, that of 1932, until 1955; this lag resulted in a deep lack of confidence in the nation's capacity to develop which has not yet been overcome. Table 8-1 illustrates the case.

Although, for the reasons advanced, recent Spanish regional experience cannot be of great direct relevance for developed countries, it can be of considerable interest to semideveloped countries, especially in regard to her overall development strategy concerning two basic choices: (1) national growth versus regional equality; and (2) directly productive versus infrastructure investment.

On the other hand, recent regional experience can be of some significance in all regional policy contexts. In effect, in a decade Spain has been transformed from an underdeveloped to an industrial economy. The time has been short enough to reveal clearly the organizational changes in the structure of firms that the process of development involves. This phenomenon, which in longer periods is smooth enough to go unnoticed, has permitted a glimpse of the interrelations between the organizational traits of business firms and the levels of economic variables (income, investment, etc.). It has also presented an opportunity to hypothesize and test some of the effects of changes in organizational factors (and policies based directly or indirectly on them) on regional economic structure. Because the speed of this reorganizational process has slowed very little, and because its impact continues to increase as the country develops, the implications of regional policy alternatives in the Spanish setting offer fruitful opportunities for further research.

Finally, before proceeding with the argument, I should like the reader to realize the main problem I have been faced with in writing this chapter: while Spain's regional growth pattern has long been one of my main research concerns, only recently has it attracted the attention of Spanish economists at large, who were previously almost exclusively concerned with national growth. This, I hope, may help to explain why I have referred so frequently to my own previous work and, hence, the paper's personal tone, which, although unintended, I have been unable to avoid.

PATTERNS OF REGIONAL GROWTH

Regional Growth Patterns from the Fifteenth to the Twentieth Century

In the fifteenth and sixteenth centuries, Spain's statistical records were among the best in the world. Some of the censuses of that period covered wider subject areas and contained finer breakdowns than those of the early nineteenth century.

Table 8-1.   Index of Spanish and Italian Official per Capita
Income Estimates

Years	Spanish (1946=100)	Italian (1946=100)	Italian in terms of Spanish
1932	120	90	96
1939	76	–	–
1946	100	100	128
1950	93	133	183
1955	121	165	175
1960	138	214	198
1964	194	261	172
1969	275	333	155
1973	415	374	115

Sources: Clark (1932; 1957); Spanish series: Pena Trapero in Lasuén et al. (1966); Spanish-Italian comparison: Sáenz de Buruaga (1973).

Thanks to these records, both the optimistic and pessimistic hypotheses on the spatial effects of development can be rejected. Indeed, contrary to the optimistic hypothesis, based on nineteenth and twentieth century experience of northwestern Europe and North America, and against the pessimistic predictions of Gunnar Myrdal, it seems easier to accept that regional development patterns in the long-run are neither conveniently convergent nor menacingly divergent. Indeed, a complete reversal of the location of the relatively developed and underdeveloped zones of Spain took place between the sixteenth and the twentieth centuries.

As recorded in the 1829 census, the population in the central zones of Spain in 1594 was around three-quarters of the national total. This is almost a complete reversal of the country's situation today, when approximately three-quarters of the population live in the peripheral zones along the seacoast and the French border. Additionally, several earlier censuses indicate that the demographic dominance of the central zones over the periphery must have been even greater during the years between 1482 and 1570.

According to several historians, summarized in da Silva (1965), several indirect indicators of income levels show that in the fifteenth and sixteenth centuries the center's dominance was also economic, in conformity with Clark's (1968) hypothesis about demographic density and relative development, and further, that from then onwards the center's economic dominance has been gradually replaced by a growing dominance of the peripheral areas.

In summary, population and output, first concentrated in the country's center (fifteenth and sixteenth centuries) have, with time, become largely concentrated in the periphery, showing today (twentieth century) almost a perfect reversal of their initial locational pattern.

Moving from the center's dominance toward the periphery's dominance, the country must have reached a period of regional homogeneity. From available data it is not possible to pinpoint the exact time at which this happened. However, comparisons of the 1587 and 1768 censuses and other data permit the hypothesis that the shift took place before the middle of the eighteenth century.

To start with, we have the clear reference of the censuses. In 1768, the Spanish population was already more densely settled in the periphery than in the center, thus reversing the pattern revealed by the 1567 census. Secondly, there are scattered data showing that during the two intervening centuries practically all central areas lost population to most peripheral areas. Thirdly, Vilar (1969), one of Spain's best economic historians, suggests that the center's maximum dominance occurred at the end of the fifteenth century, and that the reversal of the trend favoring the periphery's dominance (and therefore, moving in the direction of convergence) took place around 1640-1690.

My own view concerning the causes of this turnaround will be summarized after a brief consideration of the preliminary results of a study which I am about to publish on the evolution of Spanish regions in the nineteenth and twentieth centuries (Lasuén et al., 1974), because that will enable us to distinguish those causes on better empirical grounds.

Regional Growth Patterns 1860-1969

The aforementioned study is a shift-share analysis of the growth of Spanish provinces and regions from 1860 to 1969, broken down by decades and for up to sixteen employment categories, depending on the different periods under study. Preliminary results contained in Tables 8-2, 8-3, and 8-4 show that, in spite of the civil and colonial wars and the other frequent discontinuities in the adoption of the Industrial Revolution, the growing dominance in population density of the periphery over the center was accompanied by a growing parallel dominance in the level of economic development of the periphery, as can be deduced from the evolution in the industrial, service, and agricultural employment profiles of the provinces and regions.

With respect to industry (Table 8-3) only—services behaved similarly and agriculture just the opposite—it is seen that:

1. Throughout the period in question (1860-1969) the periphery enjoyed larger (absolute and relative) net industrial employment shifts than the center.
2. This was due to the fact that in the analyzed period the periphery had positive competitive and industry-mix effects (the first one being nearly half the second), while the center (with the exception of Madrid) had a negative competitive effect almost as large as the positive industry-mix effect.
3. The periphery's relative advantage began in the first stage of the period, as

Table 8-2. Net Regional Employment Shifts in the Agricultural Sector, 1860-1969

Period	Regions		
	Madrid	*Center*	*Periphery*
1860-1910			
Net employment shifts	68,563.63	75,647.68	95,415.65
Competitive effect	64,635.95	75,669.60	− 18,698.24
Industry mix effect	4,027.73	121,485.46	119,113.96
1910-1930			
Net employment shifts	−106,603.50	−238,435.05	−717,657.40
Competitive effect	− 75,035.94	290,593.07	−215,557.09
Industry mix effect	− 31,567.61	−134,738.75	−502,100.54
1930-1950			
Net employment shifts	44.88	−231,227.63	−155,944.18
Competitive effect	4,352.43	− 10,656.19	6,303.81
Industry mix effect	− 4,307.55	−220,571.44	−162,247.91
1950-1969			
Net employment shifts	− 22,918.74	−1,544,861.99	−910,944.86
Competitive effect	6,716.92	−137,601.45	130,884.70
Industry mix effect	− 29,635.66	−1,407,260.57	−1,041,829.59
1860-1969			
Net employment shifts	− 86,705.75	−2,113,692.76	−2,184,437.88
Competitive effect	− 13,004.90	37,610.87	− 96,339.70
Industry mix effect	− 73,700.88	−2,222,987.25	−2,088,098.25

shown in Table 8-3. In the subperiod 1860-1910 the periphery enjoyed positive competitive effects against the clearly negative effects of the center.

4. Ever since, with the exception of the Civil War impact in Cataluña (1930-1950), the competitive effects of the periphery have been clearly positive (while in the center, with the exception of Madrid, they have been negative).

5. The evolution of the industry-mix effects has been less significant; in fact, from the time the Industrial Revolution was consolidated (about 1910), all regions have had positive industry-mix effects, though in the periphery they have been larger than in the center.

6. As a consequence, the net shifts of the period may be imputed to the greater competitiveness of the periphery throughout the period (excepting the previously mentioned special stage 1930-1950).

Table 8-3.   Net Regional Employment Shifts in the Industrial
Sector, 1860-1969

Period	Region		
	Madrid	*Center*	*Periphery*
1860-1910			
Net employment shifts	−32,904.11	−181,620.14	38,786.21
Competitive effect	−21,014.24	− 94,490.03	115,504.23
Industry mix effect	−11,889.87	− 87,130.16	− 76,717.99
1910-1930			
Net employment shifts	43,163.47	48,064.53	357,110.93
Competitive effect	21,633.79	−134,635.20	113,801.43
Industry mix effect	21,529.68	182,699.78	244,109.59
1930-1950			
Net employment shifts	33,294.71	366,660.77	134,083.54
Competitive effect	144.63	195,744.18	−195,889.21
Industry mix effect	33,150.09	170,916.70	329,972.79
1950-1969			
Net employment shifts	365,710.19	− 15,237.03	845,398.74
Competitive effect	219,412.94	−485,230.50	193,817.37
Industry mix effect	74,297.31	469,993.57	651,581.50
1860-1969			
Net employment shifts	423,935.44	203,257.32	1,702,479.01
Competitive effect	266,317.25	−951,784.26	685,066.54
Industry mix effect	157,618.19	1,155,041.57	1,017,012.62

These are basically the same results that I obtained for a shorter shift-share analysis of Venezuela (Lasuén, 1971a). They tend to argue against the frequently used hypothesis that the two effects (competitive and industry-mix) move over time in opposite directions as development takes place, as found by Perloff et al. (1960) for the United States.

The previously mentioned Spanish data also tends to refute both the use of that hypothesis—formulated statistically by Williamson (1965)—to explain the argument that regional convergence proceeds *pari passu* with economic development, and Williamson's argument itself.

Regional Growth Patterns in the Twentieth Century

In fact, Williamson's case does not fit either the earlier long-run Spanish data, or the shorter, finer data of more recent periods. In effect,

Table 8-4. Net Regional Employment Shifts in the Service Sector, 1860-1969

Periods	Regions		
	Madrid	Center	Periphery
1860-1910			
Net employment shifts	43,484.30	−248,629.07	4,358.45
Competitive effect	58,244.64	−136,751.27	−148,256.45
Industry mix effect	− 14,760.35	−111,877.81	− 74,148.19
1910-1930			
Net employment shifts	30,587.43	− 93,550.37	190,785.41
Competitive effect	14,795.30	−149,756.97	134,961.62
Industry mix effect	15,792.14	56,206.60	55,823.91
1930-1950			
Net employment shifts	−121,671.94	342,376.71	−391,084.13
Competitive effect	− 98,704.63	397,887.53	−299,188.14
Industry mix effect	− 22,967.35	− 56,010.69	− 91,901.07
1950-1969			
Net employment shifts	298,104.31	−241,824.33	572,445.50
Competitive effect	250,635.88	−596,966.12	346,330.06
Industry mix effect	47,468.48	355,141.79	226,115.53
1860-1969			
Net employment shifts	276,784.69	−418,765.53	424,629.10
Competitive effect	256,006.50	−576,256.63	320,250.27
Industry mix effect	20,778.19	157,491.01	104,378.85

Racionero (1971) tested Williamson's thesis that regional per capita incomes tend to converge by recalculating Williamson's coefficient of variability(c) using provincial percentages of industrial employment (for which good statistics exist) instead of the unreliable income per capita figures. His results (Figure 8-1) show that instead of following Williamson's inverted 'U', Spain's provincial concentration index in the twentieth century moved in a cycle, superimposed on a growing provincial divergence trend. Further, in checking my previous hypothesis against that of Perloff et al., Racionero found that provincial concentration has been largely in the peripheral provinces, with the major exception of Madrid.

He also found in checking on the effects of the temporal and spatial patterns of innovation diffusions on regional development patterns that, for various industries, the troughs of regional (or provincial) dispersion correspond to the periods of rapid adoption of innovations and those of provincial income concentration to the periods of isolation and stagnation with little adoption of innovations.

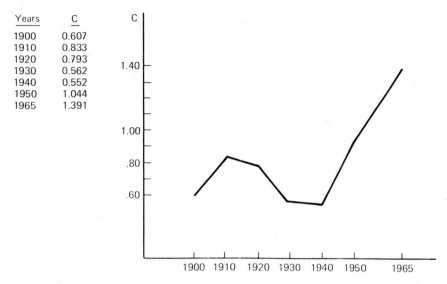

Years	C
1900	0.607
1910	0.833
1920	0.793
1930	0.562
1940	0.552
1950	1.044
1965	1.391

Figure 8-1.   Spain's Provincial Concentration of Industrial Employment

Long-Run Regional Convergence-
Divergence Factors

Racionero's three findings are also consistent with my two basic innovation diffusion hypotheses (Lasuén, 1971b, 1972a and 1973a), namely: (1) that adoptions enter through the top of the urban system (in Spain, through the periphery, with the exception of Madrid), and then spread gradually through the rest of the system; and (2) that divergences in the urban system over the long run take place because new innovations are generated and/or adopted at the top of the urban hierarchy at a faster pace and on a larger scale than the 'spread-time' and 'spread-capacity' of adoptions throughout the entire urban system.

These two hypotheses, which I had previously drawn from data measuring respectively the increasing spatial stability of the Spanish urban system (Lasuén, 1969 and 1970) and its increasing 'rank-sizeness', (Lasuén et al., 1967) help to explain the peculiar behavior of the competitive and industry-mix effects in the long-run evolution of the Spanish economy; and, in consequence, the convergence-divergence sequence of its regional structure over time. They explain, in fact, why the competitive effects of one period tend to produce reinforcing industry-mix effects in the next; and why they therefore tend to result (unless drastically changed by exogenous long-run factors) in a long-run trend toward either convergence or divergence (depending on the initial situation and the spatial pattern of innovation diffusions), with oscillating shorter cyclical movements (depending on the temporal pattern of innovation diffusions) superimposed.

Thus, summarizing, it can be hypothesized that probably the main reason for the regional divergence trends of the last century (and of previous moves toward first convergence and then divergence) has been the periphery-oriented pattern of innovation diffusions which started in the seventeenth century and has remained in effect ever since.

Short-Run Regional Convergence-
Divergence Factors

Shorter term analysis of the behavior of institutions in Spain's recent past shows other short-term factors reinforcing the long-run regional divergence trend. This is especially the case with respect to critical regional income transfers. Thus, not only do regional output trends tend to be divergent in the long-run, but regional income transfers, instead of compensating the output trends, reinforce them. This applies to both public and private transfers.

My most recent analysis of the regional structure of government revenue (Lasuén, 1960a) showed that it was clearly regressive throughout the greater part of regional activities and has remained basically unchanged to the present. Provincial taxes per active capita, in percentage of provincial value added per active capita, have been roughly the same in all provinces (with the exception of the five richest provinces, where they have been larger), in spite of great provincial income differences (larger than 100 percent). Poor regions also have received less public funds than they have paid in taxes, as can be seen in the series of budgets.

A similar situation exists with respect to private income transfers. Due to the fact that the banking system is basically a national system, both for asset and liability operations, and is concentrated in the hands of five large banks, private funds deposited in the banks' branches in less developed zones are channeled to investments in the more developed areas because returns on capital there are normally higher. The pattern is the same for savings deposited in savings banks. Although savings banks are local in their liability operations and national in their asset activities, generally (against their wishes) they are forced to follow the same spatial investment patterns as commercial banks. In effect, indirectly, the government, by law, channels the largest part of their assets toward investments in the developed zones though conditioning the savings banks to buy stocks or debentures from the large corporations registered in the stock market.

Overall Regional Convergence-
Divergence Factors

In summary, long-run factors (mostly technological) and short-run factors (mostly institutional) have interacted to reinforce divergence in the country's regional development pattern, beginning sometime at the end of the seventeenth century.

Even if the institutional factors were to reverse themselves, it is doubtful whether they could counteract the effects of the technological factors. In fact, if the hypotheses put forward are valid, it seems that the only way to moderate the long-run regional divergence trend is to reduce the dominant competitive effect of the large peripheral cities vis-à-vis the others (as the last Spanish Civil War definitively proved; see Lasuén et al., 1967). But, obviously, this procedure has the built-in danger of producing stagnation of the country (again, as the Civil War proved). In fact, it could only be imposed, I believe, as a consequence of a complete re-evaluation of the national space preferences of the country.

It is precisely this kind of reasoning that may explain the radical change in the settlement pattern of seventeenth century Spain and which may assist as well in a better assessment of present-day regional policies. The fifteenth century center-dominance pattern was probably reduced gradually,. without affecting the country's growth, because it took place as a result of the intense settlement of northerners during the fifteenth and sixteenth centuries in recently acquired southern peripheral territories; it was an open frontier situation in which the new southern resources were exploited for everyone's benefit, as in the nineteenth century United States and with similar results. Moreover, the final steps toward regional convergence were brought about during a period of stagnation (the seventeenth century). The reversal of the previous pattern in the direction of dominance of the periphery (during the late seventeenth century) coincided with a drastic reorientation of Spanish long-term national policy (until then divided between Europe and America) toward America, as a result of the European defeats. The probable explanation for the gain in competitiveness of the cities of the periphery, especially those located in the southern areas, over those of the central and northern regions, was thus due to the fact that the former were better endowed to carry on the new American-centered policy of eighteenth century Spain. Partial confirmation of this hypothesis may be seen in the fact that not all the Mediterranean periphery benefited to the extent that the southern periphery did. In its turn, this early gain in competitiveness, together with the lagged reinforcing effect of the competitive over the industry-mix effect, explains why the periphery, since that period, has been increasing its industry-mix advantage over the center.

A Framework for Regional Policy Evaluation

As for the present and future, Spain, since the end of the nineteenth century, has been forced to again follow a definitive European policy (as a result of the independence of its last remaining American possessions) and now (due to the change in its resource-mix required to pursue this policy) its periphery is once more in a better position to spearhead national development. The end result is likely to be another gain in the competitive advantage of the periphery over the center, reinforced by Spain's increasing integration into Europe.

Present and future regional policies must therefore be judged against this long-run background pattern. Both regional policy objectives and instruments must be evaluated against the long-run trend.

Given that a sound regional policy should not run counter to fundamental long-run trends, it may be concluded that the main aim of regional policy in Spain should be to direct the growth of peripheral development axes toward the center, insofar as this would be consistent with their effective continuous functioning.

Such a policy clearly has to be based on a sound infrastructure policy, whose basic allocation criteria need to equalize private and social costs so as to permit the existence of competitive effects (of any size) equally throughout the country, together with consistently equal unit costs. Most of the remaining argument is centered around this theme.

REGIONAL DEVELOPMENT STRATEGY

Strategy Before the Civil War

Against this background of long-run regional development, all pre-Civil War Spanish governments, from the right-wing Primo de Rivera dictatorship to the left-wing Popular Front, followed the same ambivalent conservative regional strategy. They tried to integrate the country by reducing regional differences through a massive infrastructure building program whose aim was to connect the outlying peripheries with the center. The program was correct in that it was based on essential infrastructure; but it was wrong in that it did not properly handle the interaction between productive and infrastructure investment, and consequently failed to generate the conditions necessary to bring about the desired decentralization of productive investment.

The results were nonetheless very impressive. Primo de Rivera's infrastructure policy was the best in the world in the opinion of the British press at the time, according to the not too sympathetic critic Madariaga (1947). All other commentators on the policy (Calvo Sotelo, 1931; Caballos, 1932; and more recently, Velarde, 1968) ranked both the quality and quantity of the roads and railroads built—900 kilometers and 100 kilometers per year respectively—very high. Even higher praise has been accorded the water resources policy of the period, designed by Pardo (1932); this policy was the predecessor to America's TVA.

Nevertheless, these efforts did not attain the goals sought. They verified once more Hirschman's (1958) hypothesis that in underdeveloped countries, productive investment does not easily follow infrastructure investment built in the underdeveloped areas. Rather, in underdeveloped countries, I would add (based on Spanish experience) that productive investment follows blindly infrastructure investment in the developed areas and shies away from that built in underdeveloped areas.

Evaluation of this period's regional policy in relation to that of post-Civil War governments can be briefly summarized. The heavy but isolated infrastructure policy of the twenties and thirties probably reduced the potential GNP rate of growth, because it channeled a higher than normal percentage of investment resources to high capital-output ratio infrastructure at a time when there were few internal and external bottlenecks to growth. But it did not bring about the desired integration of the country (the Civil War was the best proof of this) because productive investment did not follow infrastructure investment. Yet it did facilitate enormously the postwar economic policy of fast GNP growth under an infrastructure-saving strategy.

Post-Civil War Regional Development
Strategy

The economic policies of Franco's governments have been different only in their tactics. They have all followed the same "regenerationist" ideals of the prewar right- and left-wing governments. These ideals were summarized in Costa's program: "School and pantry, and seven key turns to the Cid's tomb!" No political group has ever challenged this attitude since the loss of the last colonies; it has amounted to asking the country to forget its imperial administrative specialization and to try instead the bourgeois way of a middle-class European country.

Yet, in the post-Civil War period, the regenerationist ideals were transformed into short-run development goals totally different from those which were pursued in the pre-Civil War era. Partly due to the class values of the bureaucratic and petty-bourgeois foundation on which they rested, and doubtless due also to the external political constraints they faced, post-Civil War governments buried the prewar attempt to raise Spain's development level via a free, democratically operated market process involving increasing integration into Europe. Instead, they have tried to accelerate Spain's development by means of an interventionist undemocratically controlled policy with strong anti-European, nationalistic, and autarchic content, which time has gradually eroded but not erased as effective development has taken place.

In short, since the 1930s professors' and intellectuals' interpretations of regenerationism have evolved towards the more rightist and pragmatic bureaucratic version prevailing after the Civil War. Thus, regenerationism has traveled the full circle, coming back to "Le Despotisme Illustrée" which was its main conceptual source.

Postwar governments have also had a different evaluation of and attitude toward both the regional repercussions of national development policy, and the problems regional differences have posed to the country's development (among other things, because they have directly controlled the disintegrating repercussions of the country's unbalanced regional growth). Whether consciously or unconsciously, the policies of the postwar governments have for a long time resulted in regional divergence (presently being corrected).

In brief, the actual regional policy of post-Civil War governments has for a long time favored regional divergence, thus reinforcing the effect of the country's long-run regional development pattern. It has favored maximum growth, infrastructure saving, and autarchical national development. However, these governments have also put forward a more or less coordinated formal set of regional policies, which has been partially integrated with the national development policy. The declared aim of these formal policies—partial correction of the increasing regional divergence produced by the national development policy—has been mostly rhetorical because the means made available to achieve this goal have been very limited.

Thus, in the following sections, I shall analyze the real regional impact of the national development policy; and then I shall evaluate the formal regional policies carried out by various post-Civil War governments. The procedure I shall follow in the two analyses is to study (1) the goals and (2) the means of both sets of policies, giving special attention to the uses made of the interaction of infrastructure and directly productive investment.

The Interaction of National and Regional Goals

In all countries, national goals condition regional objectives. This relationship can be analyzed in several alternative ways. The standard method is to present the stated goals at both the national and regional levels and, through analysis, to reveal the real ones—those that are actually being pursued. I shall follow a short cut by first stating the national goals in descending priority, indicating which real regional goals they permit. and then discuss the extent to which the actual formulation of formal regional goals has been a true attempt to modify the real regional effects of the national development strategy, or else simply the rhetoric of policy makers.

National Development Goals: From 1939 to the present, the desire of Spanish governments to foster national growth while maintaining political independence from external pressures has resulted in the adoption of development policies aimed at achieving economic growth and self-sufficiency. As a result, from the end of the Civil War to the present time, Spain's economic policies have been essentially autarchical. This is clearly evident from testimonies of policy makers and is substantiated in planning and legislative records, as both friends—Paris Eguilaz (1944); Robert (1943); Velarde (1968)—and foes—Hombravalla (1973), Solé Tura (1971)—of the policy recognize and document.

Autarchy and self-sufficiency doctrines which were already present in some sectors in the pre-Civil War period, as Perpiña (1952) points out, were pursued constantly, relentlessly and exclusively once they were fully adopted. This will sound like an obvious explanation of economic policies during the forties and early fifties, but one difficult to accept today, especially in view of the seven percent per capita annual rate of growth of GNP in the last decade (eight percent in the seventies) and the signs of booming international trade.

Yet, there should not be any doubt about this; according to Iberplan (1971), even though in the sixties exports increased 336 percent and imports 434 percent, and the import value per capita has lately surpassed $150, which corresponds roughly to a developed country standard (Maizels, 1963), these facts do not deny the continuous predominance of autarchical goals in Spain's present-day economic policy. In fact, Spain's current reaction against the political requirements of Common Market entry is symptomatic; *The Economist* (1973) quotes the then vice president of Spain's government, who declared in response to Chancellor Willy Brandt's conditions: "Spain will never, never accept political conditions for EEC membership." Even more revealingly clear and objective indicators of the government's desires for autarchy are its maintenance of high protectionism, its refusal to liberalize the peseta completely, and its willingness to maintain it devalued at an uncompetitive exchange rate in spite of bulging foreign reserves of close to $7 billion, making Spain sixth or seventh in the world in terms of foreign reserves.

Autarchy has in fact been the predominant goal, and it has been achieved at the expense of higher economic growth. It has meant the refusal of all external programs that could have reduced the growth constraints, but at the same time implied increased external political dependence. It has resulted in the stagnation of the forties, the moderate growth but inflation of the fifties, and the fast but below-potential growth of the sixties.

Over time, a gradual diminution of the growth constraints has taken place. But it has been accomplished unexpectedly, by the tourist boom and the overflowing of European growth. In annual round figures, and in order of importance, the following have been the most critical factors: tourist net income, $2.5 billion; foreign investment, with the accompanying transfer of technological knowhow, around $1 billion; and workers' remittances, $0.5 billion. These phenomena have permitted a reduction in the trappings of the autarchical system without reducing its spirit, which continues to exist as before but with less surveillance required.

Before analyzing the interaction between the autarchy goal and the growth constraints, and their effects on GNP growth and on regional policy, I must explain why and how autarchy has remained so dominant a goal over time in spite of the country's boom and its close and growing real integration into western Europe's economy.

The basic reason for the lasting dominance of the autarchic goals is, as I have explained at length elsewhere (Lasuén, 1972b), that the sociological base of the Spanish state is a bourgeois-bureaucratic alliance, organized under the managing principle that bureaucracy rules at the lowest possible cost in taxes to an acquiescent bourgeoisie. This base has been able to exist unaltered to the present day as a result of a number of readjustments (Lasuén 1973b). Initially more bureaucratic than bourgeois, the Spanish state has been evolving and acquiring a greater bourgeois element as a consequence of the success of its industrialization policy. The lines of that economic policy have varied, but at no time have they exceeded the limits of the implicit agreement in which the sociological basis of the state has been grounded: centralized bureaucratic direction at the least possible fiscal cost (principle of *subsidariedad*) and the greatest possible benefit to the bourgeoise.

The first challenge to this pattern was generated at the beginning of the sixties, when the tempo of development increased. Because most sectors within the public jurisdiction are in a high income elasticity and low private profitability (high social profitability) category, the rapid increase in income per capita produced a strong increase in the demand for public expenditure; but this was incompatible with the low level of taxation possible within the above-mentioned bureaucratic-bourgeois pact. The way out from the dilemma was the classic nineteenth century English solution of increasing public income by imposing a heavy import surcharge on the rising imports brought about by the trade liberalization policy undertaken, while keeping internal taxes unaltered. Since it further permitted the absorption of all benefits from a larger integration in the world economy, this Navarro-Ullastres solution favored the permanency of the Opus-Dei Administration and the strengthening of the state.

The second powerful challenge to this pattern made itself felt at the end of the last decade and at the beginning of the present one. The inexorable increase (more rapid than that of income) of the demand for goods and services from the public sector, due to the rapid rate of increase in the national income, is incompatible with the level of existing public revenue permitted by the basic sociopolitical agreement, and is also incompatible with the level of external public revenue permitted by projected international agreements (with their built-in demands for import tax reduction).

In this context, the state has two basic options: (1) reduction of the rate of development and the maintenance of the political and administrative status quo, with the possibility of greater or lesser international integration for Spain, depending on whether or not she is willing to reduce even further the potential rate of development; or (2) maintenance of the present level of development and the restructuring of economic policy consistent with the basic sociopolitical agreement. Within this second option lie three possibilities. At one extreme would be an increase in taxation and a bureaucratic centralization (in order to resist a reaction to the tax from the bourgeoisie). At the other extreme would be maintenance of the present fiscal pressure and transfer of many areas of public jurisdiction to the private sector (thus decreasing administrative centralization). The intermediate option—a light increase and readjustment in taxes and some democratization of the present economic, social, and political situation—is the one that appears to predominate in the series of currently proposed fiscal reforms.

A superficial political-economic evaluation of these options reveals that the only viable one in the present circumstances is an increased transfer of areas of public jurisdiction to the private sector, if one takes into consideration, as a criterion of the evaluation, the internal political stability of Spain as well as the necessity for greater external integration, which requires a significant tariff reduction.

Against this background, which I have recently analyzed (Ibid.), it is clear that the ruling bureaucracy's dominant interest in autarchy has been accepted permanently by the bourgeoisie because the bureaucracy has sacrificed any other goal which might have meant an increase in taxation pressure; in fact, Spain's level of taxation is the lowest of all the OECD countries, with the exception of Japan, and ranks fifty-seventh in the list of seventy-two countries analyzed by the IMF (Cansero, 1972). As a consequence, taxation has become a growing development policy concern (Fuentes, 1972).

Having explained why and how autarchy has remained the dominant goal, it is time to analyze the effects on the national and regional development patterns of the interaction between the autarchy goal and the country's growth constraints. First, I shall analyze the changing national impacts of the moving interaction above; then the actual regional effects of the national impacts.

In the forties, a low savings ratio (barely twelve percent of the GNP) together with scant public revenue (based on consumption taxes amounting to about ten percent of GNP) impeded the possibility of producing any net savings; with little foreign exchange earning power—about $20 per capita—to buy investment goods (the second growth restraint) it also produced a very small GNP growth rate. In plain words, disinclination to pursue goals which might have produced fiscal strains resulted in a low investment rate of scarcely fifteen percent of GNP (twelve percent private, three percent public), deficient capital accumulation, and an almost stagnant income per capita, far below the prewar level.

In the 1950s, remittances from workers migrating to the rest of Europe and payments from European tourists began to flow in, and although not sufficient to bolster the investment rate significantly were enough to increase investment goods imports up to about $30 per capita, making it possible for Spain to reach its prewar per capita income level by the end of the decade.

At the beginning of the 1960s, the prospect of higher tourist trade together with larger worker remittances and correspondingly greater import trade made possible the Navarro-Ullastres readjustment of the prevailing autarchy-with-low-taxes scheme to the classical model of growth-cum-trade, as already mentioned. Differential exchange rates and quotas were abolished and replaced by a high tariff policy; in turn, this furnished a significant increase without any increase in internal fiscal pressure. Parmio (1970) and Casany (1970) both show that, as a consequence, the government's revenue increase was about four percent (to arrive at about fifteen percent of GNP; twenty percent if GNP and social security were included). The government's revenue investments were dedicated, first, to government investment (basically infrastructure), then, to government net savings. These government net savings (around three percent of GNP), in their turn, were channeled through public credit banks to finance increased private productive investment.

The basis for the economic boom was thus established. It proceeded at an accelerated rate, with accumulated increases in tourist trade earnings, emigrant remittances, and expansion of exports considerably reducing the external growth constraint and enabling the country to import a yearly average of approximately $100 worth of goods per capita for the decade and up to $150 per capita per year by the end of that decade. A considerable increase in foreign investment also helped. Previously discouraged, foreign investment was now fostered, for it no longer incorporated any built-in political leverage; since all other foreign income sources were abundant, foreign investors could be turned off at will.

In spite of all these changes, the recently accelerated rate of development has not followed a smooth course, due to the persistent existence of some requirements of the autarchic policies still being pursued. For example, agricultural and industrial supply rigidities still prevail as a result of autarchical principles, which impede a compensating increase in imports in the face of changing demand; capital and money market rigidities continue to exist as a consequence of the autarchy-without-taxes and growth-cum-trade models, which attempt to maintain both the low tax base political equilibrium and the external payments equilibrium with no political ties. These rigidities have resulted in frequent shifts in monetary policy and exchange rates (frequently "stop and go" measures) when internal and external demands change, for they do not permit the existence of an alternative flexible fiscal policy.

Today, the prospects for Spain's prevailing growth model seem better than ever (Battelle, 1971). Since the end of the 1960s industrial output has become both flexible and efficient; it is likely that from now on the accelerated export boom will, after paying for required increased agricultural imports, result in a commercial surplus on top of service and transfer payment surpluses, as is indicated in a recent OECD (1972) report. This will reduce the need for sudden shifts in monetary policies, and will facilitate an "easy ride" at a seven to eight percent annual growth rate, still below the growth potential which is close to ten percent (as shown by the current yearly accumulation of two percent of GNP in the foreign reserves [Lasuén, 1972c]).

In the near future, a growth potential rate of ten percent could be achieved through increased government savings (by increased taxation) or private savings (by liberalization of the capital and money markets) and through further opening of foreign trade and finance. These policies, however, are unlikely to be followed while the present sociopolitical status quo prevails, for the reasons explained. I have indicated elsewhere how this status quo can be changed (Lasuén, 1973b).

Until it is changed, partial economic policies—sectoral and regional—will continue to be conditioned by the goals of the national growth model that has been operative for the past three decades, a model that has aimed at achieving the maximum rate of growth of income per capita consistent with, first, low taxation pressure, and second, balance of payments equilibrium based on factors controllable by the government. Its effects on the regional development process will now be analyzed.

Actual Regional Goals: The national goals have determined the regional ones. In view of the foregoing discussion, the regional implications of national policy are easily understood. Maximum growth with low government revenue and expenditure necessarily resulted in a high proportion of directly productive investment in relation to total investment (sixty percent as compared with the OECD average of forty percent), and in a correspondingly low percentage of infrastructure investment (forty percent of the total, as calculated by J. Carreras in Lasuén et al., 1966). Growth on this basis has proceeded by using up all of the excess capacity of the previously existing infrastructure stock, particularly intercity infrastructure. In effect, as shown in the study just cited, most new infrastructure investment has been intracity, especially in the area of housing (two-thirds of total infrastructure investment as against the international average of one-third).

As might be expected, this strategy has resulted in a spatially concentrated pattern of growth. In the first period, up to the middle sixties, government policies limited directly productive investments to the few main regional centers—Madrid, Barcelona, and Bilbao-San Sebastian; later policies encouraged a dispersal of directly productive investment to other large cities—Gijon-Oviedo, Zaragoza, Valladolid, Valencia, and Sevilla-Cadiz. This two-stage strategy was again the result of interaction between the growth goals and the relevant growth constraints.

Prior to the mid-sixties, Spanish entrepreneurs had to cope with an infant transport and communications sector, the lack of import capacity, a primitive distribution system hampered by government controls, and a concentration of social infrastructure in the abovementioned regional cities. In consequence, they invested in those main centers because of demand and supply considerations.

On the demand side, the new industries (mainly small workshops established by dealers or service people as a result of the drastic policy of import substitution) were bound to locate in large regional centers. They depended on proximity to the largest possible market and therefore chose the places of maximum access: the larger cities with a regional distribution tradition.

This locational trend was reinforced by supply considerations. Although many other cities had sufficient physical infrastructure, most existing social infrastructure and services were concentrated in the larger regional centers. This proved to be an essential advantage on two accounts. In the first instance, concentration of social infrastructure and services in these centers provided small firms with the needed supply of diversified inputs; secondly, the infrastructure endowments of these centers functioned as an inmigration magnet, thereby furnishing new firms with a supply of cheap labor. This migration flow in turn generated investments in education, health, housing, and services, thus reinforcing the trend, although after considerable delay and with different degrees of intensity.

The migration process has been studied in detail (Barbancho, 1960). For present purposes, I shall simply allude to the data presented in Table 8-5. Apart from international migrations, net internal migration accelerated from a net annual average of 30,000 migrants in the fifties to an annual average of 100,000 in the sixties, reaching its peak around 1964-1965.

The most effective regional policy during this period, and more so later on, was for housing. Annual housing investment, which had always been maintained around twenty to twenty-five percent of gross capital formation, produced (with a GNP that had doubled) four times as many houses in the sixties as in the fifties, with about the same total expenditure (but a rapidly declining share) of public funds (Ibid.).

As a result of this policy, the housing deficit—which was ten percent of the total housing stock in the fifties (around 700,000 units according to Cotorruelo [1960])—has recently disappeared; housing prices in real terms (in

Table 8-5. Net Internal Migratory Movements by Size of Settlement, 1961-1969

| | | Population | |
Years	Larger than 100,000	Between 10,000 and 100,000	Smaller than 10,000
1961	+ 39.955	+11.928	− 51.883
1962	+ 93.118	+22.500	−115.618
1963	+121.004	+33.091	−154.695
1964	+136.585	+43.836	−180.411
1965	+117.643	+39.391	−157.034
1966	+ 61.160	+20.887	− 82.047
1967	+ 65.801	+35.918	−101.719
1968	+ 51.655	+32.628	− 84.283
1969	+ 40.855	+33.215	− 83.070

Source: Vergara and Lorca (1970).

wage years) have come down from 5 to merely 1.5 and, as a consequence, almost seventy percent of the population (almost eighty-five percent of the workers) own their own apartments (Lasuén, 1966 and 1972d).

The indirect benefits of this policy have been at least as significant. Increased amounts of public revenue released from heavy commitment to housing have been used to finance extensive physical and social infrastructure programs since the middle of the sixties. The World Bank Report (1962) on Spain stated that the country's development was hampered by the lack of physical integration of the developed zones (in the periphery) and that the existing network would not be able to handle the prospective future demand. It also indicated that the mix of transport facilities was inadequate and unco-ordinated. As a result of this report, the First Development Plan initiated a coordinated transport program based on the modernization of the railroad system. This failed on two accounts: the calculations made were wrong because the income levels, growth rates, and income demand elasticities used proved too low; and the envisaged structure of demand of the different modes of transportation were calculated incorrectly. Transport demand evolved, as Table 8-6 shows, from rail and ship travel to road and air.

To overcome this chaos, the Second Development Plan launched three major transport programs: (1) a shipping program which has since transformed Spain into the third or fourth largest exporter; (2) an air program which has made Iberia the fifth largest European company and Spantax the world's largest charter company; and (3) a road building program which has been the country's greatest effort. The last included the *Plan Redia 1967-1972*, now practically completed (5,000 kilometers and $300 million), complemented by a privately financed express highway program, PANE, which will add 3,000 kilometers in twelve years, and 1,100 kilometers by 1975. The road program has been coupled with a strong push in the automobile industry, especially in trucks; today Spain ranks eighth in world automotive industry with a 1977 projected output of 1.5 million units.

The significant increases in government revenue already explained—which permitted the launching of the previously discussed housing and transport programs—plus the revolutionary expansion of the telephone network (up to a telephone lines per capita index that is larger than that of France) have been the key factors in this second phase of moderate regional dispersion, but there were other factors as well.

The policies referred to coincided with the gradual exhaustion of the excess capacity in physical infrastructure in the regional centers; in the presence of the constant urban infrastructure saving strategy (with the exception of housing), this exhaustion can be said to have been the factor forcing directly productive activities to look for the unused physical infrastructure existing in the other large cities, which was now a feasible alternative due to the recently built intercity infrastructure.

Table 8-6. Percentage of Total Internal Transport by Types
of Uses and Modes of Transportation

Uses		Modes		
	Rail	Road	Air	Ship
Passengers				
1960	47	50	3	–
1970	36	59	5	–
Goods				
1960	22	28	–	50
1970	15	40	–	45

Source: Third Development Plan.

At the outset of this stage, productive investment went to the large cities with unused physical infrastructure that were, in addition, in close communication with the social infrastructure of the regional centers. Lately, as in the first stage, this trend has been reinforced, for social infrastructure investment has followed the industrial and labor migration movements to the large cities. Housing policy, too, has been a major factor in this latter respect.

However brief, this background illustrates the implicit goals and the essential mechanisms of regional policy in Spain during the last three decades. Although it was not an explicit policy until the middle 1960s, its aims remained both constant in actual practice and consistent with the national growth policy, irrespective of the obfuscatory rhetoric of the bureaucracy.

Given the stock of unused infrastructure, the national growth strategy—maximum growth, balanced external payments, and low taxes—naturally resulted in infrastructure saving tactics. Since unused physical infrastructure existed in most large cities while excess social infrastructure existed only in the regional centers, the government's infrastructure saving tactics, which allowed scant social investment only after industrial and population growth had occurred, and later on only favored physical intercity infrastructure, resulted in a sequential pattern of productive investment location: productive investment occurred, first, in places with excess social and physical infrastructure until the latter were exhausted; thereafter, productive investment filtered down to places with excess physical infrastructure which were located in proximity to social infrastructure centers.

The real goals of regional policy thus have been an initial concentration of productive investment in the main regional centers, followed by the diffusion of investment to nearby smaller regional cities. The rationing of infrastructure investment—i.e., using up previously existing capacity and enlarging it only well after substantial demand exists—has followed a clear order of priorities: first, basic physical intracity infrastructure (housing); then, social infrastructure; and finally, intercity physical infrastructure.

Official Regional Goals: During the last decades there have been official regional development programs which, at face value, have run counter to the regional goals just described. All of them have been relatively minor in importance and demagogic in spirit, and have hardly affected the real goals; rather, in many instances, these minor programs, under the rhetorical cloak, have tended to reinforce the actual regional goals.

The first of these programs which could be considered as some sort of regional plan was the reconstruction program initiated shortly after the war. Known as *Areas Devastadas*, it was designed to rebuild the social infrastructure, services, and housing stock that had been destroyed during the Civil War in rural areas, excepting repair of roads and blown-up bridges. As a result, after a decade the prewar level of rural necessities was restored, even where it eventually proved to be unnecessary.

Still larger in scope were the land reclamation projects based on legislation initiated in the late thirties and forties, well analyzed by Tamames (1969). Conceived as a halfway substitute for land reform and an agricultural resource development program, it in fact aimed at agricultural import substitution consistent with the autarchy strategy. The main thrust of this effort was a vast irrigation program (close to 2 million hectares) linked to a hydroelectric power program and coupled in some instances with colonization settlements. It achieved its main real goal—self-sufficient agricultural output—only by a long, painful process and high costs. As Tamames (1972) indicates, absence of good seeds, fertilizers, and tractors forced the increased cultivation of low-yielding acreage until the middle sixties. Since that time, yields per hectare and per man have increased enormously and resulted in surpluses which are particularly bothersome, being produced as they are through subsidies to unfertile land.

The reclamation programs also resulted in the settlement of hundreds of thousands of *colons* on small, inefficient plots, and, in many instances, subsidized large landowners who thus were able to have their farms transformed into efficient producing units. The effect of this plan could have been very positive if its scale had been reduced to the irrigation of the prime land, and if it had been accompanied by all storage, transport, marketing, processing, and credit services required; or if it had been accompanied by a price policy geared to obtain the highest crop yields in every area instead of agricultural autarchy at all costs. But this was not the case, because its real aim was short-run self-sufficiency of agricultural produce. For the same reason, it did very little to help reduce regional income disparities. Rather, with few significant exceptions, most of the irrigation projects took place in the more fertile sections of the country.

The third type of program, though not proclaimed as a regional policy for reasons to be explained shortly, was the public industrialization program carried out by the state holding company, INI. It has had more important regional effects than the explicit regional programs, a fact recognized both by INI (1964) and by the World Bank (1962). Although a typical product of the autarchic strategy, INI nevertheless managed to make its main object—the industrialization of the larger cities of the nonindustrial parts of Spain that won the Civil War—compatible with the aim of overall industrialization of the country.

The fourth program was urban planning, firmly centered, as already indicated, in intracity planning. This program deserves a more lengthy comment. Urban planners, faithful to the textbooks, made known their dissatisfaction with prevailing high urban densities. But with few investment funds to enlarge urban infrastructure, they very sensibly opted for realism, and formulated tactics designed to obtain the highest possible densities on what urban land was available. The goal of these tactics was to minimize the pressure of urban demand for land throughout the country. The process was as follows (Lasuén, 1972e).

Initially, in the forties, the quantity of land demanded was much less than that available in cities, thus allowing for the existence of very low land prices. This, together with low wages, enabled the construction of housing for sale to expand in the small amounts indicated, in spite of the relative scarcity of construction materials, the general inefficiency of industry, and the population's low purchasing power, once the housing policy was liberalized.

Subsequently, in the early fifties, at the same time that the rate of economic development began its increase, the price of urban land began to rise (in absolute terms and in proportion to the increase in the prices of other factors of construction) in the industrial cities, as a consequence of the rapid increase in demand (which meant interregional migrations) and the lack of a compensatory increase in supply (as a result of limited investment in urban infrastructure).

From the middle fifties to the early sixties, the rise in the cost of land did not result in price rises for the construction of housing because the decreasing cost of other factors (e.g., materials and wages) was compensatory. In fact, migration resulted in a supply of available jobs at stable wage levels, and the cost of labor decreased as a result of an increase in productivity; industrial development also meant a decrease in the real cost of construction materials.

About the middle of the sixties, the accelerated increase in the supply of housing marked the beginning of the second phase. This time, the rise in the cost of land for housing tended to be more rapid than the rate of decrease in the cost of construction materials and labor. The housing legislation that was gradually introduced during this phase tended to avoid the implicit danger of an increase in the real cost of housing and had, as its aim, a continuing reduction in the price of housing as a percentage of income. Lacking infrastructural funds, the only solution was to increase the housing density on existing infrastructure by force. This resulted in enormous densities. For example, Madrid's center had 40,000 inhabitants per square kilometer (the center of Paris, 33,500; of Rome, 27,000). Densities in Madrid's periphery were even higher; according to Gaviria (1968) the new city districts reached 250,000 inhabitants per square kilometer.

As a consequence, congestion and land prices shot up in the regional centers and, since their peripheries could not be properly expanded for lack of infrastructure investment, productive investment was partially diverted to the other large cities or to proximate smaller cities. Table 8-7 shows the changes in growth rate in the different size cities that this process helped to induce.

With the implementation of national development plans in the 1960s, previously mentioned scattered efforts have tended gradually to coalesce into an integrated program of regional plans of the *aménagement du territoire* type, which from plan to plan have evolved in a direction which aims at the disaggregation of the national sectoral plan, and uses the framework of the urban system for development purposes. The basic argument is contained in Lasuén (1972b); its application has been the allocation of certain functions to a descending order of cities (metropolitan areas, urban areas, and market towns) in the Third Development Plan.

However, regional planning of this type has not yet achieved more than a marginal role. Its magnitude has been small, affecting the location of barely five percent of total productive investment. It has proceeded in three separate stages.

The First Development Plan (1964-1967) established seven "growth poles"; five in growing regional centers with an existing industrial base—Zaragoza, Valladolid, Sevilla, La Coruña, and Vigo; and two more in stagnant cities with growth potential—Burgos and Huelva.

The Second Development Plan (1968-1971) established four more poles in stagnant regional centers—Granada, Córdoba, Oviedo, and Logroño—which had ties with the previously selected ones, in an attempt to strengthen the poles' impact. The growth poles established within the second plan had a ten-year development period, as compared with only five years for those in the first.

In the Third Development Plan (1972-1975) it was decided to reinforce the decongestion policy applied to intensively industrialized and expanding areas, and to create "development axes" such as suggested in Lasuén (1966); an example of the latter is the "greater industrial expansion area" on the Galician coast.

A good overall evaluation of the growth pole programs is presented by Richardson (1971 and 1972), who says that the minor scale of the programs, the emphasis on direct inducement of productive investment unaccompanied by corresponding infrastructure development, and the lack of stable long-run locational objectives have been the major drawbacks in the three-stage program. These errors, however, were to be expected. The new regional plans, like the old, could not run counter to the actual regional goals of the country, irrespective of their declared content.

Nevertheless, despite the limited resources employed, some of these plans, such as the pole at Huelva, where a very efficient petrochemical complex

Table 8-7. Average Annual Rates of Population Growth per Decade, by City Size

	City Size				
Years	10,000-20,000	20,000-50,000	50,000-100,000	100,000-500,000	500,000 and over
1900-1910	19.23	10.83	9.12	43.71	10.66
1910-1920	10.12	12.15	35.23	27.55	23.08
1920-1930	7.52	39.79	9.86	40.62	34.03
1930-1940	14.85	17.19	18.51	89.12	10.79
1940-1950	2.81	9.79	24.58	18.94	53.08
1950-1960	1.48	16.95	29.62	24.85	26.86

Source: J.R. Lasuén (1967).

has been developed, have been very successful. Two partial evaluations of the growth poles setup have been made by the plan commission. In the first (1972) the poles of Huelva, Sevilla, La Coruña, and Vigo were analyzed. In the second (1973), Burgos, Valladolid, and Zaragoza were analyzed. These evaluations show that the results in the case of Huelva are the only clearly positive ones.

Instruments

Some specific regional policies have been more efficient than others in attaining their aims, and some have had greater welfare effects than have others. This section examines the cost-benefit ratios of the main policies and then their welfare effects. Before going into these, however, some general observations on both the instruments and the policy welfare effects will be made.

Regional policies can be classified under different headings: by object (specified regional goals like rural development, urban decongestion, etc.); by agent (public, private, mixed); by instrument (sectoral policies employed); by the input base on which they rely (capital, wages, etc.); and by the financing strategy they use (subventions, tax cuts, preferential credits, etc.). In general, it can be said that the most efficient direct regional policies in Spain have been those employing incentives to bolster the weakest elements in the firms' structures (capital), in the most direct way (subventions), and through the most immediate type of instrument (grants for investment projects which have been the instruments which most favor the branching out of growing firms) (Lasuén, 1969, 1970, 1971c, and 1973a). Yet at the end of the 1950s, considerable attention was being focused on the welfare aspects of regional effects of national policies. Policy debate on this subject dealt with both the short-run and long-run aspects of regional growth, but revolved primarily around the conundrums of (1) whether economic development should be concentrated or dispersed and (2) whether a concentrated or dispersed development pattern was favorable to a reduction in regional income inequalities.

A Welfare Evaluation: At this stage, it seems necessary to point out that though I feel forced to discuss Spain's regional development instruments in terms related to the traditional equity-efficiency problem, I do not think that this frame of reference is valid anymore. In fact, the equity efficiency dilemma is valid only in a purely economic planning context, where both the goals and the instruments of regional planning have a purely economic meaning. If, as the western societies demand today, it is recognized that regional planning goals are social and its instruments both economic and physical, the equity-efficiency issue disappears (Lasuén et al., 1973), although certainly at the cost of having to face newer, more difficult issues.

With this frame of reference in mind we can return to the basic polemic which began with the World Bank *Report* (1962) on the Spanish economy, which recommended industrial concentration in the developed zones; this was followed by a government publication (*Información Comercial Española*) which is normally used to sound out the public on the government's policies.

The argument expounded was, in summary, the old conservative income distribution argument couched in spatial terms. To it was added Williamson's regional convergence argument, which appeared at that time. It said, in effect, (1) that before the spatial 'pie' could be distributed, it must be increased in size; (2) that for any time span, the portions will be larger the faster it grows; (3) that it will grow faster the more concentrated the area in which this growth takes place; and finally that (4) no one is endangered because, inevitably, time series analysis shows everywhere that fast growth over time sets up forces which tend to equalize regional income per capita.

Previously, I had argued, for Latin America (Lasuén, 1959) and Spain (Lasuén, 1960b), that in certain developing countries great differences in incomes between regions posed the same problem that was posed by a sharply skewed personal income distribution—i.e., a pattern of global demand for a wider spectrum of sectoral demands than would obtain under a more homogeneous regional income distribution—an argument which is being used widely today by Prebisch (1972) and the ECLA economists in Latin America to identify large regional disparities as an obstacle to national growth.

Lacking any theoretical counter-argument, *Información Comercial Española*, a semiofficial journal, in several articles during 1968, went on defending its viewpoints on the basis of statistical evidence supporting Williamson's hypothesis, and rationalized that finding by arguing that migration increased the per capita income of the backward zones from which it originated, relatively to the decrease in the per capita income of the developed zones to which it went.

Contrary to this view, I (Lasuén, 1963) maintained that (1) the Spanish income data were not sufficiently precise or complete (as later experience has shown); (2) better data—i.e. the Italian—showed that even with the application of larger amounts of development funds, the *Mezzogiorno*'s relative income per capita was deteriorating; and (3) migration could not be conceived of as an agent of regional income convergence. In the long run, migration of the young from the backward zones could only further depress their income per capita.

Once it was clear that the dominant opinion among the bourgeoisie favored concentration, and that the larger but weaker voices of the poor regions could be silenced with the inexpensive programs which I have previously reviewed, the government embarked without qualms on a policy of industrial concentration, slightly compensated by minor industrial projects in the main cities of the poor areas.

As the different development plans evolved and created grave regional problems in both developed and underdeveloped regions, several authors joined in the polemic, primarily taking middle-of-the-road positions (as determined by their own evaluations and the weight of the available data); these included, among others, Martín Lobo (1962), Plaza Prieto (1968), and Tamames (1968).

The impact of the income data can be seen in Sáenz de Buruaga (1969) and in Gamir (1972). Both maintain that Spanish data support Williamson's convergence argument.

Recently, the whole polemic has taken on a new twist. Carreras, in his doctoral dissertation (1972) has shown (1) that all calculations of regional convergence in the past have been incorrect, for they have used regional income data which were extrapolations of indirect estimations from censuses; and (2) that available direct income estimates, however inadequate they might be, show no convergence. A similar argument is expounded by Olavarria (1973). Racionero (1972) has gone one step further; he has shown that the process of convergence, if it takes place at all, is not irrevocable. Spain, as the case in point, has shown a sequence of divergence from 1920 to 1930, convergence from 1930 to 1940, divergence from 1950 to 1960, and convergence from 1960 to 1970.

The evolution of academic opinion has been accompanied by the evolution of public opinion, and even by that of responsible businessmen from the developed zones. It also seems that the underdeveloped regions have learned not to be so easily deceived, and the developed zones have learned that concentration of old industries in rich zones creates problems for the present (the social problems of congestion) and for the future (the consolidation of an obsolete industry mix). This is, in fact, part of the summary of the important meeting on regional policy held in Bilbao in May 1973 and amply covered in *Informaciones* (May 26, 1973). In addition, it has been concluded that regional policy, and therefore its goals and means, need to be decentralized and formulated in sociopolitical terms.

It can be safely said in evaluating the polemics that most analysts today appear to agree that past reliance on regional income data has been misleading, and, therefore, that some of the conclusions based on this data must be wrong. However, re-evaluation is of little practical importance today. In fact, effective dispersion from the regional centers to the other large cities in the less developed areas was already underway, for the reasons advanced in the preceding section, when the discussion was taking place, and this dispersion has, of late, effectively reduced interurban income differentials, although it has not erased the income differentials between rural and urban areas; on the contrary, the income gap has widened in spite of the considerable modernization of agriculture (a six percent annual productivity increase), primarily because of the permanence of the autarchical agricultural price policy. Growing urban-rural income differentials have been found to be the case in the Madrid region (EVP, 1972). The same is likely to be the case for most of Spain, but not for the other major regions of industrial concentration—the Basque country and Cataluña; both appear to be typical cases of areas where the spread of innovations has permeated the countryside as well.

To recapitulate then, the consequences of the policies which have been pursued have been (1) a reduction in interurban income differentials, and (2) an increase in urban-rural income differentials, the net effect of which has been a reduction of income differentials among regions, but in two phases. Until the early sixties, both rural-urban and interregional income differentials were widening. It seems that only from the early 1960s onwards have the interurban and interregional income differentials been ameliorated, in spite of the continuous worsening of rural-urban differentials due to the growing weight of urban income in the underdeveloped areas.

A Rough Cost-Benefit Evaluation: The main policies in the first phase have already been discussed. In the order mentioned above their goals have been rural community development, agricultural resource development, and local industrial base development. The instruments used have been direct physical infrastructure policies and directly productive investment policies, respectively. Due to a lack of accurate data, it is difficult to precisely evaluate these policies, but there is widespread expert agreement that all of these programs have been characterized by cost-benefit ratios far below the average for private projects. Besides, there has been little social benefit; most rebuilt villages have been deserted, most irrigated areas produce standard low-yield crops, and most state-owned industries have already become low income elasticity producers with obsolete technology. The lower cost-benefit ratios have been achieved in those projects where bureaucratic centralization is less efficient. In descending order of efficiency they are agricultural resource development, industrial base development, and rural community development. In spite of this, it is thought that without direct implementation the results would have been far worse.

From the middle sixties onwards, the dominant goal has been government directed industrial decentralization, pursued through capital and·

other subsidies. The inducements used have been of three main types: (1) capital investment subventions (outright grants and import duty cuts); (2) tax breaks and reduced interest loans; and (3) preferential access to credit. These have been competitively awarded on the basis of criteria that have changed over time, reflecting changes in the character of the chosen cities and the overall evolution of the industrial process.

Although there exists no comprehensive evaluation of the second phase programs, from the available case studies to which I have already made reference it seems clear that both the private and social cost-benefit ratios have been much higher than those of the presixties programs. The petrochemical complex of Huelva is a case in point; although its output is small in relation to the needs of the economy, it is one of the most efficient operations of its kind in the western world.

There are two explanations for the relative success of the regional policies, in the second phase. The former planning minister, López Rodó, maintained that the main reason for the relatively high success of the program has been the structure of the plan's administrative machinery, emphasizing first the competitive element in the award of benefits, and second the simplicity of controls that it incorporates.

From personal experience as advisor to some of the applicants, I believe there is some justification for his first argument; potential investors, who were considering the possibility of establishing a plant in a certain industry and in a certain city (when that industry and city were selected for aid) were inclined to implement their plans in the specified planning periods in order to qualify for subsidies. Under the First Development Plan, this motive may have affected local entrepreneurs in the large, already industrialized cities which were selected and perhaps some firms from other cities considering locations for branch plants. Since the second plan, however, programs have continuously changed recipient industries and cities without any clear pattern; therefore, it is difficult to see why the shifting incentives have been attractive to the entrepreneurs in the old locations. His second argument, the simplicity of controls, is more difficult to evaluate. Certainly controls have been simple, but this has also probably been the cause for the charges of inefficient selection of industries and cities, and of arbitrariness in the selection of applicants.

My own evaluation of these programs has been presented before, and has been the basis for my hypothesis concerning the role of organizational changes in firms' structures as the link explaining the interaction between national and regional development patterns (Lasuén, 1969). In a nutshell, the movement of industry from cities in developed areas to the larger cities of underdeveloped regions has been the result of two sets of conditions. The sufficient conditions have been the exhaustion of excess capacity of urban physical infrastructure in the developed cities and the existence of unused capacity in the larger cities of the underdeveloped zones, coinciding with the considerable improvement in intercity transport and communications which permitted the boom to take place. The necessary condition has been the profound transformation that has occurred in the structure of firms in the developed zones (enlargement, diversification, etc.). The studies which have evaluated the development of growth poles, and similar analyses such as that of Vergara and Lorca (1970), have shown that most of the new plants in the developing areas are subsidiaries of parent firms in the developed zones, or are foreign affiliates. Therefore, although no detailed record exists, available data seem to indicate that the location of new branches of plants in developing areas has been a more important factor in employment in these developing zones than either the creation of new firms or the expansion of existing plants (as is well recorded in the British case).

These branch operations, it must be emphasized, would not have been possible ten years earlier because the size and organization of the parent firms would not have permitted it. At the beginning of the 1960s, the branch plants in the developing areas produced mostly products for local markets because the parent firms were still of the single-product type. At the beginning of the 1970s, the parent firms are increasingly becoming multiproduct, multi-plant, multicity firms producing for the national market, and they are branching out due to wage and other labor market differentials, which before appeared relevant only for multinational firms. From now on, as most large Spanish firms reach the multiproduct level and become more sensitive to such considerations, it appears that labor differentials will be more important, a development anticipated recently in the selection of Spanish plant sites by Ford, ITT, IBM, and other foreign multiproduct, multiplant firms.

PRESENT POLICIES

As expressed in the Ministry of Education's White Paper (1969c), the new policies concerning education aim at dividing up the educational system into two branches, one professional and one scientific, and at creating offshoots from these branches at many levels. Organizationally, the system is managed by an array of highly specialized educational organizations. The educational units are distributed in a geographic pattern according to the needs of the population. Because education is one of the most critical elements of social infrastructure, when the new program is fully implemented and effectively applied it will be a catalyst for the decentralization of social infrastructure. This decentralization will provide sufficient conditions for an effective outward decentralization of industry away from present industrial areas.

However, this process may take some time. As can be observed in the ministry's financing law of 1969 (1969b), the costs of this expansion program of new educational facilities, estimated by means of a UNESCO-type model (1969a), are to be paid for primarily from the national budget; revolutionary protests in the universities and high schools could result if the program's implementation is kept on schedule, and its deficient financing (due to the budget limitation) is not corrected. To avoid such protests, and given the strong political sentiments to maintain low tax pressure, the needed refinancing demands the development of a private educational system, an idea which I have advanced (Lasuén, 1972g), but which is not easily accepted. There is, therefore, a strong presumption that the program will be retarded.

The second major infrastructure program, the express highway program, does not suffer from the same limitations. This program, which is beginning to have a significant impact in the coastal areas, has been privately financed from the outset, in open recognition of the constraints on public sector financing. Though important, like all other major road programs, it is not discussed in detail here because the dominant criterion of all transport projects is that they are initiated only after substantial demand has been created. However, it should be mentioned that road programs are beginning to create or reinforce several development axes, especially those bordering on the Atlantic and the Mediterranean, as well as those which follow the main rivers—the Ebro and Guadalquivir.

The same can be said of the tourist development policy, incredible as it may seem in a country that is one of the most popular tourist spots in the world. Tourist development has not been and is not planned, apart from being subject to urban regulations and some minor inducement policies. Public infrastructure follows private construction only after a great lag.

The only new major infrastructure policy which promises to be efficient is the new urban land policy, now being discussed in Parliament. To start with, recognition of constraints on public sector financing has influenced the formulation of this new program of urban land use, as it has influenced the highway program, along lines similar to those I recommended (Lasuén, 1972e). The land use policy could be very positive, for its object is to increase the private supply of urban land in all cities in order to limit the inflation of prices, urban congestion, and pollution that have resulted from previous city planning policies.

The new program, if approved and applied, needs to be put into practice in all types of cities, for the industrial decentralization that did occur in the 1960s has already exhausted unused infrastructure capacity in the larger cities of the underdeveloped areas. The likely effect of the program would be to create an explosive expansion over the cities' boundaries, thus producing several large megalopitan areas by interlocking cities which are at present isolated.

Taking into account the likely eventual existence of differently timed effects of the new educational and urban land use policies, it can be anticipated that in the coming years the pattern of regional development may be similar growth in all metropolitan regions (both in the industrial core and in the outer areas). In effect, this would tend to take place in response to the decentralizing effect produced by the infrastructure expansion permitted in all cities by the urban land programs, as well as the larger decentralizing effects of better transport and communications networks, the appropriation of the benefits of labor market differentials, the changing structure of firms, and the slowing down of the educational expansion program. In fact, more rapid growth of intermediate-size cities could take place if the new education policy were not slowed down and if the urban land program was not adopted. In that case, the decentralization of social infrastructure, coupled with the impossibility of urban expansion in the large centers, would certainly force faster development of the unused physical infrastructure of small cities.

The official regional programs, on the other hand, will very likely manage to follow suit, and probably more effectively than in the past, because of more effective budget allocation techniques. In effect, having learned from their errors, it seems likely that the different ministries will be more willing than in the past to make mutually consistent sectoral and spatial project allocations. In addition, the multilevel planning framework (metropolitan, urban, and rural areas) now sought by Spanish planners will help in this effort.

FUTURE POLICIES

In the near future, Spain badly needs (1) an effective rural development policy, (2) a tourist development policy, and (3) an antipollution policy. It also needs a long-term regional development plan aimed at creating the best combination of natural and human environments in view of its integration into the Common Market. As Sáenz de Buruaga (1970) indicates, it is widely felt that the long-term regional plan should also provide a basis for a badly needed administrative regionalization of the country.

The first three policies have been listed separately, though they should also be part of the long-term plan. They can readily be initiated by the present government because they can be made consistent with the dominant goals of political and economic autarchy. However, the characteristics of the long-term regional plan conflict with the requirements of autarchy. Thus, the implementation of such a plan presupposes a drastic shift in political sentiments and will not, in all probability, be undertaken by the present political establishment.

Of the first three policies, the one most likely to be seriously considered, at least at the city level, is the pollution policy. Pollution control policies will probably be initiated first in the large metropolitan areas because of public concern about current dangerously high levels of pollution.

A tourist development policy ranks second in terms of probability of implementation. Given the adverse impact on the tourist trade that new reports on the pollution of Spanish beaches have had, it is likely that concerted efforts will be made to assure, by means of adequate infrastructure investment and the extension of credit facilities to private investors, that Spain's tourist attractions conform to travellers' standards of sanitation and esthetics.

Nor is there any basic obstacle to a serious rural development policy. The necessary condition for this is the implementation of a sensible agricultural price policy which will permit the country to specialize in the agricultural outputs for which it is best suited. There exist two seemingly formidable barriers to a reorganization of agricultural pricing policies. The first is a fear that reorganization would seriously undermine the autarchic goals, and the second is the fear of political reaction from farmers who are presently subsidized to cultivate inferior lands. Neither of these fears presents an insurmountable barrier. The first fear is purely psychological. Spain should and can now be a net agricultural importer without any balance of payments problem; moreover, a larger foreign trade surplus would probably result from shifting resources from agriculture to industry. As to the second, although a new agricultural price policy could engender some political unrest, this would be an easily managed problem for the population that would be affected is small. Those who would be hurt could be placated by ad hoc industrial and service development programs.

As to the long-term regional development plan, the prevailing opinion among those who are concerned with long-range goals is that the goals, standards, and methods of such a plan should be compatible with and conducive to future integration with Europe. I am currently supervising a research program to devise a preliminary draft of a long-term plan of this type. Up to now, we have come to the conclusion that the most probable political course for the Common Market to follow is not a federation of countries, but a customs union with common national policies that would permit free internal movements of goods and factors of production, as well as a common set of external policies (strategic, economic, and diplomatic). In this event, we think that a strong revival of regionalism, both economic and political, will take place. The former may emerge as a corollary to the enlargement of the market, while the latter may accompany the gradual disappearance of some of the traditional justifications for the nation-state. This means, on the one hand, that the future regional plan needs to take into account the potential integration of Spanish regions with French and Portuguese regions and, on the other, that it will not function properly unless it is administered by a decentralized regional structure of political institutions, flexible enough to deal with future political sentiments. This important point was put forward recently by J. Areilza, M. Fraga, F. Estapé and J.R. Lasuén at the previously mentioned Bilbao meeting (1973).

It is further felt that, past policies notwithstanding, this new regional plan will receive top priority in the planning process; the sectoral national plan will take second place because of the reduction in relative importance of the national goals and because of the necessary sacrifice in decision-making power the member-countries will have to make due to some important macroeconomic policy instruments, before the community's policy-making bodies.

Nevertheless, regionalization of decision-making power and spatialization of economic planning should not be taken as panaceas. As the Italian example demonstrates, greater regional divergences can result from decentralization if the underdeveloped areas are not able to set up an adequate decision-making process, while developed regions can. In addition, while advanced areas are likely to properly evaluate social needs and balance out the instruments (economic and physical) to be utilized, underdeveloped regions will most likely not have this capability, thus creating false demagogic dilemmas of the equity-efficiency type. Therefore, some measure of national intervention through direct implementation will be needed to check divergent trends, such as the direct use of public enterprises to correct regional divergences, which was recommended by Tamames (1972), and endorsed at the recent international meeting of *Mundo* (September 1973).

CONCLUSIONS

The conclusions that may be drawn fall into two categories: those which are derived from data on long-run conditions and those which derive from recent data. I shall turn my attention first to the latter.

The only general conclusion that it seems safe to draw from recent Spanish regional experience is that the spatial spread of economic growth over the different regions is greatly influenced by the organizational structure of business firms. Consequently, regional policies need to be formed with a clear understanding of organizational structures and should incorporate methods to foster necessary organizational changes and to guide their influence on regional planning objectives.

Particularly as an example for semideveloped countries with well-established urban systems, the Spanish regional experience suggests that national growth could be accelerated by an infrastructure-saving growth strategy, and that such a strategy would considerably reduce the goals of regional planning, and could perhaps limit them to management of an orderly and accelerated use of excess infrastructure capacity. In this process, if the country's own potential productive capacity is developing, the most effective policies would be the orderly absorption of, respectively, excess capacity in social infrastructure, excess capacity of physical infrastructure, and finally, the benefits of labor market differentials.

In Spain, infrastructure-building development strategies have been carried out by centralized right-wing and decentralized left-wing political structures, though both of liberal economic outlook. The infrastructure-saving development strategy has been carried out by a centralized political structure. In the history of the latter, infrastructure-saving has been more intense when the content of the government's political ideology has been less laissez faire. As a consequence, though there is no reason why an infrastructure-saving strategy cannot be effectively carried out by a decentralized political structure, it would seem necessary to conclude that the main development strategies (alternative concrete programs of the planned and accelerated material progress of a country) are related also to the concrete forms (the political structure) the country's society adopts to carry them forward. In drafting a national development program, the real and implied regional impacts and the formal regional policies should attempt to make goals and means as compatible as possible—at all levels—with the country's political structure.

On the other hand, everyone can learn something from Spain's long-run historical record of regional growth. The main conclusions that can be safely drawn are given in descending order of generality.

There seems to be no basis for the idea that either regional convergence or divergence should prevail. Both patterns are sequences of a more complex and alternate pattern, which potentially can take on many shapes. Spanish experience indicates that the long-run pattern of regional growth has been one which, starting with a high degree of divergence, proceeded toward convergence and then reverted toward an inverted divergence. This process suggests the following tentative conclusions:

1. In shift-share analysis terms, the national economic process tends either towards regional convergence or divergence depending on whether the long-run competitive effect of the leading regions, with respect to that of the lagging regions, is relatively strong or weak, because the competitive effect seems to produce industry-mix effects of the same direction and intensity, and therefore tends to consolidate either long-run cumulative convergent or divergent processes.
2. The reason why the competitive effect conditions the industry-mix effect is that regional competitiveness means a more rapid rate of and greater access to adoption of innovations, and a low level of competitiveness means a slower rate of and lesser access to innovation adoption. This process, in its turn, is controlled by the filtering down of innovation adoptions through a hierarchical urban system. At the highest levels of this system are the major cities of the more competitive regions.
3. In shorter-run periods, divergence and convergence sequences can be super-imposed on the long-run divergent trends due to accelerations or deceler-ations in the country's adoption of innovations. (The contrary would be the case in a long-run convergent trend.)

The factors determining the relative competitive-effect strength of leading regions at the beginning of the divergent or convergent long-run process are many. The relative mix of resources is of course one important determinant, but not the only one, for the relative value of a resource-mix at any point in time depends on the interaction between the patterns and policies of growth both of the country in question and of the world. What Spanish data suggests in this respect is that the long-run competitive values of a country's regions, once changed due to some transcendent political-technological reason, produce a long-term inversion in divergent or convergent regional trends. Moreover, this process is difficult to change, even given another important technological change, unless it is accompanied by intense political changes affecting the country's basic growth options.

Chapter Nine

Regional Policy in the United States

GENERAL REGIONAL TENDENCIES

This section examines general changes in national population distribution—which presumably are related to shifts in the location of economic activities—over the past several decades. Of course, mere description does not explain why they have taken place. The remaining parts of this section therefore analyze the centripetal attraction of population and economic activity to metropolitan areas, as well as the centrifugal tendencies associated with the expansion of urban fields and the decentralization of manufacturing.

The Mobility of the American Population

In general Americans are very mobile people. One need only recall such phenomena as the great westward expansion and the outmigration of southern blacks to northern cities in the past several decades. Lowdon Wingo (1972) has pointed out that public policies have on balance played a significant role in this regard:

> The United States has in the postwar period evolved a powerfully effective, implicit national urban policy whose outcome is a compound of policies, programmes and plans addressed to other, quite explicit public objectives at every level of the federal system. A key element in this implicit policy is thirty years of a national agricultural development policy which gave the U.S. the most highly capitalised and most productive agricultural establishment in the world while transferring perhaps forty million people, one-fifth of the current national population, from the nation's rural farm areas to its cities and suburbs. (P. 5)

Even today one-fifth of all Americans move to a different house every year. Between five and seven percent move to a different county every year, and of these half move to a different state. Over three-fourths of the population live outside of the state where they were born (Lansing and Mueller, 1967). If only males in the labor force are considered, the Bureau of the Census (1969) estimates that about seven percent move between counties in a year. Most of these 4.6 million intercounty movers are in the twenty-two to forty-four age group, are married, and have completed at least twelve years of school. The highest migration rates, however, were for men aged twenty-two to twenty-four, unmarried, unemployed, or in the armed services, who had attended college.

Most of the large number of persons in the labor force who move every year do so primarily for economic reasons (Lansing and Mueller, 1967). Inmigration to receiving areas is closely related to the attractiveness of their labor markets to job seekers. Active demand for labor attracts persons from both economically depressed and economically healthy areas. However, outmigration from metropolitan areas appears to be primarily spontaneous and not responsive to local labor market conditions. In other words, in the normal geographic circulation of the more mobile elements of the population there is as much movement from prosperous areas as from depressed areas. But prosperous areas replace their outmigration by attracting an even greater influx of persons from elsewhere. The depressed areas, on the other hand, are usually not able to replace their population loss. The weakness of their "pull" rather than the strength of their "push" is primarily responsible for their net migration loss (Morrison, 1972).

In addition to the economic factor there is a great deal of group migration from lagging areas. Varden Fuller (1970) points out that group migration patterns

> have been—and are still—more characteristic of the South and the southern Appalachian regions. The current migration from the rural South to northern metropolitan centers apparently depends very heavily upon kin and friendship. This is not a new pattern for the South; nor is it confined to Negroes. It is part of a cultural pattern of group self-dependence in the South as against individualistic self-dependence in the North. Other group patterns that are partly regional and partly ethnic are to be found among Mexican-Americans and in the off-reservation movements of Indians. In the North and West, individualism seems to be otherwise dominant. (P. 47)

It is particularly important to stress that while group migration may provide a valuable framework of support to the migrant, this phenomenon is not always consistent with economically rational choice. Many of the persons who belong to the groups which are of primary concern here:

. . . leave only because they have no choice; they can't eke out a living where they are. Among these can be found four major categories of desperately poor people: Southern blacks, Appalachian whites, Mexican-Americans and American Indians.

Once they reach the city, their situation often improves, often doesn't, and sometimes it gets worse. Generally these young people have made their move with little help or information about where the decent jobs are and little cash to tide them over until the right one is found. Following their relatives and old friends, they often go to precisely the places where an oversupply of unskilled labor already exists. (New Generation, 1968, p. 47)

A number of studies have indicated that the economic gains associated with rural to urban migration have in fact not been significant for many people (Fairchild, 1970; Hathaway and Perkins, 1968). On the other hand, there is evidence that among blacks, the largest minority group in the United States (with the possible exception of women), those born in the South who moved to metropolitan areas outside the South had higher incomes and less unemployment than blacks born in the North (Masters, 1972). Clearly more research is required to determine (1) whether and to what extent migration improves economic opportunities for migrants in various age, sex, race, and regional origin classes, and (2) the effects of migration on areas which are major sources of outmigration and areas which have received large numbers of inmigrants. However, in the absence of such research, it is nevertheless worth noting the major demographic shifts that recently have taken place within the United States, as well as the economic factors that have contributed to them.

Regional Demographic Trends
Differing migration and natural increase (or decrease) patterns have resulted in varied regional demographic trends. To generalize rather broadly, consistent population gains have been registered in the northeastern megalopolitan region (including nearly all of New York state), the Great Lakes urban-industrial region, the Piedmont Crescent, Florida, the Gulf Coast, the West (particularly Arizona, California, Nevada, Oregon, and western Washington), and numerous metropolitan areas in other parts of the nation.

Population losses have characterized northern New England; central Appalachia; the southern Atlantic coastal plains, central and southern Georgia; Alabama and Mississippi (excluding the Gulf Coast); the Mississippi Valley; and much of the prairie and plains areas from Canada to Mexico. Counties that have lost population only in the last decade generally are either in or bordering on these areas. About 1350 counties—well over one-third of all counties in the nation—had such heavy outmigration during the 1960s that they experienced absolute population declines. (About 500 counties had fewer births than deaths in 1970 because so many young adults had left; in 1960 there were only thirty-eight such counties and in 1950 only two.) These counties are overwhelmingly rural in nature and are heavily concentrated in the Great Plains and Corn Belt, central Appalachia, and portions of the southern Atlantic coastal plains.

In contrast to regions that have either grown or declined over a long period are a few regions that have gained population in the last decade after extended decline or stagnation. They include the Vermont-New Hampshire area, central Wisconsin and Minnesota, the Tennessee Valley (broadly defined to include counties bordering the state of Tennessee everywhere but to the west), the Ozarks, central Texas, and the Rocky Mountain regions of central Colorado and northern New Mexico. The factors behind the turnaround of these regions will be considered below. First, however, it is necessary to examine briefly the primary factor in the changing distribution of population and economic activity in the United States: the continuing growth of metropolitan areas.

Relative Advantages of Metropolitan Areas

It is customary in the United States to differentiate metropolitan and nonmetropolitan area residence categories in terms of Standard Metropolitan Statistical Areas (SMSAs). Essentially, an SMSA has a core city with at least 50,000 inhabitants, and includes the county in which the city is located as well as adjacent counties which are metropolitan in character and economically and socially integrated with the core city. In 1970, 68.6 percent of the American population lived in SMSAs; the urban population amounted to 73.5 percent of the national total. Moreover, the Bureau of the Census (1972) definition may be conservative. Berry (1972) argues that if the daily commuting fields to metropolitan area jobs are used to delimit functional boundaries for the nation's emerging urban areas, then daily urban systems so defined include even more than three-quarters of the population. The extent of urbanization thus depends on the cutoff point (of percent commuting to the metropolitan area) at which one prefers to include a given county in the daily urban system; those with an urban bias will choose a low figure and the Department of Agriculture will choose a high one.

What have been the reasons for the increasing concentration of population and economic activity in metropolitan areas? First, growing metropolitan areas benefit from external economies of agglomeration as well as from cultural and geographic amenities, and these factors provide the impetus for self-sustained future growth. Spengler (1967) estimates that whereas less than forty years ago nearly thirty percent of the labor force needed to be located close to natural resources, today only seven percent are resource-bound. Thus, the great preponderance of workers now is potentially "footloose" or must locate in proximity to consumers who themselves are relatively footloose, and economic opportunity is associated less with land and natural resources and more with the presence of capital and human skill.

It should be emphasized that the advantages of larger urban areas cannot be simply explained by the traditional economic base approach because it really never came to grips with the dynamics of the process by which an area amasses overhead capital and by which it acquires new export bases. Similarly, classical location theory, including central place theory, relied too heavily on static analyses with "other things equal." As Wilbur Thompson (1968) points out:

> The economic base of the larger metropolitan area is, then, the creativity of its universities and research parks, the sophistication of its engineering firms and financial institutions, the persuasiveness of its public relations and advertising agencies, the flexibility of its transportation networks and utility systems, and all the other dimensions of infrastructure that facilitate the quick and orderly transfer from old dying bases to new growing ones. A diversified set of current exports—"breadth"—softens the shock of exogenous change, while a rich infrastructure—"depth"—facilitates the adjustment to change by providing the socio-economic institutions and physical facilities needed to initiate new enterprises, transfer capital from old to new forms, and retrain labor. (P. 53)

In contrast, whatever advantages relatively stagnant nonmetropolitan areas may have in terms of a stable, cheap, and abundant labor force; of adequate and relatively cheap land; and of easy access to work and recreation areas, they still often have a host of disadvantages to overcome. Cheap land and low tax rates may be more than offset by low levels of public services. There may be relatively few business contacts with other producers, suppliers, or auxiliary business services. While labor may be plentiful, it may prove expensive to adapt untrained workers to the firm's needs. The local market will probably not be significant, and firms frequently find it advantageous to locate near competitors rather than at a distance. Bad connections with long distance transportation may create higher transfer costs. Nonmetropolitan areas also tend to be lacking in cultural and educational facilities and personnel, and there is often a great deal of mistrust of industrialization in rural areas, including the wariness of local "leaders" who do not wish to see the status quo altered. William Alonso (1970) argues that productivity increases with urban size because:

> urban size is a measure of the opportunities to which an inhabitant or enterprise has access. Interestingly, per capita income is also strongly correlated to population potential, which is a mathematical measure of the accessibility available to residents of the city to the population of the rest of the country. Thus, a small metropolis in an area of high population potential will usually have as high a per capita income as a larger but more remote metropolis. This phe-

> nomenon may account for the emerging megalopolitan pattern, which consists of constellations of metropoles. The nineteenth century city, which had a single dominant center of activity, has given way to the much larger metropolis, whose structure is a complex counterpoint of multiple nuclei which permit the advantages of concentration and specialization while keeping functional distances relatively small. The megalopolis, for all the negative associations this term has gathered in journalistic usage, seems to be a further adaptation permitting specialization and high connectivity among urban areas, while avoiding some of the penalties of excessive size. (Pp. 3-4)

In addition, Alonso cites evidence that incomes are more evenly distributed in larger than in smaller metropolitan areas. The sheer mass of the concentration of poverty in the ghettos of big cities may account for the contrary common impression. Evidence that per capita incomes are converging regionally would seemingly lead to the general conclusion that the market system is somehow automatically taking care of the problems of regional disparities in income and economic opportunity (Williamson, 1965; Borts and Stein, 1964). However, as will be argued later, this is by no means necessarily the case.

While the foregoing discussion indicates that metropolitan areas have many advantages over nonmetropolitan areas, two phenomena are increasingly tending to favor the growth of some nonmetropolitan areas. These are the emergence of urban fields and the decentralization of manufacturing.

The Emergence of Urban Fields

American living patterns are increasingly characterized by a spatially broader community of interests. John Friedmann and John Miller (1965) have pointed out that:

> It is no longer possible to regard the city as purely an artifact, or a political entity, or a configuration of population densities. All of these are outmoded constructs that recall a time when one could trace a sharp dividing line between town and countryside, rural and urban man. From a sociological, and, indeed, an economic standpoint, what is properly urban and properly rural can no longer be distinguished. (P. 314)

Thus, the city is no longer so much a physical entity as a pattern of localizations and connecting flows of people, information, money, commodities, and services. A number of concepts have been suggested to encompass this expanding scale of urban activity, but the most satisfactory perhaps is that of an "urban field," which has been defined in the following terms:

> Looking ahead to the next generation, we foresee a new scale of urban living that will extend far beyond existing metropolitan cores and penetrate deeply into the periphery. Relations of dominance and dependency will be transcended. The older established centers, together with the intermetropolitan peripheries that envelop them, will constitute the new ecological unit of America's postindustrial society that will replace traditional concepts of the city and metropolis. This basic element of the emerging spatial order we shall call the "urban field." (P. 313)

The urban field, in this view, represents a fusion of metropolitan areas and nonmetropolitan peripheral areas into core areas with a minimum population of 300,000 persons and extending outwards for approximately a hundred miles, that is, a driving distance of about two hours. In the past metropolitan growth has tended to draw off productive population and investment capital from hinterland areas, but in the future centrifugal forces will reverse this pattern. For one thing, the hinterlands have space, scenery, and communities that are increasingly attractive to metropolitan populations. Demand for these resources is being generated by rising real income, greater leisure, and increasing mobility. Personal income in 1972 has been estimated at $920 billion, a gain of almost fifty percent in a five year period. Over forty million Americans now work under employment conditions entitling them to three week vacations. Federal law now provides five three-day weekends each year, and a trend toward a four-day work week is clearly in evidence, with about 2000 companies now following this procedure. Earlier retirement has been encouraged by improved pension plans and higher Social Security benefits (*U.S. News*, 1972). Access to nonmetropolitan hinterlands has been vastly improved; for example, when the Interstate Highway System is complete an estimated 3.5 to 7.5 million acres will be opened for development (Friedmann and Miller, 1965).

Dollar sales of leisure equipment (an estimated $105 billion in 1972) have increased by fifty-two percent over the past five years, reflecting an accelerating desire to "get back to nature." A survey by the Department of the Interior indicates that three-quarters of the American population nine years of age and older is involved in some form of outdoor recreation. The most popular outdoor activities, with the share of the relevant population who participate, are: picnicking (forty-nine percent), swimming (forty-six percent), playing outdoor sports (thirty-six percent), attending sports events (thirty-five percent), walking for pleasure (thirty percent), fishing (twenty-nine percent), boating (twenty-four percent), bicycling (twenty-two percent), camping (twenty-one percent), nature walks (eighteen percent), and hunting (twelve percent). Moreover, about two million American families own second homes used for vacationing, and the number is increasing each year by from 150,000 to 200,000 units. In addition, about 72,000 motor homes are expected to be manufactured in 1972, up from 13,200 only four years ago. About one-third of the total mileage driven in private automobiles is devoted to getting to and from vacation areas (U.S. News, 1972). Clearly, satisfying leisure-time desires already represents a major opportunity for many nonmetropolitan areas, and growth prospects in this regard have few parallels.

The phenomena described here have been analyzed recently by the author in terms of case studies of large nonmetropolitan regions that had been declining or stagnating, but which grew relatively rapidly in the last decade (Hansen, 1973). Although employment expansion in these regions included a considerable amount of manufacturing activity, it also included a relatively large amount of workers in non-goods-producing sectors usually associated with metropolitan areas. The Interstate Highway System has helped to expand urban fields, but its role has primarily been to reinforce processes already at work. Although many nonmetropolitan counties have benefited from the continuous extension of urban fields from SMSAs, others have grown on the basis of the leapfrogging of metropolitan demand for amenities conducive to recreation, tourism, and retirement, and to second homes. This can clearly be seen in the Colorado-New Mexico Rockies and the Vermont-New Hampshire regions. The impact of this demand on local employment and income is difficult to establish, but there are indications that while tourism and related activities bring undoubted satisfactions to metropolitan populations and profit to many metropolitan-based developers, their positive impact on the local nonmetropolitan labor force is often less certain. The tourist industry does not have strong linkages to other industries and usually does not lead to the growth of complementary activities (Eichner, 1970).

Decentralization of Manufacturing

There has been considerable interest in recent years in programs that would induce greater industrialization of nonmetropolitan areas, and it is common to identify "industry" with manufacturing. However, it is essential to keep in mind that over the past two decades goods-related employment in the United States has dropped from fifty percent of nonagricultural employment to only thirty-eight percent; manufacturing employment has declined from thirty-four percent of the nonagricultural total to twenty-six percent. Meanwhile, the share accounted for by service-related employment has increased from fifty percent to sixty-two percent (Bureau of the Census, 1971). Moreover, there is abundant evidence that tertiary industry shows less ability or willingness to disperse than does manufacturing.

Wilbur Thompson's (1969) hypothesis of industrial filtering in the national system of cities maintains that invention, or at least innovation, takes place more than proportionally in the larger metropolitan areas of industrially mature regions. However, as industries age and their technology matures, skill requirements fall and competition forces them to relocate to lower wage areas. The lower an urban area in the skill and wage hierarchy, the older an industry tends to be when it arrives, and the slower its national growth rate. Intermediate level places tend to fashion a growth rate somewhat above the national average out of growing shares of slow-growing industries, but in smaller places the positive change in share weakens and erodes to zero, leading to slower than average growth and net outmigration, or even to absolute employment and population decline in the smallest places. As Thompson states:

> In national perspective, industries filter down through the system of cities, from places of greater to lesser industrial sophistication. Most often, the highest skills are needed in the difficult, early stage of mastering a new process, and skill requirements decline steadily as the production process is rationalized and routinized with experience. As the industry slides down the learning curve, the high wage rates of the more industrially sophisticated innovating areas become superfluous. The aging industry seeks out industrial backwaters where the cheaper labor is now up to the lesser demands of the simplified process. (P. 8)

There is clear evidence that in the United States the process of industrial filtering as described by Thompson is taking place. There also is evidence that the process eventually leads to an upgrading of manpower qualifications, types of industry, and incomes. These phenomena are most clearly seen in the South. The industrialization of the South was initiated in large measure by the movement of textile mills from New England and other northern areas into the Piedmont region of the central Carolinas. The textile mills in turn generated other activities. For example, Zammito (1972) remarks that:

> by 1970 there were 214 establishments in the South producing *machinery* for the textile industry. In addition, there were 65 chemical plants involved in producing synthetic fibers; the bulk of these plants were in the states where substantial textile production has concentrated. Suppliers of dyes and other processing chemicals were also stimulated by the movement of the textile industry. (P. 24)

The growth of manufacturing in the Carolinas, and especially North Carolina, was followed by similar expansion into Georgia. Decentralization next spread to the Tennessee Valley, which has managed to achieve a higher degree of industrial diversification than either the Carolinas or Georgia. More recently, the states of Mississippi and Arkansas have entered the lower rungs of the filtering process. Although Georgia is actively recruiting northern industrial firms, it is not attempting to "sell" the state on the basis of a labor force willing to work for low wages; that era has passed. Tennessee officials take a certain pride in the fact that they no longer need to tempt firms with the subsidies available in Arkansas and Mississippi. Arkansas and Mississippi are gratified with industrial growth based on low-wage, slow-growth industries, though stirrings for something better are apparent and probably will be realized.

Of course, interregional decentralization of manufacturing to the South does not in itself imply decentralization down the urban hierarchy. However, while some firms have left small New England towns in favor of larger cities in the South, the industrialization of the South has in fact been a phenomenon primarily benefiting nonmetropolitan areas. Between 1960 and 1970 manufacturing employment in the South grew at an annual rate of 4.0 percent compared to only 1.1 percent in the rest of the nation; the absolute manufacturing employment gain in the South was 1,489 thousand, which was greater than the total increase of 1,416 thousand for the remainder of the country. The nonmetropolitan South gained 753,000 manufacturing jobs between 1960 and 1970, while the metropolitan South was gaining only 736,000. The nonmetropolitan annual growth rate in manufacturing was 4.8 percent, compared to 3.5 percent for metropolitan areas. Whereas the nonmetropolitan South accounted for thirty-eight percent of total southern employment in 1970, it accounted for forty-five percent of manufacturing employment. In contrast, nonmetropolitan areas had only thirty-three percent of service employment.

The southern counties that have been the primary beneficiaries of industrial decentralization have one element of homogeneity that is even more striking than their industrial expansion: despite the fact that they are southern they have proportionally fewer blacks than the nation as a whole. The obvious general lack of extension of employment opportunities to areas with a high proportion of blacks has been rationalized on a number of grounds. Many employers believe that blacks are less productive and more prone to organization by unions. A prominent local official in northeastern Mississippi, commenting on the failure of the industrial growth characteristic of his area to spread to the Black Belt, stated that firms seeking a large pool of relatively cheap labor may need to go as far south as northeastern Mississippi but no farther. Whatever superficial merit these arguments may have, it cannot be denied that racial discrimination plays a part in the failure of firms to locate in black areas. However, the issue is not solely one of overt racism on the part of those who decide where firms will locate. Past and present discrimination against blacks in the provision of health, education and other human resource investments has created a labor force that may really be relatively less productive and marginal firms in particular cannot afford experiments based on social concern.

Without subsidies on a scale not likely to be politically feasible, lagging rural areas with large concentrations of minority groups are likely to remain poor. Yet the people of these areas can be given the option of employment in viable urban growth centers, preferably not too big or too distant from the regions where the relocatees feel they have their roots. If a federal subsidy can accelerate growth in a center that is already growing, and if this subsidy is made conditional to providing opportunities for residents of lagging areas, then it would be more efficient to try to tie into the growing area then to attempt to create growth in stagnant areas that are basically unattractive economically. It should be emphasized that this approach has little to do with the prevalent notion that a growth center should, for policy purposes, be a generator of beneficial "spread effects" to its hinterland; there is little evidence that such a policy really works in large lagging rural regions. It might be preferable to refer to the proposed growth centers as migration centers, which link external economies of urban growth to human resource development in lagging areas.

Rural Prosperity and Outmigration

Because not all nonmetropolitan areas have significant growth potential, it may be more sensible in many cases to organize an orderly retreat than to fan false hopes for future growth. The Great Plains, for example, have had heavy outmigration for several decades, and quite a few counties within or near this area declined in population during the past decade after having grown previously. There are those who view population decline with alarm, and numerous bills are before Congress to provide special assistance to these distressed areas. However, it is difficult to compare the situation in the Plains, the upper Great Lakes, northern New England, and other relatively prosperous areas with heavy outmigration to the situation in areas such as central Appalachia, south Texas, the southern Atlantic coastal plains, and the Mississippi Delta. In the Plains, for example, outmigrants have generally been well prepared to take advantage of economic opportunities in other areas. Of course, the population left behind has a relatively high proportion of older people and it is often difficult to maintain essential services for a widely dispersed population. On the other hand, agriculture is viable and there is relatively little poverty. In addition to savings and farm income there is considerable income from the federal government in the form of farm subsidies and social security benefits. There also are viable small towns, though they probably should be developed as service centers for rural hinterlands rather than as growth centers capable of halting and even reversing outmigration.

POLICY ISSUES AND GOALS

Regional policies generally are responses to situations that are perceived to be problems. The regional policies introduced in the 1960s evolved from a concern in the mid-1950s for assisting areas that were economically depressed but not underdeveloped in the usual sense. Pittsburgh represents a classic example in this regard; the basic problem is one of specialization in declining sectors and poor adaptability to alternative uses of local resources. Chinitz (1969; see also Cameron, 1970) has identified other models of regional problem areas that became eligible for federal assistance during the 1960s. The "not-so-poor depressed rural area" is characterized by high unemployment, income somewhat below the national average, and a basically rural setting. Examples of such areas, whose economies usually are based on declining primary activities, include the upper Great Lakes region, the Pacific northwest and northern New England. "Poor depressed rural areas" are largely confined to the South, where many of the classic conditions of underdevelopment still exist. Appalachia, and particularly central Appalachia, represents a special case where the population is white, poor, unemployed, and relatively isolated. Large city ghettos and Indian reservations are yet other special cases. Finally, there is the " 'rich' and rapidly growing distressed area," primarily found in California. Here incomes are high and employment growth is rapid, but high unemployment has provided a basis for assistance under regional legislation. The principal reason for this perhaps peculiarly American phenomenon is that the rate of inmigration has been more rapid than the rate of growth of jobs. There is evidence that this model may no longer be relevant, and in any case it is doubtful whether such areas should have benefited from depressed area legislation in the first place.

Reduction of unemployment is one of the principal rationales for regional policy. However, the data in Table 9-1 show that among the nation's broad regions, the South—which is generally acknowledged to be the most significant problem region—actually has the lowest unemployment rate. Moreover, even though the unemployment rate for minority races in the South is 8.8 percent compared with 4.9 percent for the total regional labor force, this figure is still below the national rate of 9.9 percent for minority races. Participation rates in the South for the total labor force and minority races is about the same as the corresponding national rates, though the minority race rate is relatively low in the east south central states of Kentucky, Tennessee, Alabama, and Mississippi.

The data in Table 9-2 indicate that the major problem in the South is low income rather than high unemployment or low participation rates. This is particularly the case for blacks. In 1970 Southern black families had a median income of $5,226, compared with the corresponding national figure of $9,867 for all families.

It is important to recognize that in a nation as large as the United States the broad regional differences shown in Tables 9-1 and 9-2 often mask significant intraregional differences. Thus, the lagging counties which constitute the regional commission (see Map 9-1) and Economic Development Administration areas, to be discussed later, are very often located in relatively prosperous states. Because the problems that have given rise to regional policies cut across multistate regions and even states, the remainder of this section is devoted to two broad issues that have affected national regional policy: the disparities between rural and urban areas, and those between central cities and suburbs in metropolitan areas.

Table 9-1. Civilian Labor Force and Unemployment, by Race
(Persons Sixteen Years Old and Over), Region, and Ten Largest
States, 1971

Region and state	Civilian labor force (1,000) Total	Minority races	Participation rates[1] Total	Minority races	Unemployment Number (1,000) Total	Minority races	Rate[2] Total	Minority races
United States	84,106	9,324	60.2	60.9	4,999	922	5.9	9.9
Northeast	20,203	1,727	59.0	60.0	1,261	160	6.2	9.3
New England	5,063	171	62.4	63.8	351	28	6.9	16.2
Massachusetts	2,472	86	61.6	59.7	164	11	6.6	13.0
Middle Atlantic	15,140	1,556	58.0	59.6	909	132	6.0	8.5
New York	7,562	888	57.8	60.7	495	71	6.6	7.9
Pennsylvania	4,826	401	57.3	57.4	261	35	5.4	8.8
New Jersey	3,017	305	59.4	59.8	172	29	5.7	9.6
Northcentral	24,033	1,751	61.3	59.4	1,330	225	5.5	12.8
East northcentral	17,436	1,473	61.1	59.6	1,049	196	6.0	13.3
Illinois	4,747	501	61.6	55.1	244	51	5.1	10.2
Ohio	4,434	393	60.3	63.5	287	60	6.5	15.2
Michigan	3,617	372	60.3	59.9	276	52	7.6	13.9
West northcentral	6,597	278	61.8	58.3	281	29	4.3	10.4
South	25,448	4,584	59.8	61.1	1,247	402	4.9	8.8
South Atlantic	12,665	2,631	60.2	63.6	571	194	4.5	7.4
Florida	2,764	402	55.0	64.8	135	32	4.9	7.9
East southcentral	5,091	829	58.2	55.6	265	84	5.2	10.1
West southcentral	7,692	1,124	60.1	59.9	411	124	5.3	11.0
Texas	4,715	525	62.1	64.3	234	51	5.0	9.7
West	14,422	1,262	60.7	63.4	1,161	135	8.1	10.7
Mountain	3,366	136	61.3	59.6	204	16	6.1	11.5
Pacific	11,056	1,126	60.5	63.9	957	120	8.7	10.6
California	8,374	810	60.5	64.4	735	101	8.8	12.5

[1] Percent of each group in civilian labor force.
[2] Percent of civilian labor force.
Source: Bureau of the Census (1972), p. 222.

Rural-Urban Disparities

Most of the major issues concerning the spatial distribution of
population and economic activity in the United States have been anticipated in
the foregoing discussions. Interregional income disparities are reflected in the
data on poverty status presented in Table 9-3. In 1969 it was estimated that 17.1
percent of the nonmetropolitan population was in poverty status, in contrast to
only 9.5 percent of the metropolitan population. Even more striking, however, is

Table 9-2.　Money Income: Percent Distribution of Families and Unrelated Individuals, by Income Level, Race, and Region, 1970

Item	Total (1,000)	Income level (percent distribution)										Median income
		Under $1,000	$1,000-$1,999	$2,000-$2,999	$3,000-$3,999	$4,000-$4,999	$5,000-$5,999	$6,000-$6,999	$7,000-$9,999	$10,000-$14,999	$15,000 and over	
Families												
All races	51,948	1.6	3.0	4.3	5.1	5.3	5.8	6.0	19.9	26.8	22.3	$9,867
White	46,535	1.4	2.4	3.7	4.6	4.9	5.5	5.8	20.1	27.9	23.7	10,236
Northeast	11,382	1.0	1.7	3.3	3.7	4.5	4.6	5.3	19.3	29.7	26.8	10,939
Northcentral	13,485	1.4	1.9	3.3	4.6	4.7	5.2	5.4	20.2	29.1	24.4	10,508
South	13,391	1.6	3.7	4.9	5.0	5.5	6.7	6.9	21.0	25.2	19.7	9,240
West	8,277	1.5	2.0	3.5	5.1	4.9	5.0	5.7	19.9	28.0	24.4	10,382
Black	4,928	3.5	8.1	9.5	9.2	8.2	9.3	7.7	18.1	16.9	9.5	6,279
Northeast	938	2.1	3.4	6.6	7.7	7.8	9.1	7.7	20.9	22.5	12.2	7,774
Northcentral	1,040	3.0	6.7	7.5	6.7	6.0	9.3	6.3	18.5	24.4	11.6	7,718
South	2,538	4.5	11.5	11.1	11.1	9.6	9.8	8.2	16.9	10.7	6.6	5,226
West	412	2.0	2.8	11.0	6.3	6.6	6.5	8.0	17.6	23.1	16.0	8,001
Unrelated Individuals												
All races	15,357	11.9	22.5	14.2	10.0	7.7	6.4	5.8	12.3	6.3	2.8	3,137
White	13,413	10.8	21.8	14.3	9.9	7.8	6.5	5.9	12.7	6.9	3.3	3,283
Black	1,746	20.0	28.4	11.9	10.9	6.7	5.8	5.0	9.0	1.7	0.6	2,117

Source: Bureau of the Census (1972), p. 323.

Table 9-3.   Persons in Poverty Status, by Type of Residence, 1969 (Number of persons in thousands)

Residence type	All races			White			Black		
		Below poverty level			Below poverty level			Below poverty level	
	Total	Number	Percent of total	Total	Number	Percent of total	Total	Number	Percent of total
United States	199,849	24,289	12.2	175,231	16,668	9.5	22,349	7,214	32.3
Metropolitan	130,017	12,320	9.5	112,440	8,200	7.3	15,824	3,855	24.4
Central city	57,781	7,760	13.4	44,392	4,527	10.2	12,439	3,068	24.7
Metro ring	72,236	4,560	6.3	68,049	3,674	5.4	3,384	786	23.2
Nonmetropolitan	69,831	11,969	17.1	62,791	8,468	13.5	6,525	3,359	51.5

Source: U.S. Bureau of the Census, "Consumer Income," Current Population Reports, P-60, No. 76, (Washington, D.C.: Government Printing Office, 1970).

the degree of poverty found among the nonmetropolitan black population; over half of these persons lived in poverty conditions.

It was noted earlier that some investigations have indicated that regional income disparities are narrowing over time. This position is usually based on state data. But many regions comprising the poorest parts of states continue to lag far behind the rest of the country in per capita income. Reference already has been made in this regard to such areas as central Appalachia, south Texas with its large number of disadvantaged Mexican Americans, much of the upper Great Lakes region, the Ozarks, the southern Black Belt, and Indian reservations. Moreover, even if per capita regional incomes are converging, the pace is so slow as to be politically and socially unacceptable to many persons. Finally, it is not even certain interregional income differences are narrowing in a broadly regional sense. E.J.R. Booth's analysis (1964; see also Keuhn, 1971) of per capita income trends in major multistate regions from 1880 to 1960 concludes that the hypothesis of any recent approach to interregional income parity in the United States must be rejected. "This conclusion is not modified by considerations of differential price movements, by the form chosen to represent the trends, nor even by longer-term trends" (p. 51).

Because nonmetropolitan areas account for the vast majority of counties with relatively low incomes and relatively high net outmigration there has been considerable pressure to "do something" for these places. It also is argued that many of the problems experienced by large, congested metropolitan areas could be ameliorated by curbing rural to urban migration, or at least diverting migration flows to smaller urban centers. However, even if nonmetropolitan areas were to retain their people it is not clear that this would really help the big cities in solving their problems. Preliminary estimates indicate that four-fifths of the recent growth of metropolitan areas is a consequence of natural increase (births in relation to deaths), while the remainder is as much as result of international migration as net inmigration from nonmetropolitan areas (Alonso, 1970).

If rural to urban migration no longer constitutes the burden that it perhaps once did for large cities, there is yet another argument for policies to restrain the expansion of major metropolitan areas. This appraoch is based on evidence that most Americans appear to prefer living in rural areas or small towns and cities. A Gallup Poll survey released in 1968 found that fifty-six percent of the respondents would prefer living in rural areas or small towns, if jobs were available. In comparison with a poll taken two years earlier, the proportion of persons expressing a preference for city or suburban living dropped by seven percentage points.

The data in Table 9-4 were obtained from a probability sample of 1700 persons, using a questionnaire designed by the staff of the Commission on Population Growth and the American Future. While only twelve percent of the respondents resided on farms or in open country not on farms, thirty-four percent would prefer to live in such areas. At the other end of the spectrum, over twice as many respondents lived in large cities as would prefer to live there, and twice as many persons lived in suburbs of large cities as would prefer to live there. It is not surprising, therefore, that fifty-two percent of the respondents thought that the federal government should discourage or should not encourage further growth of large metropolitan areas. Similarly, fifty-eight percent felt that the federal government should encourage people and industry to move to smaller cities and towns.

Of course, as Sundquist (1970) notes, most people "are not in reality free to live just anywhere. The vast majority are employees who must live where there are jobs, and the location of jobs is not their choice. The concentration of the country's population is the result of employer-created job patterns that the people have had to follow" (p. 90). Although the present distribution of jobs and people is largely the result of market forces, other factors have also created a bias toward metropolitan areas. Wilbur Thompson (1969) has pointed out that most semiskilled production workers have implicitly abandoned any influence they might have had on the location of their jobs by quoting a spatially invariant wage through their unions.

Reinforcing this skill bias through which managers and professional people lock the semiskilled production workers into their preferences for metropolitan areas is an age bias in migration. The more affluent, the better educated, and the young are the more mobile persons who not only have preferred cities but have not hesitated to move to them. With time and aging many city people may prefer the environment of nonmetropolitan areas, but they will tend not to move because of heavy financial and psychic investments in home, friends, and local institutions, and of the shorter remaining life span over which the costs of moving must be recaptured (Thompson, 1972).

Despite these considerations it must be admitted that we still are largely ignorant of the individual and social residential location preferences that economists and others presumably are trying to satisfy when they speak of making spatial resource allocation more rational. For example, in the survey results presented in Table 9-4, there may be a considerable difference between preferring to live in a small town or small city within easy commuting distance of a metropolitan area, and preferring to live in such places in relative isolation from metropolitan areas. It seems probable that the metropolitan resident who states a preference for a small town or city has the first alternative in mind, whereas the last may appeal more to the person actually residing in a nonmetropolitan area. A residential preference survey made in Wisconsin in fact suggests that what most people want is the best of both worlds, that is, rural or semirural residence within reasonable commuting distance to metropolitan amenities (National Area Development Institute, 1972a). This interpretation is of course consistent with the proposition that urban fields are, or should be, a fundamental unit of analysis in the regional economics of the United States.

Table 9-4.   Actual and Preferred Place of Residence of Americans Sixteen Years of Age and Older (percent)

	Actual Residence	Preferred Residence
Farm	5	14
Open country not on a farm	7	20
Small town	20	19
Small city	13	11
Medium-size city	14	10
Large city	16	7
Suburb of medium-size city	14	12
Suburb of large city	12	6

Source: Commission on Population Growth and the American Future (1972).

American regional policy, however, is more oriented toward the vague rhetorical objective of achieving rural-urban balance, a phrase encountered again and again in legislative proposals. Implicit in such arguments is the notion that each American should be guaranteed the right to a good job no matter where he lives. In other words, economic efficiency should be constrained by considerations of equity. Rural to urban migration in this context is a phenomenon that should not only be halted, but reversed. The consequences of this reasoning will be discussed subsequently.

Intrametropolitan Problems

Probably the most pressing urban problem in the United States is that of the ghetto, or slum. The data in Table 9-3 indicate that the incidence of poverty in central cities is over twice that in metropolitan rings, and that it is still greater in nonmetropolitan areas. The plight of the black population is particularly apparent. About one-quarter of the metropolitan black population was below the poverty line in 1969, whereas this was the case for only seven percent of the white metropolitan population. Moreover, contrary to whites, there is little difference between the incidence of poverty among central city and metropolitan ring blacks. It was pointed out earlier that degree of equality of income distribution may be directly related to size of city. Nevertheless, the sheer mass of the concentration of poverty in the slums of larger cities, and particularly those in the North, poses a clear challenge to regional policy. Hoover (1971) points out that "concentrated poverty, inadequate housing, and denial of opportunity give rise to a festering social conflict and a potentially catastrophic polarization of interests and attitudes, with increasingly geographic aspects as the ghettos crystallize and the contrast between the poor black central city and rich white suburbia heightens" (p. 345).

Even if the complex issues of racial discrimination and slum poverty were to be solved there still would be a number of major problems facing the large cities. Economic obsolescence and decay in downtown areas is widespread; though related to the problem of central city ghettos, this phenomenon would probably have arisen in any case because of the rapid suburbanization of metropolitan population and economic activity. Traffic congestion is yet another challenge to the cities, and contributes to the general pollution of the metropolitan environment. The failure of metropolitan areas to respond adequately to these problems is related to the fragmentation of government and fiscal responsibility into rival independent jurisdictions. In 1962, for example, the average SMSA contained eighty-seven local government units (seventy-six of which could levy property taxes), comprising 1.5 counties, twenty municipalities, twelve townships, twenty-eight school districts, and twenty-six special districts (Ibid., p. 374).

The role of the federal government is critical in dealing with metropolitan problems because of its financial capacity to make grants for housing, welfare, education, transportation, and community facilities, as well as to implement revenue sharing with local government. As yet, however, no clear and consistent goals and strategies have been formulated to guide metropolitan development policies. In particular, choices still must be made concerning the extent to which and conditions under which the white suburbs should be opened to the nonwhite population, on the one hand, and the extent to which the central cities should be transformed on the other.

REGIONAL DEVELOPMENT POLICY

The New Regionalism

Regional policy in the United States is primarily based on legislation passed in 1965, during the heyday of President Johnson's Great Society programs. There had, of course, been a number of prior experiments in regional development legislation. For example, during the 1930s such New Deal programs as the Tennessee Valley Authority, rural electrification, and the Civilian Conservation Corps were based on public works and resource development and conservation. Following the Second World War a large number of local industrial development groups attempted to attract economic activity, but there were many more of these groups than there were new plants; moreover, many communities denied themselves badly needed public services in order to subsidize marginal firms. In the early part of the 1960s there was a renewal of interest at the federal level in helping depressed areas. The Area Redevelopment Act of 1961 and the Accelerated Public Works Act of 1962 provided for public facilities in declining and stagnating communities. However, funds were not sufficient to overcome basic problems, planning was carried out on too small a scale, and little attention was given to human resource development.

Although a public works bias was carried over in the 1965 legislation, the two regional development acts passed in that year—the Appalachian Regional Development Act (ARDA) and the Public Works and Economic Development Act (PWEDA)—represented an unprecedented effort to deal comprehensively with regional problems characterized by high unemployment and low income.

The Appalachian Program

The ARDA established the Appalachian Regional Commission (ARC) for the purpose of coordinating a six year (since extended) joint federal-state development effort—the largest such program yet undertaken in the United States. The ARC (1970) maintains that its social goal is to provide the people of Appalachia with the health and skills they require to compete for opportunity wherever they choose to live. The economic goal is to develop in Appalachia a self-sustaining economy capable of supporting rising incomes, improving standards of living, and increasing employment opportunities.

The Appalachian program involves portions of thirteen states—stretching from northeastern Mississippi to southern New York—but the only whole state included is West Virginia. Given this vast expanse of territory it is not surprising that the ARC itself distinguishes "four Appalachias," each with its own needs and potentials. The ARDA gave the ARC a broad range of functions and a somewhat narrower set of programs to administer, as well as general guidelines for these purposes. The ARC was given specific program and funding authority in nine functional areas: health, housing, vocational education, soil conservation, timber development, mine restoration, water survey, water and sewer facilities, and highways. The commission also was given supplemental grant authority and provided with program funding linkages to local development districts.

Strictly speaking, the ARC is not a federal agency, but rather a cooperative venture in which the federal government and relevant states participate as equals. The commission is composed of the governors (or their representatives) of the thirteen states and a federal cochairman appointed by the president. The regional, state, and local development district levels each have their own responsibilities. At the regional level the ARC attempts to assess Appalachia's future role in the national economy and is concerned with developing regional programs, planning for public facilities, cooperating in interstate programs, and undertaking social and economic analyses. The role of state planning is to determine areas with significant potential for future growth; formulate long-run programs and annual project plans geared to each Appalachian subarea in the state; and establish local development districts within which federal, state, and local planning efforts are to be coordinated. The multicounty development districts are responsible for communicating local needs and aspirations to the states, identifying local development projects, and coordinating their local execution.

In contrast to the wide scattering of public investments that had characterized earlier efforts to aid depressed areas, the ARDA specified that those "made in the region under this Act shall be concentrated in areas where there is the greatest potential for future growth, and where the expected return on public dollars will be the greatest."

What degree of project concentration has actually been achieved by the ARC? Probably the best indication of success in this regard is provided by the data in Table 9-5. The four-level categorization shown there was developed by the ARC and applied to each state plan. Level 1 was defined as the highest level of growth potential in each state. Level 4 areas were not designated as growth areas, while the other levels represent different degrees of intermediate situations. The data presented in Table 9-5 do not include projects that were made before growth areas were defined, and they do not include certain outlays that could not be localized. For all of Appalachia, sixty-two percent of investment funds went to the dominant growth areas of each state during the first five years of the ARC's operations. Only fourteen percent went to areas that were felt to have no growth potential. Kentucky's low proportion of Level 1 investments reflects the fact that it has only one Appalachian county that is part of a multistate SMSA. The relatively low Level 1 outlays in Georgia, North Carolina and Tennessee reflect state decisions to promote growth away from the largest SMSAs. Moreover, those states with the highest proportions of Level 4 investments for the most part concentrated their funds in human resource projects rather than those more directly associated with economic development.

The issue of investment in human resources has been a key one in the history of the Appalachian program. The original ARDA made highway development a substantial part of the program on the ground that lack of accessibility was holding back the progress of the region. Of the initial $1.1 billion authorization, $840 million was allocated to highway construction over a five year period, while another $252 million was allocated to a number of other social and economic programs for a two year period. Bringing the two types of outlays down to a two year basis and adding matching state funds meant that about $480 million was authorized for highways and approximately $281 million for eleven other major categories.

The ARDA's initial emphasis on highway construction was severely criticized in some quarters (Munro, 1969; Hansen, 1966). On the other hand, there has been strong support for the highway program within the ARC, primarily because it has been regarded as the matrix within which human resource investments will prove their effectiveness. Thus, Ralph Widner (1971), the very able executive director of the ARC during its first six years, could argue in reviewing the Appalachian experience that:

> the critics argued that it makes far better sense to invest in people than in the concrete of highways. Most of us would agree.
> But how carefully thought through is that criticism? If children

Table 9-5. Concentration of Appalachian Program Investments in Growth Areas, by State, 1965-1970

State	Growth area levels			
	1 *(percent)*	*2* *(percent)*	*3* *(percent)*	*4* *(percent)*
Alabama	84.3	1.4	–	14.3
Georgia	33.2	27.1	–	39.7
Kentucky	2.2	45.8	42.0	9.9
Maryland	86.0	14.0	–	–
Mississippi	87.2	6.9	–	5.9
North Carolina	17.3	36.5	43.4	2.8
New York	80.5	9.9	–	9.6
Ohio	87.2	9.7	–	3.1
Pennsylvania	86.1	4.8	2.9	6.2
South Carolina	68.6	9.1	–	21.3
Tennessee	38.7	26.5	24.3	10.5
Virginia	61.5	–	–	38.5
West Virginia	67.3	3.0	9.5	20.2
Region	62.1	13.9	10.3	13.7

Source: Newman (1972), p. 156.

cannot get to a school for lack of decent transportation, if a pregnant mother cannot get to a hospital for lack of a decent road, if a breadwinner cannot get to a job because the job 30 miles away cannot be reached in a reasonable time, then is such an investment an investment in people or an investment in concrete? (P. 19)

Moreover, in practice there has been a complete reorientation of nonhighway funds during the life of the ARC. From an original preference for physical resource investments in the ARDA, the ARC has moved to a three-to-one preference for human resource projects in terms of actual project expenditures. And this comparison understates the case because it leaves out the human resource emphasis of supplemental fund allocations. Finally, under one of the more innovative sections of the ARDA, the ARC is given funds to supplement local funds in the financing of federal grant-in-aid programs so that the local contribution can be reduced to as low as twenty percent of the project's cost. Newman (1972) maintains that through August 1971, $215 million had been appropriated for supplemental funds; almost eighty-two percent of this total was spent on human resource development.

The reasoning behind the shift in emphasis toward human resource investments has been stated by Newman in the following terms:

By investing heavily in the most mobile form of resources—people—
the commission was able to minimize the chance that its investments
would be wasted. Though no one could be sure that any particular
set of public facility investments could contribute to the development of a self-supporting economy in the more lagging portions of
the region, it was clear that better health and education for the
people of those areas was a necessary precondition for such development if it was to occur, and, if it did not, individuals could carry
them wherever opportunities were available. (P. 150)

This approach would seem to be a milestone on the road from
place-oriented policies toward approaches recognizing that the welfare of people
is, or should be, the principal objective of economic policy.

The Title V Commissions

Title V of the PWEDA authorized the secretary of commerce to
designate, with the cooperation of the states involved, multistate regions
containing common problems of economic distress or lag that extend beyond
the capability of any one state to solve. Once a region has been designated, the
relevant states are invited to participate in a regional commission patterned in
structure on that for Appalachia. In 1966 and 1967, regional commissions were
established for the Ozarks (comprised of 134 counties in Arkansas, Oklahoma,
Missouri, and Kansas), the Four Corners (comprised of ninety-two counties in
New Mexico, Utah, Arizona, and Colorado), New England (covering all six states
in the region), the Coastal Plains (made up of 159 tidewater counties in Georgia
and the Carolinas), and the Upper Great Lakes (comprised of 119 counties in
northern Minnesota, Wisconsin, and Michigan). In 1972 the Upper Missouri
Regional Commission was designated, covering the whole states of South
Dakota, North Dakota, Nebraska, Wyoming, and Montana.

The Title V commissions have not received the magnitude of funds
made available to the Appalachian program. During their first six years federal
expenditures for all of the Title V commissions amounted to a little over $100
million, while those for Appalachia came to $1.3 billion. The ARC was
established as an independent agency whereas the other commissions operate
under the secretary of commerce. In contrast to the ARC, the Title V
commissions had little or no advance planning (New England is an exception)
and they have had greater political problems. The Title V commissions only have
funding powers for planning and demonstration project efforts, along with a
supplemental grant program. They lack their own cluster of specific programs,
and few systematic attempts have been made to build needed linkages between
regional and state developmental planning efforts. Moreover, although a few
growth centers have been designated or approved, the Title V commissions
following this strategy have had difficulty in implementing it in view of their
limited program and funding authority, as well as the political risks involved.

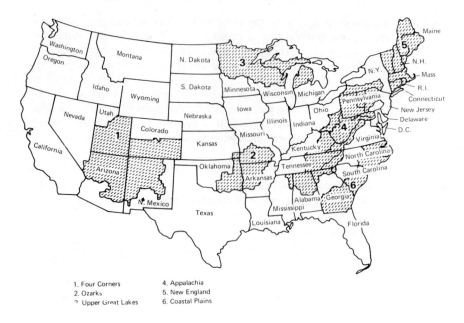

1. Four Corners   4. Appalachia
2. Ozarks   5. New England
3. Upper Great Lakes   6. Coastal Plains

Map 9-1.   Economic Development Regions

Finally, there has been little or no coordination between the activities of the Title V commissions and the Economic Development Administration even though both are lodged in the Department of Commerce (Walker, 1972).

The Economic Development Administration

The EDA was created by the PWEDA to assist the regional commissions (a role it has never effectively assumed) and to provide assistance in its own right to areas characterized by chronic economic distress. Eligibility for EDA assistance is based on one or more of the following general economic conditions: (1) a substantial or persistent unemployment level for an extended period of time; (2) a median family income at a level of less than forty percent of the national level; and (3) an actual (or prospective) abrupt rise in unemployment resulting from the closing of a major employer.

To implement its development goals the EDA has at its disposal a wide range of program tools, including grants and loans for public works and development facilities; industrial and commercial loans; and an extensive program of technical, planning, and research assistance. As of June 30, 1971, the EDA (1971) reported that it had approved 2,305 public works projects amounting to nearly $1.1 billion. About half of these expenditures were for water and sewer projects. There were 302 approved business development projects involving $262.7 million in loans and $23.0 million in working capital.

A total of $64.6 million was provided for technical assistance and $25.6 million for planning grants. All programs together received $1.44 billion. California received the most money, $109 million, followed by Kentucky ($82 million), Mississippi ($79 million), Georgia ($65 million), and West Virginia ($58 million).

In addition to the multistate regions discussed earlier, the PWEDA called for three other categories of institutions for dealing with regional development problems. "Redevelopment areas" include counties, labor areas, and certain cities where unemployment and low incomes pose particularly urgent assistance problems. "Economic development districts" are multicounty organizations within which counties and communities work cooperatively on mutual needs and opportunities. "Economic development centers" are communities or localized areas with fewer than 250,000 persons where resources are to be used rapidly and effectively to create more jobs and higher incomes for the population of the surrounding area. Although these growth centers need not be within depressed areas, they are intended tᴏ promote economic development in redevelopment areas within the districts of which the centers and redevelopment areas are a part.

Early in its existence the EDA experimented with a "worst first" strategy whereby areas with the most severe difficulties in each category of aid eligibility were to receive top priority for funds from the agency. The worst first strategy, insofar as it was implemented, was inconsistent with the notion of clustering investments in the growth centers of EDA districts. On the other hand, the EDA's experience with the growth center approach has left much to be desired. For example, an evaluation carried out within the agency itself (1972) concludes that:

> EDA's experience in funding projects in economic development centers has not yet proven that the growth center strategy outlined in the Agency's legislation and clarified in EDA policy statements is workable. The Agency's approach to assisting distressed areas through projects in growth centers has resulted in minimal employment and service benefits to residents of depressed counties. (P. 5)

Of course, this lack of success does not necessarily mean that a growth center strategy would not be workable. It may rather reflect the nature of the centers selected by the EDA. Brian Berry (1967) has pointed out that

> examination of the gradients of influence of smaller centers indicates clearly that there seems little sense in trying to use small urban places as growth centers—their regional influence is too limited. Indeed, very few cities of less than 50,000 population appear to have any impact on their regional welfare syndrome, although admittedly the few that do are located in the more peripheral areas. (P. 12)

The growth centers that have been designated by the EDA are generally smaller than this 50,000 population level. As of April 15, 1970 there were eighty-seven EDA-designated economic development districts with 171 development centers (126 economic development centers and forty-five redevelopment centers; the latter were in redevelopment areas whereas the former were not). Only thirty of the development centers had a population greater than 50,000 and only thirteen had a population greater than 100,000. Forty-two of the centers had fewer than 10,000 persons. Moreover, between 1960 and 1970, sixty-one percent of these development centers had population growth below the national average; thirty-eight percent of the development centers (and over half of the redevelopment centers) experienced population declines.

At this writing the White House favors elimination of the EDA in favor of revenue sharing measures to be discussed later. However, in June 1973 Congress approved a bill to authorize up to $430 million for an extension of the agency until mid-1974. It appears that the president will approve the measure, but that the EDA will be phased out during the coming year.

General Evaluation

The United States, like nearly all other industrialized nations of the West, has developed an elaborate system of aids to promote the growth of economically lagging regions. Regional development policy thus conceived has been inspired by two major concerns. The first is based on equity and the second on the notion that even the metropolitan populations have a stake in nonmetropolitan development because rural to urban migration has been a major contributor to the problems of the big cities. In both instances the motivation seems to have been well-meaning but misplaced.

The regional legislation of the mid-1960s was strongly influenced by the liberal, free market bias that is characteristic of the United States. Public works projects that would induce and support private economic initiatives, as well as more direct incentives to businessmen (one hesitates to invoke the term entrepreneur in this context) were viewed as the keys to the economic development of lagging regions. This approach ignored not only the failure of similar policies in other countries, but also the theoretical and empirical evidence—forthcoming at an accelerated pace from the early 1960s on—that investment in human resources has been a major source of economic development (Denison, 1962; Schultz, 1961). Most regional development policies and proposals have continued in the traditional mold. However, there have been a few exceptions among the regional commissions, most notably the Appalachian Regional Commission. Although the legislation that created the ARC had a marked public works emphasis, particularly with respect to highway construction, the subsequent evolution of the ARC's own policies has demonstrated clear recognition of the importance of human resource investments. Without denying the need for the expansion of infrastructure in the narrower sense, the ARC's goal of providing "the people of Appalachia with the health and skills they require to compete for opportunity wherever they choose to live" represents a landmark in the evolution of American regional policy. It also raises the question of place-oriented versus people-oriented investments and their relation to migration policy, as well as the issue of the role of growth centers.

The selective nature of outmigration from lagging areas means that they tend to lose their most vital people—the best workers, the young, the better educated. Moreover, there is evidence that when employment opportunities appear in a lagging area there is a return movement of workers. Since these returnees are frequently more highly skilled than the members of the local work force, the hard-core unemployed of the area may find little relief for their problems (Parr, 1966). Thus, outmigration may cause cumulative difficulties in a lagging region, and the benefits from an increase in local employment opportunities may help return migrants more than the local residents. (Of course, the positive multiplier effects of any new activity will indirectly benefit the community as a whole, especially if leakages to other areas are minimal.)

Whatever may be the consequences of outmigration from lagging areas, it is clear that policies that merely try to check migration—even by attempting to subsidize the industrialization of rural areas—do little service to either the nation or the individuals concerned, at least from an opportunity cost viewpoint. Return migration in particular shows that the real problem of lagging regions is underinvestment in their human resources, rather than migration as such which is a symptom rather than a cause.

Labor mobility demonstration projects in the United States have yielded some evidence that it is possible to divert migration away from large cities where an unemployed worker would arrive with little or no funds and no immediate employment prospects, toward medium-sized cities where the demand for labor is strong and chances for adjustment better. However, there is little political support for programs based on comprehensive worker relocation assistance.

Within the larger industrial centers it would appear that while employment opportunities are potentially available to minority groups in the central city ghettos, they have been denied these opportunities as much because of housing discrimination as because of employment discrimination (Kain, 1968). There is clear evidence that blacks (and other minorities) are not concentrated in central cities so much because they are poor as because they cannot obtain housing in the suburbs where new jobs increasingly are being created (Kain and Persky, 1968). Residents of urban ghettos, like those of lagging rural areas, are badly in need of better education, job training, and generally expanded investment in human resources, but they also need better access to suburban employment sites. Among the means that can be employed toward this end are improved transportation between the ghetto and suburban jobs, expansion of low-income housing outside of the ghetto, vigorous enforcement of open housing statutes, and rent subsidies. Policies which are based on refurbishing the ghetto, and which therefore assume the permanence of the ghetto, will not resolve the employment problems of big cities. Rather, what is called for is a change in their structure. Of course, if minority groups prefer to live in their own communities, what may be called for is a policy of concentrated decentralization within metropolitan areas.

FUTURE DIRECTIONS

Although the United States has not committed many resources to altering spontaneous trends in the location of population and economic activity, and does not have an overall strategy in this regard even in principle, there are indications that public policy may play a greater role in the future.

The issue of population growth has received wide national attention in recent years, but primarily in terms of aggregate growth. The government's Commission on Population Growth and the American Future reflected the sentiments of many groups when it recently recommended eventual stabilization of the national population as a means of "buying time" to cope with a host of economic, social, and environmental problems. However, a substantial decline in the birth rate has removed some of the raison d'être for policies aimed at zero population growth. Increased attention thus may be focused on the commission's finding that eventual aggregate population stability would still leave a distribution problem of nearly comparable magnitude.

These demographic issues are closely related to a remarkable increase in public concern about the quality of the environment. Cumberland (1971) has argued that:

> regions today are forced to compete for growth, whether they wish to or not, especially by placing major responsibility to finance public sector services upon local government. The result has been pressures for excessive growth in some areas, as evidenced by exhaustion of local water supplies and massive water transfers, overloading of waste removal facilities, urban congestion, breakdown of transportation facilities, and in the intensive settlement of areas unsuitable for development because of periodic drought, brush fires, flooding, seismic activity, earth slides, and other natural phenomena. (P. 138)

Those who share this view maintain that the larger public interest of the nation requires that restrictions be placed on uncontrolled regional growth so that there can be more effective management of water resources, wilderness areas, recreational sites, and the quality of the environment. An Environmental Protection Agency has been established to deal with these issues and its powers of enforcement have thus far clearly been more than nominal. Legislation is also pending in Congress to establish a national system of land use planning. Measures for dealing with the interrelationships between regional development and environmental quality thus appear to be more than a passing fad, and are likely to play an increasingly important part in influencing spatial resource distribution.

While the spontaneous decentralization of manufacturing has benefited some rural areas, particularly in the South, congressional advocates of nonmetropolitan development have sought to use spatial decentralization of federal facilities as a deliberate national policy. A provision of the Agricultural Act of 1970 called for location of federal offices and installations "insofar as practical" in areas of "lower population density," and executive agencies were directed to give "first priority in the location of new offices and other facilities" to areas of 50,000 population or less. However, these measures have in fact had little practical effect. The Rural Development Act of 1972 contains even stronger language encouraging federal decentralization, and the administration has recently stated that "it should be emphasized . . . that the location of federal government facilities in rural areas and the development and vigorous implementation of policies and procedures for accomplishing this are integral parts of this Administration's program for sound and balanced rural development" (National Area Development Institute, 1972b). It is nevertheless likely that federal facilities, like other tertiary activities, will continue to be located primarily in or very near metropolitan areas. A major study (EDA, 1970) of the impact of federal activities on regional development concludes that:

> The fundamental requirements of the American economic system—natural resources, labor, capital, and markets—are influenced to some extent by more than forty federal programs which provide assistance to public agencies, private institutions and individuals. But the geographic impacts of these programs, in the aggregate, are modest: They are largely confined to accelerating pre-existing trends toward economic concentration in metropolitan areas or to curbing slightly prevailing trends of economic decline.
>
> At best, even with substantially modified priorities, funding, and administrative processes, the capacity of these programs to alter—and particularly to reverse—geographic patterns of economic development is extremely limited. Isolated shifts in the outcome are possible. These, however, would probably demand greater political consensus and professional expertise than is currently at hand. (P. 11)

In another attempt to influence spatial resource allocation in the United States, the Congress in 1971 called for the establishment of a national urban growth policy, and for a Report on Urban Growth from the president in every even-numbered year. The report is to include data on the state of urban development as well as recommendations for programs and policies to carry out a national urban policy. However, the president has shown little interest in developing such a policy. Thus, as Wingo (1972) observes, at present "putative national urban policy is simply the working out of laws, programmes, administrative decisions and regulations, and judicial rulings which have accumulated over the past two generations" (p. 11).

If individual federal programs cannot be counted upon to alter current spatial distribution trends, it does not necessarily follow that the federal government has no possibility of playing a significant role in this regard. Indeed, the Appalachian Regional Commission experience has demonstrated that a multiprogram approach directed toward an entire region can produce positive results. The impact of the Appalachian program is still difficult to evaluate in terms of the usual indicators of economic progress, but Americans are overly prone to expect quick results from infusions of money. Without denying the importance of economic infrastructure in the narrow sense, the Appalachian Regional Commission has, for the first time in the history of regional policy in the United States, made a clear move in the direction of emphasizing human resource development as a major, and perhaps the major, element in long-run economic growth. Moreover, the generally positive results of the Appalachian program led to the introduction, in 1972, of a bill in the United States Senate to create regional development commissions that would cover the entire nation. At present the future of this initiative is in doubt because of uncertain presidential support. At times there has been warm executive backing for the establishment of a national system of regional commissions but at other times the pendulum has swung the other way—where it appears to be at this writing. The present head of the powerful Office of Management and Budget, an agency within the executive department, recently was chairman of a presidential commission that recommended abolition of the regional commissions on the ground that they constitute an unnecessary layer of government—a curious conclusion given that the commission staffs are very small and that they have had a coordinating and suggestive role (like French "indicative planning" but unlike "compulsory" Soviet-type planning), and little direct control of specific projects and programs.

It was pointed out earlier that there are both economic and administrative arguments against defining regional commission areas primarily in terms of economic distress, as has been the case. This tendency now represents, however inadvertently, the principal threat to the commissions' existence. For mixed reasons there has been considerable reaction to the War on Poverty programs of the 1960s. In many respects the inefficient and often ineffectual results of these efforts have been all too evident. Nevertheless, it would be unfortunate if questions of rational spatial resource allocation were to become identified with the issue of poverty elimination.

If the fate of the regional commission approach is uncertain, a more promising future seems assured for the multicounty planning units that have proliferated in recent years. During the 1960s the problem of coordinating a host of new federal agencies and programs concerned with economic development became acute. Proposed solutions were as numerous as the federal agencies involved; by 1967 there were over a dozen types of federally-initiated local coordinating structures differing not only in name, structure, and function but also in the elements of the local communities' social, economic, and political structures upon which they were based. In response to this maze of frequently conflicting approaches the Office of Management and Budget put pressure on the states to create multicounty planning units within which all federal programs would be coordinated. The agency's Circular A-95, dated July 24, 1969, sought to establish a "network of state, regional and metropolitan planning and development clearinghouses" to receive and disseminate information about proposed projects; to coordinate applications for federal assistance; to act as a liaison between federal agencies contemplating federal development projects; and to perform the "evaluation of the state, regional or metropolitan significance of federal or federally-assisted projects." At this writing many states have made noteworthy strides in implementing effective multicounty planning schemes. Future progress will depend in large part on the ability of state governors to create economically feasible planning units and to compel the various federal agencies to coordinate their activities within this context. Even more important, if the A-95 review process is to be effective there must be regional plans against which the consistency of various projects and programs can be evaluated. At present such plans are largely nonexistent.

The impetus that the system of federal "categorical" grants-in-aid has given to multicounty planning efforts may abate with the substitution of President Nixon's revenue sharing measures. More than any recent president, he has made decentralization of federal government authority an explicit goal. The first Nixon administration witnessed the enactment of the most significant measure in a generation designed to improve the fiscal position and the decision-making potential of state and local governments. This was the program of general revenue sharing, which will pump $30.1 billion into state and local treasuries over the next five years, with few strings attached on how the funds will be used. On the other hand, the future of the president's far more sweeping program of special revenue sharing faces stiff congressional opposition. This legislation is designed to eliminate most of the hundreds of special purpose, categorical grant-in-aid programs that have been passed in the last two decades. They would be replaced with six broad categories of assistance. Many categorical aid programs have strong supporters on key congressional committees and many state and local officials fear that special revenue sharing would reduce the amount of overall assistance they get from Washington. Moreover, the kind of decentralized decision making implied by revenue sharing would be more politically appealing if more progress had been made in improving the governmental structures of both metropolitan areas and multicounty rural planning districts. In fact, much remains to be done in developing units of government capable of dealing with problems whose dimensions are broadly regional in nature. In particular, disadvantaged minorities may well find no substitute at the local level for the advocacy they received under expiring federal programs.

In conclusion, it may be useful to note briefly some recommendations (with which I am in basic agreement) made by the Commission on Population Growth and the American Future concerning the future development of urban and regional policy in the United States.

At the national level, it is recommended that the federal government develop a set of national population distribution guidelines to serve as a framework for regional, state, and local plans and development. Action should be taken to increase freedom of choice of residential location through the elimination of current patterns of racial and economic segregation and their attendant injustices. To anticipate and guide future urban growth there should be comprehensive land use and public facility planning on an overall metropolitan and regional scale. Vigorous and concerted efforts should be undertaken to promote free choice of housing within metropolitan areas; federal and state governments should ensure provision of more suburban housing for low- and moderate-income families; and more extensive human capital programs should be developed to equip black and other deprived minorities for fuller participation in economic opportunities. Future programs for declining and chronically depressed rural areas should emphasize human resource development, and worker relocation counseling and assistance should be provided to enable individuals to relocate with a minimum of risk and disruption. Finally, it is recommended that a growth center strategy be developed to expand job opportunities in urban places that have a demonstrated potential for future growth and that are located in proximity to declining areas. The types of growth centers envisioned by the commission's final report (1972) are:

> expanding cities in the 25,000 to 350,000 population range whose anticipated growth may bring them to 50,000 to 500,000. Somewhat lower and higher limits should be considered for the sake of flexibility. Not every rapidly-growing city within this range should be eligible. Only those cities that could be expected to benefit a significant number of persons from declining regions, as well as the unemployed within the center, should be eligible. Thus, growth centers should be selected on the basis of commuting and migration data, as well as data on unemployment and job opportunities, and physical and environmental potential for absorbing more growth. (Pp. 125-26)

The population sizes of the growth centers proposed here may be overly conservative, but this should not preclude at least some demonstration projects linking investments in growth centers to human resource investments in lagging areas and comprehensive relocation assistance programs. It is also important that policy efforts in these regards give greater attention to market forces than has been the case in the past. Efforts to reverse market forces are likely to be not only inefficient but ineffective as well, though the very notion of regional policies implies some modification of laissez faire spatial resource allocation. Of course, when we speak of making spatial resource allocation more rational it also is implied that we know more than we actually do at present about the locational preferences of the people whose welfare we are trying—in some sense—to increase. This neglected area of research hopefully will receive more attention in the near future.

Chapter Ten

Regional Economic Policy in Canada

THE BACKGROUND

The vast size of Canada, second only to that of the USSR, and the fact that its population, though growing rapidly in recent years, still totals little over twenty-one million, results in areas of concentrated economic activity being interspersed with extensive areas where such activity is virtually nonexistent. As will be seen from Map 10-1, the heavy concentration of manufacturing activity extending in a fairly narrow belt between Quebec and Windsor is in striking contrast to the several hundred miles which separate the main manufacturing centers of the western provinces.

One of the conventional ways of viewing the country is to see it in terms of five main regions: the Atlantic region, consisting of the four most easterly provinces of Newfoundland, Prince Edward Island, Nova Scotia and New Brunswick; Quebec, with its predominantly French speaking population and culture; Ontario, the largest province in terms of population and industrial output; the three prairie provinces of Manitoba, Saskatchewan, and Alberta; and the most westerly province, British Columbia, 3,000 miles by air from Newfoundland and separated from the rest of Canada by the immense barrier of the mountains. The foregoing regions are separated not only by geographic distance but also by dissimilarities in outlook and culture, dissimilarities which increase as one proceeds north, crossing the sixtieth parallel to the very sparsely populated areas of the Yukon and Northwest Territories.

Since the turn of the century the regional distribution of population and industry across the country has varied greatly; there has been a strong secular shift to the west, and the relative decline of the Atlantic provinces shows little sign of slowing down. Within the western provinces themselves, moreover, the shift has been westward, with Alberta and British Columbia gaining

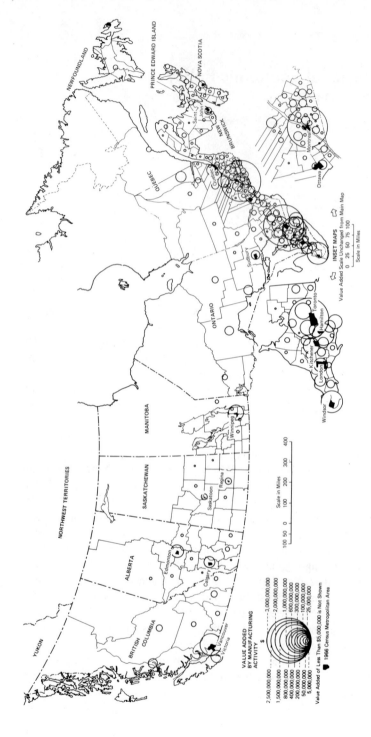

Source: Manufacturing and Primary Industries Division, D.B.S.

Map 10-1. Distribution of Manufacturing Activity by County or Census Division, 1967

population rapidly in contrast to the situation in Saskatchewan and Manitoba. Although government action through immigration, transportation, and various other policies has contributed significantly at different times to economic growth in different regions and to the current spatial patterns of population and industrial development, for the most part demographic and industrial trends have resulted from the powerful forces of expanding and declining opportunities in the private economic sector. Some areas have benefited substantially from such forces while others have suffered, but there are many which have remained chronically depressed and it is these in particular which have given rise of late to so much concern.

As noted below, income disparities are of prolonged duration and thus far efforts to reduce them have met with only very limited success. Provincial per capita incomes varied at the beginning of the 1970s between sixty-three and 118 percent of the national average, a much wider dispersion than would be characteristic of main regions in the United Kingdom. Unemployment rates, based on a twelve month moving average, showed a similar divergence, with Quebec and the Atlantic Provinces varying around eight percent and the Prairies and Ontario between four percent and five percent, percentages which would be regarded as intolerably high by European standards.

The catastrophic depression of the 1930s led to the introduction of fiscal transfers from the federal government to the poorer provinces to enable them to maintain a standard of public services closer to the national average. Some of the provinces were hit extremely hard by the depression and their governments found themselves in dire financial straits. With many adjustments in scope and magnitude the transfers have continued over the past quarter of a century and are now running at over a billion dollars a year. In addition to such transfers the federal government has made conditional grants to provinces for various purposes, including hospital insurance, assistance to the aged and disabled, road construction, vocational school training, airport development, and various resource projects. But conditional grants and shared cost programs of one sort and another have had a mixed reception for while they have undoubtedly tended to standardize certain services across the country they have also presented problems of administrative control and have influenced the direction of provincial expenditures in ways which did not always express the priorities of individual provincial governments. That apart, there has been a growing belief in the desirability of policies of regional development which would reduce the need for large and continuous transfers.

The fact that there are ten provincial governments in Canada in addition to the federal government complicates the task of policy formulation and implementation. Depending on how it is interpreted, the constitution can seriously inhibit federal action. Decisions have to be made as to which level of government has the power to do what, as well as the form that cooperation between the different levels of government should take. Provincial governments have substantial powers under the constitution; they are closer to the people geographically as well as in sentiment than is the national parliament in Ottawa; and in some parts of the country regional, rather than national loyalties, remain the dominant ones. Recognition of this is important to an understanding of the Canadian scene.

In the early 1960s the federal government embarked on a number of programs designed to assist the lagging regions and its expenditures on that objective have grown rapidly in recent years. On a per capita basis they are now many times greater than those in the United States and, unlike the situation there, regional issues in Canada often dominate the political scene. Efforts to aid depressed regions, however, need to command widespread support. As the late Lester B. Pearson (1955), a former prime minister of Canada, remarked: "Statesmen find it worth making great efforts, and displaying great restraint in order to devise policies which will if possible obtain popular support in all the main regions affected. When this cannot be achieved, it is at least virtually essential to obtain from all sections an acquiescence that is willing and understanding rather than grudging or forced" (p. 45).

Constant discussion of regional policies takes place between the federal government and the provincial governments. Currently there is a strong and growing desire on the part of the latter for more decisions to be made by them and the federal government is relaxing the degree of centralized control.

In the discussion which follows, attention is focused on three issues:

1. the goals we are pursuing,
2. the action we have taken, and
3. evaluation.

GOALS

Numerous declarations have been made expressing a desire to reduce the extent of regional economic disparities. Though it would be true to say that the reduction of unemployment and the raising of incomes in the poorer parts of the country have been two specific issues which have commanded the most attention of successive governments, these goals, as well as various methods of attainment, have been subject to frequent revisions. Different governments at different times have shifted both direction and emphasis. As observed below, the areas which have been designated for assistance have been greatly increased and institutions have come and gone.

The preservation of national unity is perhaps the most fundamental objective underlying policies of regional assistance. Speaking in Moncton in May 1968 prime minister Trudeau expressed his view as follows:

> The inhabitants of the less favored regions of Canada are often cut off from our national life because they lack the opportunity to participate in it fully. And I am convinced that the need to attack

the primary causes of regional inequality constitutes one of the great priorities of no matter what Canadian government.

I believe firmly that Canadian unity cannot be truly assured until all Canadians from sea to sea will have the feeling that they possess this equality of opportunity which will permit them to participate fully in a just society.

Geographic isolation, he went on to say, was one factor contributing to the difficulties which some communities faced but there was also the problem of ethnic isolation. The Indian, the Eskimo, and the Metis populations were isolated in Canada and in a way which needed to be corrected. In addition there were other groups associated with a marginal economy of primary resources—specifically fishing, forestry, and subsistence farming. Such groups were in regions which very often lacked the well-developed service industries "which offer a just and decent standard of living." Such regions typically contain only a scattered population and public services such as health, transportation, and education are at a substandard level. Industry is not attracted to such areas and the resultant poverty cycle—poor education, poor training, and poor health services—which perpetuated economic inequalities from generation to generation had to be broken. That, the prime minister continued, is what we are talking about when we refer to economic disparities in Canada. National unity and social justice both demanded action. Unity, he added, was not just a matter of different languages, it was also a matter of poverty, and a strong government was necessary

> qui pourra redistribuer les bienfaits, qui pourra redistribuer les impôts et les bénéfices en prenant dans les régions riches pour aider les régions pauvres.

Numerous statements, particularly to the Standing Committee on Regional Development (1968), were subsequently made to spell out more precisely what it was that the government had in mind. Speaking in 1970 the minister of regional economic expansion referred to two main objectives—the alleviation of regional disparities across the country, and the fight against unemployment and underemployment. Policy was aimed not only at alleviating the present disparities between the financial capabilities of provinces but also at stimulating development activity so as to reduce the urgency and the importance of the federal government contribution through transfer payments. Earlier, in May 1969, his deputy minister had referred to regional economic expansion as a planned, consistent, prolonged effort to remove the adjective 'slow growth' from the economies of substantial parts of Canada and expressed the probability that in the circumstances of the time regional economic expansion would help to maximize national expansion but that was not the decisive reason for it. The prime motivations were not economic; they were nationalism and social justice.

A more qualified statement by the Department of Regional Economic Expansion was made in a report prepared for the Organization for Economic Cooperation and Development (1969) which stated that the goal of policy was to disperse economic growth widely enough across Canada to bring employment and earning opportunities in the slow growth regions as close as possible to those in the rest of the country but without generating an unacceptable reduction in the rate of national economic growth (p. 237). This, however, was not to be interpreted as meaning that there would be more jobs in every county and a new industrial plant at every cross roads. Some mobility was essential to economic efficiency. Therefore, the objective of regional policy was to facilitate the generation of new opportunities for employment and income at some points in all regions, so that economic growth would take place mostly by movement and change within each region, rather than by massive attrition of whole regions.

Given the availability of unemployed labor, the possibility that investment in the poorer regions might contribute more to national output than investment elsewhere has been suggested once or twice, and there has been an occasional reference to the possibility that in times of inflation output in the depressed areas might be increased without contributing to the inflationary pressure elsewhere, but neither possibility has figured prominently in federal pronouncements. Far more important has been the question of migration and the attitudes of governments towards it. Migration is a sensitive political issue and those provinces which have been losing population are anxious to see the loss reduced. In the main the federal government has not wished to commit itself on the subject. It has hesitated to express views on the sort of demographic distribution it would like to see between the main regions of the country, contenting itself for the most part with statements about the impracticality of providing employment opportunity in every small and remote community.

From time to time, however, no doubt in response to the political climate, statements have been made suggesting a broader concern. Thus, speaking in New Brunswick in May 1969, the minister referred to the emigration of young adults from the region as having reduced the proportion of the population of labor force age to a figure significantly lower than that of Canada as a whole. The working population had thus to support a relatively larger number of persons who were either too old or too young to work and this they had to do on incomes significantly lower than the Canadian average. He went on to say that "it is evident that this drain of people must be stopped, or at least greatly slowed."

Questions as to what constitutes a region have been the subject of some academic enquiry but by and large much of the discussion on regional disparities in Canada centers on provincial data. The fact that data are more readily available at the provincial than the subprovincial level and that provincial governments play an important role in regional policies are two of the reasons why regional socioeconomic disparities of one sort and another are usually discussed in terms of provincial boundaries. But interprovincial comparisons may not be those most deserving of attention. Averaging at the provincial level conceals the fact that there are many wealthy people in the Atlantic provinces who need no help from governments and many quite poor ones in Ontario, Alberta, and British Columbia who do. Moreover, the wealthy cities of central Canada contain more people in "sorry economic circumstances," depending on how that term is defined, than do the poor rural areas of the Atlantic provinces, although the *proportion* of poor people in the latter is admittedly greater.

When it comes to measuring disparities at the regional level (in whatever way we define the region) we are confronted with the fact that disparities can take a great variety of forms and their measurement presents ample scope for subjective judgments. Apart from questions of data reliability, and random and cyclical influences, which complicate the drawing of secular trends, we can say that per capita income disparities between the Atlantic provinces and Ontario over the past half century or so have increased and we can say with equal justification that they have decreased. In percentage terms they have decreased somewhat; in absolute terms, even allowing for changes in the value of money, they have increased.

Regional differences in female labor force participation rates have at times been mentioned as a matter of concern but it is not always easy to know what conclusions can be drawn from such differences. In and of itself, a low female participation rate does not necessarily indicate the need for corrective action. In like manner, the fact that per capita incomes are lower in rural areas reflects in part lower housing costs and somewhat larger families. Disparities in real income between rural and urban areas are likely to be less than the dollar figures would suggest. There are some people in rural parts of the country who, given a choice, may in any event prefer to accept a lower income for a more relaxed pace of life. It is not intended to suggest that such disparities in employment and income are thereby less deserving of attention, but it is important to look behind the statistics. The heavy unemployment rates in British Columbia or the low income levels in Prince Edward Island suggest a degree of distress which may be misleading.

ACTION TAKEN

Canadian governments have adopted a wide variety of regional policies and programs and for the purposes of this discussion it has seemed convenient to categorize them under the following headings:

1. Equalization payments (i.e., fiscal transfers to the poorer provincial governments);
2. Aid to depressed agricultural and rural communities;
3. Industrial location incentives (i.e., direct aid to industry)·
4. Aid to special areas, mainly urban centers;
5. Aid to the Atlantic region exclusively;

6. Other federal action; and
7. Action by provincial governments.

Equalization Payments

During the world depression of the 1930s a number of provinces, particularly those mainly dependent on raw material exports, ran into extremely severe financial difficulties and in some cases fiscal transfers from the federal government became essential to prevent a collapse of their public services. These fiscal transfers of a redistributive nature have continued since. The rationale behind these grants was stated by the minister of finance, in a 1966 address to the Tax Structure Committee in Ottawa, as follows:

> where circumstances, whether natural or man-made, have channeled a larger than average share of the nation's wealth into certain sections of the country, there should be a redistribution of that wealth so that all provinces are able to provide to their citizens a reasonably comparable level of basic services, without resorting to unduly burdensome levels of taxation.

The yield of provincial tax fields varies greatly from province to province and since the Second World War five-year fiscal agreements involving the redistribution of revenues in favor of the poorer provinces have been one of the important elements of Canadian policy. Under the last equalization formula, adopted in 1967, the federal government undertook to equalize to the national average all revenues raised by the provincial governments. In implementing this program, provincial revenue sources were classified into sixteen categories, and for each category the national average tax rate which would produce revenue equal to what all provinces were collectively gathering from this source was determined. Where the revenue a province could derive from each of the sixteen tax sources at the average national tax rate for that source fell below the national average per capita, the federal government undertook to pay an equalization payment equivalent to the amount by which the provincial ability to raise taxes at the national average tax rate fell below the national average yield per capita.

The payments are made unconditionally and the provinces may use the funds for any purpose that they wish. There is widespread approval of the principle underlying the transfers but, as might be expected, differences of opinion exist concerning the formula which should govern their magnitude. The sums involved are considerable; currently they amount to a billion dollars a year and are expected to increase to $1.5 billion in 1976/1977. For every hundred dollars each province raises from its own revenue sources the amount of equalization among all provinces currently ranges from a low of twelve dollars for Manitoba to a high of sixty-five for Newfoundland. Ontario, Alberta, and British Columbia receive nothing. Equalization payments to Newfoundland and

Prince Edward Island (the two poorest provinces), together with other conditional and unconditional grants, constitute about half the provincial revenues of each.

In 1964 the Department of Finance undertook an elaborate enquiry to attempt to discover whether individual provincial governments were net recipients of or contributors to federal disbursements, taking into account all the sums received by Ottawa and all the payments made out of the federal treasury involving fiscal transfers, public works, crown corporations, and other federal bodies (Department of Finance, 1964). For a number of reasons, conceptual and other, it proved impossible to reach any clear answer.

Input-output tables may help to clarify the picture. They are being prepared by the federal government and by some provinces. The federal government is supporting the provincial effort and is anxious to maintain close channels of communication among those involved in their preparation so that provincial tables will be compatible with each other. The long-run objective should be a system which will permit all the provincial tables to be operated jointly for interregional impact analysis.

Aid to Rural Areas

The number of urban poor exceeds the number of rural poor but at the time of the 1961 census the percentage of low income families was almost three times as high in rural areas as in metropolitan centers. The 1971 census showed little change. Approximately one million of Canada's rural poor are located in seven areas, mostly in the Atlantic provinces and eastern Quebec, and many depend in large measure on a subsistence type of farming for their prime support.

Recognition of the problem led in January 1957 to the appointment of a Special Land Use Committee of the Senate to consider and report on land use in Canada and ways of increasing agricultural production and the incomes of those engaged in it. In eastern Canada in particular it was felt that some of the poorer agricultural land would be more suitably used for forestry and water conservation and that the farmers involved should be resettled in more rewarding surroundings.

An extensive investigation of land use resulted from the Senate enquiry, and the studies and ideas which emerged therefrom were largely instrumental in shaping federal legislation in the form of an act passed in 1961 "to Provide for the Rehabilitation of Agricultural Lands and the Development of Rural Areas in Canada." This act, commonly known as ARDA, provided for joint federal-provincial action to facilitate the economic adjustment of rural areas; to increase standards of living and income, and employment opportunities; and to improve the use and productivity of resources in those areas. The act was administered at the outset by the Department of Agriculture since that department at the time seemed to be the only one which would permit federal-provincial action of the type envisaged.

Following some eighteen months of experience, it was obvious that changes were necessary. The second agreements which were signed with the provinces covered the five year period 1965-1970. They introduced an important change in emphasis and the federal administration which hitherto had been the responsibility of the Department of Agriculture was transferred to the Department of Forestry and Rural Development. Resource development projects received less weight and financial assistance was given to encourage farm consolidation to reduce the number of small farms and thereby permit more profitable operation. Rural and not just agricultural adjustment measures received increased attention. (McCrorie, 1969) Of particular importance was the encouragement given for the implementation of comprehensive plans in specially selected areas. Legislation passed in 1966, and since rescinded, established a Fund for Rural Economic Development (FRED) for this purpose. In a further administrative change ARDA has now been brought under the wing of the new Department of Regional Economic Expansion, and a third set of agreements, of a less uniform nature, have now been negotiated and are designed to cater more closely to the situations and needs within individual provinces.

It was apparent that measures to improve the physical qualities of land did little to improve the lot of the poorest farmers whose handicaps lay in their deficiencies of skill and education as much as in the quality of the land they were cultivating. In practice, provincial governments have not confined projects to those that benefit low income groups exclusively; indeed most ARDA resource programs have tended to favor the middle-income farmer who is more responsive to advice.

Characteristically, the small scale farmer has a level of education much lower than the national average. Depending on individual circumstances, investment in his education and technical training as well as financial aid to move elsewhere is likely to promise larger returns both to him and to society than other types of expenditure. Admittedly, without further training and the provision of alternative employment there is little point in encouraging him to leave the land and join the urban labor force; otherwise he faces the risk of merely replacing rural poverty with urban poverty. But whatever one's views on that issue, solutions to farm and rural poverty called for broader policies than those encompassed in the conventional framework of land use and improvement.

The FRED legislation marked a step in this direction. FRED provided a means of financing and carrying out comprehensive rural area development programs in areas which suffered from particularly severe distress. The selection of the areas required joint agreement by the federal and provincial governments, while to qualify the areas had to have widespread low incomes and major adjustment problems. In addition to being mainly rural and depressed, they also had to have recognized development potentials, a combination which was difficult to achieve, the more so since industrial development was the responsibility of another agency. But, subject to these restraints and following a study of the problems and potentials of the area, a strategy of development and related programs was agreed upon jointly by the two governments. Agreement covered respective responsibilities for the cost and implementation of the necessary measures.

Action under the legislation began with tremendous verve. Several ambitious plans were introduced involving a total outlay of over a billion dollars, but hardly had the programs got under way than the legislation under which they were implemented was repealed with the introduction of the Government Organization Act of 1969. Meanwhile, five areas had been selected for the plans; action in these will be continued. They include two in New Brunswick— Mactaquac and the northeast; the lower St. Lawrence, Gaspe, and Iles de la Madeleine in Quebec; the Interlake area in Manitoba; and Prince Edward Island.

With the exception of Prince Edward Island, where the whole province was covered, a feeling developed that the areas in question were too small and too isolated to be the subject of effective independent plans, and in the absence of integrated programs with other areas offering more scope for development there was little hope for significant improvement in their economic condition. In response to political and other pressures a number of changes have been made in the plans since their inception. They are under constant review. Although they are similar in some respects—education, training, and mobility figure prominently in all of them—the plans are not replicas, and the needs of the individual areas are addressed according to their individual circumstances. Increased mobility in the Interlake area of Manitoba, for example, presents particular difficulties and since many of the residents are Indians and Metis, alternatives to migration are emphasized.

In eastern Quebec the main thrust of the plan was to change the economic structure of the area to meet the requirements of a modern economy. Attempts were to be made to attract new industry and encourage modernization, as well as to phase out obsolete units in the resource sector, but again as elsewhere education, training, and mobility were stressed. Originally, the plan envisaged the outmigration of some 20,000 people but this had to be abandoned because of political opposition.

As in other countries, new patterns of rural life are emerging in Canada. There is a growing disposition of some people to live outside the cities and to commute into them for work. Rural dormitories surround the larger centers and the income of many who reside in them and commute into the cities will often be significantly higher than those who work locally. Such people are not part of the rural scene in the sense of deriving their income from rural pursuits and their inclusion in statistical averages of rural incomes is apt to be misleading. In looking at the rural scene it is necessary to distinguish not only between various groups of people resident therein but also between various types of rural area. Some are closely linked to urban areas; others are remote therefrom. The latter are typically tied to a resource base; agriculture, forestry, mining, or recreation and the incomes therefrom can vary from one extreme to another.

There is a continuing outmigration of the rural farm population in terms of aggregate figures for the country as a whole, and there is an accompanying outmigration of those involved in the provision of services to that population. At the same time there is a growing trend for farmers to combine farming with other jobs and their classification for employment purposes becomes increasingly difficult. Multiple job holding is becoming very common.

Like many other countries Canada is confronted with patterns of settlement which have lost their rationale. The feeling seems to be emerging in Canadian discussions of the subject that we should move towards the encouragement of an interconnected system of towns and cities, linking communities together more effectively than they are at present and reducing the isolation of remote communities. In this way rural and urban development are viewed as interrelated rather than distinctly separate objectives.

As was to be expected, the magnitude of the proposed FRED expenditures led to extensive questioning of the direction in which the federal government was heading in its regional policies. Outlays on one front almost inevitably lead to recommendations for outlays on another. It is not much use embarking on a program unless all the necessary steps are taken to fulfill it, but 'total systems' approaches may entail a far greater degree of government participation in economic affairs than many wish to see. Moreover, the coordination of various government departments in the task is fraught with numerous difficulties not the least of which are the different priorities and rivalries that exist between departments. There was a widespread feeling that the Department of Forestry and Rural Development, which was administering certain policies, was extending its influence too widely, that it lacked the mandate for such an expansion, and that it was not the appropriate body for such a task. It was these considerations among others which led to the decision to establish a new Department of Regional Economic Expansion, known as DREE.

Direct Incentives to Industry

Although much of the government's initial concern with development related to rural areas it was obvious at the outset that there were many other areas of the country in need of special assistance, areas where unemployment was chronically heavy and incomes low. The Area Development Agency (ADA) established in 1963 was entrusted with the task of assisting such areas. A number of areas were designated and various financial incentives were granted automatically to secondary manufacturing industry that established in them.

Like ARDA, ADA has been subject to numerous changes. It is now being phased out but, pending demise, has been incorporated with ARDA, FRED, the Atlantic Development Council (ADC), the Canadian Council on Rural Development (CCRD), and certain other agencies in the Department of Regional Economic Expansion (DREE), which was established in 1969. The Regional Development Incentives Act (RDIA) and related legislation make provision for incentives in support of the establishment, modernization, or expansion of manufacturing and other types of facilities. The incentives may take the form of grants or loan guarantees. Whereas originally small areas of heavy unemployment were singled out for assistance under ADA, the emphasis has now shifted to large areas with greater potential for expansion. Indeed, the anomalous situation has now been reached where more than half the country qualifies for federal regional assistance of one form or another. Aid to industry, which hitherto was automatic, is now discretionary, and applications are reviewed on their merits alone.

In considering the criteria for granting assistance a variety of factors (as stated below) are taken into account. Inevitably a substantial degree of judgment is involved, particularly when it comes to deciding how much of an incentive is necessary to induce the applicant to establish in the designated area. The maximum incentive grant varies according to the region.

The provision of capital incentives to industry constitutes one of the major policy tools which DREE has adopted for the purpose of job creation. For some time this has been one of the more controversial aspects of federal policy. As noted, under the old ADA policy incentives were given automatically to certain types of industry, mainly manufacturing, that established or expanded in designated areas. Since aid was given automatically it was inevitable that those firms which would have established in the designated areas anyway received windfall gains. It was for this reason that grants under DREE were made discretionary. A grant is offered only if and to the extent that it is deemed necessary to encourage a firm to locate or expand in a designated area. In principle this appears to be eminently sensible.

Clearly there is no point in subsidizing firms to establish in designated areas if that is where they are going to go in any case. In like manner there is little or no advantage in aiding firms whose prospects of long-run profitability are highly questionable. DREE is seeking applicants who expect to be successful but who will not go to the depressed areas without some subvention. The trick is to decide who they are. How does one read the mind of the applicant? A recent EFTA study (1971) comments as follows: "The difficulty in finding a foolproof system of avoiding payments for what would have happened in any event lies in the problem of establishing motive. If a firm is to set up a branch in an area where it knows the government is ready to offer incentives, but that these incentives are available only to firms who would not otherwise have gone there, it is unlikely to present itself as other than a reluctant mover" (p. 95). In spite of certain obvious merits, it may be that discretionary aid is too difficult to handle administratively.

The criteria for incentives assessment were outlined by the minister in testimony to the Standing Committee on Regional Development. They include questions relating to the market, manpower requirements, sources of supplies, expected rates of return, public and private costs, likely effects on other industries, and the incentives needed.

The question remains as to how far the incentives do in fact influence the decisions of firms to locate in the designated regions. The question is a crucial one, for such influence constitutes a prime objective of the incentive program. The answer has its roots in the determinants of industrial location in general. One aspect of the latter which affects the Canadian scene is American investment. A dominant share of much Canadian industry is owned or controlled in the United States and the location of Canadian subsidiaries introduces special factors (Ray, 1967).

Looking at the influence of federal incentives specifically on locational decisions, one enquiry (Springate, 1972) cast considerable doubt on their impact. The reasons for their seemingly modest effect were seen in the factors which influence business behavior. The feeling is prevalent in business circles that the choice of location should be determined by "sound business judgment" rather than by "government interventions" and sound business judgment depends on such factors as expected long-run viability, ready accessibility to markets, adequacy of the labor force, and the minimization of risk. There is a strong preference for the traditional zones of economic concentration, for apart from their other advantages it is in these that risks appear to be less. It is not enough just to receive grants which will offset the estimated added costs of a poor location for the present; the matter is not one which concerns only the present, it concerns an uncertain figure as well, and it is even more difficult to put a figure on the latter than on the former.

Companies are reluctant to take the greater risks involved in establishing in the more depressed areas partly because of the consequences for the decision maker if the results prove unsatisfactory or lead to failure. There is a degree of risk beyond which management is not willing to go.

Given the uncertainty of estimation of costs and revenues it is difficult to see how grants can be tailored with precision, and if the projected costs submitted by the applicant appear too high the application may be considered nonviable and thus be rejected, while if they are too low the sum received will be less than it might have been. It is not surprising, therefore, that firms present their cases in ways which will maximize the potential grant. This is not imputing dishonesty to business, it is a natural response to the system. Accepting the argument that firms determine their location with only a limited regard for the incentives offered combined with the fact that half the country is designated for grants, it is difficult to doubt Springate's contention that for many recipients the grants constitute windfall gains. To the extent that funds are available, firms will naturally collect them if they can.

To the extent that grants are awarded on the basis of the demonstrated need of applicants, it is the weaker firms that will receive the most. Seemingly, in exercising discretion in the awarding of grants no attempt is made to formally modify the industrial structure of a region; there is no strategy or plan relating to structure. There is a prevalent view, however, that industrialization is linked strongly to urbanization and efforts to strengthen urban centers in areas of the country requiring assistance have thus been made. Before proceeding to that topic, however, it is worth noting three studies of the efficacy of the former ADA program. The first was a joint study by Yeates and Lloyd (1968), the second by Larsen (1969), and the third by Comeau (1969).

The studies had a number of points in common, but that by Yeates and Lloyd differed from those by Larsen and Comeau in one critical respect. Underlying the Yeates and Lloyd conclusions was the simplifying assumption that the mere receipt of aid by a firm was evidence in itself of the effectiveness of the program. A firm that received aid was considered to have been established or expanded because of it. Proceeding from this assumption, data were collected on the types of firms involved and their linkages with others. The conclusion was then reached that the program had had impressive results.

Larsen and Comeau, in contrast, were much more cautious in linking receipt of aid to the efficacy of the incentive program. Thus Larsen, in describing the purpose of his study, stated that although his study would attempt to throw light on the forces which attracted new plants and induced the expansions of existing plants, it would not be possible to separate the specific impact generated by ADA's assistance program from the impacts of the many other forces at work. He went on to say that there was considerable evidence that a large proportion of the aided plants would have established or expanded in New Brunswick without ADA assistance, pointing out that in such cases aid constituted a windfall profit and not an inducement to invest. Comeau arrived at much the same conclusion in his study of experience in Nova Scotia.

In referring to the difficulty of carrying out a cost-benefit enquiry in terms of ADA assistance and jobs created, Comeau mentioned two factors: first, the uncertainty surrounding the actual estimates of job opportunities and of capital assistance, and second, the uncertainty of the effects of aid on entrepreneurial decisions. As he noted, there is no way of actually measuring what part of the cost incurred in the form of ADA assistance was actually required to achieve the increases in employment and income which followed. Enquiries of firms suggested that perhaps one-half to three-fifths of the results recorded could be attributed to the Area Development Agency as a cause, though Comeau describes this as probably a generous estimate.

What Springate has observed, however, is that even with discretion in the granting of aid, windfall gains appear to have continued, although it may well be that such gains are less than they were before. Indeed it is hard to believe the results could be otherwise.

Apart from the foregoing issue, one observation which can be drawn from the aforementioned studies is that manufacturers were much readier to locate or expand their activities in the southern Georgian Bay area than in New Brunswick or Nova Scotia, an observation which should occasion little surprise. An area close to the industrial heartland can be expected to attract manufacturing more readily than one on the periphery.

The Special Areas

As shown in Map 10-2, there are several types of special area which qualify for assistance. One type is associated with the notion of growth centers. It is well recognized that the preferred location of manufacturing industry is in or close to the larger urban centers and that the future prosperity of a depressed region will require the focusing of aid in those localities which offer the greatest promise of sustained expansion. It is hoped by those who advocate such a course of action that such expansion will filter down to the outlying peripheral areas so that the region as a whole will benefit from the results, the filtering down being aided to some extent by the conscious development of a number of smaller centers. With reservations, most provinces pay at least some lip service to such a strategy and the federal government likewise subscribes to it.

Essentially, the advocates of the growth center approach argue that the propulsive forces of most regional development have their origin (or best prospects of emerging) in specific centers or areas and these are the places in which aid should be concentrated. Thus, to quote a recommendation of the Atlantic Development Council (1971), the development of a strong secondary manufacturing base in the Atlantic region will best be promoted through the existence of strong "growth centers" which possess an adequate population, the necessary kind and variety of facilities and services, good community and cultural amenities, and a sufficient concentration of industrial activities to permit firms to realize economies of scale and agglomeration (p. 6).

Growth center policy, however, may create islands of prosperity with detrimental effect on other parts of the region. By attracting activities from outlying areas a center may grow at the expense of those areas rather than stimulate their expansion. This is not a sufficient reason for discouraging the growth of strong centers—the alternative may be a lack of any growth in the region—but it does indicate the need for caution in their adoption and particularly the need for care in applying the experience to Canada of densely populated countries with vastly different patterns of settlement. It may make admirable sense in some countries to conceive of growth centers as consisting of towns with a population of 100,000 or more, but such a figure accounts for the entire population of Prince Edward Island. Moreover, some rural areas in Canada are several hundred miles from sizeable cities and the growth of such cities is of no relevance whatever to their prosperity.

To the extent that experience in the United States can serve as a guide it seems that centers of less than 40,000-50,000 population are unlikely to have any significant regional influence unless they happen to be located in the more peripheral areas. Proximity to metropolitan areas is important in improving the social and economic conditions of rural areas and attempts to develop sparsely populated rural areas independently thereof seem to be doomed to failure (Hansen, 1971).

The twenty-three "special areas" which have been designated under the federal regional development legislation were selected in consultation with

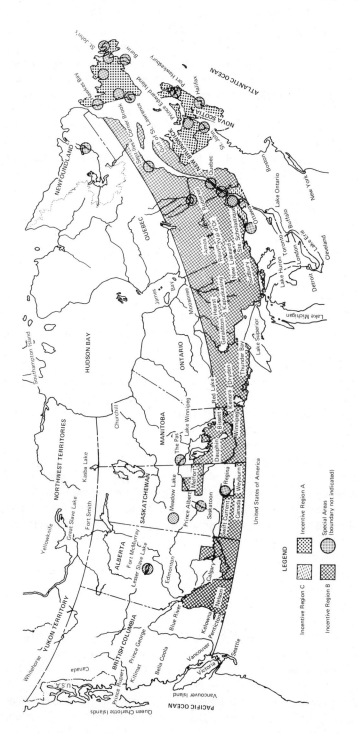

Map 10-2. Designated Regions and Special Areas

the provincial governments concerned and the proposed courses of action in them are the subject of joint bargaining and plans with those governments. It is customary to observe two conditions in their selection. First, such areas must show a relatively good potential which, once developed, can be expected to have an impact on the whole region, thus creating more and better jobs for its residents. Second, the construction of new or more comprehensive infrastructure must, right from the start, be required for the development of these areas. Not all of them, however, can be considered to fall under the rubric of growth centers. They have been classified officially into seven categories of which the first includes .the relatively large population centers in eastern Canada of St. John's, Halifax, Dartmouth, Moncton, St. John, Quebec City, and Trois Rivieres. It was believed that their faster growth could have major repercussions throughout the region. They have shown some natural potential for growth and they are big enough to offer a fairly wide range of educational, business, financial, and personal services. However, without substantial public assistance and additional private investment, those centers were considered unable to realize their growth potential.

Other classifications included some of the smaller population centers of eastern Canada, specifically Corner Brook, Happy Valley, Strait of Canso, and Sept-Iles-Port Cartier, where significant industrial developments are already in progress or the potential for growth is clearly established.

In Saskatchewan, the two major population centers of Regina and Saskatoon (with populations of 140,000 and 130,000 respectively), have been designated. Additional special areas in the prairies include The Pas, Meadow Lake, and Lesser Slave Lake; the development of these three areas depends not only on the stimulation of resource-based activities and improvement of community infrastructure facilities, but also on the provision of special counseling and work preparation to enable the seriously disadvantaged people (particularly those of native ancestry) to gain access to new employment opportunities.

In Newfoundland another group of special areas constituted "resettlement areas" where the objective is largely to facilitate the resettlement of people from the outports into larger communities. Special development action in these areas was, therefore, to stimulate new employment opportunities and to provide improved social facilities.

In the central provinces, Lac St. Jean and Renfrew-Pembroke were designated with a view to developing the wood-based industries on which they are heavily dependent. Ste. Scholastique was designated because it contains the site of the new Montreal International Airport.

What is striking about the above list is the great diversity of places included. Clearly, not all of them are regarded as growth centers in the conventional sense; some have been included because of their weakness and others because of their potential strength. In terms of per capita income Sept-Iles is among the richest in the country—it recently headed the list—whereas Lesser Slave Lake is among the poorest. Regina and Saskatoon fall in between.

As was to be expected, other places have sought special area status and ministers, feeling impelled to call a halt somewhere, have felt obliged to resist their requests.

The evaluation of the special area expenditures is in some ways even more complicated than that of the Industrial Incentives Program. Not only, as noted above, are the special areas heterogeneous, the programs themselves cover a wider range, involving grants and loans of many kinds. Certain general observations can be made, but ideally it would be desirable to look at each individual case in turn.

The implicit if not express assumption underlying much of the expenditures is that improvement in infrastructure will attract industry. But as is widely recognized, such an assumption may or may not be valid. Admittedly, whether or not industry is attracted by infrastructure expenditures, there may be a clear case on social grounds for improving roads, housing, water supplies, and so on—industrial development, after all, is but a means to an end, not an end in itself—but the question then arises as to how we are to judge such expenditures. We are faced with the fact that if we interpret regional development broadly enough almost any expenditures can be considered appropriate. There is virtually no limit to the range of activities on which money might be spent. How then are they to be assessed?

In a DREE publication (Regional Development and Regional Policy, 1972) reference is made with regard to the special area concept to "an effort to reinforce market forces through a set of coordinated special programs, applied selectively, where the objective is to assist the so-called 'little economies' to participate effectively in the mainstream of the general process of economic growth and social change in Canada" (p. 63). Unless market forces will be reinforced (or it is believed that they will be) expenditures presumably will not be regarded as appropriate by the department. It would seem, however, from some of the expenditures which have been undertaken, that the restraint is not especially circumscribing.

Formally, in both the choice of the special areas and the expenditures incurred thereunder, there is federal-provincial cooperation and joint planning. In practice, planning has often amounted to little more than bargaining over specific projects and allocating the respective financial responsibilities for them. The priorities desired by the provincial governments do not always coincide with those of the federal government, and agreements once made are subject to substantial revisions.

Aid to the Atlantic Region

The one large region of the country which immediately comes to mind in discussions of poverty and unemployment is the Atlantic region, comprising as stated above the four provinces of Newfoundland, Prince Edward Island, New Brunswick, and Nova Scotia. These provinces have a combined population of some two million and although they differ from each other in many respects they all display characteristics typical of peripheral areas. Their relative poverty and high levels of unemployment have persisted throughout living memory and have been the subject of countless studies and reports. In the Constitutional Conference of 1968 the premiers of these provinces urged the adoption of a national policy regional in application and of massive size to deal with the difficult question of regional economic disparity. Only rarely does unemployment in the region as a whole drop below six percent and in times of recession it has been far higher than this.

Numerous steps have been taken at one time or another to improve the lot of the region. One of these was the introduction of legislation in 1962 establishing the Atlantic Development Board, a body charged with the responsibility of enquiring into and reporting on programs and projects for fostering the economic growth and development of the region. The board was subsequently provided with funds to undertake projects directly. Though changes in emphasis began to emerge in time, it confined its expenditures very largely to those on infrastructure. At the outset most of the outlay was on power development, but the sums expended thereon were later exceeded by those on roads.

The board was superseded in 1969 by an Atlantic Development Council as part of the major reorganization of administrative machinery undertaken at the time the new Department of Regional Economic Expansion was established.

During its short life the board was subjected to a number of criticisms, the view that it was overly concerned with expenditures on infrastructure and not enough with the development of a strategy of development being one of them.

In spite of efforts to achieve it, the board failed to receive the strong cooperation and good will of the individual provinces. A number of background studies on subjects including agriculture, forestry, fisheries, mineral resources, water resources, education, and urban centers were prepared under its auspices (ADB 1968-70). But although these studies furnished much valuable information on economic aspects of the Atlantic provinces, the board itself never reached the point of preparing a comprehensive plan for the region. It was only after the board was superseded by the council, which had advisory powers only, that a strategy of development was formulated for the decade 1971-1981 (ADC, 1971).

The council wanted to see a much clearer strategy evolve and to enlist a greater participation of local people in the planning process, the contention being that one cannot plan *for* people, one has to plan *with* them. It is one thing, of course, to express this hope for greater local participation and another to accomplish it. Like many others, the council placed less emphasis on heavy expenditures on infrastructure, and more on education and technical training, the development of growth poles, and the grouping of industries to increase their economies of operation. The industrial complex approach should, in the opinion of the council, receive special attention for the region's main growth centers. It was realized, however, that the potential impact of the growth centers would be dissipated if more than a small number were selected in each region, so the question of their selection assumed an obvious importance.

The strategy which was recommended focused on the creation of increased job opportunities primarily through the manufacturing sector, and secondary manufacturing in particular. Again this will not be easy. Employment in manufacturing at the national level is growing much more slowly than that in service industries. In considering the type of industries to be encouraged it was observed that the attraction of an assortment of nonrelated industries should not be regarded as constituting a successful development effort, the best avenue for substantial and sustained regional development lying in the attraction of growth industries using modern technology and having supply and market relationships with other industries within the region.

The expansion and increased productivity of existing firms was considered crucial to the success of the development effort and, based on this, the council recommended the establishment of a Regional Management Institute.

In general (and it is hard to quarrel with this) it was felt that the region should build on those things in which its endowment, location, and environment were unique, or in which it had inherent advantages. Since, for example, the region is marine-oriented efforts should be made to develop and excel in the skills, sciences, and undertakings related to ocean environment. An estimated required capital investment of $25 billion was envisaged for the decade ahead.

The reaction of the federal government to the proposed strategy was, in the main, favorable. A qualified approval was given to much of it but serious reservations were expressed with regard to the specific employment targets which were set involving the provision of jobs for future as well as present members of the labor force.

The government was loath to commit itself on that score and understandably so. Apart from the political hazards entailed in commitments to specific employment targets which might prove unattainable for reasons quite unrelated to anything DREE did or did not do, there was a fundamental demographic question involved. The council wanted to see a reduction in the heavy migration out of the region. In effect, the government was being asked to commit itself to a particular regional distribution of population. It is one thing to attempt to keep unemployment levels down to acceptable levels; it is another to provide employment for a particular size of labor force.

In the past, rivalries between the four Atlantic provinces have frustrated efforts to attack the problems of the region as a unit but latterly there appears to be a growing realization of the advantages that could accrue from greater political and economic integration. There is no doubt that on several grounds such a step would make good sense. The individual provinces have little to gain and much to lose by competing with each other to attract new industry, particularly when such competition entails the granting of concessions of one sort and another.

Other Federal Policies

In addition to the various forms of specific regional assistance outlined above there are many national policies which have important regional implications. Included among these are shipping subsidies, fishing and agricultural subventions, international trade policies, and defense expenditures. Indeed, one of the difficulties in attempting to assess the influence of the federal government on regional development is that virtually every action which the government takes has some regional implications.

Confining attention to transportation and manpower specifically, the former has been the subject of action and debate from the time of confederation in 1867, when it was one of the crucial underpinnings of the new Canadian nation. Responsibility for capital costs of road, rail, water, and air transport is shared by federal and provincial governments, the federal share being much greater in some regions than others. Under the Maritime Freight Rates Act and the Atlantic Region Freight Assistance Act, which provide federal subsidies for the movement of goods by rail and motor truck respectively in the Atlantic region, there is a current budget of some $20 million a year. The sum would be increased considerably if one included contributions to the costs of maintaining ferry services between the mainland and Prince Edward Island and Newfoundland. The western provinces for their part benefit by special subventions for the movement of grain. There are frequent demands for changes in transportation policies and for improved transportation services in the Atlantic provinces especially.

As for manpower programs, lack of vocational training and skills combined with the factor of geographic distance constitute barriers to movement of the labor force from less to more prosperous areas of the country and the federal government through its department of Manpower and Immigration has been attempting in various ways to reduce the significance of those barriers. Though not conceived primarily as regional policies, such programs relate to them. Assistance in the acquisition of skills and in moving to new opportunities in more promising areas are aspects of that relationship.

The Manpower Mobility Program assists certain individuals in exploring the possibilities of jobs elsewhere and in moving to other areas where job prospects are brighter. Grants are provided to cover removal and travel expenses as well as re-establishment expenses and in some cases a special allowance favoring larger families is made for homeowners who buy or sell a house when they move. It is recognized in this regard that home ownership can inhibit mobility.

Though conceptually they would seem to have much to recommend them, a recent study of the impact of manpower programs has cast considerable doubt on their efficacy (Dymond, 1973). Expenditures of a billion dollars since their inception appear to have produced relatively little in the way of benefits. It would seem that trainees benefit only marginally compared with nontrainees in terms of finding employment and that only a small number have been induced to move and of these some have returned to their original locations. Cultural and other adjustments have proved too great.

Provincial Policies and Programs

To confine attention to the federal role in regional development is to see half only of the Canadian picture. Provincial governments have been active too, in some cases especially so.

There are several features of the provincial scene relating to regional development which are worth noting at the outset, namely:

1. the wide diversity of economic and social situations prevailing in different parts of the country;
2. the differences in political orientation and attitudes towards regional objectives;
3. the variations in professional sophistication and administrative style;
4. the multitude of policies, programs, and institutions involved specifically with regional development or which, while not falling specifically under a regional development rubric, have none the less an important bearing thereon;
5. the fluidity of policies, programs, and administrative arrangements, often though not necessarily related to changes of government at the provincial or federal level.

It will be apparent from the foregoing that any attempt to obtain a comprehensive view of the prominent features of regional policies as pursued by provincial governments constitutes a major undertaking, quite apart from the added dimension of appraisal. Even within the limited context of such institutions as development corporations or industrial parks the task of investigation can be one of considerable dimensions if more is to be attempted than the pointing up of certain issues and experience.

All provinces, without exception, attach importance to the attraction of industry. For most of them, indeed, this is where the main thrust of their regional development effort lies, and this is reflected in the magnitude of their subventions of one sort and another to industry and by infrastructure expenditures designed to induce or facilitate industrial expansion. Among their activities can be cited the preparation of market studies; the provision of various advisory services and technical help; financial aid of one kind and another; tax concessions; loans; grants and equity participating; the building of factories; and the leasing of facilities. Aid has also been extended to resource industries, including in this regard roads to resources and reduced royalty demands.

In a regional development context expenditures on social welfare and individual adjustment typically play a minor role. It is in terms of industrial growth that the solutions to regional disparities are seen. Where such growth appears impractical the emphasis frequently shifts to migration of the labor force, although official declarations on that subject tend to be muted.

In general, it is in the poorer provinces that provincial governments have been most active in attempting to attract new industry and many of the ventures which they have helped to finance have proved extremely costly to the governments in question (Mathias, 1971).

One can only speculate what the net effect of all this activity is on the industrial structure and the location of industry across the country. It seems certain that incentives are to some extent self-cancelling, the incentives offered in one province being offset by those offered in another.

In the framing of policies all governments pay at least lip service to the view that public participation in the formulation of plans and programs for individual regions is essential to their success. The differences occur not in the expression of the need for public participation but in the manner of its interpretation. Participation is a many-faceted concept and some officials, anxious to hasten the pace of change, often regard it as an impediment to effective action or as a will-o'-the-wisp. Administrative secrecy and lack of publicity is one of the more common obstacles to effective public participation, and the larger the bureaucracy the more difficult the problem of communication becomes.

With regard to the distribution of population, almost all provincial governments recognize the inevitable demise of many small communities but while some, such as Newfoundland, have hastened the process, others are more disposed to let events run their own course. No province, however, denies the impracticability of providing adequate services to small isolated groups of people. At the other extreme, governments in Ontario and British Columbia have wondered about the desirability of permitting continued growth in Toronto and Vancouver and there are indications of disenchantment with unrestrained expansion. The Toronto region has been the subject of detailed proposals in this regard.

Provincial boundaries have only a limited economic relevance and regional planning by provinces in isolation is inadequate and in some cases makes little sense. To the extent that it is feasible, closer collaboration between the provinces in the formulation of regional objectives and plans is clearly to be desired. Indeed, as noted in the concluding comments, regional development ought to be tied in to national developments and the secular changes occurring in specific industries. We are still a long way from this and what has happened in a number of cases is that firms have been aided to establish in areas of heavy unemployment notwithstanding misgivings about overproduction in the industry as a whole.

As will be apparent from the trend of discussion up to this point, the main preoccupation of governments involved in regional issues has been with unemployment and low incomes but, while this is entirely understandable, regional planning calls for more than this. The distribution of economic activity and social capital affects the employed as well as the unemployed, the wealthy as well as the poor. The preservation and improvement of the environment, the provision of recreational space, and the curbing of the disadvantages associated with excessive concentrations of people and industry are matters which also merit attention. Regional planning confined to areas of distress falls short of what is needed, moreover, and from a purely political point of view it is less likely to command widespread support.

One would naturally like to know which provincial and federal policies have been successful, which have failed and why, and what lessons can be drawn from different plans, procedures, and administrative arrangements.

Until quite recently evaluation in recorded form has been one of the most neglected aspects of government policy. Evaluation and some reflexions on the future are the subject of the concluding section.

EVALUATION AND FUTURE TRENDS

Any evaluation of the efficacy of federal policies of regional development depends upon an identification of the objectives being pursued and the priority accorded to them. To the extent that the objectives lack precision, or change, or receive a different priority over time, as in fact they do, the task of evaluation becomes increasingly complex. As noted above, there has been an almost continuous change in goals, policies, institutions, and administrative arrangements over the past decade, and further important changes are currently being contemplated.

The two goals, however, which have received most emphasis thus far are the reductions in disparities in regional unemployment rates and per capita income. Although data and definitional problems arise in connection with both of these goals, it is possible to draw certain conclusions regarding the manner in which they appear to have been changing. As observed in Table 10-1, in the Atlantic provinces (the region which has attracted most attention over the past decade) there has been some improvement in incomes when expressed as a percentage of the national average although, with the exception of Newfoundland, there is little to suggest that the pace of improvement has quickened.

It will be noted that the minima have risen throughout the entire periods but the maxima in Nova Scotia and New Brunswick have not. There is no convincing evidence of acceleration since the early 1960s. It will be observed too that the improvement in the minima over the entire period extending over forty years is very modest, amounting to around ten percent in Prince Edward Island, seven percent in Nova Scotia, and only four percent in the case of New Brunswick. As the Department of Regional Economic Expansion has observed

Table 10-1.   Range of Personal Income per Capita in the Maritime Provinces as a Percentage of the National Average

	1927-1945	*1946-1962*	*1963-1970*
Prince Edward Island	49.1-56.9	50.4-59.2	59.8-64.5
Nova Scotia	68.1-82.2	73.1-82.3	75.1-77.2
New Brunswick	63.2-70.2	65.2-72.5	67.3-71.8

(To avoid annual fluctuations, figures are based on three-year averages)

from time to time, the task of reducing disparities can be expected to be a long-term one. Newfoundland, which became a province of Canada at the end of the Second World War, has done better; per capita income there has risen from under fifty percent in 1950 to over sixty percent in 1970.

With regard to absolute disparities in current dollar terms, Prince Edward Island fell below the national average in the late twenties by some $200 compared with over $1,000 now. The corresponding figures for Nova Scotia are $142 and $718, and for New Brunswick $164 and $889. Even allowing for changes in the value of money, it is doubtful if this constitutes any improvement.

With regard to the data on unemployment, there is little to suggest any significant closing of regional differentials since the early 1960s. The interpretation of data, however, merits a word of caution. There has been an increasing disposition of late to question the significance of the conventional measures of unemployment. As with income figures, they can be misleading as indicators of distress. Life styles vary substantially across the country and, given these differences, comparisons of income and employment levels have to be made with care. Seasonal work is traditional in some parts of the country and those involved in it are not necessarily disposed to exchange the pattern for year-round employment. In like manner not all rural residents hanker after the higher incomes of the cities, particularly when such incomes are accompanied by higher prices and a quicker pace of life. More sophisticated indicators of regional inequalities are needed than those conventionally used in the past.

The foregoing considerations aside, if we are to measure the efficacy of the Department of Regional Economic Expansion in terms of reducing unemployment we are immediately faced with a multiplicity of variables bearing on unemployment levels and it becomes a matter of considerable difficulty to isolate the specific impact of the department itself. The need to look at a medium- or a long-run time horizon rather than a short one in assessing the impact of the department on employment levels is not merely a matter of the inevitable delays involved in the completion of structural changes; there are also the complications in the short run of random year to year changes as well as those associated with fluctuations in the business cycle.

As for many of the secular changes occurring in the fortunes of particular areas, these will often arise independently of anything the department does or does not do. The discovery and depletion of natural resources; changes in consumer demand or international trading patterns; or technological developments influencing the location of industry may result in improvements or deterioration in the fortunes of particular areas. One of the major issues at the present time relates to the uneven distribution of natural resources and the question of how much freedom the fortunate provincial governments within whose boundaries oil and gas, in particular, exist shall have in determining the price of their disposal at the expense of the "have not" provinces.

With regard to the future, a number of revisions to policy based upon past experience and criticisms are currently being contemplated. Greater flexibility in policy is being sought in the light of regional potentialities and aspirations and general development agreements are being negotiated with individual provinces bearing these in mind. Administratively, one of the most important changes currently being undertaken relates to the decentralization of decision making. It has frequently been contended that too many decisions are being made in Ottawa. The intention now is to delegate more power to the regions and there has been a substantial redistribution of staff accordingly. The objective is to increase the number of trained and responsible people with authority to make decisions in the field, people who both have more knowledge of local conditions and are able to speed up the decision-making process.

The question of the appropriate degree of centralization and decentralization is, however, a complex issue and satisfactory compromises are especially difficult to achieve. It will be necessary to ensure that national goals and interests are not overlooked. There is uneasiness in many quarters about the inadequacy of guidelines at the national level—within which the industrial structure of individual regions might be steered. Looked at in isolation, it may seem wise for one region to embark upon a particular course of action but unwise in the light of what others may be doing, or in the framework of national objectives. In the determination of those objectives, however, provincial governments will want a voice. They are becoming increasingly unwilling to leave initiatives and decisions to Ottawa, an unwillingness by no means confined to the operations of DREE but extending over a wide range of national economic policies including taxation and revenue sharing, urbanization, transport, and manpower, as well as others.

It is of paramount importance in Canada, with its federal structure, that the federal and provincial governments reach agreement on the direction policies should take. Current debates on environmental control, the nature and magnitude of foreign investment, and the increasing concentration of population in a few major urban centers reflect dissatisfaction in many quarters with the laissez faire decisions of the market place. But national policies designed to modify the forces at work have to be framed with regional interests in mind.

Thus, given the inadequacy of Canadian investment in their region, governments in the Atlantic region are anxious to foster rather than discourage foreign investment, and, unlike the situation in Ontario, where unemployment is heavy the creation of jobs assumes more importance than the protection of the environment. The stronger provinces are inclined to go their own way and are apt to identify national interests with their own. In the Atlantic region, which would benefit by presenting a common front, internal rivalries are strong, making it even more difficult to reach a consensus.

Individual provinces have offered a great variety of incentives to firms in an effort to influence their location, at times in competition with each other and often with inadequate evaluation of their potential viability. Losses have been heavy and in some cases, to avoid the unemployment resulting from failure, enterprises have been taken over by governments, leading to a compounding of losses. There has been a lack of expertise and realism in the attempts to develop some of the less promising areas. The powerful influence of market forces has been underestimated.

Misgivings have not been confined to industrial incentives. The attitude towards infrastructure expenditures has undergone a number of changes, receiving considerable emphasis at one time and less at another. These swings in attitude reflect in part the uncertainty surrounding their contribution to the process of development.

Controversy continues on the merits of growth centers and while there is little doubt that measures to foster them will continue, experience thus far does not suggest that they have a strong popular appeal. Indeed, a task force established to examine social development in New Brunswick revealed little enthusiasm for them even in those parts of the province which could be expected to benefit most and there was opposition in other parts. The concept appears to be more popular with administrators anxious to have some rationale for spatial expenditures than with the public at large.

So far as equalization payments are concerned there is nothing to suggest any reduction in their magnitude over the next few years and, as noted above, they contribute very substantially to the spatial income redistribution process in Canada. The recipient provinces are free to spend the sums as they wish and are not tied to specific objectives as is the case under the shared cost programs.

As for the designation of regions to be the recipients of various types of federal aid, there have been many changes over the years, one way or another, and, to varying degrees, half the labor force of the country now falls within those regions. Their boundaries may be extended still further. Consideration is currently being given to expanding the operations of DREE into the sparsely populated northern parts of the provinces which hitherto have been excluded. What the future configuration of the designated regions will be is a matter of doubt. But no matter how the boundaries are drawn, depressed areas need to be seen in the context of the very rapid developments which are taking place elsewhere. The relative prosperity of the poorer regions may depend as much on what is happening in the richer regions as it does in their own. To be effective, regional policies may have to be concerned with both.

One thing is certain, if we are to achieve a high standard of living as a nation, we must encourage the creation of an industrial structure which is innovative, flexible, and responsive to change. Policies have to be seen in this context. Aid to regions which undermines or threatens to undermine the international competitiveness of Canadian industry is most unlikely to command the widespread support necessary for its continuance.

Bibliography

Chapter 1
Preliminary Overview
Niles M. Hansen

Alonso, W. 1970. The Question of City Size and National Policy. Center for Planning and Development Research, Institute of Urban and Regional Development, University of California, Berkeley, Discussion Paper no. 125, June.

_____. 1971. The Economics of Urban Size. *Regional Science Association Papers*, vol. 26.

Brown, A.J. 1972. *The Framework of Regional Economics in the United Kingdom*. London: Cambridge University Press.

Cameron, G. 1970. Growth Areas, Growth Centres and Regional Conversion. *Scottish Journal of Political Economy* 17, no. 1, pp. 19-38.

Clark, C. 1945. The Economic Functions of a City in Relation to its Size. *Econometrica* 13, no. 2, pp. 97-113.

Commission of the European Communities 1971. *Regional Development in the Community*. Brussels.

_____. 1973. *Report on the Regional Problems in the Enlarged Community*. Brussels.

Davis, K. 1969. *Basic Data for Cities, Countries and Regions*. World Urbanization 1950-1970, Population Monograph Series no. 4. Berkeley: University of California Institute of International Studies.

Hansen, N.M. 1971. *Financing Rural Development*. Lexington, Kentucky: National Area Development Institute.

_____. 1972. *Growth Centers in Regional Economic Development*. New York: The Free Press.

Hirsch, W.C. 1968. The Supply of Urban Public Services. In *Issues in Urban Economics*, eds. H. Perloff and L. Wingo. Baltimore: Johns Hopkins.

Hirschman, A.O. 1958. *The Strategy of Economic Development.* New Haven: Yale University Press.

Kuklinski, A.R., ed. 1972. *Growth Poles and Growth Centres in Regional Planning.* Paris and The Hague: Mouton.

Neutze, G.M. 1967. *Economic Policy and the Size of Cities.* New York: Augustus M. Kelley.

Newman, M. 1972. *The Political Economy of Appalachia.* Lexington, Mass.: D.C. Heath.

Nichols, V. 1969. Growth Poles: An Evaluation of Their Propulsive Effect. *Environment and Planning* 1, no. 2, pp. 193-208.

OECD Observer. 1973. April.

Richardson, H. 1969. *Regional Economics.* New York: Praeger.

Robinson, E.A.G. 1969. *Backward Areas in Advanced Countries.* New York: St. Martin's Press.

Smith, D.M. 1971. *Industrial Location.* New York: John Wiley and Sons, Inc.

Thompson, W.R. 1968. Internal and External Factors in the Development of Urban Economies. In *Issues in Urban Economics,* eds. H. Perloff and L. Wingo. Baltimore: Johns Hopkins.

Wingo, L. 1972. Issues in a National Urban Development Strategy for the United States. *Urban Studies* 9, no. 1, pp. 3-27.

Chapter 2
Regional Economic Policy in France, 1962-1972
Rémy Prud'homme

Anfré, J. 1969. Entreprises Multirégionales et Concentration des Sièges Sociaux. *Economie et Statistiques,* September, pp. 27-41.

Aydalot, P.; Noel, M.; and Pottier, C. 1971. *La Mobilité des Activités Economiques.* Paris: Gauthier-Villars.

Bertrand, P. 1970. Le Déséquilibre des Migrations Paris-Province s'atténue. *Economie et Statistique,* March, pp. 3-25.

Borel, N. 1969. Les comptes régionaux des Ménages en 1966 et 1967. *Etudes et Conjoncture,* August, p. 109.

Chinitz, B. 1961. Contrasts in Agglomerations: New York and Pittsburgh. *The American Economic Review,* May 1961, pp. 279-289.

Commissariat Général du Plan. 1963. "Le Niveau Supérieur de l'Armature Urbaine Française." Mimeographed. Paris. (Often referred to as Hautreux and Rochefort Report.)

_____. 1971. "Etude Relative à la Composition de l'Emploi par Establissements." Mimeographed. Lille: Centre d'Analyse du Développement.

DATAR 1969. *La Politique d'Aménagement du Territoire, Project de Loi de Finances pour 1970.* Paris: La Documentation Française.

_____. 1972. *La Politique d'Aménagement du Territoire, Project de Loi de Finances pour 1972.* Paris: La Documentation Française.

Durand, P. 1972. *Industrie et Régions.* Paris: La Documentation Française.

Le Fillâtre, P. 1964. La Puissance Economique des Grandes Agglomérations Françaises. *Etudes et Conjoncture,* January 1964, pp. 1-40.

Falise, M. and Lepas, A. 1970. Les Motivations de Localisation des Investissements Internationaux de l'Europe du Nord-Ouest. *Revue Economique*, January 1970, pp. 103-109.

Guichard, O. 1965. *Aménager la France*. Paris: Laffont-Gauthier.

INSEE 1965. *L'Espace Economique Français*. Paris: Imprimerie Nationale and P.U.F., Fascicule 1, Demographie Générale.

_____. 1967. *L'Espace Economique Français*. Paris: Impremerie Nationale and P.U.F., Fascicule 2, Population Active.

INSEE and DATAR 1970. *Statistiques et Indicateurs des Régions Françaises*. Paris: INSEE.

_____. 1972. *Statistiques et Indicateurs des Régions Françaises*. Paris: INSEE.

Keller, P., and Simula, P. 1971. "La Localisation Industrielle en Milieu Urbain." Mimeographed. Toulouse: Institut d'Etudes de l'Emploi.

Lamarre, H. 1972. La Localisation Industrielle Devient Une Science Exacte. *L'Usine Nouvelle*, July 1972, pp. 125-140.

Lajugie, J. 1969. Le Shéma Français d'Armature Urbaine. In Société Canadienne de Science Economique et Congrès des Economistes de Langue Française, *Développement Urbain et Analyse Economique*, pp. 347-380. Paris: Cujas.

Lanversin, J. 1970. *L'Aménagement du Territoire et la Régionalisation*. Paris: Librairie Générale de Droit et de Jurisprudence.

Monod, J. and Castelbajac, P. 1971. *L'Aménagement du Territoire*. Paris: P.U.F.

Muel, P.A.; Bolton, P.; and Cazin, F. 1970. *Etudes de Demographie Régionale*, Les Collections de l'INSEE, Série R., no. 4. Paris: INSEE.

Office Statistique des Communautés Européennes. 1972. *Statistiques Régionales*. Annuaire. Luxembourg.

Prud'homme, R. 1972. "La Production D'Equipements Collectifs en France Pendant le 5ème Plan." Report for the Commissariat Général du Plan. Mimeographed. Paris: BETURE.

Rimareix, G. 1970. *La Politique de rénovation rurale*, Notes et Etudes Documentaires no. 3708. Paris: La Documentation Française.

Ruault, J.P. 1965. Les Revenus des ménages en 1962. *Etudes et Conjoncture*, December.

Schiray, M. and Elie, P. 1970. *Les Migrations Entre Régions et au Niveau Catégories de Communes de 1954 à 1962*, Les Collections de l'INSEE, Série D, no. 4. Paris: INSEE.

SODIC 1967. "Etude de l'Incidence des Implantations Industrielles sur le Marché du Travail." Mimeographed. Paris.

Strawczynoki, E. 1971. Le processus de choix de localisation. *La Vie Urbaine*, no. 3.

Chapter 3
Regional Economic Policy in the United Kingdom
G.C. Cameron

Atkins, D.H.W. 1973. Employment Changes in Branch and Parent Manufacturing Plants in the U.K., 1966-1971. *Trade and Industry*, 12, no. 9.

_____. 1972. *The Framework of Regional Economics in the United King-dom.* Cambridge: Cambridge University Press.

Brown, A.J. 1968. Regional Problems and Regional Policy. *Economic Review*, November.

Brown, Lord George. 1972. *In My Own Way.* London: Penguin.

Cameron, G.C. and Clark, B.D. 1966. *Industrial Movement and The Regional Problem.* University of Glasgow, Social and Economic Series Occasional Paper no. 5. Edinburgh: Oliver and Boyd.

_____. 1970. Growth Areas, Growth Centres and Regional Conversion. *Scottish Journal of Political Economy*, February.

Cambridge University Department of Applied Economics, 1972. N.I.E.S.R. *Economic Review*, June.

Civil Service Department. 1973. *The Dispersal of Government Work From London.* Cmnd 5322. (The Hardman Report.) London: Her Majesty's Stationery Office.

Crosland, Anthony. 1971. *Population of the United Kingdom.* First Report of the Select Committee on Science and Technology. House of Commons Session 1970-1971. London: Her Majesty's Stationery Office.

Department of the Environment. 1971. *Long Term Population Distribution in Great Britain*, SBN 11 750415 7. London: Her Majesty's Stationery Office.

Expenditure Committee (House of Commons). 1973. Subcommittee on Regional Incentives. Session 1972-1973. London: Her Majesty's Stationery Office.

Firn, J. Forthcoming. "The Components of Regional Economic Growth." Mimeographed. Department of Social and Economic Research, University of Glasgow.

Forsyth, D.J. 1972. *U.S. Investment in Scotland.* London: Praeger Press.

Foster, C.D. 1973. Public Finance Aspects of National Settlement Patterns. In *Cities, Regions and Public Policy*, eds. Gordon C. Cameron and Lowdon Wingo, pp. 79-98. Edinburgh: Oliver & Boyd.

Hart, P. and Macbean, A. 1961. Profitability in Scottish Companies. *Scottish Journal of Political Economy*, November.

Keeble, D. 1972. Industrial Mobility. In *Spatial Problems of the British Economy*, Eds. Michael Chisholm and Gerald Manners. Cambridge: CUP.

Logan, R.I. 1972. Transport, Communications and Industrial Mobility. Ph.D. thesis, University of Glasgow.

Luttrell, W.F. 1962. *Factory Location and Industrial Movement.* London: National Institute of Economic and Social Research.

Mulvey, C. 1974. *Structure, Growth and Performance of West Central Scotland.* University of Glasgow Urban and Regional Discussion Papers.

McCallum, J.D. 1973. U.K. Regional Policy 1964-1972. In *Cities, Regions and Public Policy*, Eds. Gordon C. Cameron and Lowdon Wingo. Edinburgh: Oliver & Boyd.

McCrone, G. 1969. *Regional Policy in Britain.* University of Glasgow Social and Economic Series. London: Allen & Unwin.

_____ . 1973. The Location of Economic Activity in the United Kingdom. In *Cities, Regions and Public Policy*, Eds. Gordon C. Cameron and Lowdon Wingo. Edinburgh: Oliver & Boyd.

Moore, B. and Rhodes, J. 1973. Evaluating the Effects of British Regional Policy *Economic Journal*. March.

Organisation for Economic Cooperation and Development. 1973. OECD Economic Surveys—United Kingdom—January.

Ridley, A. 1972. Regional Policy—Theory and Practice. Paper presented at Urban Studies Conference on Regional Policy, Oxford. 1972.

Samuelson, P.A. 1969. Discussion in *Backward Areas in Advanced Countries*. Ed. E.A.G. Robinson, pp. 378-379. London: Macmillan.

Simpson, J. 1974. *Discrimination and Subsidies—the Northern Ireland Area*. University of Glasgow Urban and Regional Discussion Papers.

Thomas, R.L. and Storey, P.J.M. 1971. Unemployment Dispersion as a determinant of Wage Inflation in the U.K. 1925-1966. Manchester School of Social & Economic Studies. June.

Upson, R. 1974. *The Scope For Discrimination in Government Incentives*. University of Glasgow Urban and Regional Discussion Papers.

West Central Scotland Plan. Forthcoming. *West Central Scotland Plan Team*, Glasgow.

West, E.G. 1973. *Regional Policy for Ever*. London: Institute of Economic Affairs.

Wilson, T. 1973. British Regional Policy in the European Context. *The Banker*, February, p. 168.

Chapter 4
Regional Policies in West Germany
Günter Krumme

Akademie für Raumforschung und Landesplanung (1967). *Stadtregionen in der Bundesrepublik Deutschland 1961*. Hannover: Jänecke.

Albert, W. 1970. Zielgewinnung und Entscheidungsfindung für Infrastrukturprogramme. In *Theorie und Praxis der Infrastrukturprogramme*, eds. R. Jochimsen and E.E. Simonis. Berlin: Duncker & Humblot.

Bayerische Staatsregierung. 1972. *Raumordnungsbericht 1971*. München.

Beirat für Raumordnung beim Bundesminister des Innern. 1972. *Empfehlungen Folge 3*. Bonn.

Blake, C. 1972. The Effectiveness of Investment Grants as a Regional Subsidy. *Scottish Journal of Political Economy*, 19, no. 1, pp. 63-71.

Borries, H.W. v. 1969. *Ökonomische Grundlagen der westdeutschen Siedlungsstruktur*. Hannover: Jänecke.

Böventer E.v. 1969a. Regional Economic Problems in West Germany. In *Backward Areas in Advanced Countries*, ed. E.A.G. Robinson. London: Macmillan.

_____ . 1969b. Determinants of Migration into West German Cities, 1956-1961, 1961-1966. Papers, Regional Science Association, 23: 53-62.

_____. 1971. Die räumlichen Wirkungen von öffentlichen und privaten Investitionen. In *Grundfragen der Infrastrukturplanung für wachsende Wirtschaften*, eds. E. Arndt and D. Swatek. Berlin: Duncker & Humblot.

British Overseas Economic Surveys (BOES). 1955. *The Federal Republic of Germany: Economic and Commercial Conditions in the Federal Republic of Germany and West Berlin.* London: Her Majesty's Stationery Office.

Brösse, U. 1971. Regionalpolitische Konsequenzen aus einer Standortuntersuchung über die Zulieferindustrie. *Informationen (Institut für Raumordnung)*, vol. 21, no. 7, pp. 177-183.

Brösse, U. et al. 1971. *Industrielle Zulieferbeziehungen als Standortfaktor.* Forschungs- und Sitzungsberichte no. 65, Akademie für Raumforschung und Landesplanung. Hannover: Jänecke.

Bundesanstalt für Arbeit (BAA). 1972. *Ausländische Arbeitnehmer 1971.* Nürnberg.

Bundesministerium für Arbeit und Sozialordnung (BAS). 1964. *Die Standortwahl der Industriebetriebe 1961-1963.* Bonn.

Bundesministerium für Arbeit und Sozialordnung (BAS 1966). *Die Standortwahl der Industriebetriebe 1964 und 1965.* Bonn.

Bundesministerium für Arbeit und Sozialordnung (BAS 1968). *Die Standortwahl der Industriebetriebe 1966 und 1967.* Bonn.

_____. 1971. *Die Standortwahl der Industriebetriebe 1968 und 1969.* Bonn.

Bundesministerium für Ernährung, Landwirtschaft und Forsten (BELF). 1971. *Landwirtschaft im Umbruch.* Bonn.

Bundesministerium für Wirtschaft (BfW). 1969. *Intensivierung und Koordinierung der regionalen Wirtschaftspolitik.* Bonn.

_____. 1972. *Durch 460,000 neue Arbeitsplatze mehr Wohlstand fur unsere Fördergebiete.* Bonn.

Bundesregierung (BROB 1970). *Raumordnungsbericht 1970.* Bonn: Deutscher Bundestag, 6. Wahlperiode.

Commission of the European Communities 1969. *A Regional Policy for the Community.* Luxemburg.

Frankfurter Allgemeine Zeitung (FAZ). 1971. Ein Programm für die Regionalpolitik. August 8.

Gerfin, H. 1964. Gesamtwirtschaftliches Wachstum und regionale Entwicklung. *Kyklos*, 17, no. 4, pp. 565-593.

Gerlach, K. and Liepmann, P. 1972. Konjunkturelle Aspekte der Industrialisierung peripherer Regionen—dargestellt am Beispiel des ostbayerischen Regierungsbezirks Oberpfalz. *Jahrb. für Nationalökonomie und Statistik*, 187, no. 1, pp. 1-21.

German Press and Information Service. 1973. *Bulletin*, Supplement, January 23, p. 7.

Jochimsen, R. and Treuner, P. 1967. *Zentrale Orte in Lündlichen Räumen.* Mitteilungen aus dem Institut für Raumforschung, Heft 58. Bad Godesberg.

Julitz, L. 1972. Die Schwächeren Bundesländer holen auf. *Frankfurter Allgemeine Zeitung*, August 26.

Jürgensen, H. and Thormählen, T. 1972. Regionale Entwicklungspläne. In *Neue Wege der Wirtschaftspolitik*, ed. E. Dürr. Berlin: Duncker & Humblot.

Koch, T.P. 1968. Zur Mindestgrösse von Industriestandorten. *Informationen. (Institut für Raumordnung)*, vol. 18, no. 24, pp. 691-714.

Krengel, R.; Stanglin, R.; and Wessels, H. 1968. Anwendung von Input-Output Techniken in der Arbeitsmarktforschung. *Mitteilungen (Institut für Arbeitsmarkt- und Berufsforschung Erlangen)*, no. 3, pp. 127-43.

Krumme, G. 1972. Development Centers and Central Places in West German Regional Planning Schemes. *The Review of Regional Studies*, 2, no. 2, pp. 215-234.

Kunz, D. and Spöri, D. 1971. Eine neue Technik für die regionale Wirtschaftsförderung. *Informationen (Institut für Raumordnung)*, vol. 21, no. 23, pp. 607-617.

Monheim, H. 1972. Zur Attraktivität deutscher Städte. *Informationen (Institut für Raumordnung)*, vol. 22, no. 11, pp. 289-296.

Noé, C. 1971. Zur Regionalpolitik als Innere Entwicklungspolitik. In *Regionalpolitik als Entwicklungspolitik*, ed. Rainer Thoss. Münster: Institut für Siedlungs- und Wohnungswesen, pp. 7-28.

OECD. 1970. *The Regional Factor in Economic Development: Policies in 15 Industrialized OECD Countries*. Paris.

Shonfield, A. 1965. *Modern Capitalism: The Changing Balance of Public and Private Power*. New York: Oxford University Press.

Statistisches Bundesamt. 1955-1972. *Statistische Jahrbücher für die Bundesrepublik Deutschland*. Wiesbaden.

Stöckmann, W. 1971. *Die Wohnort- und Arbeitsplatzmobilität der Bevölkerung in Ländlichen Räumen*. Frankfurt: Metra-DIVO.

Streit, M. 1966. *Uber die Bedeutung des räumlichen Verbund im Bereich der Industrie*. Köln: Carl Heymanns.

Wall Street Journal. 1971. Outside Firms' West German Subsidiaries. November 2, p. 6.

Weber, A. and Meinhold, W. 1951. *Agrarpolitik*. Berlin: Duncker & Humblot.

Welt. 1973. Gegen regionalen Kahlschlag. January 2.

Wieting, R.G. and Hübschle, J. 1968. *Struktur und Motive der Wanderungsbewegungen in der Bundesrepublik Deutschland*. Basel: Prognos AG.

Wirtschaft und Statistik. 1972. Bevölkerungsentwicklung in Stadt und Land 1961 bis 1970. No. 11, pp. 626-628.

Zimmermann, H. et al. 1972. Regionale Präferenzen: Zur Wohnortorientierung und Mobilitätsbereitschaft der Arbeitnehmer in der BRD. *Informationen (Institut fur Raumordnung)*, vol. 22, no. 15, pp. 379-399.

Chapter 5
Regional Policy in Italy
Vera Cao-Pinna

Allione, M. 1968. Esperienze di pianificazione regionale in Italia. *Programmazione economica e regioni*. Rome: Associazione nazionale per la programmazione economica.

343 Public Policy & Regional Economic Development

Arfé, G. 1962. Il problema delle diversità e degli squilibri regionali nella cultura politica italiana, dalla caduta della Destra all'avvento del Fascismo. In *Gli squilibri regionali e l'articolazione dell'intervento pubblico*, pp. 160-163. Milan: Lerici.

Bandini, M. 1956. Offensiva contro la riforma. *Rivista di politica agraria*, no. 2

Cacace, N. 1973. Le Partecipazioni Statali ed il Mezzogiorno: analisi delle carenze passate e prospettive di programmi futuri. *Quaderni ISRIL*, III, no. 4.

Cao-Pinna, V. 1965. Modèle de croissance de l'économie italienne. *Quaderni del Centro di studi e piani economici*. Turin: Boringhieri.

Centro di Studi e Piani Economici 1971. Le proiezioni territoriali del "Progetto 80". Rome.

Chenery, H.B. 1962. *Politiche di sviluppo per l'Italia meridionale*. Rome: SVIMEZ.

D'Antonio, M. 1967. *Commento al piano economico nazionale*. Bologna: Cappelli.

DiNardi, G. 1960. I provvedimenti per il Mezzogiorno. In *Economia e Storia*, pp. 494-520. Milan: Giuffre.

Fiorelli, F. and Novacco, N. 1963. *Politica di localizzazione dell'industria e sviluppo del Mezzogiorno*. Milan: Giuffrè.

Food and Agriculture Organization 1960. The Agrarian Reform in Italy. New York.

Fortunato, G. 1911. Il Mezzogiorno e lo stato italiano. (Reprinted in 1925). Florence: Vallecchi.

Graziani, A. 1968. La politica del Mezzogiorno: sue realizzazioni e sviluppi. *Nord e Sud*, nella società e nell'economia di oggi, pp. 150-153.

————. 1972. *L'economia italiana: 1945-1970*. Bari: Il Mulino.

Graziani, A. et al. 1973. *Incentivi investimenti industriali nel Mezzogiorno*. Milan: F. Angeli.

Ilses 1965. *Ricerca sul grado di convenienza all'insediamento delle industrie, in relazione ai vigenti incentivi diretti*. Milan: Instituto Lombardo di Studi Economici e Sociali.

Indovina, F. 1967. *Esperienze di pianificazione regionale*. Padova: Marsilio Editori.

La Malfa, U. 1962. Problemi e prospettive dello sviluppo economico italiano. An addendum to the *Report*, to the Parliament, on the Italian economic situation in 1961. Ministry of the Budget. Rome.

Legitimo, G. 1960. Considerazioni sulla nuova politica d'intervento nei territori depressi dell'Italia centrosettentrionale. *Annali* della Facoltà di Economia e Commercio in Verona.

Leon, P. 1973. Calcolo economico e progetti speciali. *Economia Pubblica*, nos. 1-2. Milan: Angeli.

Lombardini, S. 1967. *La Programmazione*. Turin: Einaudi.

Lutz, V. 1962. *Italy: A study in Economic Development*. Oxford: Oxford University Press.

Luzzatto, G. 1962. Gli squilibri economici fra regione e regione e l'unità nazionale. In *Gli squilibri regionali e l'articolazione dell'intervento pubblico*. Milan: Lerici.

Ministry of the Budget and Economic Planning. 1965. Programma economico nazionale per il quinquennio 1966-70.

_____. 1969. *Progetto 80*. Milan: Libreria Feltrinelli.

_____. 1971. Documento Programmatico Preliminare: elementi per l'impostazione del programma economico nazionale 1971-75.

Molinari, A. and Turco, C. 1959. Il problema delle zone industriali in Italia. *Informazioni*. Rome: SVIMEZ.

Novacco, N. 1972. Il Mezzogiorno come fattore determinante per il superamento della crisi e per il concretarsi di nuove prospettive di sviluppo sociale. Discussion paper presented at the Economic Conference of the Demo-Christian party, Perugia.

Petriccione, S. 1972. I progetti speciali tra la teorizzazione e l'empirismo. *Il Globo*. Rome.

Pilloton, F. 1960. *Effetti moltiplicativi degli investimenti della Cassa per il Mezzogiorno*. Rome: SVIMEZ.

Rossi Doria, M. 1959. La riforma: sei anni dopo. *Dieci anni di polititica agraria nel Mezzogiorno*, pp. 139-144. Bari: Laterza.

Ruffolo, G. 1973. *Rapporto sulla programmazione*. Roma: Laterza.

Salvemini, G. 1900. La questione meridionale e il federalismo. *Scritti sulla questione meridionale*. Reprinted in 1955. Turin: Einaudi.

Saraceno, P. 1961. La mancata unificazione economica italiana a cento anni dall'unificazione politica. *L'economia italiana dal 1861 at 1961*. Milan: Giuffrè.

_____. 1968. La politica di sviluppo di un'area sottosviluppata, nell'esperienza italiana. *NORD-SUD*, May 1968.

SVIMEZ. 1955. Schema di sviluppo dell'occupazione e del reddito in Italia, nel decennio 1955-64. Rome.

_____. 1962. Un secolo di statistiche italiane Nord-Sud: 1861-1961. Rome.

Tagliacarne, G. 1972. *Il reddito prodotto dalle provincie italiane, 1963-1970*. Milan: Angeli.

Valarché, J. 1956. Réforme agraire en Italie. *Revue Economique et Sociale*. Paris.

Vicinelli, P. 1972. I compiti della "Cassa" nel quadro della nuova legislazione per il Mezzogiorno. *Realtà del Mezzogiorno*, no. 11. Rome.

Chapter 6
Regional Policy in the Netherlands
Ad. J. Hendriks

Centraal Plan Bureau. 1970. *De Nederlandse Economie in 1973*. The Hague.

Vanhove, N.D. 1962. *De doelmatigheid van het regionaal-economisch beleid in Nederland*. Gent and Hilversum.

Weber, A. 1909. *Ueber den Standort der Industrien. Reine Theorie des Standorts*. Tubingen.

Chapter 7
Regional Economic Policy: Problems, Analysis, and Political Experiments in Sweden
Åke E. Andersson

SOU 1951:6 Holm P., De lokaliseringsbestämmande faktorerna. (Determining factors in decisions on location.)

SOU 1963:49 Törnqvist G., Studier i industri lokalisering. (Studies in industrial location.)

SOU 1970:14 Urbaniseringen i Sverige. (Urbanization in Sweden.) Essays by Hägerstrand T., Bylund E., and other geographers.

SOU 1970:15 Regionalekonomisk utveckling. (Regional economic development.) Essays by Andersson, Å, Siven, C., and other economists.

SOU 1971:16 Regional utveckling och planering. (Regional development and planning.) ERU-report with a theoretical appendix by Andersson,Å.

SOU 1974:2 Ortsbundna levnadsvillkor. (Locally determined conditions of living.) A number of empirical reports and theoretical analyses of regional differences in standard of living.

SOU 1974:3 Produktionskostnader och regionala produktionssystem. (Costs of production and regional production systems.) A number of empirical and theoretical studies of regional differences in productivity.

SOU 1974:4 Regionala prognoser i planeringens tjänst. (Regional forecasting for economic planning.) A number of theoretical and practical methods of forecasting and planning of long term economic development in regions.

Rehn G., "The problem of stability: An analysis and some policy proposals," in *Wages Policy under Full Employment.* Ed. Ralph Turvey, London 1952.

Meddelanden från konjunkturinstitutet.Kap. IX. Serie A:17. Stockholm 1950.

Lind T., Serck-Hanssen J., "Regional Subsidies on Labour and Capital." Swedish Journal of Economics 1972:1, vol. 74, pp. 68-83.

Koopmans T., Beckmann M., "Assignment problems and the location of economic activities." *Econometrica,* vol. 25, pp. 53-76, Jan. 1957.

Chapter 8
Spain's Regional Growth
J.R. Lasuén

Alcaide, J. 1973. La renta española. *Ya,* May 16, 1973.

Barbancho, A.G. 1960. *Los movimientos migratorios en España.* Madrid.

Battelle Institute, 1971. *La economía española en 1975: Aplicación de un modelo econométrico.* Geneva.

Caballos, J.G. 1932. *Historia económica.* Madrid.

Calvo Sotelo, J. 1931. *Mis servicios al estado.* Madrid.

Cansero, J.E. 1972. Política Fiscal. In *Política Económica de España,* ed. J. Gamir. Madrid: Guadiana.

Carreras, J. 1972. Ph.D. Thesis, University of Barcelona.

Casany, E. 1970. Los Fondos de inversión en el proceso de formación del ahorro. *Haciende Pública Española,* no. 12.

Castañe, J. 1973. Report to the University of Deusto Meeting on Regional Development, Bilbao.

Censo de Población de la Corona de Castilla en el Siglo XVI, de orden del Rey. 1829. Madrid: La imprenta real.

Clark, C. 1957. *Conditions of Economic Progress.* (Spanish version by J. Vergara and M. Paredes. Madrid: Alianza Editorial, 1967.)

_____. 1968. *Crecimiento Demografico y Utilización del Suelo* (Spanish version by M. and E. Paredes) Madrid, 1968.

Comisaria del Plan, IDE, Volume I (1972). Madrid.

Comisaria del Plan, IDE, Volume II (1973). Madrid.

Cotorruelo Sendagorta, A. 1960. *La política económica de la vivienda en España.* Madrid, Instituto Sancho de Moncada.

Da Silva, J.G. 1965. *Developpement Economique Subsistence Déclin.* Paris. Mouton & Co.

De Madariaga, S. 1947. *España.* Buenos Aires.

The Economist. 1973. April 28-May 4, 1973.

EVP. 1971. *Estudio de Viabilidad del Mercado Central de Madrid.* Madrid.

_____. 1972. *Estudio de Renta en la Región Central.* Madrid.

Fuentes, E., ed. 1972. *Hacienda pública española.* January-April.

Gamir, L. et al. 1972. *Política Económica de España.* Guadiana.

Gaviria, M. 1968. Gran San Blas. Análisis Socio-Urbanistico de un barrio neuvo español. *Arquitectura,* May-June.

Hirschman, A.O. 1958. *The Strategy of Economic Development.* New Haven: Yale University Press.

Iberplan. 1971. *Report for the Ministry of Commerce: 1970.*

IBRD. 1962. *The World Bank Report on the Spanish Economy, the Economic Development of Spain.* Madrid.

_____. 1972. *Growth and Change in Spanish Industry.* Washington.

Informaciones. 1972. Interview with J.R. Lasuén, January 22.

Instituto Nacional de Industrie. 1964. *Report to the IV Congress on Regional Economics.* Madrid.

Lasuén, J.R. 1959. Las Balanzas de Pago Sudamericana. *De Económica,* no. 63.

_____. 1960a. Estructura y desarrollo económico. *Anales de Economía,* no. 66.

_____. 1960b. Developpement régional et national. *Cahiers de L'ISEA,* June.

_____. 1963. Today's Problems in Regional Planning. *II World Conference on Regional Planning.* Rhodes.

_____. 1966. chapter in *España ante la integración europea.* Barcelona.

_____. 1967. Urbanization Hypothesis and Spain's Cities' System Evolution. *Round Table on Regional Planning.* The Hague: Institute of Social Studies.

_____. 1969. On Growth Poles. *Urban Studies*, June.
_____. 1970. Urban Hierarchy, Stability and Spatial Polarization. *Urban Studies*, January.
_____. 1971a. Venezuela: An Industrial Shift-Share Analysis 1941-1961. *Regional and Urban Economics* 1, no. 2.
_____. 1971b. "An Open System Model of Multi-Regional Economic Development." Monograph. Universidad Autónoma de Madrid.
_____. 1972a. Multiregional Economic Development. An Open Systems Approach. In *Information Systems for Regional Development*, eds. T. Hagerstrand and A. Kuklinski. Lund University.
_____. 1972b. La política de desarrollo económico precisa. *III Semana Económica Internacional*. Barcelona.
_____. 1972c. Política económica española 1972. *Boletin HOAC*, June.
_____. 1972d. El sector de la vivienda. *Joint Housing Seminar, U.S.A.-Spain*. Madrid.
_____. 1972e. La política del suelo. *Revista Arquitectura*, June.
_____. 1972f. Desarrollo regional y proceso de urbanización. United Nations Seminar on Urban Land Policies, Madrid 1971. Monograph. Ministry of Housing.
_____. 1972g. La política universitaria. *Indice*, no. 319. Madrid.
_____. 1973a. Urbanization and Development—The Temporal Interaction Between Geographical and Sectoral Clusters. *Urban Studies* 10.
_____. 1973b. *Sectores prioritarios del Desarrollo español*. Madrid: Guadiana.
Lasuén, J.R. et al. 1966. *La Vivienda y la Actividad Económica; XIV: Criterios de la Política de Vivienda*. Studies for revision of the National Housing Plan. Madrid.
Lasuén, J.R.; Lorca, A.; and Oria, J. 1967. City Size Distributions and Economic Development. *Ekistics*, August.
Lasuén, J.R. and Rubio, R. 1974. *La evolución de las regiones españolas 1860-1969*. Confederación Cajas de Ahorro.
Lasuén, J.R.; Vergara, J.; and Rubio, R. 1973. An Approach to Regional Planning. United Nations Seminar on the integration of physical and economic planning. New York, September.
Maizels, A. 1963. *Industrial Growth and World Trade*, Cambridge, 1963.
Martin, Lobo, M. *Realidad y perspectiva de la planificación regional en España*. Edición del Movimiento. Madrid.
Ministerio de Educación. 1969a. *Modelo español de desarrollo educativo*. Madrid.
_____. 1969b. *Ley General de Educación y Financiamiento de la Reforma Educativa*. Madrid.
_____. 1969c. *Libro Blanco de la Educación*. Madrid.
OCED. 1972. *Report*. Madrid.
Olavarria, J. 1973. Report to the University of Deustó Meeting on Regional Development. Bilbao.
Pardo, M.L. 1932. *La conquista del Ebro y nueva política hidréulica; La confederación del Ebro*. Madrid.
Paris Eguilaz, J. 1944. *La expansión de la económía española*. Madrid.

Parmio. J. 1970. Hacienda pública española y europea: Sus fuentes de financiación. *Hacienda Pública Española*, no. 12.

Perloff, H.; Dunn, E.S., Jr.; Lampard, E.E.; and Muth, R.F. 1960. *Regions and Economic Growth*. Lincoln: University of Nebraska Press.

Perpiña, R. 1952. *De estructura económica y economía hispanica*. Madrid: Rialp.

Plaza Prieto, J. 1968. El desarrollo regional y España. *Estudio de Historia Social, Económica y Demográfica de España*. Madird.

Prebisch, R. 1972. Opening speech to the ILPES Seminar on Regional Development, Villa del Mar. Chile.

Racionero, L. 1971. Un modelo espacial del desarrollo español. Doctoral Thesis, Universidad Autónoma de Madrid, Facultad de Ciencias Económicas. 1972.

Richardson, H.W. 1971. Regional Policy Development in Spain. *Urban Studies*. February.

_____. 1972. Algunos aspectos de la política de desarrollo. *OECD Report*, June.

Robert, A. 1943. *Un problema nacional; la industrialización necesaria*. Madrid: Espasa-Calpe.

Ros Hombravella, J. et al. 1973. Capitalismo español de la autarquía a la estabilización. *Cuadarnos pare el Diálogo*.

Saenz de Buruaga, G. 1969. *Ordenación del territorio, El caso del País Vasco y su zona de influencia*. Madrid: Guadiana.

_____. 1970. 'Desarrollo Regional-Desarrollo de las Regiones' en *Ciudad y Territorio*. Madrid.

_____. 1973. 'España e Italia: Un Análisis Económico Comparativo' in *Información Comercial Española*. January.

Solé Tura, J. 1971. *Introducción al Régimen español*. Barcelona. Ariel.

Tamames, R. 1968. *España ante el II Plan de desarrollo*. Barcelona. Nova Terra.

_____. 1969. *Estructura económica de España*, 4th ed., Madrid.

_____. 1972. *Estructura económica de España*, 6th ed., Madrid.

_____. et al. 1972. 'La Empresa Pública', Study by Iberplan. Madrid.

Velarde, J. 1968. *Política económica de la Dictadura*. Madrid. Guadiana.

Vergara, J. and Lorca, A. 1970. 'Spatial Distribution of Spain's Economic Growth', monograph, Universidad Autónoma de Madrid; also UNRISD, Geneva, 1971/72.

Vilar, P. 1969. *Oro y Moneda en la Historia 1450-1920* (translated by A. Saez Buesa, J. Sabater Borrell, 2nd edition, Esplugas de Llogregat, Barcelona, Ariel 1972), original 1969.

Williamson, J.G. 1965. 'Regional Inequality and the Process of National Development' in *Economic Development and Cultural Change*, July.

Chapter 9
Regional Policy in the United States
Niles M. Hansen

Alonso, W. 1970. The Question of City Size and National Policy. Center for Planning and Development Research, Institute of Urban and Regional Development, University of California, Berkeley, Discussion Paper no. 125, June.

Appalachian Regional Commission. 1970. *Annual Report.* Washington, D.C.: ARC.

Berry, B.J.L. 1967. Spatial Organization and Levels of Welfare: Degree of Metropolitan Labor Market Participation as a Variable in Economic Development. Paper presented to the Economic Development Administration Research Conference, October 9-13, Washington, D.C.

_____. 1972. Growth Processes in the Urban System: New Forces and Trends. Paper prepared for the Second Advanced Seminar on Growth Centers and Public Affairs, University of Texas, Austin, October 12, 1972.

Booth, E.J.R. 1964. Interregional Income Differences. *Southern Economic Journal,* 31, no. 1, pp. 44-51.

Borts, G.H. and Stein, J.L. 1964. *Economic Growth in a Free Market.* New York: Columbia University Press.

Cameron, G.C. 1970. *Regional Economic Development: The Federal Role.* Baltimore: Johns Hopkins.

Chinitz, B. 1969. The Regional Problem in the U.S.A. In *Backward Areas in Advanced Countries,* ed. E.A.G. Robinson. New York: St. Martin's Press.

Commission on Population Growth and the American Future. 1972. *Population and the American Future.* Washington, D.C.: Government Printing Office.

Cumberland, J.H. 1971. *Regional Development: Experiences and Prospects in the United States of America.* Paris and The Hague: Mouton.

Denison, E. 1962. *The Sources of Economic Growth in the United States and the Alternatives Before Us.* New York: Committee for Economic Development.

Economic Development Administration. 1970. *Federal Activities Affecting Location of Economic Development,* vol. 1. Washington, D.C.: EDA.

_____. 1971. *Annual Report.* Washington, D.C.: EDA.

_____. 1972. *Program Evaluation: The Economic Development Administration Growth Center Strategy.* Washington, D.C.: EDA.

Eichner, A.S. 1970. *State Development Agencies and Employment Expansion.* Ann Arbor, Michigan: University of Michigan and Wayne State University Institute of Labor and Industrial Relations.

Fairchild, C.K. 1970. *Worker Relocation: A Review of U.S. Department of Labor Mobility Demonstration Projects.* Washington: E.F. Shelley and Co.

Friedmann, J. and Miller, J. 1965. The Urban Field. *Journal of the American Institute of Planners* 31, no. 4, pp. 312-19.

Fuller, V. 1970. *Rural Worker Adjustment to Urban Life.* Ann Arbor, Michigan: University of Michigan and Wayne State University Institute of Labor and Industrial Relations.

Hansen, N.M. 1966. Some Neglected Factors in American Regional Development Policy: The Case of Appalachia. *Land Economics* 42, no. 1, pp. 1-9.

_____. 1973. *The Future of Nonmetropolitan America.* Lexington, Mass.: D.C. Heath.

Hathaway, D.E. and Perkins, B.E. 1968. Occupational Mobility and Migration from Agriculture. In President's National Advisory Commission on Rural Poverty, *Rural Poverty in the United States.* Washington, D.C.: Government Printing Office, pp. 185-237.

Hoover, E.M. 1971. *An Introduction to Regional Economics.* New York: Alfred A. Knopf.

Kain, J.F. 1968. Housing Segregation, Negro Employment, and Metropolitan Decentralization. *Quarterly Journal of Economics* 82, no. 2, pp. 175-97.

Kain, J.F. and Persky, J.J. 1968. Alternatives to the Gilded Ghetto. Harvard University Program on Regional and Urban Economics, Discussion Paper No. 21.

Keuhn, J.A. 1971. Income Convergence: A Delusion. *Review of Regional Studies* 2, no. 1, pp. 41-51.

Lansing, J. and Mueller, E. 1967. *The Geographic Mobility of Labor.* Ann Arbor, Mich.: University of Michigan Survey Research Center.

Masters, S.H. 1972. Are Black Migrants from the South to the Northern Cities Worse Off than Blacks Already There? *Journal of Human Resources* 7, no. 4, pp. 411-23.

Morrison, P.A. 1972. *Population Movements and the Shape of Urban Growth: Implications for Public Policy.* Santa Monica, Calif.: Rand Corporation.

Munro, J.M. 1969. Planning the Appalachian Development Highway System: Some Critical Questions. *Land Economics* 45, no. 2, pp. 149-56.

National Area Development Institute. 1972a. *Area Development Interchange* 2, no. 6, March 15.

_____. 1972b. *Area Development Interchange* 2, no. 20, October 15.

New Generation. 1968. Vol. 50, no. 3.

Newman, M. 1972. *The Political Economy of Appalachia.* Lexington, Massachusetts: D.C. Heath.

Parr, J.B. 1966. Outmigration and the Depressed Area Problem. *Land Economics* 42, no. 2, pp. 149-59.

Schultz, T. 1961. Investment in Human Capital. *American Economic Review* 51, no. 1, pp. 1-17.

Spengler, J.J. 1967. Some Determinants of the Manpower Prospect, 1966-1985. In *Manpower Tomorrow: Prospects and Priorities.,* ed. Irving H. Siegal. New York: Augustus M. Kelley.

Sundquist, J.L. 1970. Where Shall They Live? *The Public Interest,* no. 18, pp. 88-100.

Thompson, W.R. 1968. Internal and External Factors in the Development of Urban Economies. In Harvey S. Perloff and Lowden Wingo, Jr., *Issues in Urban Economics.* Baltimore: The Johns Hopkins Press.

_____. 1969. The Economic Base of Urban Problems. In *Contemporary Economic Issues,* ed. Neil W. Chamberlain. Homewood, Illinois: Richard D. Irwin.

_____. 1972. The National System of Cities as an Object of Public Policy. *Urban Studies* 9, no. 1, pp. 99-116.

U.S., Bureau of the Census 1969. *Current Population Reports*, Series P-20, no. 188, "Mobility of the Population of the United States: March 1967 to March 1968." Washington, D.C.: Government Printing Office.

———. 1971. *Statistical Abstract of the United States: 1971.* Washington, D.C.: Government Printing Office.

———. 1972. *Statistical Abstract of the United States: 1972.* Washington, D.C.: Government Printing Office.

U.S. News and World Report. 1972. April 17, pp. 42-45.

Walker, D. 1972. Interstate Regional Instrumentalities: A New Piece of an Old Puzzle. *Journal of the American Institute of Planners* 38, no. 6, pp. 359-68.

Widner, R.R. 1971. Appalachia After Six Years. *Appalachia* 5, no. 6, pp. 14-21.

Williamson, J.G. 1965. Regional Inequality and the Process of National Development: A Description of the Patterns. *Economic Development and Cultural Change* 13, no. 4, pt. 2, pp. 1-84.

Wingo, L. 1972. Issues in a National Urban Development Strategy for the United States. *Urban Studies* 9, no. 1, pp. 3-27.

Zammito, J.H. 1972. *Dynamics of Southern Growth.* Memphis, Tennessee: Morgan, Keegan and Co.

Chapter 10
Regional Economic Policy in Canada
T.N. Brewis

Atlantic Development Board. 1968-70. *Background Studies*, nos. 1-7. Ottawa: Queen's Printer.

Atlantic Development Council. 1971. *A Strategy for the Economic Development of the Atlantic Region 1971-81.* Fredericton, N.B.

Atlantic Provinces Economic Council. 1972. The Growth Centre Concept. *Sixth Annual Review, The Atlantic Economy.* Halifax, Nova Scotia. (Also 1972 Conference papers.)

Comeau, R.L. 1969. *A Study of the Impact of the Area Development Agency Program in Nova Scotia.* A Report submitted to the Area Development Agency, Department of Regional Economic Expansion, Ottawa.

Department of Finance. 1964. Reply of the Minister of Finance to Question No. 741 by Mr. Balcer, July 22.

Department of Regional Economic Expansion. December 1969. *Salient Features of Regional Development Policy in Canada. Ottawa.*

———. February 1972. *Regional Development and Regional Policy.*

Dymond, W.R. 1972. *Canadian Manpower Policy: A Policy in Search of a Problem* University of Ottawa, Faculty of Management Sciences, Working Paper No. 73-1, December.

EFTA. September 1971. *Industrial Mobility, Regional Policy in EFTA.* Geneva.

Hansen, N.M. 1971. The Problem of Spatial Resource Allocation. *Growth and Change* 2, no. 2, pp. 22-4.

Larsen, H.K. 1969. A Study of the Economic Impact Generated by ADA Assisted Manufacturing Plants Located in the Province of New Brunswick. A Report Submitted to the Area Development Agency.

Mathias, P. 1971. *Forced Growth.* Toronto: James, Lewis & Samuel.

McCrorie, J.N. 1969. *ARDA: An Experiment in Development Planning.* Special Study No. 2 prepared for the Canadian Council on Rural Development. Ottawa: Queen's Printer.

Pearson, L.B. 1955. *Democracy in World Politics.* Toronto: Saunders.

Ray, M.D. 1967. *Regional Aspects of Foreign Ownership of Manufacturing in Canada.* Waterloo, Ontario: University of Waterloo.

Springate, D.J.V. 1972. *Regional Development Incentive Grants and Private Investment in Canada.* Ann Arbor, Michigan: University Microfilms.

Standing Committee on Regional Development House of Commons. *Minutes of Proceedings and Evidence.* Annual.

Yeates, M.H. and Lloyd, P.E. 1968. A Study of the Impact of the Area Development Agency Program in the Southern Georgia Bay Area, Ontario. A report submitted to the Area Development Agency, Ottawa.

About the Contributors

Niles M. Hansen is Professor of Economics and Director, Center for Economic Development, at the University of Texas. He is the author of *French Regional Planning, France in the Modern World, Rural Poverty and the Urban Crisis, Intermediate-Size Cities as Growth Centers, Location Preferences, Migration and Regional Growth*, and *The Future of Nonmetropolitan America*, and the editor of *Growth Centers in Regional Economic Development*.

Rémy Prud'homme, born in 1936 at Saumur, France, taught at the Universities of Phnom-Penh, Lille and Paris XII, and recently joined the Environment Directorate of the Organization for Economic Cooperation and Development as Deputy Director. He is the author or editor of *The Economy of Cambodia, Urban Gaming Simulations*, and *Urban Economic Accounts*, and has written a number of papers on urban, regional and environmental affairs for professional journals.

Gordon C. Cameron is Titular Professor in Applied Economics, University of Glasgow, Scotland. He has held visiting research and teaching appointments at the Universities of Pittsburgh and California (Berkeley) and at Resources for the Future, Washington, D.C. From 1968 to 1973 he was editor of the *Urban Studies* journal and is currently a counselor of the Regional Science Association. He has been a consultant to the Organization for Economic Cooperation and Development, the Ford Foundation, the World Bank and the Netherlands Economic Institute.

Gunter Krumme is Associate Professor of Geography at the University of Washington. He holds degrees in Business Economics (Dipl.oec.publ., Munich) and Geography (Ph.D., Washington) and has taught at University College, London, the University of Hawaii, and Columbia University. His major interests relate to regional and spatial aspects of industrial and organizational change.

Vera Cao-Pinna is a member of the Economics Faculty of the University of Rome. She is a leading authority on input-output analysis and has contributed many articles to professional journals. She also has served as a consultant on regional development and other problems to numerous organizations and national governments.

Ad J. Hendriks, professor of regional economic research, is associated with the Netherlands Economic Institute at Rotterdam. He is involved in research on regional and urban development planning at the national and the local levels.

Åke Andersson is a member of the Economics Faculty at the University of Göteborg, Sweden. He is the author of numerous scholarly publications dealing with econometric analyses and public policy issues, and has lectured widely throughout Europe and the United States.

José-Ramon Lasuen is presently Head of the Department of Economic Theory at the Autonomous University of Madrid. He was a Research Associate at Resources for the Future, and later Dean of the Economics Faculty of the Autonomous University of Madrid. Among his honorary titles are Dean Honoris Causa of the Autonomous University of Madrid and Doctor Honoris Causa of the International Academy (World Fraternity of Scholars). He is also Board Director of the *European Economic Review* and President of Lasuén Asociados, General Consultants.

Thomas Brewis is Professor of Economics and Director, School of Commerce, Carleton University, Ottawa, Canada. He is the author of *Canadian Economic Policy*, *Regional Economic Policies in Canada*, and *Growth and the Canadian Economy*.